Beginning iOS Storyboarding with Xcode

Easily Design and Develop Your App, from Concept and Vision to Code

Rory Lewis

Yulia McCarthy

Stephen M. Moraco

Apress®

Beginning iOS Storyboarding with Xcode

ISBN-13 (pbk): 978-1-4302-4272-7

ISBN-13 (electronic): 978-1-4302-4273-4

President and Publisher: Paul Manning
Lead Editor: Matthew Moodie
Technical Reviewer: Matthew Knott
Editorial Board: Steve Anglin, Mark Beckner, Ewan Buckingham, Gary Cornell, Morgan Ertel, Jonathan Gennick, Jonathan Hassell, Robert Hutchinson, Michelle Lowman, Matthew Moodie, Jeff Olson, Jeffrey Pepper, Douglas Pundick, Ben Renow-Clarke, Dominic Shakeshaft, Gwenan Spearing, Matt Wade, Tom Welsh
Coordinating Editor: Brigid Duffy
Copy Editor: Corbin Collins
Compositor: Bytheway Publishing Services
Indexer: SPi Global
Artist: SPi Global
Cover Designer: Anna Ishchenko

Distributed to the book trade worldwide by Springer Science+Business Media, LLC., 233 Spring Street, 6th Floor, New York, NY 10013. Phone 1-800-SPRINGER, fax (201) 348-4505, e-mail orders-ny@springer-sbm.com, or visit www.springeronline.com.

For information on translations, please e-mail rights@apress.com, or visit www.apress.com.

Apress and friends of ED books may be purchased in bulk for academic, corporate, or promotional use. eBook versions and licenses are also available for most titles. For more information, reference our Special Bulk Sales–eBook Licensing web page at www.apress.com/info/bulksales.

The source code for this book is available to readers at www.apress.com.

To my mother, Adeline. Thank you for those 13 hours! Love you.

—Rory

To my amazing mom—the most caring and supportive person I've ever known. Thank you for your endless love!

—Yulia

To Donna, my wife of 31 years, my best friend and travelling companion through this life and around this beautiful planet. Without your support and encouragement, many of my efforts throughout our time together would not have been possible, nor nearly as enjoyable. I look forward to our upcoming years together.

To my son Steve, for sharing in our many endeavors together, for your graphics contribution to our first joint iOS app, 9CardGolf in the App Store, but most importantly for being a shining example to me, and I hope to others, of constant self-motivation and constant learning, and for maintaining a youthful passion for learning about the universe in which we live. I look forward to seeing where you go with your photography passion and the life ahead of you.

—Stephen

Contents at a Glance

Contents

Foreword: About the Authors

The three authors have found a beautiful way to lead the beginner into Storyboarding and at the same time show the old school coders of Objective-C a new exquisite methodology for learning and debugging this incredible tool. Essentially, you have a guru of explaining complex Objective-C to beginners, a former Apple iOS intern, and a super-successful, old-school coder showing many people from many different walks of life the alpha and omega of Storyboard creation, debugging, and tweaking.

Dr. Rory Lewis   Stephen M.   Yulia McCarthy
                        Moraco

Dr. Rory Lewis

Rory and I met in L.A. in 1983. He reminds me of one of my favorite film characters: Buckaroo Banzai—always going in six directions at once. If you stop him and ask what he's doing, he'll answer comprehensively and with amazing detail. Disciplined, colorful, and friendly, he has the uncanny ability to explain the highly abstract in simple, organic terms. He always accomplishes what he sets out to do, and he'll help you do the same.

Why You'll Relate to Dr. Lewis

While attending Syracuse University as a computer-engineering student, Rory scrambled to pass his classes and make enough money to support his wife and two young daughters. In 1990, he landed a choice, on-campus job as a proctor in the computer labs in the L.C. Smith College of Engineering. Even though he was struggling with subjects in the Electrical Engineering program, he was always there at the Help Desk. It was a daunting experience for Rory because his job was only to help his fellow students with computer lab *equipment* questions, yet he invariably found his classmates asking deeper and harder questions: "Dude, did you understand the calculus assignment? Can you help me?!"

These students assumed that, because Rory was the proctor, he knew the answers. Afraid and full of self-doubt, he sought a way to help them without revealing his inadequacies. Rory learned to start with: "Let's go back to the basics. Remember that last week when the professor presented us with an equation…?" By going back to the fundamentals, restating and rebranding them, Rory began to develop a technique that would, more often than not, lead to working solutions. By the time his senior year rolled around, there was often a line of students waiting at the Help Desk on the nights Rory worked.

Fast-Forward 17 Years

Picture a long-haired, wacky professor walking through the campus of the University of Colorado at Colorado Springs, dressed in a stunning contrast of old-school and dropout. As he walks into the Engineering Building, he's greeted by students and faculty who smile and say hearty hellos, all the while probably shaking their heads at his tweed jacket, Grateful Dead t-shirt, khaki pants, and flip-flops. As he walks down the hall of the Computer Science Department, there's a line of students standing outside his office. Reminiscent of the line of students that waited for him at the Help Desk in those early years as a proctor in the computer lab, they turn and greet him, "Good morning, Dr. Lewis!" Many of these UCCS students aren't even in his class, but they know Dr. Lewis will see them and help them anyway.

Past—Present—Future

Dr. Lewis holds three academic degrees. He earned a Bachelor of Science in Computer Engineering from Syracuse University. Syracuse's L.C. Smith College of Engineering is one of the country's top schools. It's there that Intel, AMD, and Microsoft send their top employees to study for their PhDs.

Upon completing his BS (with emphasis on the mathematics of electronic circuitry in microprocessors), he went across the quad to the Syracuse University School of Law. During his first summer at law school, Fulbright & Jaworski, the nation's most prolific law firm, recruited Rory to work in its Austin office, where some of the attorneys specialize in high-tech intellectual-property patent litigation. As part of his clerking experience, Lewis worked on the infamous *AMD v. Intel* case; he helped assess the algorithms of the mathematics of microprocessor electrical circuitry for the senior partners.

During his second summer in law school, Skjerven, Morrill, MacPherson, Franklin, & Friel—the other firm sharing the work on the *AMD v. Intel* case—recruited Rory to work with them at their Silicon Valley branches (San Jose and San Francisco). After immersing himself in law for several years and receiving his JD at Syracuse, Lewis realized his passion was for the *mathematics* of computers, not the legal ramifications of hardware and software. He preferred a nurturing and creative environment rather than the fighting and arguing intrinsic in law.

After three years away from academia, Rory Lewis moved south to pursue his PhD in Computer Science at the University of North Carolina at Charlotte. There, he studied under Dr. Zbigniew W. Ras, known worldwide for his innovations in data mining algorithms and methods, distributed data mining, ontologies, and multimedia databases. While studying for his PhD, Lewis taught computer science courses to computer engineering undergraduates, as well as e-commerce and programming courses to MBA students.

Upon receiving his PhD in Computer Science, Rory accepted a tenure-track position in Computer Science at the University of Colorado at Colorado Springs, where his research is in the computational mathematics of neurosciences. Most recently, he co-wrote a grant proposal on the mathematical analysis of the genesis of epilepsy with respect to the hypothalamus. However, with the advent of Apple's revolutionary iPhone and its uniquely flexible platform—*and market*—for mini-applications, games, and personal computing tools, he grew excited and began experimenting and programming for his own pleasure. Once his own fluency was established, Lewis figured he could teach a class on iPhone apps that would include *non*-engineers. With his insider knowledge as an iPhone beta tester, he began to integrate the parameters of the proposed iPad platform into his lesson plans—even before the official release in April 2010.

The class was a resounding success, and the feedback was overwhelmingly positive, from students and colleagues alike. When approached about the prospect of converting his course into a book to be published by Apress, Dr. Lewis jumped at the opportunity. He happily accepted an offer to convert his course outlines, class notes, and videos into the book you are now holding in your hands.

Why Write This Book?

The reasons Dr. Lewis wrote this book are the same reasons he originally decided to create a class for both engineering and non-engineering majors: the challenge and the fun! According to Lewis, the iPhone and iPad are "… some of the coolest, most powerful, and most technologically advanced tools ever made—period!"

He is fascinated by the fact that, just underneath the appealing touchscreen of high-resolution images and fun little icons, the iPhone and iPad are programmed in Objective-C, an incredibly difficult and advanced language. More and more, Lewis was approached by students and colleagues who wanted to program apps for the iPhone and would ask his opinion on their ideas. It seemed that with every new update of the iPhone, not to mention the advent of the expanded interface of the iPad, the floodgates of interest in programming apps were thrown open wider and wider. Wonderful and innovative ideas just needed the proper channel to flow into the appropriate format and then out to the world.

Generally speaking, however, the people who write books about Objective-C write for people who know Java, C#, or C++ at an advanced level. So, because there seemed to be no help for the average person who has no such knowledge but who has a great idea for an iPhone/iPad app, Dr. Lewis decided to launch such a class. He realized it would be wise to use his own notes for the first half of the course and then explore the best existing resources he could find.

As he forged ahead with this plan, Lewis was most impressed with *Beginning iPhone 3 Development: Exploring the iPhone SDK*. This best-selling instructional book from Apress was written by Dave Mark and Jeff Lamarche. Lewis concluded that their book would provide an excellent, high-level target for his lessons, a "stepping-stones" approach to comprehensive and fluent programming for all of Apple's multitouch devices.

After Dr. Lewis's course had been successfully presented, and during a subsequent conversation with a representative from Apress, Lewis happened to mention that he'd only started using that book about halfway through the semester, as he had to bring his non-engineering students up to speed first. The editor suggested converting his notes and outlines into a primer—an introductory book tuned to the less-technical programming crowd. At that point, it was only a matter of time and details—like organizing and revising Dr. Lewis's popular instructional videos to make them available to other non-engineers excited to program their own iPhone and/or iPad apps.

So, that's the story of how a wacky professor came to write this book. We hope you're inspired to take this home and begin. Arm yourself with this knowledge and begin now to change your life!

Ben Easton
Author, Teacher, Editor

Stephen M. Moraco

Stephen has more than 30 years of experience in software engineering. He's developed projects writing in high-level languages such as PL/I, RPG, ANSI C, C++, C#, Objective-C, and assembly languages for more microprocessors than he can count on two hands. Prior to joining Hewlett-Packard/Agilent Technologies 1989, he was an embedded-systems designer/developer. Stephen is a past member of the Large-scale Logic Analyzer Team, building system recovery media and writing triggering/capture drivers for multichannel custom data capture ASICs. As a software process engineer, he worked with medium-sized R&D teams developing techniques to improve the rate of release and initial release quality of software products. Stephen also designed and wrote an operating system for optical drives produced by Hewlett-Packard.

Stephen's profession is also his hobby. He is a strong believer in constant learning and of constantly practicing what he's learning. All during his career Stephen developed on non-work-related projects as a form of self-training. He enjoys designing and building his own hardware/software systems for home control and general experimentation. Stephen also developed firmware for key integration systems that fly aboard amateur radio satellites and developed hardware and software for testing these systems.

Stephen and his son Steve both enjoy building large LEGO models and working with LEGO Mindstorms robotics. Son Steve is studying photography, and together they've volunteered with Colorado First LEGO League for the past five years, with Dad refereeing the Mindstorms Robotics tournaments for 9–14 year-olds throughout Colorado while son Steve documents the excitement of the events though his photography.

In the fall of 2009, father Stephen and son Steve took an Objective-C, iOS programming class together at the University of Colorado at Colorado Springs. Shortly thereafter Stephen started his company Iron Sheep Productions LLC, the name under which he sells the hardware and software he's developed. After a successful 22-year career with Hewlett-Packard/Agilent Technologies, Stephen is now a retired professional software engineer and … a successful iPhone and iPad app programmer who sells his apps on the iTunes store.

Yulia McCarthy

Yulia is a Senior iOS Developer at InspireSmart Solutions, Inc., a local Denver firm specializing in innovative mobile business solutions. After graduating from one of the best classic universities in Russia with a BS in Mathematics, she went on to conquer the snowy peaks of Colorado, pursuing her dream of snowboarding and adventure. Soon she decided to pursue a graduate career in Computer Science at University of Colorado at Denver where, after taking an iPhone development class with Dr. Lewis, she quickly converted into a Mac user and transferred all her passion and incredible ability to program and solve complex problems into developing iPhone and iPad apps, which has been her new passion ever since. Her amazing talent soon attracted iOS recruiters at Apple, and now Yulia is even more inspired and devoted to Cocoa Touch programming after her invaluable experience as an iOS Apps and Frameworks intern at Apple's headquarters in Cupertino, California during the summer of 2011. She believes that life is all about constantly reaching for new horizons and challenging yourself. As a programmer, this concept is very close to Yulia's heart.

From Russia to UC Denver to Apple's iOS Division at Cupertino, Yulia believes that everything is possible if we follow our dreams.

About the Contributing Author

Ben Easton is a graduate of Washington & Lee University and has a BA in Philosophy. His eclectic background includes music, banking, sailing, hang gliding, and retail. Most of his work has involved education in one form or another. Ben taught school for 17 years, mostly middle-school mathematics. More recently, his experience as a software trainer and implementer reawakened his long-time affinity for technical subjects. As a freelance writer, he has written several science fiction stories and screenplays, as well as feature articles for magazines and newsletters. Ben resides in Austin, Texas, and is currently working on his first novel.

About the Technical Reviewer

Matthew Knott is a Learning Platform developer and SharePoint expert. He has been programming since a young age and hasn't stopped learning since. An experienced C and C# developer, Matthew has recently started developing iOS apps to mobilize the Learning Platform. He lives in Wales, United Kingdom, with his wife and two children and likes to write on his blog (mattknott.com) from time to time.

Introduction

In editions of Rory's previous book *iPhone and iPad Apps for Absolute Beginners* (Apress), there were only two ways to teach the reader how to make an iOS app user interface. The first was to write everything in code, and the other was to use Interface Builder to compose a Windows-based app. But things have changed with Storyboarding … boy, have they!

Storyboarding first appeared with Xcode version 4.2. When we first saw the scenes that made up an app, we thought Storyboard was fantastic. It was wonderful how Storyboard allowed us to navigate a path through out app in a visual way. Almost immediately Rory found freshmen students coming into his office, knee-deep in trouble using Storyboards. Meanwhile Xcode experts were pooh-poohing Storyboards. This book helps the novice understand the power of Storyboards and can help even experts in Xcode to unleash it.

In this book you'll discover how Xcode's Interface Builder's support for Storyboarding in iOS 5 makes designing your iOS apps so much easier. Storyboarding lets you graphically arrange all your views within a single design canvas, where you can then define the app's logical flow and even assign transition animations. You'll be able to learn how to use Storyboards to quickly go from concept to a fully functional iOS application.

First, we go over the fundamental concepts of Storyboarding and the technology behind it. We then walk you through building seven complete projects that advance you through using various Storyboarding features, covering the most important aspects you need to know to successfully create your own apps from start to finish. By the end of this book, you'll eventually see how to use Storyboarding with almost every application template offered by Xcode and you'll learn which Storyboarding techniques are most suitable in certain scenarios.

Working with Storyboarding involves much more than simply dragging and dropping View Controllers onto a canvas. In this book we show how to start from scratch and build complete apps using Storyboarding. Along the way we demonstrate using common iOS technologies as Map Views, Page View Controllers, Split View Controllers, Core Data, Table Views, and more—and we tell you how they all fit together with the new Storyboarding feature.

What You'll Learn

In Chapter 1, we help you to get started in iOS development by walking you through Apple's iOS Developer Program registration process and installing Xcode and other tools you'll be using throughout this book.

Chapter 2 talks about the basics of Storyboard structure and introduces the main Storyboarding concepts, including standard view transitions, passing information around, and creating custom transitions between the views.

Chapter 3 explains how to create a map-driven app using Storyboarding and how to transition to other scenes from a Map View. It also demonstrates several important Storyboarding concepts, such as triggering manual segues and instantiating View Controllers designed in the Storyboard from within the code. Additionally, you'll learn how to easily parse JSON data from a remote server (such as Flickr) using nothing but the new iOS 5 API.

In Chapter 4, you'll find out how to develop a fun utility app using Storyboarding targeted for the iPad. You'll learn the foundation of many apps, which is how to place controls on the settings screen of a utility application and to return those settings to the Main View of the app via the Settings View delegate protocol. You'll get a good grasp of the main Storyboarding specifics of the iPad environment, including Split View Controllers, Popover View, and iPad-specific segues. As a part of building this chapter's project, you'll also demonstrate how you can use a build-it media framework to enable your app to play audio files.

In Chapter 5, we explore a very special Xcode template: the Page-Based Application template. Unlike other templates, it doesn't let you opt out of using Storyboarding. In this chapter, you'll learn the powerful tools that let you create Page View Controller transitions. We dig deep into the ins and outs of how to use the UIPageViewController to build an iPad brochure with beautiful, built-in page-curl animations and custom layout.

Chapters 6–8 bring to you a whole new world of Storyboarding features that dramatically change the way to program Table Views. We walk you through a more advanced Table Views-based project that utilizes Core Data in the back end. You'll learn critical Storyboarding techniques such as Dynamic Cell Prototyping and designing Static Table Views. Most importantly, in this chapter we show you how to design your entire app workflow entirely in the Storyboard before doing any coding at all.

In Chapters 9–11 you'll learn to develop a cool game app that stretches your knowledge of how segues can be used to provide much more complex navigation paths between screens.

Who Should Read This Book?

This book is for readers of Rory Lewis's last book, *iPhone and iPad Apps for Absolute Beginners,* but it's also for the beginner who's never programmed but who can use the Storyboarding tool in Xcode to get up and running fast. This book is also for experienced iOS developers who want to learn Storyboarding to quickly cut down on app development and debugging time.

For the beginner who has never programmed, *Beginning iOS Storyboarding with Xcode* shows how to extract those cool and innovative app ideas you have in your head into a working app ready for sale on the App Store. Even if you're an intermediate or pro-level Objective-C developer, you can still learn the ins and outs of Xcode's new Storyboarding feature—and find new ways of building and debugging your new Storyboarding app. Yup: This book is for you, too.

Regardless of your skill level, we're extremely happy to have you on board and hope you enjoy the ride. Let's get to Storyboarding!

Preliminaries

This introductory chapter will make sure that you have all the required tools and accessories to proceed fully and confidently. Three types of readers are likely reading this book. One group can skip to Chapter 2 immediately without reading Chapter 1. Another group may only need to read one small section in Chapter 1 and then move on to Chapter. The third group should read Chapter 1 very carefully before moving on.

- *Group 1*: You own a Mac. You have experience coding with Xcode on your Mac. You have an up-to-date iOS SDK and an up-to-date version of Xcode. You also have experience with DemoMonkey, and it's installed on your machine. If all this is true, meet me in Chapter 2.

- *Group 2*: You own a Mac. You have experience coding with Xcode on your Mac. You have an up-to-date iOS SDK and an up-to-date version of Xcode. However, you don't have experience with DemoMonkey or it's not installed on your machine. Please check out the section "Installing DemoMonkey" in this chapter and then meet me in Chapter 2.

- *Group 3*: You are a seeker of knowledge and have begun travelling down a wonderful road. We need to check your backpack and make sure you have all the tools you'll need for your journey. So let's start right here.

Necessities and Accessories

In order to program for the iPhone and/or iPad, and to follow along with the exercises, tutorials, and examples presented in this book, you'll need to have 6 minimal requirements which you may not completely understand right now but that's OK just roll with me for a second, I'll explain everything as we go through these steps.

> **NOTE:** Whenever we say *iPhone* or *iPad*, we're referring to any iPhone or iPad OS device, including the iPod touch. Also when we say *Macintosh HD*, yours may be named something different.

Briefly, you will need six things:

- An Intel-based Macintosh
- The correct operating system for your Mac (OS X 10.7.4 Lion or later)
- Be a registered developer or be simulator-based (discussed in detail later in this chapter)
- To have the correct operating system for your iPhone (iOS 5 or above)
- To have the correct Software Development Kit (SDK) for your iPhone that runs a program called Xcode (version 4.3 and above)
- To install and run DemoMonkey

Let's go into each of these in a bit more detail.

Getting a Mac

If your Mac was manufactured after 2006, you're okay. One of the authors purposefully programs everything on a MacBook bought in 2008. All the videos on the net are screencast from Dr. Lewis's MacBook from 2006; or if he broadcasts from his 2010 iMac, he first runs it on his MacBook bought in 2006.

- You don't need the latest revved-up Mac. If you haven't bought one yet, we suggest you get a basic, no-frills MacBook Air.

- If you do own an older Mac, you may be able to add some RAM. Make a free appointment at the Genius Bar at an Apple Store and ask whether they can increase the RAM on your older model Mac, and if so, ask about the maximum the RAM can be increased. Then ask explicitly: "Can this old computer run Lion, *at least* 10.7.1, and Xcode 4.3 or later?" Note that some of the apps in this book will work using Xcode 4.3 on Snow Leopard. But if possible, try to get Lion (at least Mac OS X 10.7.4) and iOS SDK 4.3.

- If you don't have a Mac, you'll need to buy one if you want to follow along with this book and or program Objective-C to make iPhone apps. Keep in mind that, as mentioned, we have made a point to code and run every program in this book on Apple's smallest and cheapest model, the MacBook. Apple has discontinued the MacBook; it now sells the MacBook Air for $999, which is more advanced than the Author's MacBook. You can purchase a MacBook on eBay and other such sites. See Figure 1-1.

Figure 1-1. *The authors use the cheapest 2006 Mac on the market, the MacBook, to perform all the coding and compiling in this book. Many of the authors' students purchase the MacBook Air for $999 as illustrated here.*

Getting OS X

You will need the correct version of OS X. At the time of this writing, that version is OS X 10.7.4. We need to make sure that you have the latest greatest operating system inside your Mac. We see a lot of emails and forum questions revealing that many of you will think: "*Ah, my code probably did not compile correctly because Dr. Lewis has a different version of OS X or/and iOS on his machine...*"

> **NOTE:** Even if you think everything is up to date, we suggest you follow along with the procedure in this section and make sure your system has the latest OS X and the latest iOS inside it. We say this because as you follow along in this book and tackle all the programs, there will be times when your code doesn't work the first time you run it.

To make sure your system is recent enough to follow along with the book, please do the following:

1. Close every program running on your Mac so that only the Finder is running.

2. Click the little apple in the upper left-hand corner of your screen and select About This Mac. You'll see the window shown in Figure 1-2. Make sure it says OS X 10.7.4.

Figure 1-2. *Here you can see that Dr. Lewis's MacBook is using is OS X 10.7.4.*

Now to make sure you have the latest software on your Mac:

1. With all your programs closed except for the Finder, click the apple in the upper left-hand corner again and select Software Update… as illustrated in Figure 1-3.

2. If updates are available, click Continue and follow the instructions and four screen prompts, as shown in Figure 1-3.

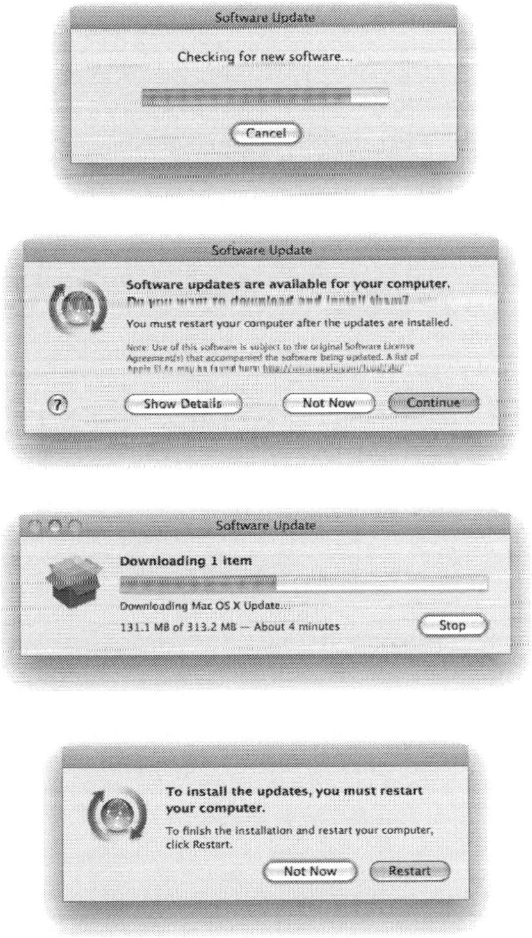

Figure 1-3. *Top: Checking for new software. Second from top: Download the new software. Second from bottom: Wait for software to download. Bottom: Click Restart to have your Mac properly install the new software.*

If by the time you are reading this book, you realize that your version of OS X or iOS makes my pictures seemed dated, don't freak out. We have an online forum where we and volunteers love to help others. We always update the forum with news about recent updates of OS X and iOS. You can visit the forum here:

www.rorylewis.com/ipad_forum/
http://bit.ly/oLVwpY

Become a Developer

You will need to become a registered developer via the iPhone/iPad Software Development Kit (SDK) for $99. Or you can pay $0 for an introductory set of bells and whistles.

Making Your Choice

If you are a student, it's likely that your professor has already taken care of this, and you may already be registered under your professor's name. If you are not a student, you need to decide which type of developer you would like to be. Here are your options:

- *$0 option.* You can go to the App Store and download Xcode for free. This is fine, but bear in mind that unless you become a developer ($99), you will only be able to see the apps you code and program in this book running on the iPhone or iPad *Simulator.* That means you can't run them on a real physical iPad or iPhone. You also won't be able to sell your apps on the iTunes store. Lastly, you won't be able to log in to the developer site to view code snippets and updates, beta-test new products, or be a part of the Apple online community. This may be a very good choice for the person who isn't sure whether they want to continue with Xcode and programming. If that's the case, then download the latest version of Xcode from https://developer.apple.com/xcode/ and meet me at Figure 1-13.

- *$99 option.* If you do want to run your apps on a physical device such as a real iPad or iPhone, sell apps on the iTunes store, and be a part of the developer group at Apple—simply continue reading.

Installing Xcode

Let's get started installing Xcode.

1. Go to `http://developer.apple.com/programs/ios/` or
   `http://bit.ly/rrrdjc`. You'll see a page similar to the one
   shown in Figure 1-4. Click the Enroll Now button.

Figure 1-4. *Click the Enroll Now button.*

2. Click the Continue button, as illustrated in Figure 1-5.

Figure 1-5. *Click the Continue button.*

3. Most people reading this book will select the "I need to create a new account for…" option (arrow 1 in Figure 1-6). Next, click the Continue button (arrow 2). (If you already have an existing account, then you have been through this process before; go ahead with the process beginning with the "I currently have an Apple ID…" option, and I'll meet you at step 6, where you'll log in to the iPhone/iPad development page and download the SDK.)

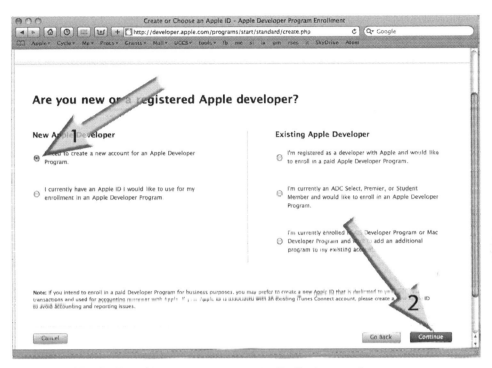

Figure 1-6. *Click the "I need to create a new account ..."option to proceed.*

4. You are probably going to be enrolling as an individual, so click the Individual link shown in Figure 1-7. If you are enrolling as a company, click the Company option to the right and follow the appropriate steps; Skip to step 6.

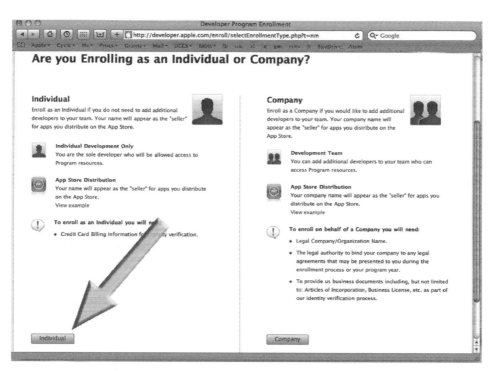

Figure 1-7. *Click the Individual option.*

5.   Enter all your information as shown in Figure 1-8 and pay your fee of $99 for the Standard Program. This provides all the tools, resources, and technical support you will need. (If you're reading this book, you really don't want to buy the Enterprise program at $299—it's for commercial in-house applications.) After paying, save your Apple ID and username; then receive and interact with your confirmation email appropriately.

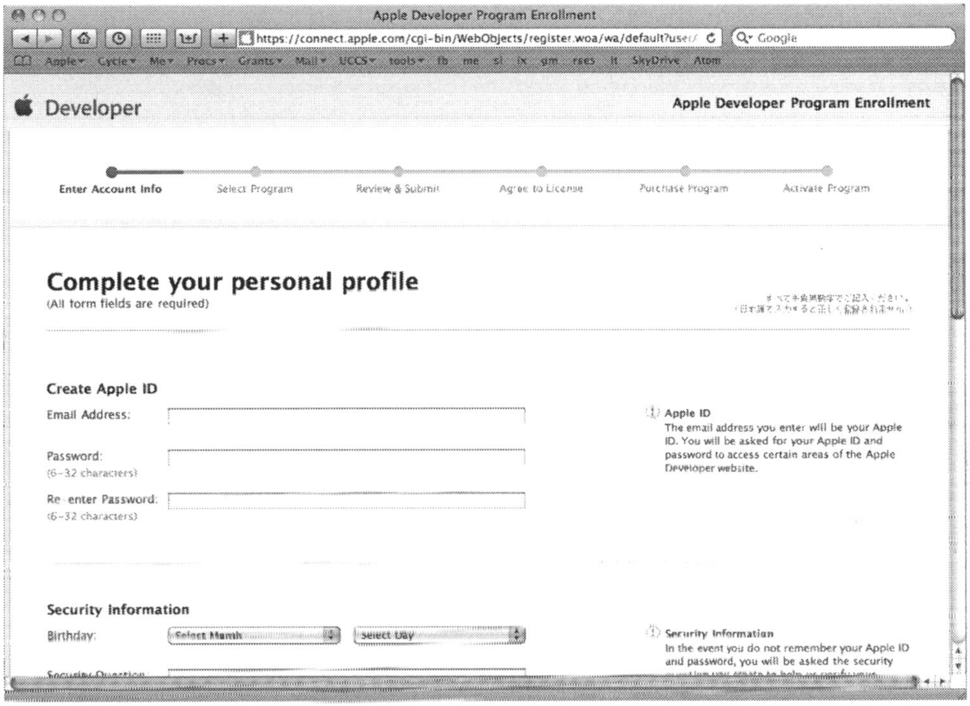

Figure 1-8. *Enter all your information accordingly.*

> **NOTE:** Before you move on to step 6, make sure you have received your confirmation email and chosen a password to complete the last step of setting you up as a bona fide registered Apple developer. Congratulations!

6. Use your Apple ID to log in to the main iOS development page at `http://developer.apple.com`. This page has three icons for the three types of Apple programmers. As shown on Figure 1-9, click the iOS Dev Center icon, which leads to the download page for iOS development software.

Figure 1-9. *For now click on the iOS Dev Center icon as indicated by the arrow. Later you may want to also program apps for the Mac Computer or the Safari Web Browser.*

7. After logging in with your username and password as described in step 6, you will see a screen similar to Figure 1-10. The iOS Dev Center contains all the tools necessary to build iOS apps. Later on you will spend time here, but for now just go to the Developer Page of the latest build of the iOS SDK. Click the icon indicated by the arrow.

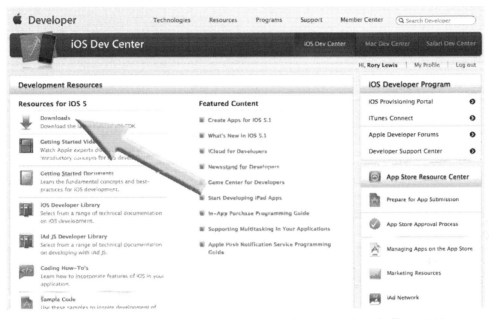

Figure 1-10. *The Downloads link takes you to the bottom of the page as shown in Figure 1-11.*

> **NOTE:** At the time of writing, Xcode 4.3 and iOS SDK 5 are the latest environments. There is a great chance that by the time you read this book these may have larger numbers. This is not a problem—just go on to step 8. If by chance there is something that has really thrown us a curve ball, it will be discussed and solved for you in our forum located at www.rorylewis.com/ipad_forum/ or http://bit.ly/oLVwpY.

8. For now we want you to click on the latest version. The figures in this section show the latest version at the time of print. These *will* be different by the time you read this. Right now the latest version is Xcode 4.3 for Lion, so click the link indicated by the arrow in Figure 1-11.

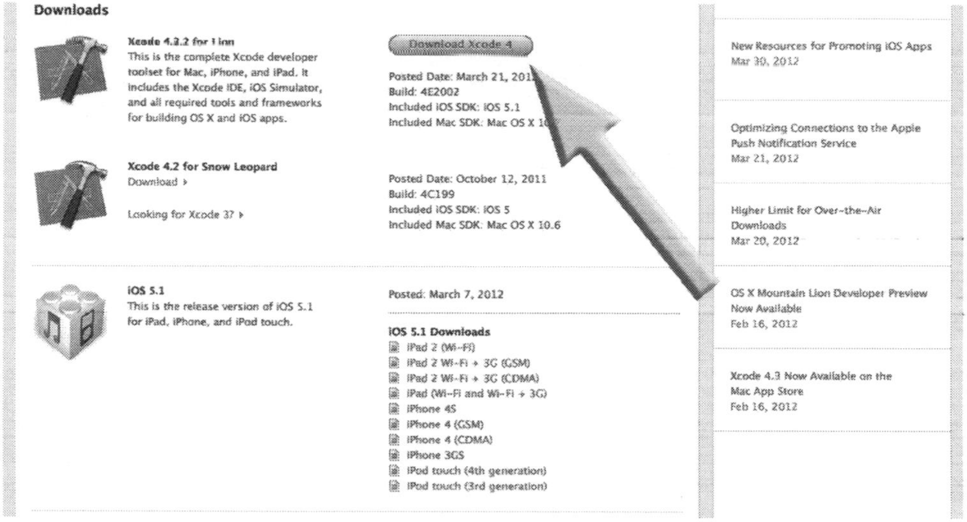

Downloads

Xcode 4.2.2 for Lion
This is the complete Xcode developer toolset for Mac, iPhone, and iPad. It includes the Xcode IDE, iOS Simulator, and all required tools and frameworks for building OS X and iOS apps.

Download Xcode 4

Posted Date: March 21, 2012
Build: 4E2002
Included iOS SDK: iOS 5.1
Included Mac SDK: Mac OS X 10

Xcode 4.2 for Snow Leopard
Download ▸

Looking for Xcode 3? ▸

Posted Date: October 12, 2011
Build: 4C199
Included iOS SDK: iOS 5
Included Mac SDK: Mac OS X 10.6

iOS 5.1
This is the release version of iOS 5.1 for iPad, iPhone, and iPod touch.

Posted: March 7, 2012

iOS 5.1 Downloads
- iPad 2 (Wi-Fi)
- iPad 2 Wi-Fi + 3G (GSM)
- iPad 2 Wi-Fi + 3G (CDMA)
- iPad (Wi-Fi and Wi-Fi + 3G)
- iPhone 4S
- iPhone 4 (GSM)
- iPhone 4 (CDMA)
- iPhone 3GS
- iPod touch (4th generation)
- iPod touch (3rd generation)

New Resources for Promoting iOS Apps
Mar 30, 2012

Optimizing Connections to the Apple Push Notification Service
Mar 21, 2012

Higher Limit for Over-the-Air Downloads
Mar 20, 2012

OS X Mountain Lion Developer Preview Now Available
Feb 16, 2012

Xcode 4.3 Now Available on the Mac App Store
Feb 16, 2012

Figure 1-11. *Clicking the Download Xcode 4 button takes you to the Xcode 4 Developer page.*

9. Click the View in Mac App Store button. Remember that if it's a later version than shown in Figure 1- 12 things may look slightly different, but we have confidence in you.

Xcode 4

Xcode is Apple's powerful integrated development environment for creating great apps for Mac, iPhone, and iPad. Xcode includes the Instruments analysis tool, iOS Simulator, and the latest Mac OS X and iOS SDKs.

The Xcode interface seamlessly integrates code editing, UI design with Interface Builder, testing, and debugging, all within a single window. The embedded Apple LLVM compiler underlines coding mistakes as you type, and is even smart enough to fix the problems for you automatically. Learn more ›

Download Xcode 4 for free.

Xcode 4.3.2 for Lion

Xcode in the Mac App Store has been repackaged, and is now distributed as a stand-alone application. This replaces the Install Xcode package, and adds support for delta updates. Xcode includes a new "Downloads" preference pane to install optional components such as command line tools, and previous iOS Simulators.

Note: To get the latest version of Xcode, you will need to click the "View in Mac App Store" button to the right and download from the new Xcode product page. The update from Xcode 4.2 will not show up in the Mac App Store "Updates" tab. Updates will work as normal for Xcode 4.3 and later.

View in Mac App Store

What's New in Xcode

Xcode 4 User Guide

Figure 1-12. *Click the View in Mac App Store link.*

10. Click the Install button, as shown in Figure 1-13. As the download continues, the Install button changes to say "Installing." When it has completed downloading Xcode and iOS SDK, it changes to "Installed." Included with Xcode's iOS SDK is Apple's Integrated Development Environment (IDE). This is the programming platform that contains a suite of tools, sub-applications, and boilerplate code that enable programmers to do their jobs more easily.

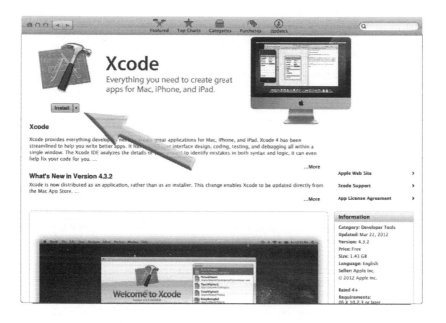

Figure 1-13. *Click Install and then wait for the download to complete.*

With your Xcode and iPhone/iPad Simulator tools installed and ready to access easily, you're almost ready to roll.

ABOUT DEMOMONKEY

Before you load the final tool—called DemoMonkey—let's step back and have a look at where we're going.

Through the years we have found that the most efficient means to teach students code is to take what we call the subsystem approach, teaching you what pieces or sections of code will serve you in which situations. In this book we will use a cool program you may have seen if you watched the latest WWDC: it's called DemoMonkey. Essentially, you drag a heading explaing what needs to be done from the DemoMonkey palette, and as you drop it into your code at the appropriate section of your Xcode file, it magically transforms into code that the author of the DemoMonkey file wrote. Before you can download and compile the Xcode project that creates DemoMonkey, you need to make sure Xcode works.So in the next section you first run a simple app to make sure all is in order in Xcode land.

Getting Ready for Your First iPhone/iPad Project

Before starting on your first Storyboarding app, you need to make sure that everything runs. Assuming you've already downloaded and installed Xcode, open up Xcode.

1. Press Command + Shift + N (⌘⇧N), simultaneously. This will open a new window that showcases the different types of project templates in the land of Xcode.

2. Figure 1-14 displays the project templates: Master-Detail Application, OpenGL Game, Page-Based Application, Single View Application, Tabbed Application, Utility Application, and Empty Application. Click Single View Application as shown in Figure 1-14 and then click Next.

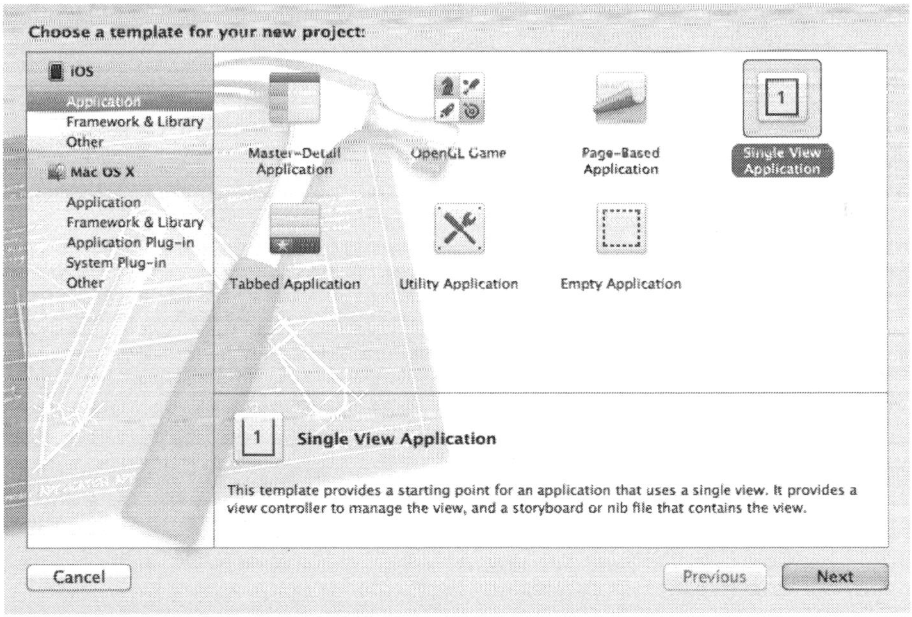

Figure 1-14. *Select the Single View Application and then click Next.*

3. On your screen you should see something very similar to Figure 1-15. First call your project test as indicated by arrow 1. Choose iPhone (arrow 2) and then click Next (arrow 3).

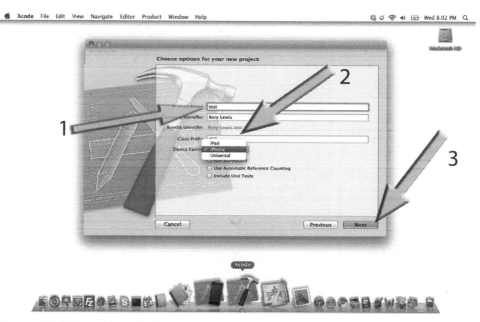

Figure 1-15. *Let's go for a test drive.*

> **NOTE:** For this test we are not using Storyboarding; we just want to see that Xcode builds a simple app. So keep everything unchecked—yes, including "Use Storyboard" for now (as shown in Figure 1-15).

4. Figure 1-16 shows the initial view of Xcode's IDE. Click the
    ViewController.h file as indicated by the arrow.

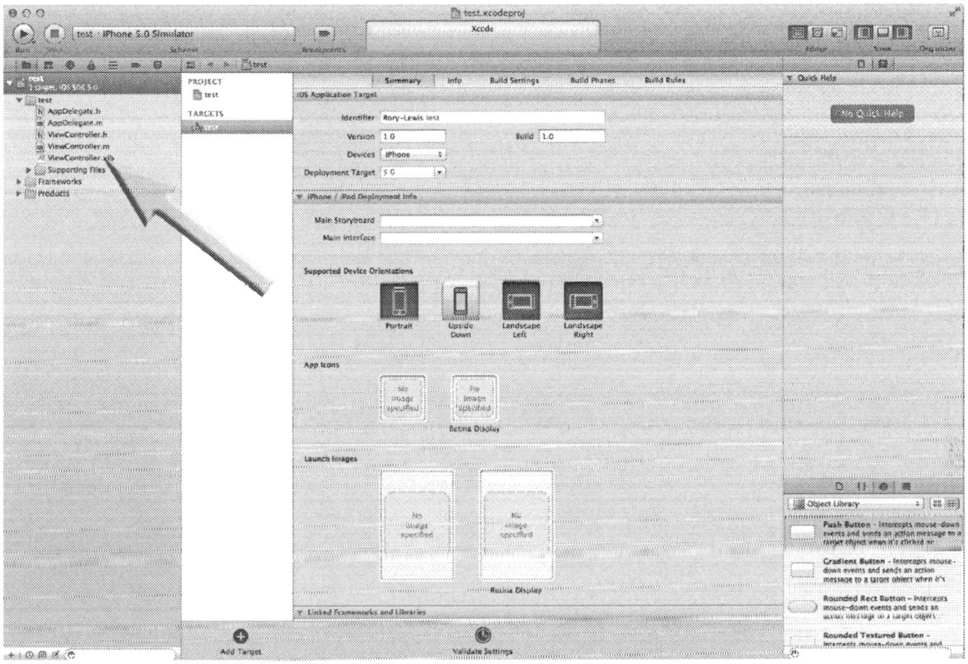

Figure 1-16. *The Initial Integrated Development Environment (IDE) screen.*

5. This will bring up the screen shown in Figure 1-17 where we want you to run your blank app by clicking on the "go" button, as indicated by the arrow. Oh yeah!

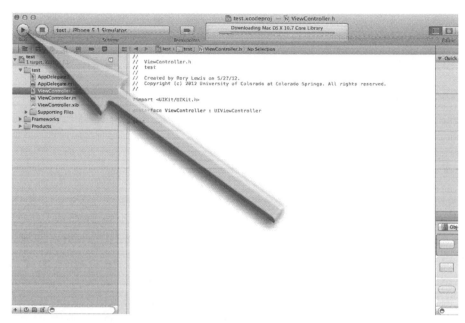

Figure 1-17. *Run it!*

6.   The iPhone Simulator pops up, as illustrated in Figure 1-18.

Figure 1-18. *Your first test drive.*

Congratulations! You've loaded Xcode and you've taken it for a test drive. Now let's get DemoMonkey running and start Storyboarding.

Installing DemoMonkey

DemoMonkey is an optional tool intended to help you follow along with the book projects. You only need it if you choose to use our .demoMonkey files for each chapter, which will allow you to drag and drop ready-to-use code snippets into the Xcode for most of the steps. Otherwise, you can still type the code yourself, and if you choose not to use DemoMonkey for this book, you can skip the rest of this chapter.

DemoMonkey will make life easier for you and let you focus more on the code you are using—but you will still be challenged in this book, and that's simply part of our pedagogy. The issue is really how to handle things when you get challenged.

> **NOTE:** When you do find yourself in one of those tough spots, you can always reread the section, rewind the video examples, or—most importantly—go visit the forum where there are often many people, including us, online and ready to help you immediately. We may refer you to somebody else's solution or we may help you directly. So go to the forum, say "hello" to the crowd, and become immersed by first seeking help from others and then going back to help others at the forum, located at www.rorylewis.com/ipad_forum/ or http://bit.ly/oLVwpY.

With your Xcode running and building apps, you can now install DemoMonkey.

1. Apple provides DemoMonkey as an OS X sample code project that is available for download to anyone. Go to http://developer.apple.com/library/mac/#samplecode/DemoMonkey/Introduction/Intro.html or http://bit.ly/v3BuKI, as shown in Figure 1-19. Click Download Sample Code as indicated by the arrow and save the zip file into a desired location on your machine.

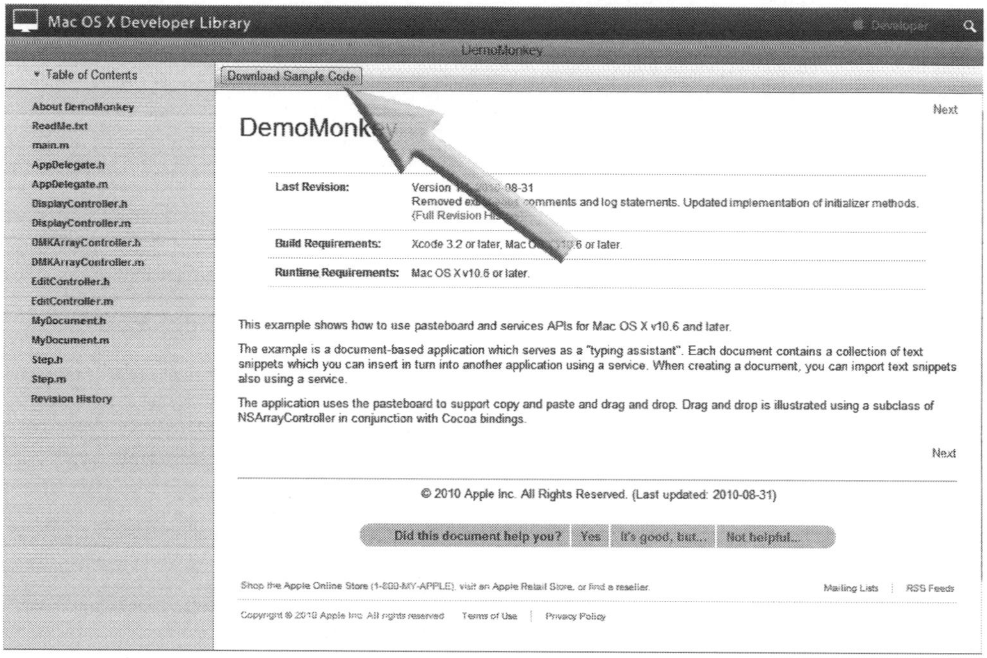

Figure 1-19. *Download Sample Code*

2. Unzip the zip file by double-clicking it, open the folder, and then double click on the DemoMonkey.xcodeproj file, as indicated by the arrow in Figure 1-20. Once the Xcode project is open, press Command + B (⌘B) simultaneously to compile the project.

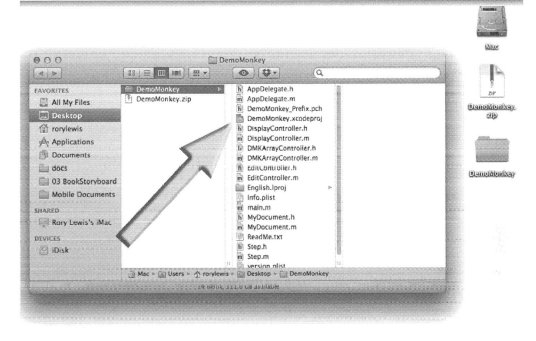

Figure 1-20. *Open the DemoMonkey Xcode project inside your DemoMonkey folder.*

3. After the "Build Succeeded" message shows up, expand the Project Navigator, right-click on the DemoMonkey.app icon, and then choose Show in Finder from the context menu, as shown in Figure 1-21.

Figure 1-21. *Expand the Project Navigator and choose Show in Finder from the context menu.*

4. Lastly, once Finder opens the folder containing the application you just built, drag the DemoMonkey.app to your Applications folder, as shown in Figure 1-22.

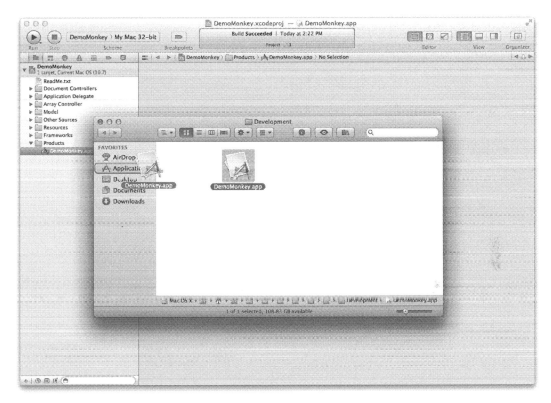

Figure 1-22. *Drag the DemoMonkey.app to your Applications folder.*

> **NOTE:** If for some reason you were unable to reproduce the steps in this section, you
> can download a compiled DemoMonkey.app from our site using this link:
> www.rorylewis.com/docs/02_iPad_iPhone/Storyboarding%20Book/Stor
> yboarding%20Video%20Tutorials.html. Then simply drag it to your
> Applications folder.

You're ready to roll now!

Fundamentals

With the release of iOS 5, Apple has given iOS developers an updated SDK with more than 1500 APIs, among which Storyboarding is one of the most intriguing.

So what is Storyboarding? And how can it make your life as iOS developer easier?

For our introduction to Storyboarding, we will navigate our way through this awesome new tool. Storyboarding allows one to lay out the workflow of your app using the new Storyboards feature built into the design tools of Xcode. Created for apps that use Navigation and Tab Bars to transition between Views, Storyboards ease the development by managing the View Controllers for you. You can specify the transitions and segues that are used when switching between Views without having to code them by hand. Storyboarding enables you to interact seamlessly and link all the screens in your application without the cumbersome code you had to write for the transitions between the screens and the controls used to trigger the transitions. This allows you to see every possible path through your application graphically, greatly reducing the amount of code you need to write for a complex multi-View application.

Before we dive into all the nuts and bolts of creating apps using Storyboarding, let's take a quick tour of what lies behind this new developer tool.

As you may already know, since the release of Xcode 4, Interface Builder (IB) has been completely integrated within the Xcode IDE so there is no longer a separate application for building your user interface (UI). Selecting an interface file (`.nib`/`.xib`) in your project simply opens the IB Editor within Xcode, where you tweak your UI just the way you want it.

Storyboard is a new IB file, introduced in Xcode 4.2, which allows you to view the entire UI of your app in one place, including the transitions between the parts of your app and the triggers that initiated those transitions, so you can very conveniently get an overview of the app. It is very similar to a `.nib/.xib` file except that it manages multiple View Controllers for you and allows you to specify the transitions used when switching from one View to another without having to code them manually. You can think of a Storyboard as a collection of mini `.xibs` and transitions and/or relationships between them.

With the built-in Storyboarding feature, you can now lay out the workflow of your app visually before writing any code at all! It also reduces the amount of code you need to write for complex multiscreen applications.

Ever wondered what lies behind the mysterious `.storyboard` files? The answer may surprise you: it's XML (Extensible Markup Language)—yes, good ol' XML that's so widely used in web-server communication and a variety of web applications. So, at the low level, Storyboard is just a text document formatted in a special way that defines an object graph of your application UI, and which iOS interprets at runtime to render the UI elements, based on the rules specified in the document. This XML file keeps track of all the attributes for every UI element in the Storyboard as well as transitions and/or relationships between them.

In fact, you can check it out for yourself. Open Xcode and create a new project. Select the Single View Application template in the first dialog screen. Hit Next. Name the project whatever you like, but make sure the Use Storyboards option is checked. Save it to your preferred location. Once the new project opens up, you'll see that Xcode has created a file for you called `MainStoryboard.storyboard`. Select the file in the Project Navigator as shown in Figure 2.0A. Now click the Version Editor icon in the top right-hand corner of the main toolbar and then click the Log mode icon in the bottom right-hand corner as shown in Figure 2-0B. You can now see the XML behind your Storyboard file. Not very pretty, huh? Imagine how complex and hard to read it gets after you add tons of UI elements to it? Luckily, Interface Builder nicely renders it for you in the form of graphical elements that are much more pleasant to interact with than raw XML.

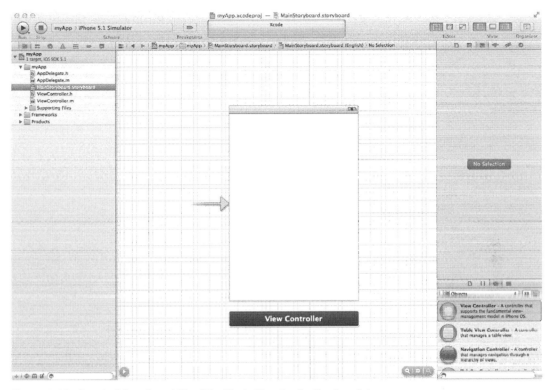

Figure 2-0A. *Standard Storyboard file of the Single View Application template*

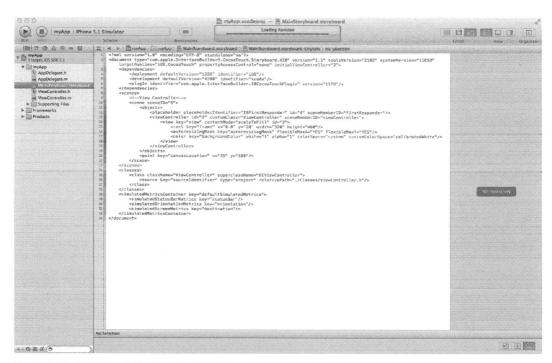

Figure 2-0B. *Storyboard file viewed as XML document*

Now that you know the secret behind the Storyboard implementation, let's take a quick peek at how it looks at first sight.

As you probably noticed, the basic Storyboard created by the Xcode for Single View Application template is almost identical to any regular `.xib` file you may have seen before, with just a few exceptions: there's an incoming arrow pointing towards the main View, and there's a black container below the main View that says "View Controller." Both of these elements serve a very clear purpose. Because Storyboard can have multiple View Controllers, you need a way to specify which one of those should load when the app starts; the arrow is pointing towards the View Controller that will be the first View presented to the user when the app is launched. To change the Initial View Controller of your application, drag and drop the arrow onto any View Controller in the Storyboard that you want to be presented first.

What about the black container? It's a so-called Dock for each View Controller scene. As we mentioned earlier, Storyboard can be seen as a collection of nibs, and each one of them has a View Controller class it's controlled by (default or custom) and a First Responder.

NOTE: First Responder is a placeholder object that represents the first object in the responder chain, which is determined dynamically at runtime by the UIKit framework. This object first receives many kinds of events like touches, key events, action messages, and so on. In iOS applications, there is no single First Responder object— the First Responder is always the View that is the target of a touch, which is typically the currently selected object or the object with the current focus in the frontmost window.

The Dock gives you easy access to the two objects just described, which you would normally see at the top of the Document Outline in a regular nib file. You can see the icons representing View Controller and First Responder placeholder objects by clicking the Dock as shown in Figure 2-0C. You can use these referencing icons to quickly connect the IBOutlets and specify IBAction for your UI elements. Each View Controller in the Storyboard has a set of those two objects, so you can conveniently edit all the necessary details of each Storyboard scene by focusing on just one particular screen at a time. Additionally, the Dock may contain other objects added to a scene, such as Gesture Recognizers, Navigation Items, and others. You'll get a better understanding of how to use them when you get to actual coding.

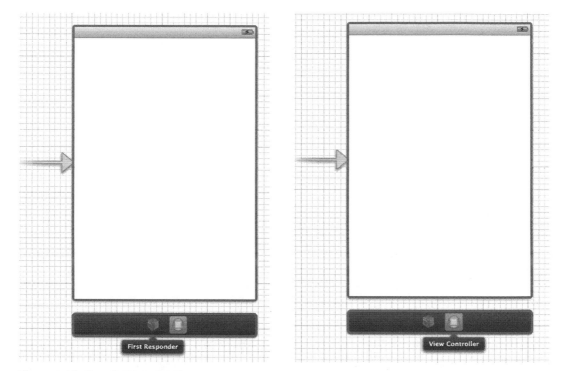

Figure 2-0C. *Scene's Dock with First Responder and View Controller objects*

We'll give you a short overview of the main high-level concepts you should understand before we start Storyboarding apps.

Figure 2-0D depicts the main components of a standard Storyboard file that gets created for you by Xcode when you pick a Master-Detail Application template for your project. We'll now explain the role those key components play and how they fit together.

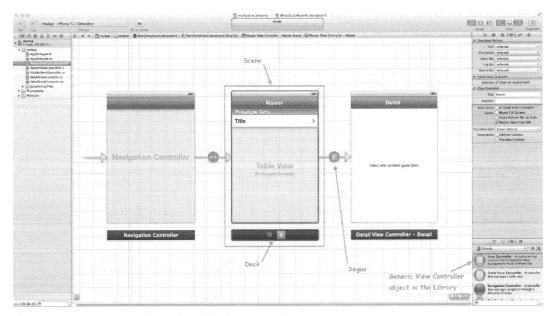

Figure 2-0D. *Storyboards' Master-Detail Application template*

There are two main concepts in Storyboarding: scene and segue.

Scene is a View Controller that either represents a screen in the app or just one major component area (like a split View pane in a Split View Controller). You can do everything here you used to do in a nib file: drag and rearrange UI elements (like labels, text fields, and images), resize them, set their properties in the Attribute Inspector, and so on.

Segue defines navigation in your Storyboard. It indicates how to get from point A to B. You usually create a segue by picking an event source (like a button or a table View cell) and choosing a scene to transition to. You can also choose the type of animation you want to use. All Apple built-in animations are available to you by making a simple selection. Additionally, you can even create your own custom animations for custom segues.

As a result, you use scene and segue to build your application UI.

> **NOTE:** You can have multiple Storyboards in your app. You just need to specify the name of the main one in your [appName]-Info.plist under the "Main storyboard file base name" key, which has the default value MainStoryboard.

You start with a View Controller object that represents your first scene (the initial View Controller). To get View Controllers for your Storyboard, you select Objects and Controllers from the Object Library (just as you did with all other UI elements in nib files) and drag the View Controllers you need onto the Storyboard canvas. Each View Controller always manages a single scene of your app.

> **NOTE:** On the iPhone, each scene represents the contents of a single screen. For iPad applications, a screen can be composed of the contents of more than one scene (as in the case of a Split View Controller).

One of the most important concepts is how data is passed around. Here is a very classic scenario: a Master-Detail application where you display some data in a Table View, and when user taps on a cell, a Detail View is presented that displays additional information about the selection. In this case you must send a reference to the selected object to the Detail View so it knows exactly what to display.

Storyboarding comes with an API for that. A method called `prepareForSegue:sender:` on every `UIViewController`, and it is intended to be overridden. You can write code here that will take effect whenever each segue fires.

Segues are UI elements just like labels and Image Views are. You can select a segue in the Storyboard and inspect its properties. You can distinguish between segues by checking each segue's identifier property, which can be set in the Attributes Inspector. We show you how to do that and we cover several other major Storyboarding aspects in this chapter.

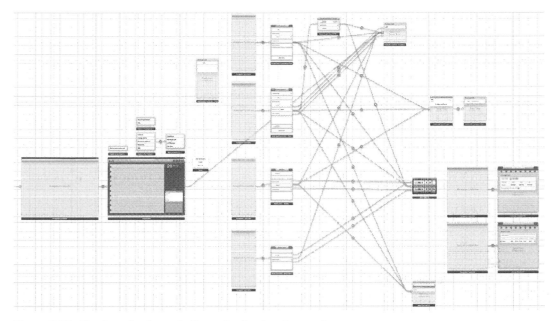

Figure 2-0F. *Storyboarding in use in the professional environment.*

To illustrate that Storyboards are indeed used quite extensively, even for large-scale projects, Figure 2-0E shows one of nine Storyboard-based projects being used at one of the author's clients. This figure is indicative of how, even at the professional level, Storyboards are here to stay.

So without further ado, let's get going.

helloAlien: A Quick Example Application

We'll start by introducing you to our four fundamental concepts of Storyboarding:

- Easily create transitions between views with little or no code.
- Pass information back from a Secondary View to a Main View.
- Send information to a Secondary View from a Main View.
- Transition between views with user-created visual effects.

In our example application we demonstrate these four concepts by

- Creating a button that invokes a transition from a Main View to a Secondary View .

- ▓ Passing a Yes/No value from a Secondary View (Alien View) to the Main View.

- ▓ Sending user-entered text to the Secondary View (Alien View) from the Main View.

- ▓ Create a custom segue (pronounced "segway") which implements a fade-out/fade-in between the two views.

To do this we'll write a simple app that asks an Alien whether he's out there. Going to the Secondary View, you'll see there is a switch that the Alien can switch on—if, of course, the Alien exists. If the Alien switches the switch to the on position, when you go back to the Main View, a message appears saying he does exist. You can then say something to the Alien, and you'll see the message out there in outer Alien space in the Secondary View. Lastly, you'll create a custom segue that transports you from the Main View to the Secondary View in a beautiful way. So let's get to it!

Preliminaries

As in all the chapters, we supply you with a video of Dr. Lewis writing and running the code exactly as described here in the book. You can also download the code that's from the video and used precisely "as is" here in this book. And you can download the DemoMonkey files and images used in each chapter.

These download files are at `http://bit.ly/sMRvAP` as illustrated in Figure 2-1.

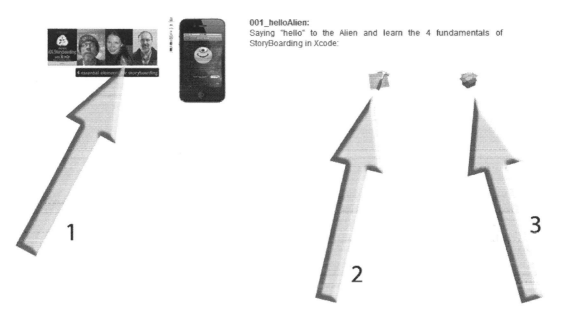

Figure 2-1. *Videos, code, and files for this chapter*

In Figure 2-1, arrow 1 points to an image from the video of this chapter, located at http://bit.ly/tNKUij. Arrow 2 points to an Xcode icon that links to the Xcode of this chapter, located at http://bit.ly/QSYAV6. Arrow 3 points to an icon that links to all the files necessary for this chapter, including the images and the DemoMonkey files located at http://bit.ly/Qxr16s. If you need more help, go to the forum http://bit.ly/oLVwpY.

Before you start, make sure you've downloaded the images and DemoMonkey file at http://bit.ly/Qxr16s and that you have opened them up on your desktop.

Step1: Create a Button That Segues to a Secondary View

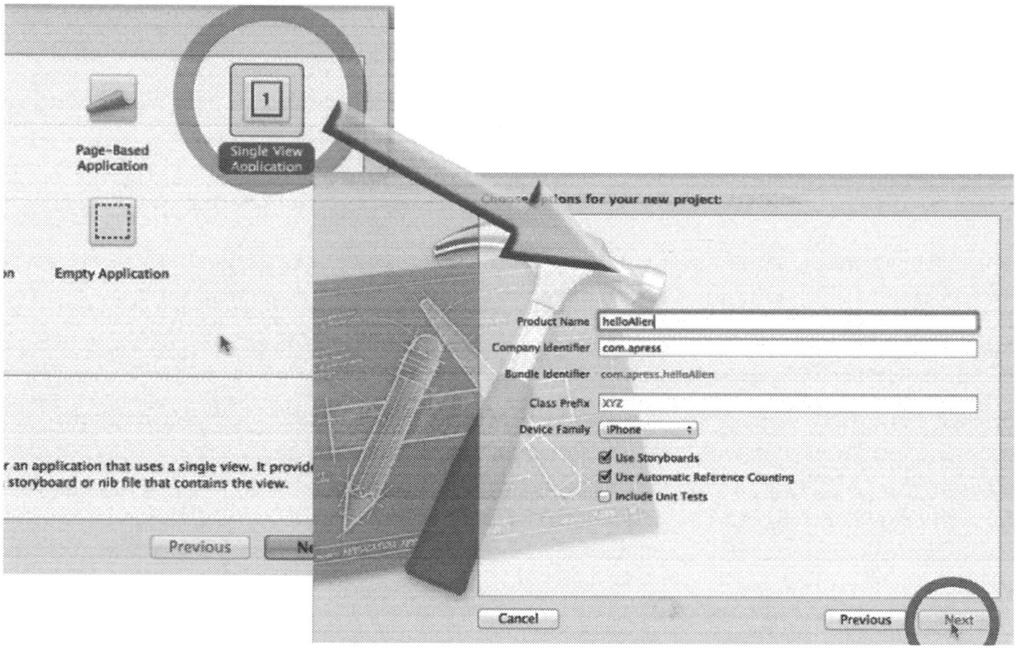

Figure 2-2. *Start a Single View Application.*

1. Open Xcode and click ⌘+⇧+N (File ➤ New ➤ Project), as shown in Figure 2-2. Select Single View Application and press Enter/Return. Name it helloAlien. We've used the Company Identifier com.apress. You can name yours whatever you like, but if you feel there is a chance you will need to compare your code to ours at any time, go ahead and name it com.apress like ours so that there will be less chance of confusion. We won't use a class prefix. Make sure to select iPhone and check both Use Storyboard and Use Automatic Reference Counting. Click Next, and you will be prompted for the location where you want to save your project. Choose a location and click Create.

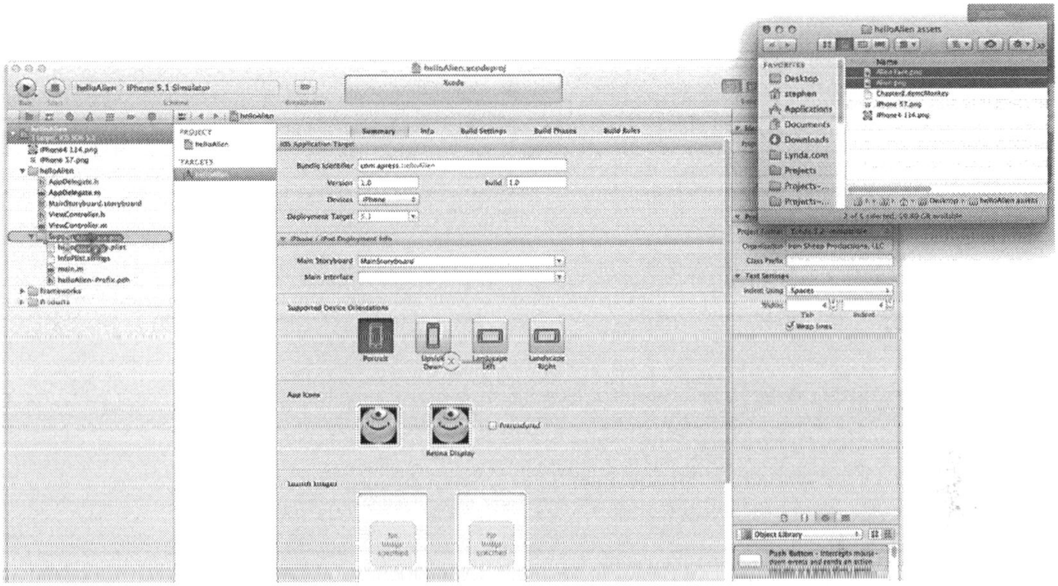

Figure 2-3. *Drag in the images.*

2. Navigate to your Target Settings by clicking the project icon at the root of the Navigation tree and drag the two Alien icon image files named iPhone 57.png and iPhone4 114.png into the icon boxes (Figure 2-3). The IPhone57 image goes into the regular icon box, and the iPhone4 114 image goes into the Retina box. Also drag the Alien.png and Alien Face.png image files into your Supporting Files folder. Make sure to check "Copy Items into destination group's folder."

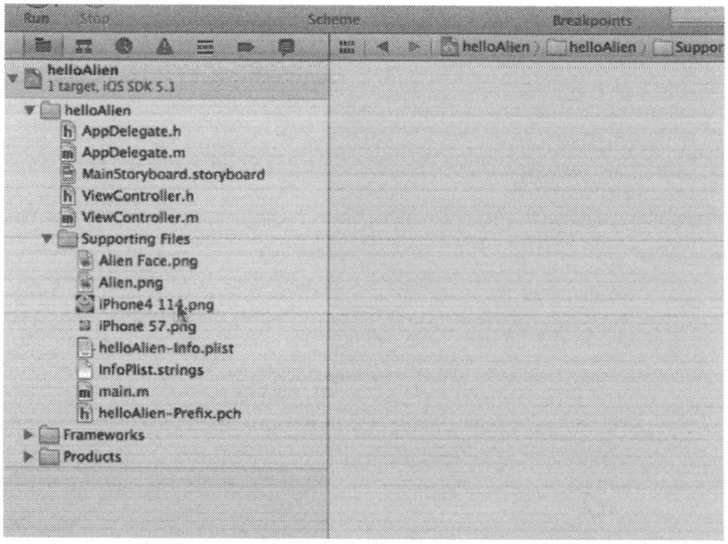

Figure 2-4. *Also drag the icons from the root folder to the Supporting Files folder.*

3.   Once these files are copied into your `Supporting Files` folder, drag the icon image files into your `Supporting Files` folder as shown in Figure 2-4. Deselect the Landscape Left and Landscape Right images within the Supported Device Orientations section, because this application only supports the Portrait orientation.

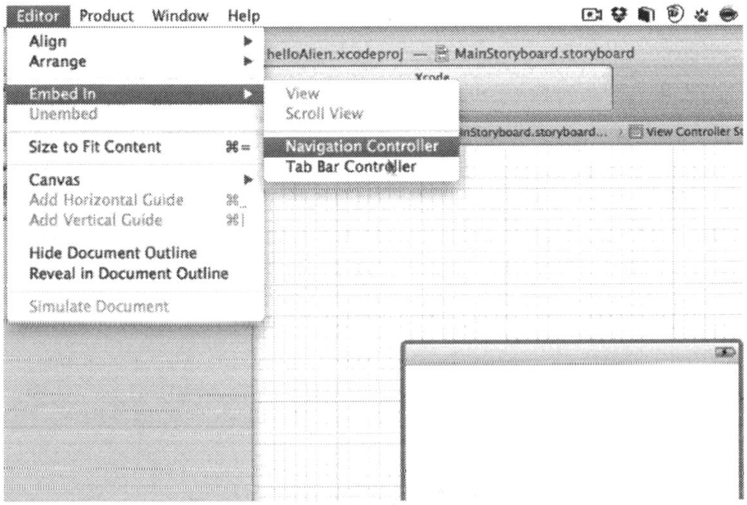

Figure 2-5. *Add a Navigation Controller.*

4. To make handling view transitions simple, we'll let a Navigation
    Controller coordinate the transitioning for us. Open the
    Storyboard file by going to the Project Navigator pane on the
    left and click MainStoryboard.storyboard to open it. It's in this
    new Storyboard file that you'll define most, if not all, of the
    views (called *scenes* in Storyboarding) in the application and
    specify the transitions between them. Now select the View
    Controller (by single-clicking the black bar below it). With the
    View Controller selected, click Editor ➤ Embed In ➤ Navigation
    Controller as shown in Figure 2-5. This will place a Navigation
    Controller to the left of your existing View Controller Scene and
    connect the two with an arrow indicating the relationship
    between them. It will also add a Navigation Bar to your existing
    View Controller. The Navigation Controller places buttons on the
    Navigation Bar to indicate how/when you can return to views
    you have left. You'll see this in action shortly when you run the
    newly created application.

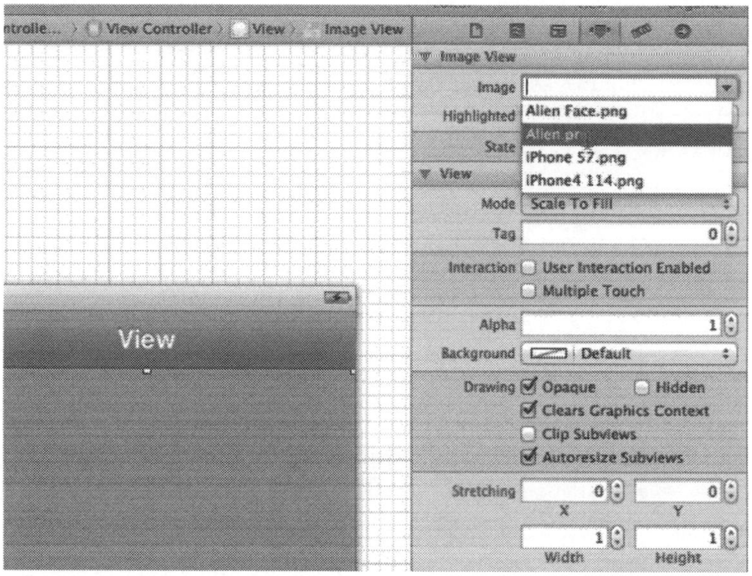

Figure 2-6. *Assign Alien.png to the Main View.*

5.   You're going to name the current View to *View*. Double-click the center of the View Controller's Navigation Bar and enter the name *View*. (You'll see this name being used in buttons created by the Navigation Controller — you need to return to this view from another view when you run this app.) Now add an image to your view by dragging an Image View onto the existing View Controller Scene's canvas. Let it autosize to the full View size and center it in the View as you drag the Image View onto the View. Go to the Attributes Inspector and select Alien.png as the image it should show. The image will appear showing what the Scene now looks like. See Figure 2-6.

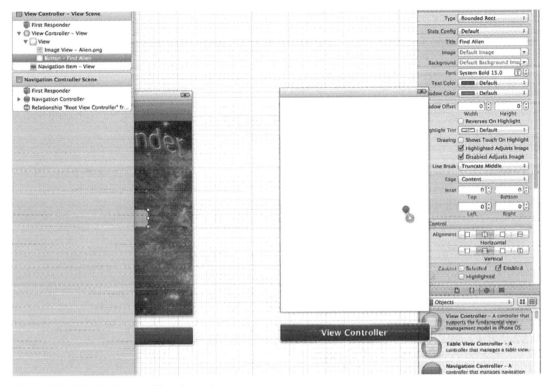

Figure 2-7. *Add a button and View Controller.*

6. Next you need to add a button to this scene and add a new
   View Controller Scene that will become the Secondary "Alien"
   View. First drag a Round Rect button onto the canvas and name
   it *Find Alien* by first double-clicking it. Stretch the button so the
   text shows and then center the button within the view. To add a
   new scene, drag a View Controller from the Object Library to the
   right-hand side of the existing View Controller scene. Hold it
   there for a second, and the existing scene will shift to the left.
   Once it does, place the new View Controller to the right of the
   Main View Controller scene that has shifted to the left. This is
   illustrated in Figure 2-7.

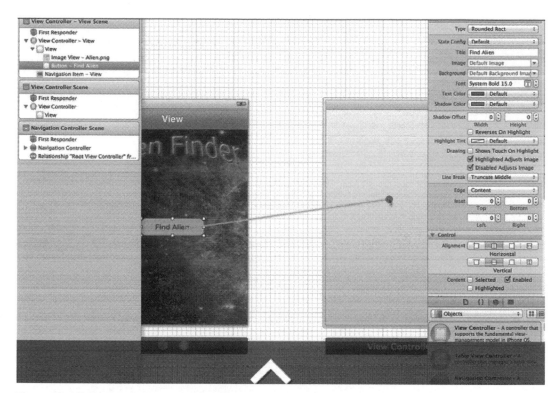

Figure 2-8. *Connect the button to the new View Controller.*

7. You now need to perform one of the coolest things
    Storyboarding can do—seamlessly connect segues from one
    view to the next. In this case you want to connect the button
    you just created to segue to the new scene you've added. In the
    olden days this took huge amounts of code. Now you just
    Control-drag. To connect the Find Alien button to the new View
    Controller, Control-drag from the Find Alien button to the new
    View Controller as shown in Figure 2-8.

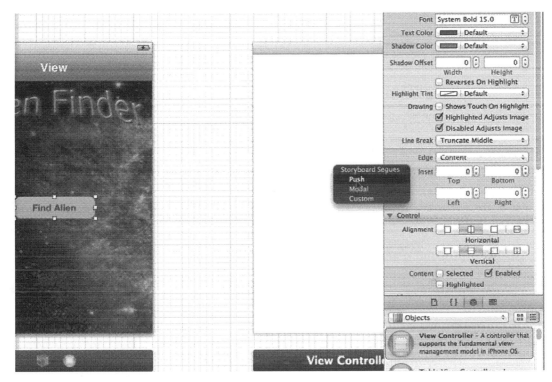

Figure 2-9. *Select Push.*

8. Once you've Control-dragged over to the new View Controller,
    let it go and you will see a menu as shown in Figure 2-9 where
    you set the Storyboard segue transition style. Use the Push
    style for now. Select the Push transition style from the
    Storyboard Segues pop-up menu.

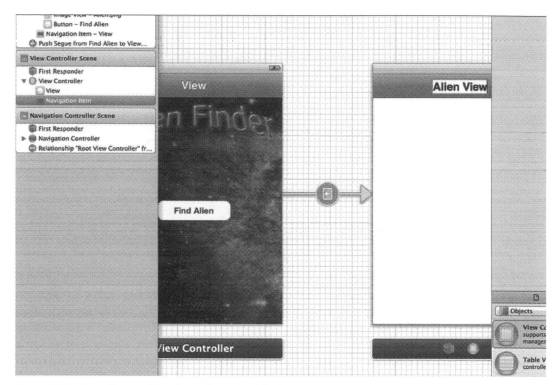

Figure 2-10. *Name the new View Controller and set the image.*

9.   Name this second View Controller *Alien View*. To do this, as you did with the first view, double-click the new View Controller's Navigation Bar and name it *Alien View*. While we're here let's create the Alien's Image View. Drag an Image View onto the View Controller's canvas. With the image View still selected, in Attributes Inspector select Alien Face.png as its Image. This is illustrated in Figure 2-10.

Figure 2-11. *The segue works! No Code!*

10. Believe it or not, you already have a running app! Run it by clicking the Run button in the top left-hand corner of Xcode, and as shown in Figure 2-11 it works beautifully. Click the button, and you go to the Alien View. Click the back button entitled View on the left-hand side of the Navigation Bar in the Alien View, and you return to the Main View. Beautiful!

Step 2: Pass Information Back from a Secondary View (Alien View) to the Main View

In this step we show the typical pattern for passing information back from a Secondary View to the Main View. You do this most often by describing the communication as a protocol, and with the Main View setting itself up as the delegate of the Secondary View. Let's see how this is done.

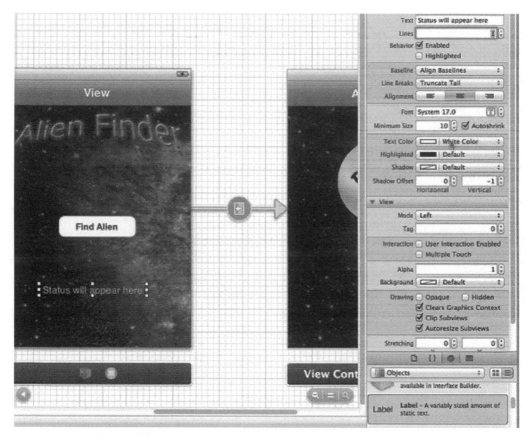

Figure 2-12. *Drag a label onto the Main View.*

1. When passing back results from the Alien View, you need some
    way to display the fact that the results have been returned.
    You're going to show text on the Main View that changes based
    on the value returned. Add a label where you can indicate
    whether the Alien exists. Drag a label onto the Main View under
    the button. Center it, set the text color to white, and enter
    Status will appear here into the Text box as shown in
    Figure 2-12.

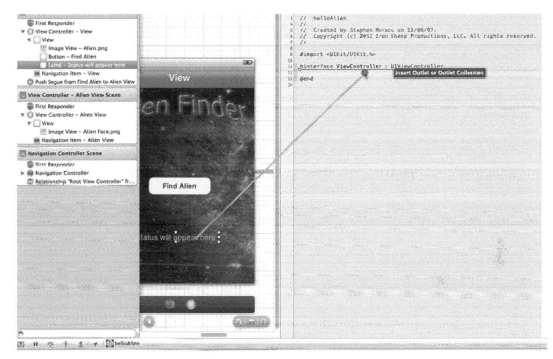

Figure 2-13. *Control-drag from the Label to ViewController.h.*

2. To be able to set the label text from our code, you need to have a connection to this new label. Let's create the Label's IBOutlet (your connection). Open the Assistant (its icon is in the white circle in Figure 2-13) and make sure it has correlated the ViewController.h file onto the right-hand pane of the Split View. Control-drag from the label to the ViewController.h file, dropping it directly under the @interface ViewController line as shown in Figure 2-13.

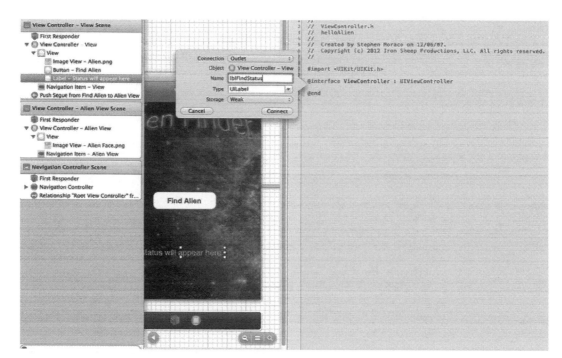

Figure 2-14. *Control-drag from the Label to ViewController.h.*

3. After you drop the connector into the ViewController.h file, a connection dialog box appears. Keep this connection type as an Outlet and name it lblFindStatus. (The lbl prefix reminds you that a label is connected to this outlet.) This dialog is illustrated in Figure 2-14.

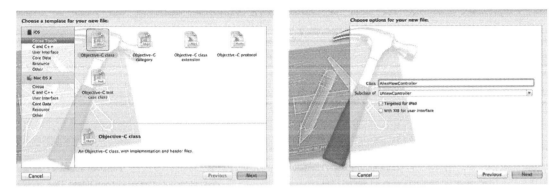

Figure 2-15. *Add a new View Controller subclass.*

4. You now need to add custom code to the View Controller for your Alien View. Do this by creating a new derived View Controller class. Select the helloAlien group in the Project Navigator (so the new files are placed within this group). Press ⌘+N and select the Objective-C class option as shown on the left in Figure 2-15. After clicking Next, name the new class AlienViewController, select the UIViewController subclass option as shown on the right in Figure 2-15, and click Next. Don't change any options—save them. Note that the two new files (AlienViewController.h and .m) were placed below the Supporting Files group. Drag them back above the group so they appear with the rest of the files.

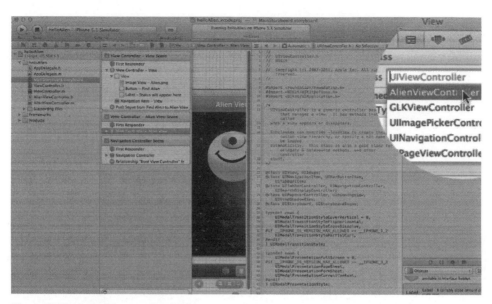

Figure 2-16. *Assign the new Detail View.*

5. You need to assign the new `AlienViewController` class you've just created to your Alien View. Go back into the Storyboard file and select the Alien View—but you need to be precise here. In Document Outline Navigator, go to the View Controller – Alien View Scene ➤ View Controller – Alien View and click it to select it. With it properly selected, in the Utilities' Identity Inspector in the Custom Class area select the class `AlienViewController` as illustrated in Figure 2-16.

NOTE: In the remainder of this chapter you're going to do things like Apple Developers do onstage at conferences like WWDC. You're going to drag snippets of code into your project while we describe what you're doing. This is intended to save you a lot of time (because you don't have to type the code), yet still give you an opportunity to study the code with each drag-and-drop. To get started, open the DemoMonkey file you downloaded along with the images you've already placed into this project. Locate the file named `Chapter2.demoMonkey` and continue on the next page.

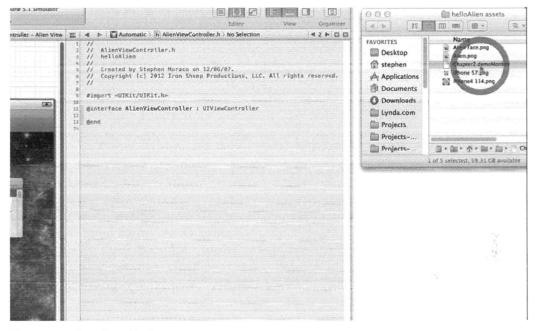

Figure 2-17. *Open DemoMonkey.*

6. Open the `Chapter2.demoMonkey` file. The window first appears very small as you see in Figure 2-17. Simply grab a corner and stretch the window so that the lines are visible.

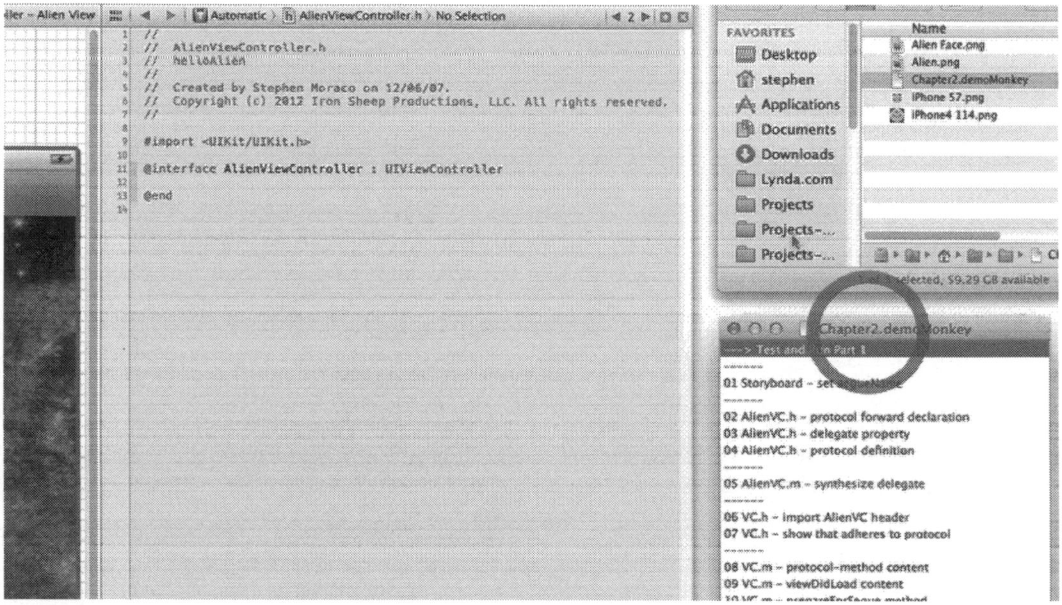

Figure 2-18. *Expand the DemoMonkey window and place it on the side.*

7. In Figure 2-18 you can see that we've placed the DemoMonkey file to the right of the Xcode window and stretched it so that the lines can be seen. Some of them may be off the bottom of the screen, depending on your display resolution. If they are, scroll the DemoMonkey window when you need to get to these off-screen lines.

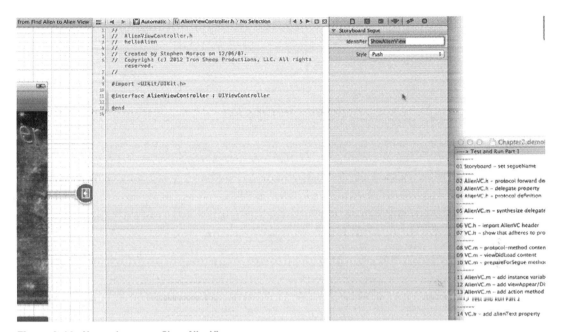

Figure 2-19. *Name the segue ShowAlienView.*

8. In order for the code to know which segue is taking place, give each segue a name. The code can then look for this name to know which segue has occurred and take the actions appropriate to the named segue. To name the segue, select it by clicking the circled icon in the middle of the segue arrow and then choosing the Attributes Inspector in the Utility area as shown in Figure 2-19. Click in the Identifier text box and then drag the "01 segueName" DemoMonkey snippet onto the Identifier text box and drop it there. The name ShowAlienView appears in the Identifier box.

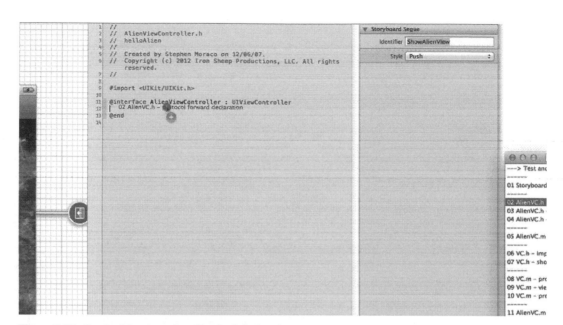

Figure 2-20. *Create delegate protocol forward-declaration.*

9. You'll use a delegate protocol to talk back to the Main View's
    controller. So, let's create it now:

    a. Open the `AlienViewController.h` file, insert a
        declaration of the name of your new protocol by
        dragging the "02 AlienVC.h - protocol forward
        declaration" snippet to just under the `#import
        <UIKit/UIKit.h>` line.

    b. Add your delegate property by dragging in the "03
        AlienVC.h - delegate property" snippet to just under
        the `@interface AlienViewController :
        UIViewController` line.

    c. Create a definition for your
        `AlienViewControllerDelegate` protocol. Do this by
        dragging "04 AlienVC.h - protocol definition" and
        placing it after the `@end` line of the interface (at the end
        of the file) as shown in Figure 2-20.

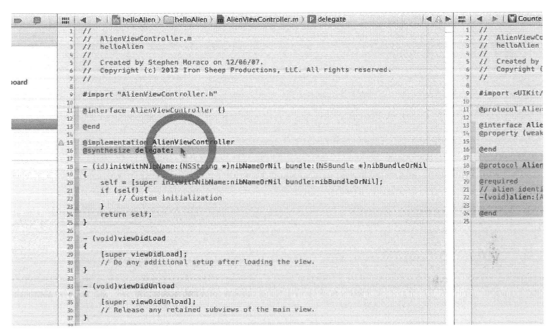

Figure 2-21. *Synthesize the AlienViewController Delegate property.*

10. Quick recap: You've declared the protocol and declared the delegate property that refers to an object which must conform to this protocol. Now you need to synthesize the delegate property. To do that, first open the `AlienViewController.m` file and simply drag out from "05 AlienVC.m - synthesize delegate" and drop it under the `@implementation AlienViewController` line as shown in Figure 2-21.

> **NOTE:** In Xcode, to *synthesize* means to generate code. In this case you're generating the setter and getter for your delegate property. The purpose of the `@synthesize` directive is to save work for coders because we no longer have to write the setter and getter methods for every property we create.

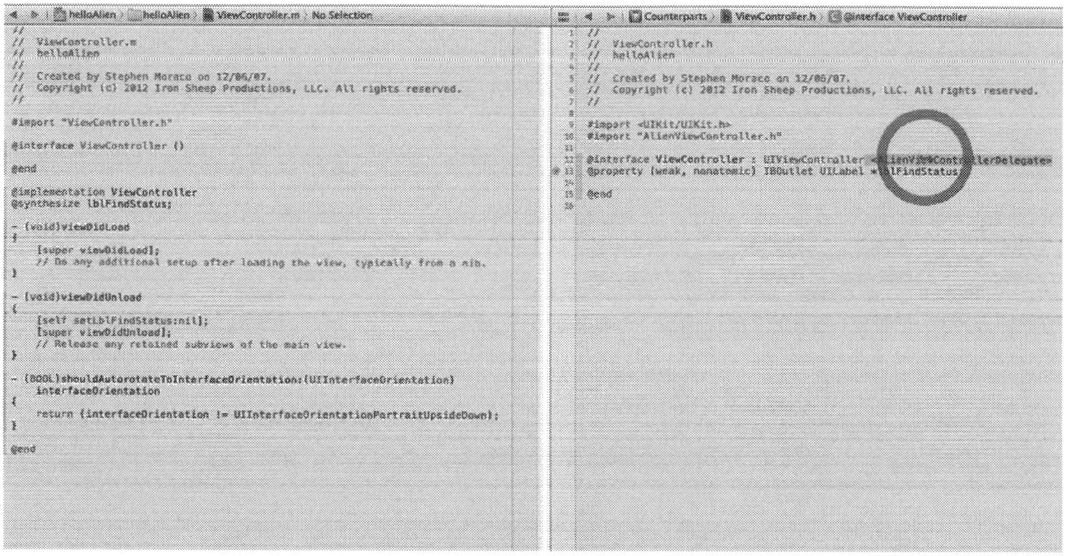

Figure 2-22. *Make the Main View Controller adhere to the AlienViewControllerDelegate protocol.*

11. You now want to make sure that the ViewController adheres to the AlienViewControllerDelegate protocol you've just created. To do that, first open the ViewController.h file and drag "06 VC.h - import AlienVC header" to just below the #import <UIKit/UIKit.h> line. Now you need to add @interface ViewController : UIViewController onto the protocol conformance declaration by dragging "07 VC.h - show that adheres to protocol" as shown in Figure 2-22.

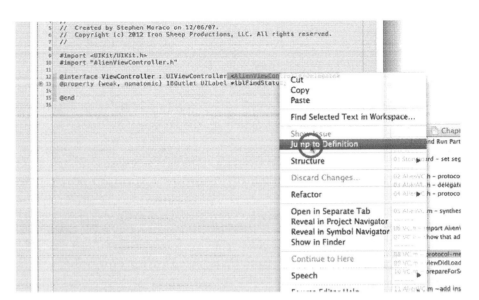

Figure 2-23. *Select Jump to Definition .*

12. Next add the new protocol method to the code. Copy the
method signature directly from the protocol declaration so you
get it exactly correct. Click the protocol name (found in the < >
brackets) and then select the right-mouse menu item Jump to
Definition to jump directly to your new protocol. (Note you may
have to build (press ⌘+B) the code once to get this name
recognized.)

> **NOTE:** Why did we use this Jump to Definition technique? Because you have to learn
> about a very large number of protocols and object interfaces when writing code for
> iOS. The best way to learn is to refresh what you know about a protocol or interface
> each time you use it. By going directly to the protocol declaration, you get a chance
> to remind yourself of the other methods declared to be part of the protocol. See?
> Continuous training as you work!
>
> If you've been around in the code business for a while, did you notice that you don't
> have to know which file the protocol is declared in? Xcode found it for you
> automatically. Thank you, Xcode (and the developers who built it)!

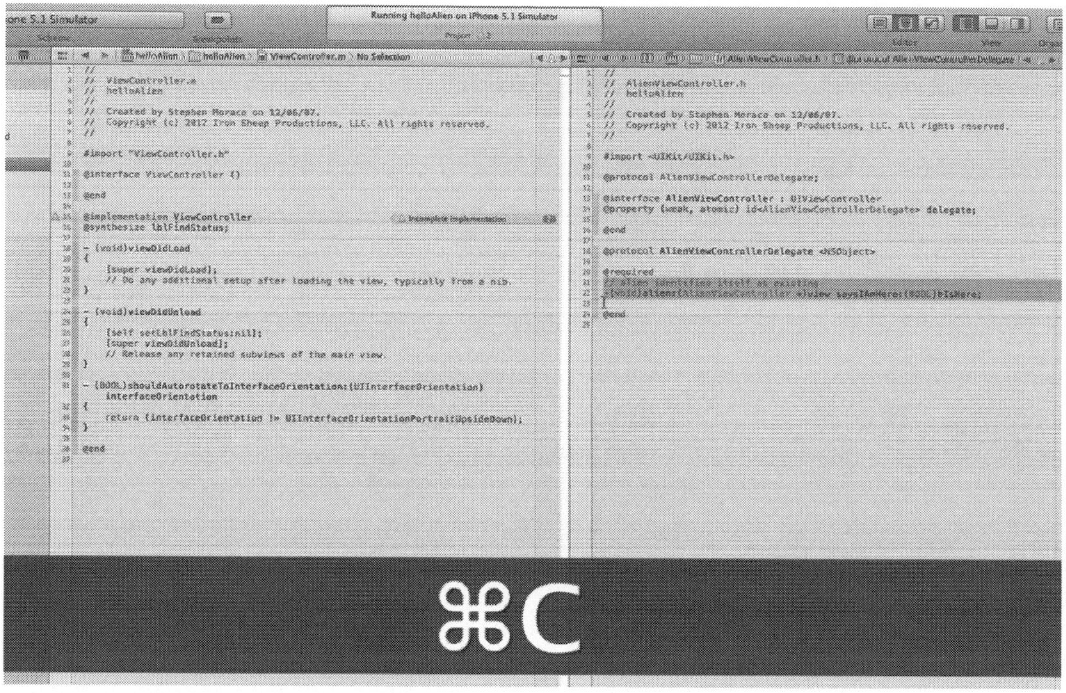

Figure 2-24. *Grab the method from the protocol.*

13. Now select and copy the signature of the `alien:saysIAmHere:` method as shown in Figure 2-24 (the code you're grabbing is highlighted).

NOTE: Did you notice the `@required` directive just above the method line you're copying? That means any object that indicates it conforms to your delegate protocol (in this case, the `ViewController`) *must* have implemented the method `alien:saysIAmHere:`. When you state `@required` in your protocol definition, and you state in another class that you conform to the protocol, the compiler generates an error when you haven't yet implemented one or more of the `@required` methods of the protocol. This helps ensure that you've written all the code you minimally need to handle the protocol.

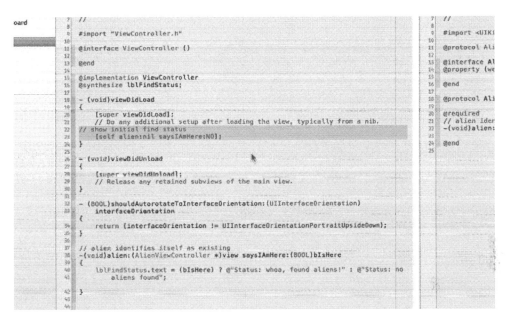

Figure 2-25. *Paste the delegate method.*

14. Continuing with the creation of the delegate protocol method: Go back to the VicwController.m file. Paste the method you just copied right before the @end as shown in Figure 2-25. Add the curly braces in place of the semicolon and add the code from "08 VC.m - protocol-method content" inside these braces that tells you a message (writes text to your new label) when the Alien is found. We happen to say Status: whoa, found aliens! but you of course can insert anything you want. The new method now looks like this:

```
-(void)alien:(AlienViewController *)view saysIAmHere:(BOOL)bIsHere
{
  self.lblFindStatus.text = (bIsHere) ? @"Status: whoa, found aliens!" :
@"Status: no aliens found";
}
```

> **NOTE** This code simply places one of two messages into the onscreen label depending on the state of the parameter bIsHere. Notice too that you're writing this message text to the .text property of the User Interface object, which you know should be a label due to the lbl prefix of the name.

15. You have the segue name ShowAlienView and you have added the delegate protocol method to ViewController so that it knows what to do when the Alien View tells it whether an Alien is present. But now you need to initialize the displayed text when the application first starts to say that you've not found an Alien yet. So, staying in the ViewController.m file, go to the viewDidLoad method and drag in another line of code "09 VC.m - ViewDidLoad content" so the method now looks as follows:

```
- (void)viewDidLoad
{
 [super viewDidLoad];
    [self alien:nil saysIAmHere:NO];
}
```

> **NOTE** This code invokes the same new protocol method, but within ViewController, not from AlienViewController. You're not the AlienViewController so pass nil as the first parameter, and the state you initially want is "NO alien found," so pass NO as the second parameter. Conveniently, the viewDidLoad method happens once when you first start the application, so the onscreen label is set as you need, when you first see it.

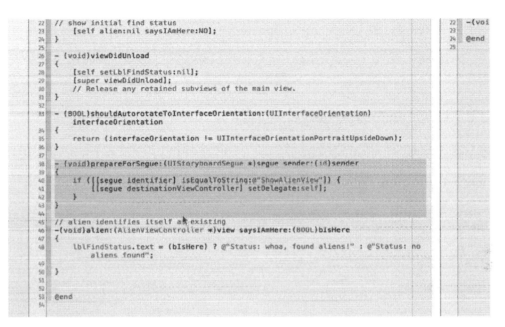

Figure 2-26. *Add prepareForSegue method.*

16. Now you need to tell the `AlienViewController` that
    `ViewController` can handle data it sends to its delegate. Do this
    by telling the `AlienViewController` that `ViewController` is the
    delegate. The `prepareForSegue` method exists just so you can
    do things like this. Let's add a `prepareForSegue` method and set
    the `AlienViewController` delegate property. Dragging "10 VC.m
    - prepareForSegue method" to just under
    `shouldAutorotateTo...`: yields:

```
- (void)prepareForSegue:(UIStoryboardSegue *)segue sender:(id)sender
{
    if ([[segue identifier] isEqualToString:@"ShowAlienView"]) {
        [[segue destinationViewController] setDelegate:self];
        }
}
```

> **NOTE:** This method first checks to see whether the segue is the one you want
> (ShowAlienView). If it is, you set the destination view's delegate property to self
> (this ViewController instance). Now when the destination view appears and
> wants to pass information to the delegate by invoking the alien:saysIAmHere:
> method, the matching method in ViewController is invoked which then sets your
> label text.

Figure 2-27. *Set initial state of switch to Off.*

17. You now have the segue named ShowAlienView setting the delegate property to the ViewController instance so that it can display alien-exists statuses. But our Alien needs to be able to tell you that it exists! So how about a simple "exist" switch? Go add a switch to the Alien View along with a description label. Open the Storyboard file, select the Alien View Controller Scene, and drag a switch onto the Alien View. Set the Switch State to Off as shown in Figure 2-27.

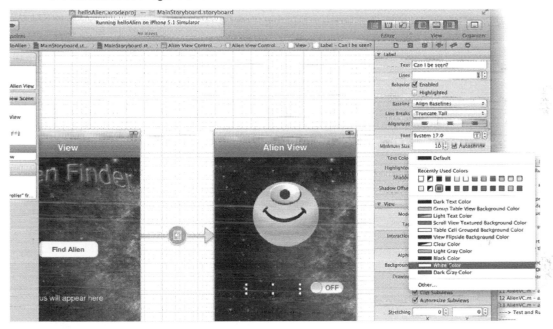

Figure 2-28. *Left-aligned with white text*

18. You also need instructional text, so drag a label onto the canvas to the left of the switch. Make it left-aligned, set the Text Color to white, and set the Text to *Can I be seen?* as shown in Figure 2-28.

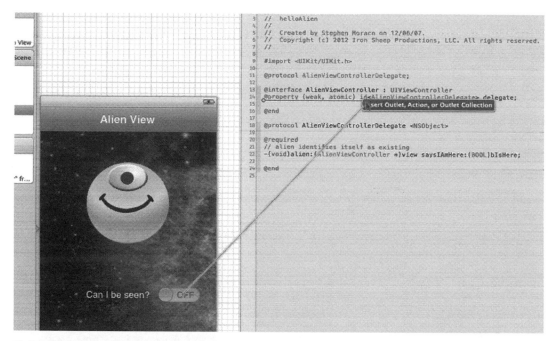

Figure 2-29. *Add an IBAction for the switch.*

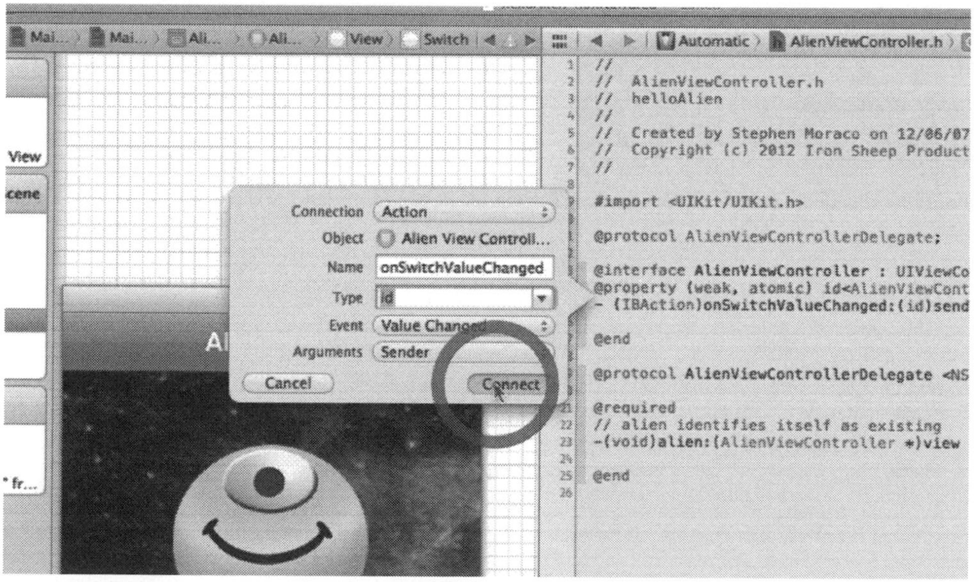

Figure 2-30. *Name the IBAction method onSwitchValueChanged.*

19. Now you need to add an IBAction method for the switch. Open the Assistant Editor and make sure the AlienViewController.h file is to the right of the Alien View. Control-drag from the switch to the blank line after the delegate property as shown in Figure 2-29. Select Action from the Connection drop-down and enter the name *onSwitchValueChanged* as shown in Figure 2-30.

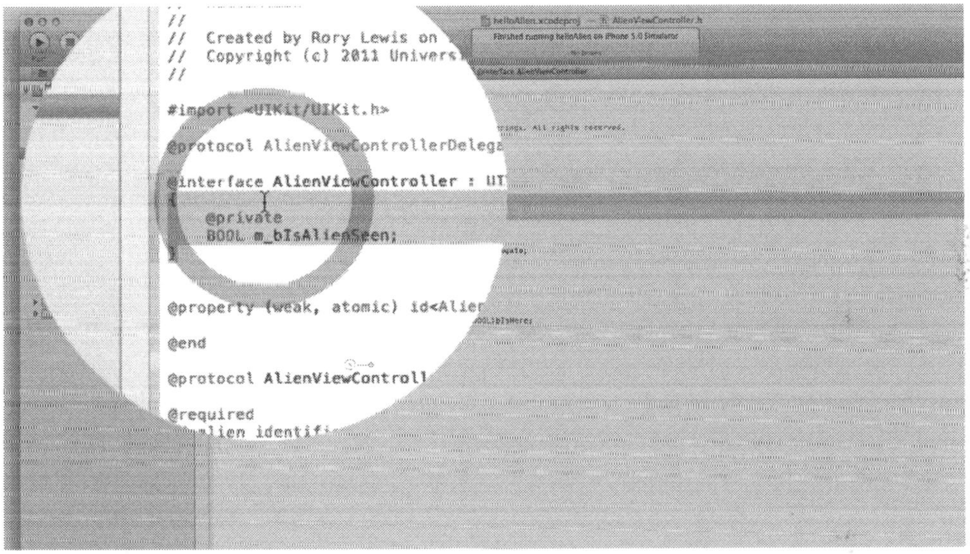

Figure 2-31. *Create a variable to hold the value of the switch.*

20. Xcode has generated a method shell for this in the implementation file that you now need to code to get the value from the switch. But before you do this, you need to first create a variable that will hold the switch state. So, let's first declare this variable. Go to the AlienViewController.m file and drag "11 AlienVC.m -add instance variable" just to the right end of the @interface AlienViewController () line, so that you now have the code as shown In Figure 2-31:

```
@interface AlienViewController () {
@private   // unneccessary, but reminds us!
    BOOL m_bIsAlienSeen;
}
```

21. You need to set up the initial state of this variable and return the state of this variable to your delegate. Conveniently, you can use `viewWillAppear` to set the initial state and `viewWillDisappear` to report the switch value as you're leaving. To add these two methods, drag "12 AlienVC.m -add viewWillAppear/Disappear methods" to just after the `viewDidLoad` method, so that we now have the code as shown in Figure 2-32.

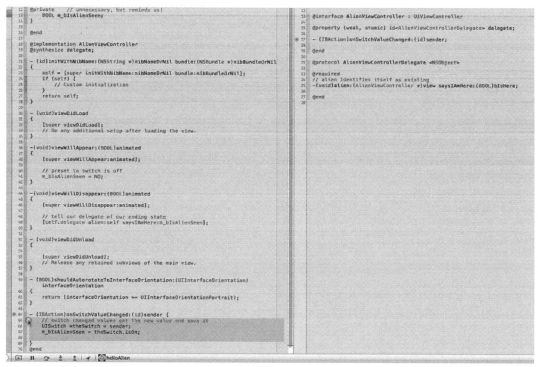

Figure 2-32. *Add the two methods viewWillAppear and viewWillDisappear.*

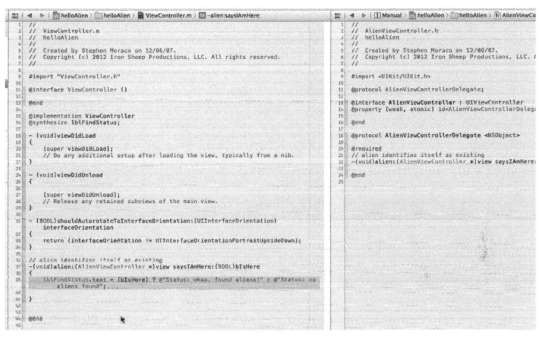

Figure 2-33. *Add code to capture the current switch value when it changes.*

22. Finally, you're in a position to capture the switch value whenever it's changed. Drag "13 AlienVC.m - add action method content" inside the curly braces of the `onSwitchValueChanged:` method so that the code appears as shown in Figure 2-33.

Figure 2-34. *Whoa! Found the Alien!*

23. You've completed the code modifications for Step 2. Let's run the code in the iPhone Simulator to see if you have it all working! Click the Run button at the top left of the Xcode window. When the Simulator starts, click Find Alien to go to the Alien View. Your new switch should be there. Toggle the switch to On and click the back button (top left of Navigation Bar) to return to the Main View. Did your Status: text change? Did you find your Alien? Figure 2-34 illustrates this test sequence.

Step 3: Send Information Out to the Secondary View (Alien View)

In this section we're going to demonstrate a common technique for passing information out to the destination view. In this case, you're going to add a text field to your Alien Finder main screen and pass the text on to the Alien's universe! Let's get started.

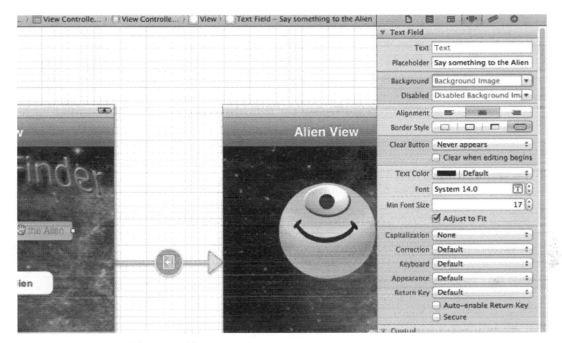

Figure 2-35. *Say something to the Alien.*

1. You now want to send a message to the Alien once he tells us
   he exists. Drag a text field onto the Main View above the Find
   Alien button. Center the text and enter *Say something to the
   Alien* as the Placeholder text (this text informs the user of the
   purpose of the Text Field) as illustrated in Figure 2-35.

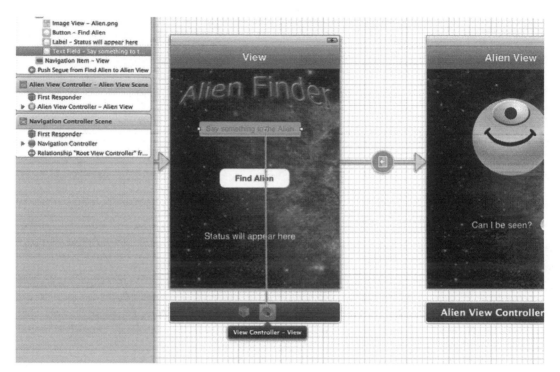

Figure 2-36. *Control-drag from the Text Field down to the View Controller icon.*

2. You now need to assign the View Controller as the Text Field's delegate so that it can know when the editing is done—so you can dismiss the keyboard. Control-drag from the "Say Something to the Alien!" Text Field down to the View Controller icon right below as shown in Figure 2-36.

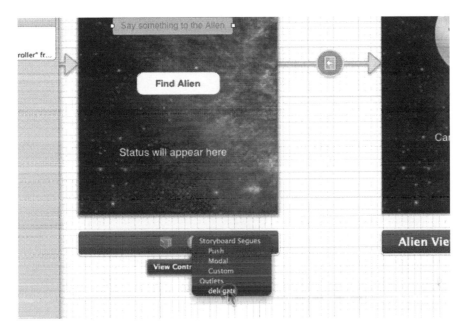

Figure 2-37. *Connect to the "delegate" outlet.*

3. In the drop-down menu, connect it to the "delegate" outlet as illustrated in Figure 2-37.

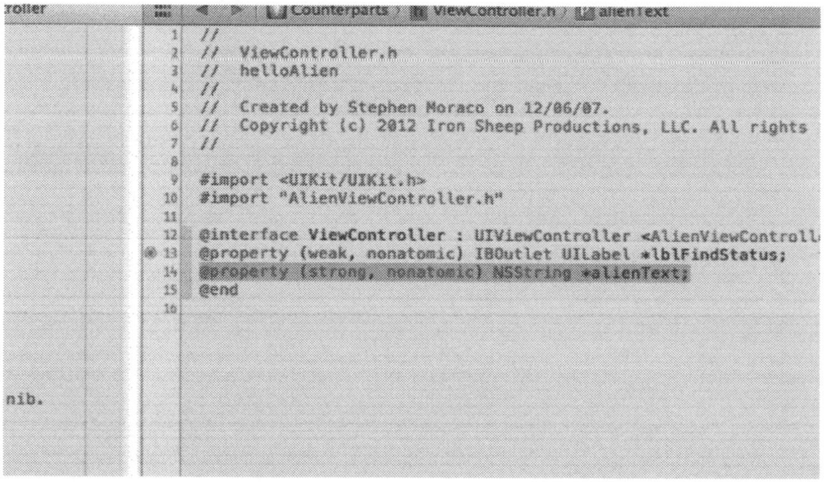

Figure 2-38. *Create the property for the string message to the Alien.*

4. Next create and synthesize a property for your message string
    to the Alien. Go to the ViewController.h file and under the
    lblFindStatus property add a new property by dragging "14
    VC.h - add alienText property" as illustrated in Figure 2-38. To
    synthesize it, go back to the ViewController.m file under the
    lblFindStatus synthesis and add the new property synthesis by
    dragging "15 VC.m - synthesize AlienText property" into place.

```
39    - (void)prepareForSegue:(UIStoryboardSegue *)segue sender:(id)sender
40    {
41        if ([[segue identifier] isEqualToString:@"ShowAlienView"]) {
42            [[segue destinationViewController] setDelegate:self];
43        }
44    }
45
46    // alien identifies itself as existing
47    -(void)alien:(AlienViewController *)view saysIAmHere:(BOOL)bIsHere
48    {
49        lblFindStatus.text = (bIsHere) ? @"Status: whoa, found aliens!" : @"Status: no
          aliens found";
50
51    }
52
53    #pragma mark ---- <UITextFieldDelegate> Methods
54
55    - (BOOL)textFieldShouldReturn:(UITextField *)textField
56    {
57        // the user pressed the return, so dismiss the keyboard
58        [textField resignFirstResponder];
59        return YES;
60    }
61
62    - (void)textFieldDidEndEditing:(UITextField *)textField
63
64    {
65        // Capture the new text from out text field
66        self.alienText = textField.text;
67    }
68
69    @end
```

Figure 2-39. *Controlling the text editing to the Alien.*

5. When you enter text, you need two sets of code—one method to dismiss the keyboard, and the other to capture the text that was entered in the text field. You'll do this with textFieldDidEndEditing and textFieldShouldReturn delegate methods that are provided by the UITextFieldDelegate protocol. All you need to do is to add implementation for both methods. Staying in the ViewController.m file, drag "16 VC.m - add Text Editing support methods" as illustrated in Figure 2-39.

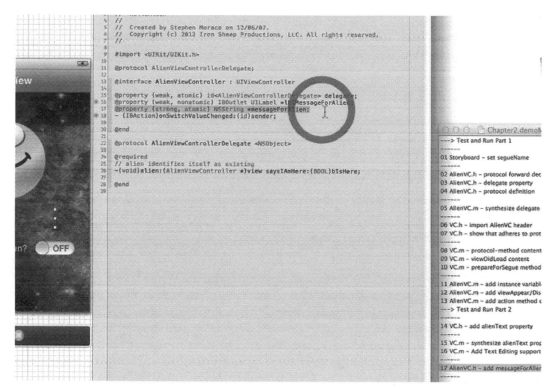

Figure 2-40. *The property for the message to the Alien*

6. You need to create and synthesize a property, but this time it's for you to capture the text you're sending to the Alien. In the `AlienViewController.h` file, add a property by dragging in "17 AlienVC.h - add messageForAlien property" as illustrated in Figure 2-40.

```
11   @interface AlienViewController () {
12   @private     // unnecessary, but reminds us!
13       BOOL m_bIsAlienSeen;
14   }
15
16   @end
17
18   @implementation AlienViewController
19   @synthesize delegate;
20   @synthesize lblMessageForAlien;
21   @synthesize messageForAlien;|
22   - (id)initWithNibName:(NSString *)nibNameOrNil bundle:(NSBundle *)nibBundleOrNil
23   {
24       self = [super initWithNibName:nibNameOrNil bundle:nibBundleOrNil];
25       if (self) {
26           // Custom initialization
27       }
28       return self;
29   }
30
31   - (void)viewDidLoad
32   {
33       [super viewDidLoad];
34       // Do any additional setup after loading the view.
35   }
36
37   -(void)viewWillAppear:(BOOL)animated
38   {
39       [super viewWillAppear:animated];
40
41       // preset to switch is off
42       m_bIsAlienSeen = NO;
43   }
44
```

Figure 2-41. *Synthesize the message to the Alien property.*

7. In the AlienViewController.m file, under the lblFindStatus
    synthesis, add the new property synthesis using "18 AVC.m
    synthesize messageForAlien property" as illustrated in
    Figure 2-41.

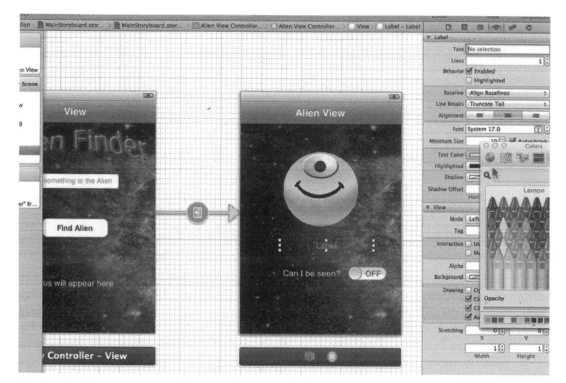

Figure 2-42. *Create a means for Alien to receive the text.*

8. Now you need to create a means to have the Alien receive the
    text being written to the Alien. Go to Storyboard and drag a
    label onto the Alien View. Center it, make it yellow, and empty
    out its text as illustrated in Figure 2-42.

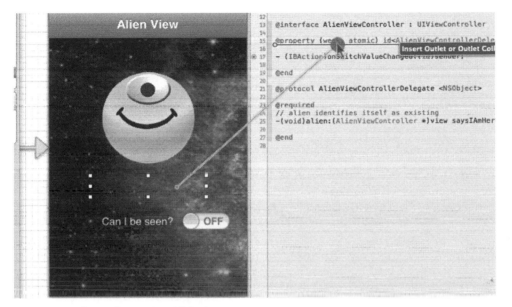

Figure 2-43. *Create the new label IBOutlet.*

9. You need an outlet for the label you created in step 41, so open
    the Assistant Editor and Control-drag from the label to the
    header file and drop it below the messageForAlien property as
    illustrated in Figure 2-43.

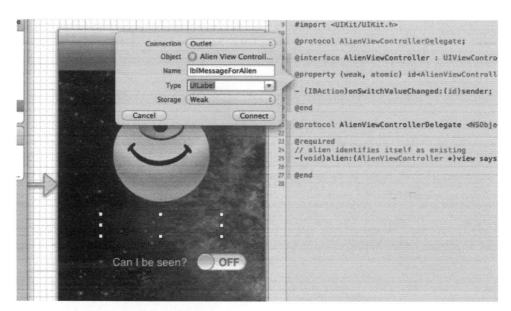

Figure 2-44. *Name it lblMessageForAlien.*

10. Keep it as an Outlet and name it `lblMessageForAlien` as illustrated in Figure 2-44.

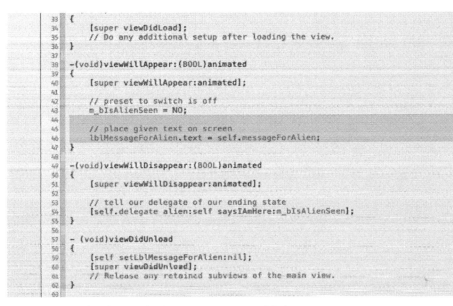

Figure 2-45. *Add code to assign text to your onscreen label.*

11. You need to make sure that the viewWillAppear method will show the label's text. Go to the AlienViewController.m file and drag in "19 AlienVC.m - add viewWillAppear content" as shown in Figure 2-45 and illustrated here:

```
-(void)viewWillAppear:(BOOL)animated
{
    [super viewWillAppear:animated];
    // preset to switch is off
    m_bIsAlienSeen = NO;

    // place given text on screen
    lblMessageToAlien.text = self.messageForAlien
}
```

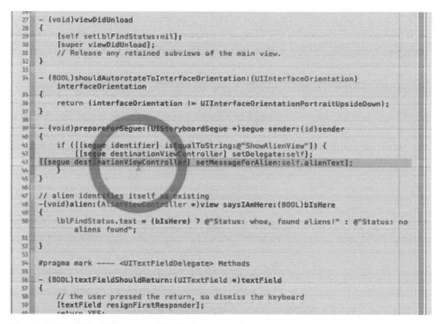

```
27  - (void)viewDidUnload
28  {
29      [self setLblFindStatus:nil];
30      [super viewDidUnload];
31      // Release any retained subviews of the main view.
32  }
33
34  - (BOOL)shouldAutorotateToInterfaceOrientation:(UIInterfaceOrientation)
        interfaceOrientation
35  {
36      return (interfaceOrientation != UIInterfaceOrientationPortraitUpsideDown);
37  }
38
39  - (void)prepareForSegue:(UIStoryboardSegue *)segue sender:(id)sender
40  {
41      if ([[segue identifier] isEqualToString:@"ShowAlienView"]) {
42          [[segue destinationViewController] setDelegate:self];
43  [[segue destinationViewController] setMessageForAlien:self.alienText];
44      }
45  }
46
47  // alien identifies itself as existing
48  -(void)alien:(AlienViewController *)view saysIAmHere:(BOOL)bIsHere
49  {
50      lblFindStatus.text = (bIsHere) ? @"Status: whoa, found aliens!" : @"Status: no
        aliens found";
51
52  }
53
54  #pragma mark ---- <UITextFieldDelegate> Methods
55
56  - (BOOL)textFieldShouldReturn:(UITextField *)textField
57  {
58      // the user pressed the return, so dismiss the keyboard
59      [textField resignFirstResponder];
```

Figure 2-46. *Adjust the prepareForSegue method.*

12. Lastly, and this should look quite familiar to you, pass the text to
    the Alien View by setting the Alien View property to the value of
    the Main View property. Open ViewController.m and scroll
    down to the prepareForSegue: method. Drag "20 VC.m - add
    prepareForSegue content" placing it within the if statement
    after the setDelegate: call as shown in Figure 2-46.

Figure 2-47. *Hello Mr. Alien!*

13. You've completed modifying the code. Run the code on the
    iPhone Simulator once again to prove that your changes work
    as expected. When the Main View appears, enter text into your
    new text field. Click Find Alien, and when the new view appears,
    there's your message out in the Alien universe! Figure 2-47
    shows what your result should look like.

Congratulations. You've just completed adding the code to receive text from the
user, passing it as a string from the source view to the destination view, and
showing it on the destination view when the view appears. Easy, right?

Step 4: Custom Segue

This section demonstrates the ease with which you can substitute a custom
segue you created for the default segue you've been using.

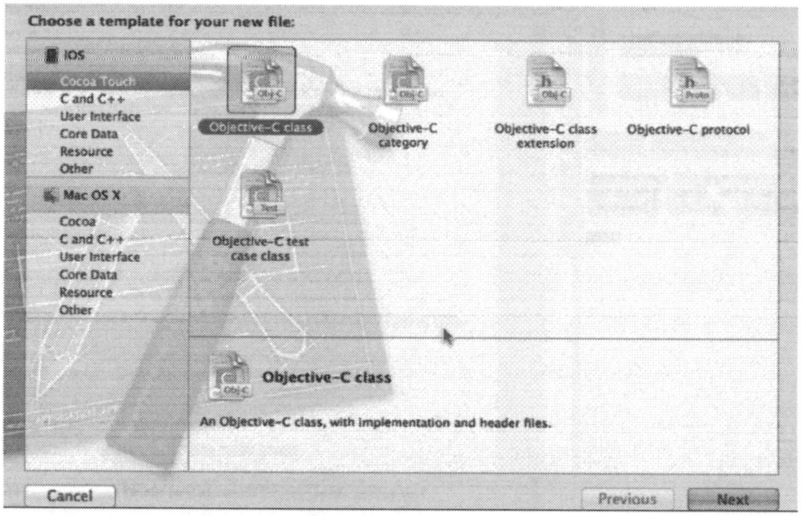

Figure 2-48. *A new class for your segue override*

1. To create a new view transition for segue use, you now can
    simply create a specialized class of UIStoryboardSegue and
    override the default perform method. Let's create the new
    derived class by clicking the helloAlien group in the Project
    Navigator and pressing ⌘+N as illustrated in Figure 2-48. The
    new dialog appears. Choose "Objective-C Class" and click
    Next.

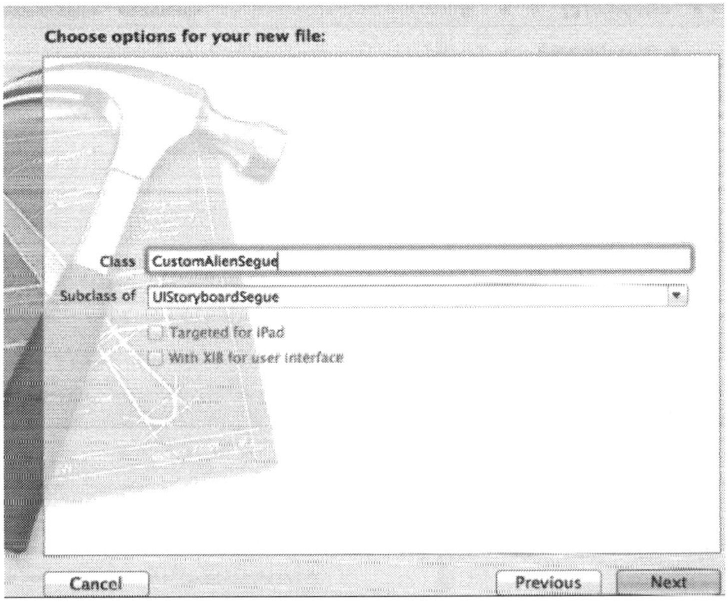

Figure 2-49. *Name it CustomAlienSegue.*

2. In the "Choose options for your new file" dialog, enter the name
    CustomAlienSegue for your class. Make it a subclass of
    UIStoryboardSegue as is illustrated in Figure 2-49. Click Next to
    create the class files.

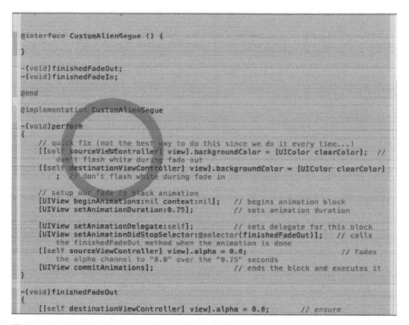

```
@interface CustomAlienSegue () {

}

-(void)finishedFadeOut;
-(void)finishedFadeIn;

@end

@implementation CustomAlienSegue

-(void)perform
{
    // quick fix (not the best way to do this since we do it every time...)
    [[self sourceViewController] view].backgroundColor = [UIColor clearColor]; //
        don't flash white during fade out
    [[self destinationViewController] view].backgroundColor = [UIColor clearColor]
    ;   // don't flash white during fade in

    // setup our fade to black animation
    [UIView beginAnimations:nil context:nil];   // begins animation block
    [UIView setAnimationDuration:0.75];          // sets animation duration

    [UIView setAnimationDelegate:self];          // sets delegate for this block
    [UIView setAnimationDidStopSelector:@selector(finishedFadeOut)];   // calls
        the finishedFadeOut method when the animation is done
    [[self sourceViewController] view].alpha = 0.0;          // Fades
        the alpha channel to "0.0" over the "0.75" seconds
    [UIView commitAnimations];                   // ends the block and executes it
}

-(void)finishedFadeOut
{
    [[self destinationViewController] view].alpha = 0.0;   // ensure
```

Figure 2-50. *Paste the new CustomAlienSegue code.*

3. In the CustomAlienSegue.m file, delete all the code, leaving just
    the comments at the top of the file. Now add your custom
    implementation by dragging in "21 CustomAlienSegue.m -
    replace implementation" as illustrated in Figure 2-50.

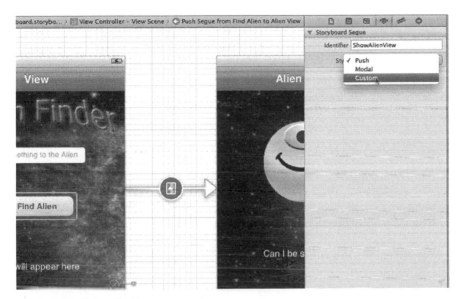

Figure 2-51. *Select the Custom segue type.*

4. You need to tell the Storyboard to use your custom segue. So
    go to the Storyboard file and select the segue (by clicking the
    circle in the middle of the segue arrow between the two View
    Controllers). In the Utility area's Attribute Inspector, change the
    Storyboard Segue Style from Push to Custom in the drop-down
    menu as illustrated in Figure 2-51.

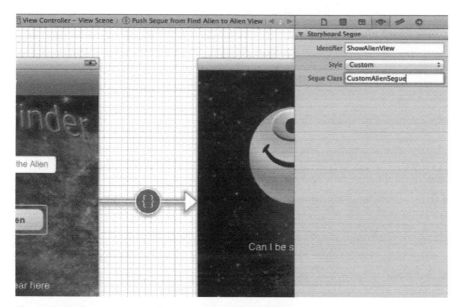

Figure 2-52. *Enter your new class name CustomAlienSegue.*

5. A Segue Class option appears. Enter the custom segue's name,
    CustomAlienSegue, as illustrated in Figure 2-52.

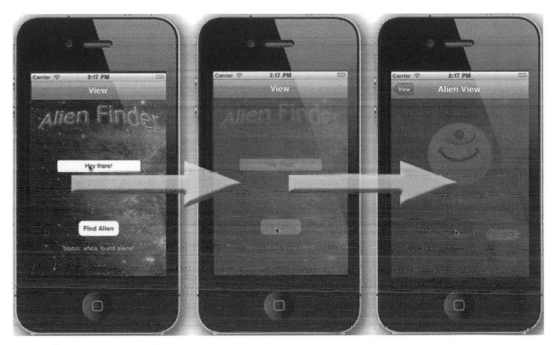

Figure 2-53. *Custom segue fade.*

6. You've completed the modifications for Step 4 of this chapter's four steps. Run your application in the iPhone Simulator to see the result of your latest work. When your application starts, click Find Alien and watch your new custom seque in action (shown in Figure 2-53). If the Main View faded out to black, and your Alien View faded in from black, then you've activated the custom seque correctly. Congratulations!

> **NOTE:** Are you wondering what the custom segue does? We use a couple key facts
> to make a quick and simple effect. The `UIStoryboardSegue` object, upon which
> our custom class is based, knows which `viewController` is going away and which
> `viewController` is going to be shown. Also, to show or hide a User Interface object
> (our views), you can adjust its alpha setting. An alpha value of 1.0 is showing, and a
> value of 0.0 is hidden. This alpha change can be animated. Using these facts, we
> created three methods as follows:

We override the only `UIStoryboardSegue` method perform. In our perform method, we tell the leaving view to animate a fade-out (by adjusting its alpha from 1.0 to 0.0 over time). But we also want to fade-in the appearing view, so we tell the animation to call our `finishedFadeOut` method when the fade-out is complete. In this `finishedFadeOut` method, we tell the view that's going to be shown to do a fade-in animation (again, by adjusting its alpha this time from 0.0 to 1.0 over time) and when it's been completed to call our final `finishedFadeIn` method. In our last method we simply set our first view, which is no longer showing, back to a faded-in state. See? Simple!

Storyboarding with MapView

For your second Storyboarding app, you'll build a really fun Navigation-Based Application that uses MapKit and CoreLocation frameworks. You'll use Flickr as a data source for retrieving photos taken around a specific location and annotate them on a MapView. The Storyboard topics include setting different transition types for segues, building Storyboard scenes utilizing MapView and a static TableView, and initializing segue transitions to other views from MapView's callouts. We will also demonstrate several handy programming techniques, such as dealing with NSURL and parsing some basic JavaScript Object Notation (JSON) data received from a remote server, which has become a great deal simpler with the release of iOS 5.

Figure 3-1 is a screenshot of the final app. The left-hand image illustrates the map zoomed over our location here in Colorado Springs, Colorado. You see a number of blue pins, indicating images taken near the specified location, that have been uploaded to our Flickr account associated with this app and that now appear on the MapView. Selecting the southernmost pin, you see the image titled "Great Sand Dunes," which has been parsed from the Flickr server. Clicking the blue chevron disclosure button, as directed in the app's Storyboard, takes you to the detail view of that image with a back button allowing the user to return to the main view. The image shown is the photo we shot while camping near the famous Sand Dunes in Colorado, located exactly as indicated on the map. The GPS location of the photo was automatically captured by my iPhone as we took the picture. We later uploaded this image to the Flickr site.

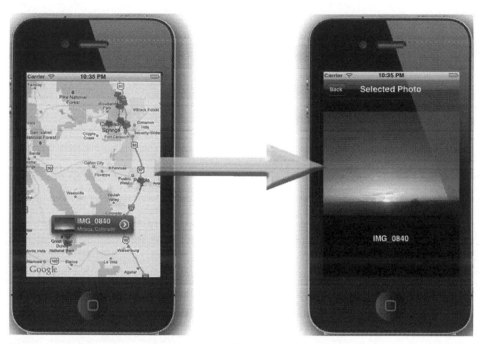

Figure 3-1. *This is the final version of this chapter's app.*

For this exercise, you'll focus on the Storyboarding aspect, so for now, allow us to suggest that you simply use our Flickr account and get the hang of the Storyboarding aspect. Once you do that setting up your own Flickr account will be trivial. We say this because the learning curve in this app is quite steep, and you may not want to be distracted about which images, Flickr account, and so on are being used. There will be enough to occupy your mind as you move through this very exciting and very cool app.

flickrPhotoMap: A Single View App

We have divided this project into three phases:

- Creating a simple MapView scene, setting up the data connection, and displaying geotagged photos on the map

- Creating a secondary scene in Storyboard and making the app transition to that scene by clicking each annotation callout's disclosure button

▨   Creating a modal segue to an additional scene that lets users rate the photo once they click on the callout's thumbnail

In each step we apply the basic Storyboarding techniques from Chapter 2 to a real-life scenario and we demonstrate how iOS 5 Storyboarding makes dealing with more complex UI elements, like MapView and TableView, a lot less intimidating.

Preliminaries

As with all chapters, here we supply you with all the files and code necessary for this project. However, we don't show the images on where to go because they all reside at http://bit.ly/sMRvAP, as illustrated in Figure 3-2.

Looking at Figure 3-2, arrow 1 shows an image from the video of this chapter that links to the video, arrows 2 and 3 point to download icons for the Xcode project and all files necessary for this chapter, including the images and the DemoMonkey files. If you need more help, go to the forum at http://bit.ly/oLVwpY. Before you start, make sure you have downloaded the images and DemoMonkey files at http://bit.ly/sMRvAP and that you have them opened up on your desktop.

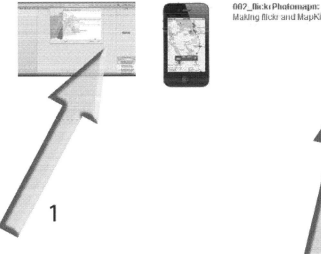
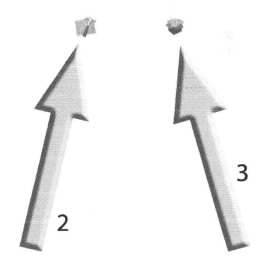

Figure 3-2. *Videos, code, and files for this chapter*

Before embarking on the three steps, keep in mind that:

- In Step 1 you'll set up the code behind the Storyboard features you'll enact in Step 2.

- Step 2 will be the Storyboarding.

- Step 3 will be a combination of code and Storyboarding as you tweak our very cool app.

Step 1: Setting Up the Data Connection and Displaying Geotagged Photos on a Map

In the first step you'll create a single-View scene in which, upon the app start, you'll download the information about our geotagged photos from our Flickr account and display annotations on the map representing locations where the photos were taken. Note that for this application to run successfully, you must be connected to the Internet. You can follow along using the API key we have set up for this book, but if you want to use the Flickr service *in your own project* you will need to apply for your own unique API key. You can apply for an API key online at www.flickr.com/services/api/misc.api_keys.html.

1. Open Xcode, press ⌘⇧N, and select a Single View Application. Name it FlickrPhotoMap. Name the Company Identifier com.storyboarding. We will not use a Class Prefix. Make sure to select iPhone in the Device Family drop-down and check both Use Storyboard and Use Automatic Reference Counting, as shown in Figure 3-3. Once created, save it onto your desktop.

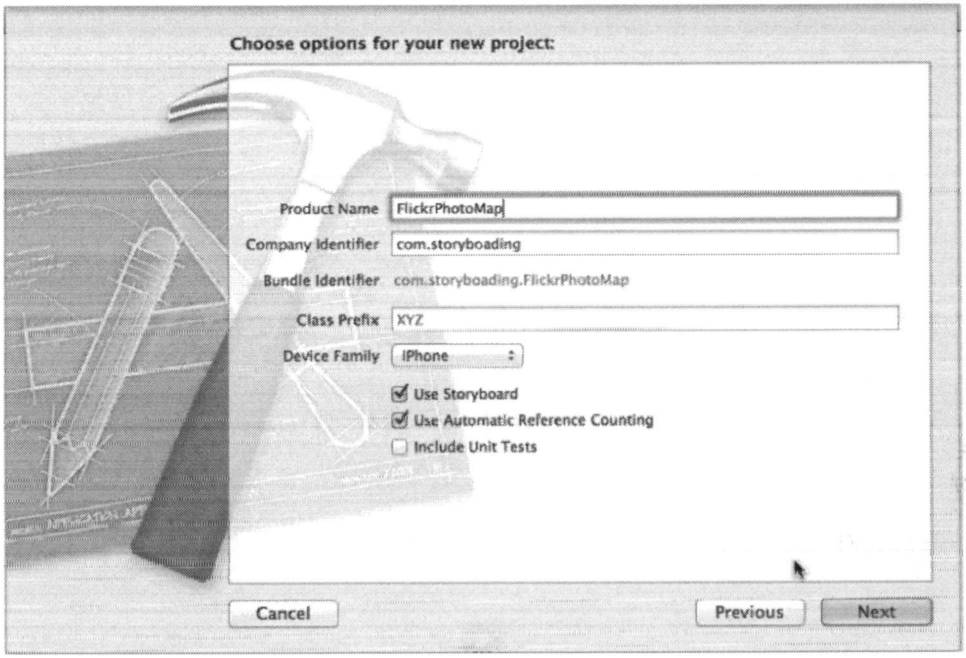

Figure 3-3. *Start with a Single View Application template.*

NOTE: In this app you'll be using MapView and Reverse Geocoding. To use those features you must link required frameworks to your project. Click the project title at the top of the Navigation tree. In the target settings on the right, select the Build Phases tab, open up the Link Binary With Libraries section, and click the plus button at the bottom. Then, in the pop-up window, search for *MapKit*, as shown in Figure 3-4, select it in the list, and click the Add button. Repeat the steps again to add the CoreLocation framework.

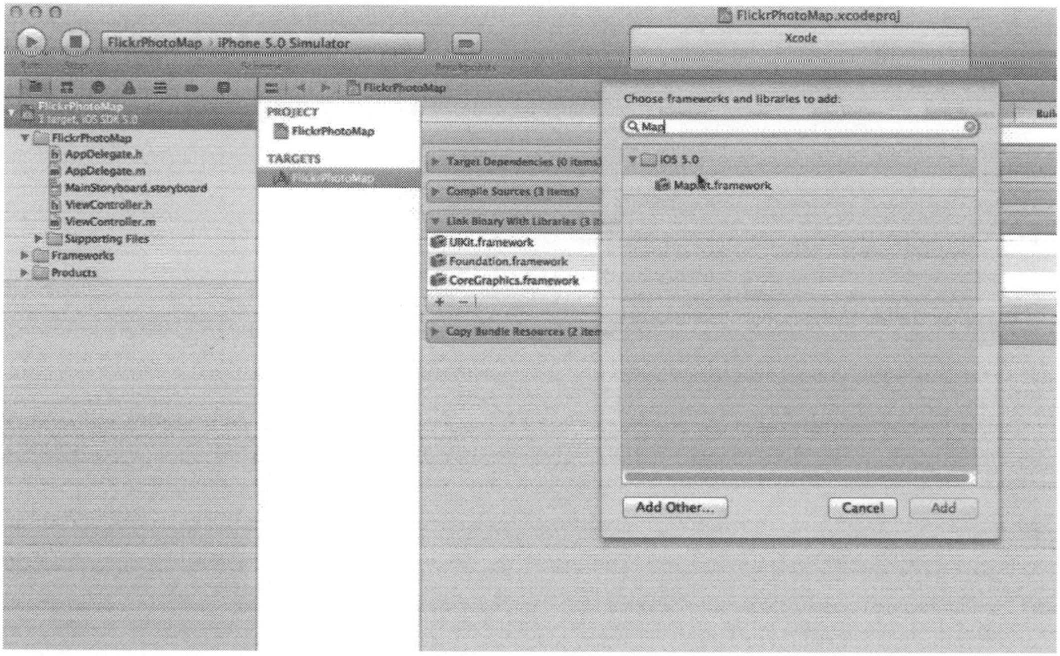

Figure 3-4. *Add MapKit and CoreLocation frameworks to the project.*

2. If the newly added framework files end up outside the project Navigation tree, drag them into Frameworks group as shown in Figure 3-5. You also need to drag the Images folder into the Xcode project. The folder is located in your download pack from the author's site. Navigate to the Images folder and drag the entire folder, in as shown in Figure 3-6. Also make sure the box "Copy items into destination group's folder (if needed)" is checked, as shown in Figure 3-7.

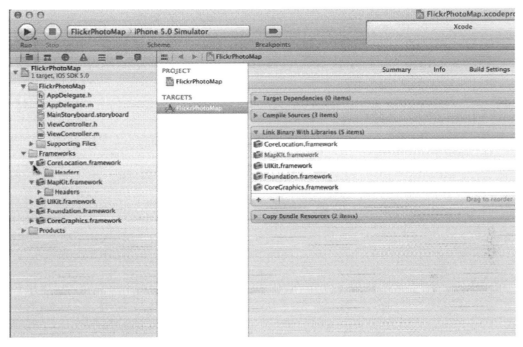

Figure 3-5. *Move newly added files to the Frameworks folder.*

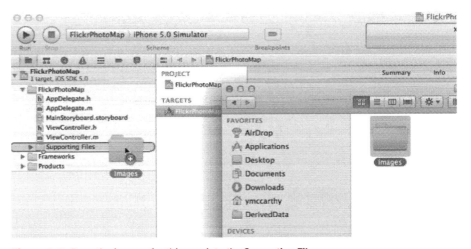

Figure 3-6. *Drag the images for this app into the Supporting Files group.*

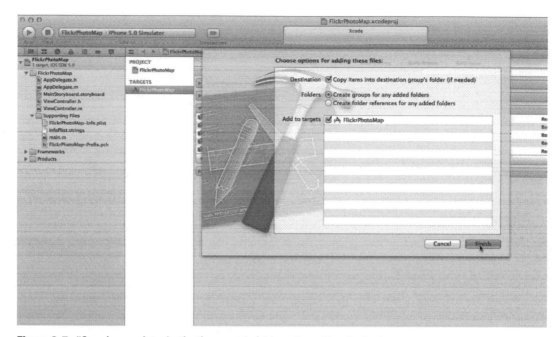

Figure 3-7. *"Copy images into destination group's folder…" must be checked*

3. Now select both ViewController.h and ViewController.m files and hit Delete. In the confirmation dialog, click Move to Trash, not Remove References.

4. You will now create your own main View Controller. Hit ⌘N and select the Objective-C class option as shown in Figure 3-8. Click Next, select the UIViewController subclass, and name it MapViewController, as shown in Figure 3-9. Do not change any options. Save it.

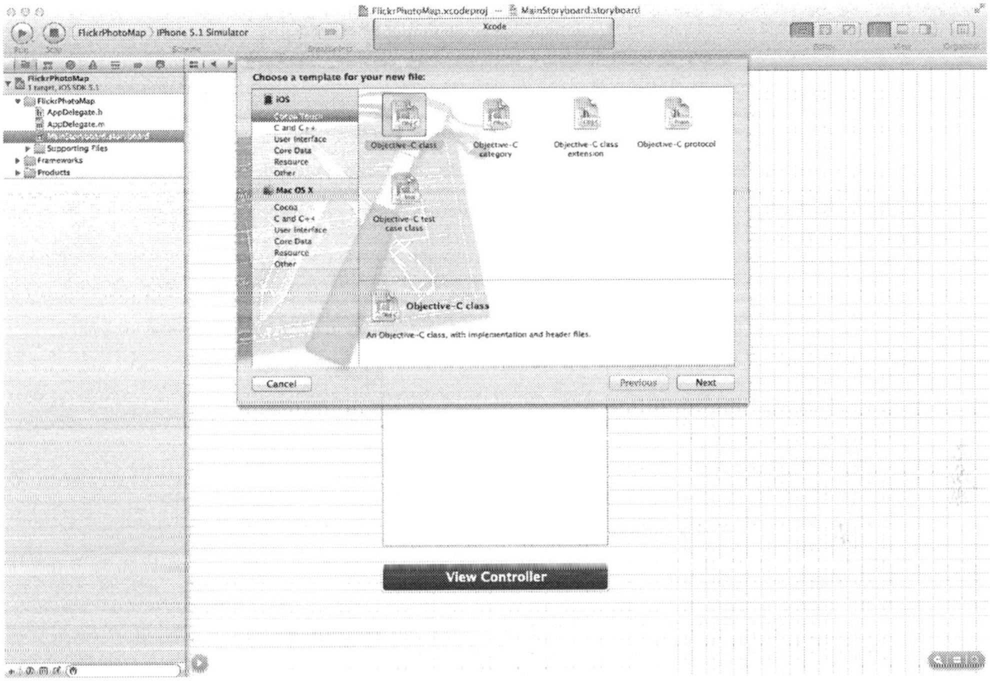

Figure 3-8. *Create a new Objective-C class.*

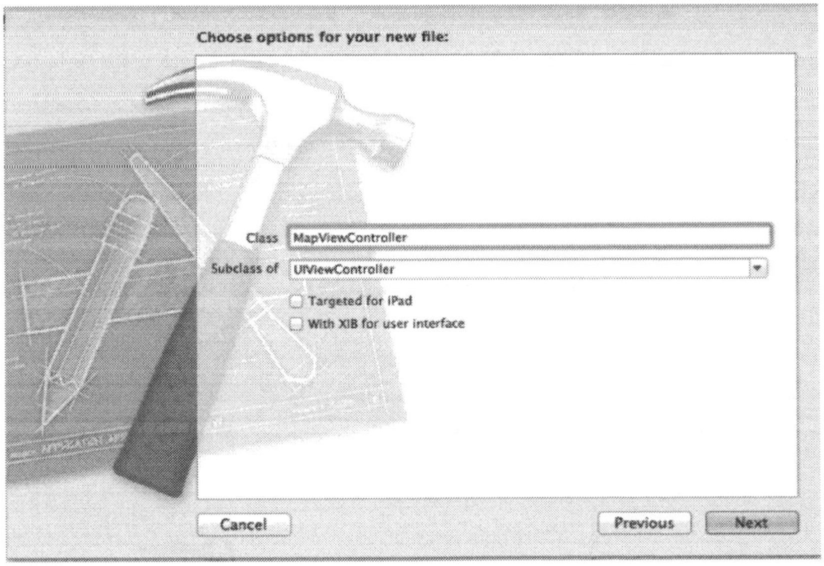

Figure 3-9. *Name new class MapViewController.*

5. Now go to the `MainStoryboard.storyboard` file, select the View Controller icon at the bottom of the main scene as shown in Figure 3-10, open the Utilities Pane, select the Identity Inspector, and change the Custom Class to `MapViewController`. Save the changes.

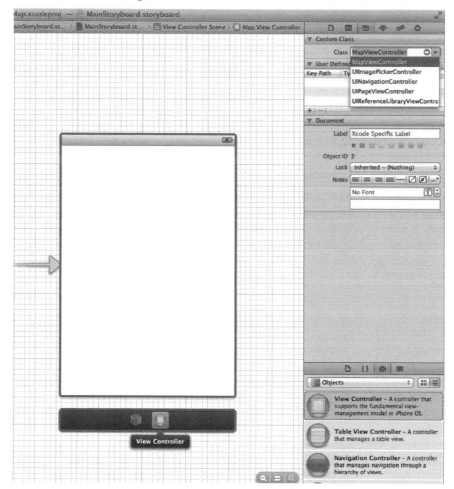

Figure 3-10. *Select View Controller icon at the bottom of the main scene.*

6. Find MapView in the Object Library and drag it to the View Controller canvas as shown in Figure 3-11.

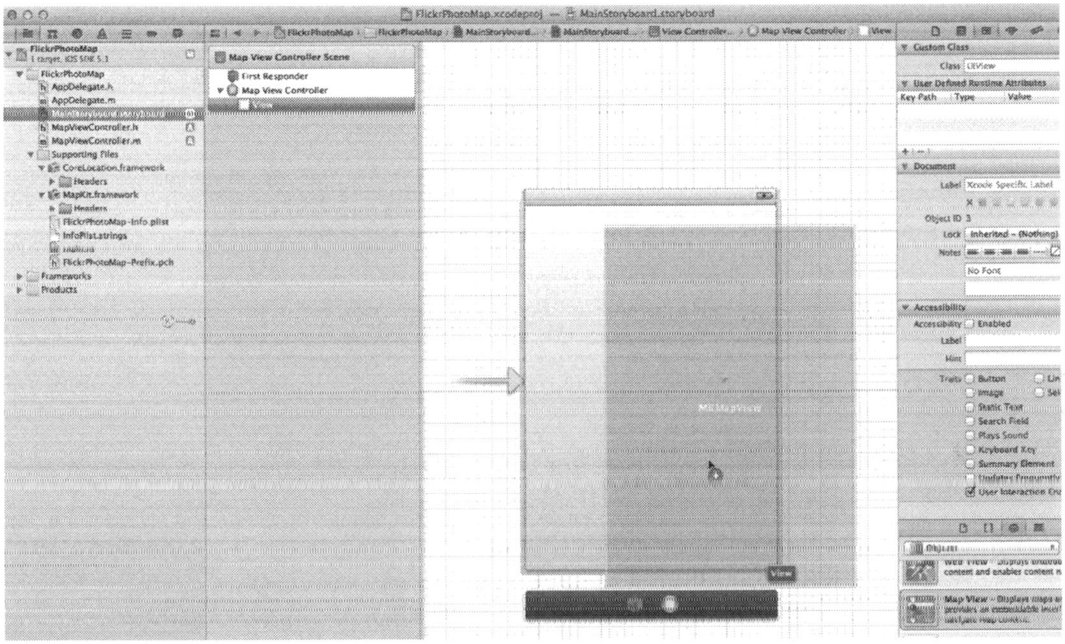

Figure 3-11. *Place a MapView onto the main view.*

7. Also place an Activity Indicator on top of the MapView as shown in Figure 3-12, because it may take time to download data from the Internet, and it would be helpful to see the progress. Center it towards the top. Then, while it's still selected, go to the Attributes Inspector and check the Hides When Stopped option.

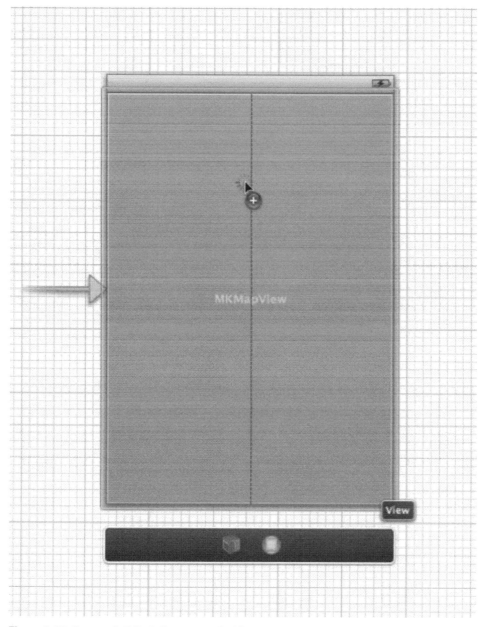

Figure 3-12. *Drag an Activity Indicator onto the View.*

8. Click the Assistant icon. If Assistant doesn't display the
    MapViewController.h file automatically, you can select it from
    Recent Files submenu under the Related Files Options menu (at
    the top of the screen divider as circled on Figure 3-13). You'll
    now create and connect IBOutlets for your MapViewController
    class. Control-drag from MapView onto the
    MapViewController.h file and drop it right before @end as shown
    in Figure 3-13. Name it mapView.

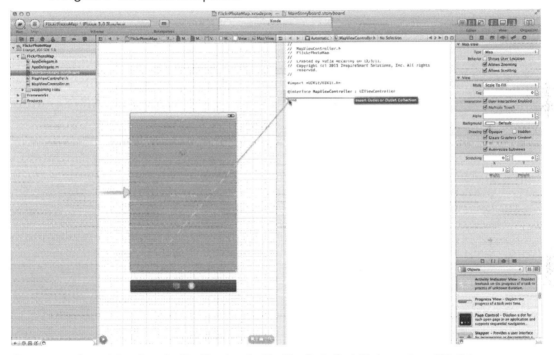

Figure 3-13. *Control-drag from the MapView into the MapViewController.h file to create an IBOutlet.*

9. Repeat the process to create an IBOutlet for the Activity Indicator and name it activityIndicator as shown in Figure 3-14.

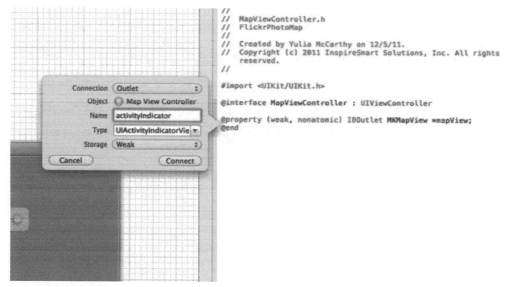

Figure 3-14. *Create IBOutlet for the Activity Indicator.*

10. To be able to access MapKit features, you must import the framework's header. Add #import <MapKit/MapKit.h> and specify that your MapViewController class is going to implement the MKMapViewDelegate protocol: add <MKMapViewDelegate> at the end of the line with class name declaration as shown in Figure 3-15.

```
#import <UIKit/UIKit.h>
#import <MapKit/MapKit.h>

@interface MapViewController : UIViewController <MKMapViewDelegate>

@property (weak, nonatomic) IBOutlet MKMapView *mapView;
@property (weak, nonatomic) IBOutlet UIActivityIndicatorView *activityIndicator;
@end
```

Figure 3-15. *Import MapKit header files.*

11. Turn off the Assistant. Open the `MapViewController.m` file. If Xcode has already created an empty private declaration section like the one highlighted on Figure 3-16, remove it and replace it with the code shown in Figure 3-17 (you can also achieve that by dragging and dropping the DemoMonkey step "01 MapViewController.m Private Declarations + API Constants" right before `@implementation`). Here you simply declare constants, variables, and signatures of the methods you need in this View Controller. You're going to use these variables and methods to request and process the data from the Flickr service. You'll discover what role each of these data members plays in the following steps. As mentioned earlier, to get access to the Flickr API, you must supply a unique API key in your web request. In this case, we also need to provide a user ID, because we only want to download photos from our own Flickr account. Both of those constants are defined here.

```
//
//  MapViewController.m
//  FlickrPhotoMap
//
//  Created by Yulia McCarthy on 5/28/12.
//  Copyright (c) 2012 InspireSmart Solutions, Inc. All rights reserved.
//

#import "MapViewController.h"

@interface MapViewController ()

@end

@implementation MapViewController
@synthesize mapView;
@synthesize activityIndicator;
```

Figure 3-16. *Default private declaration section created by Xcode*

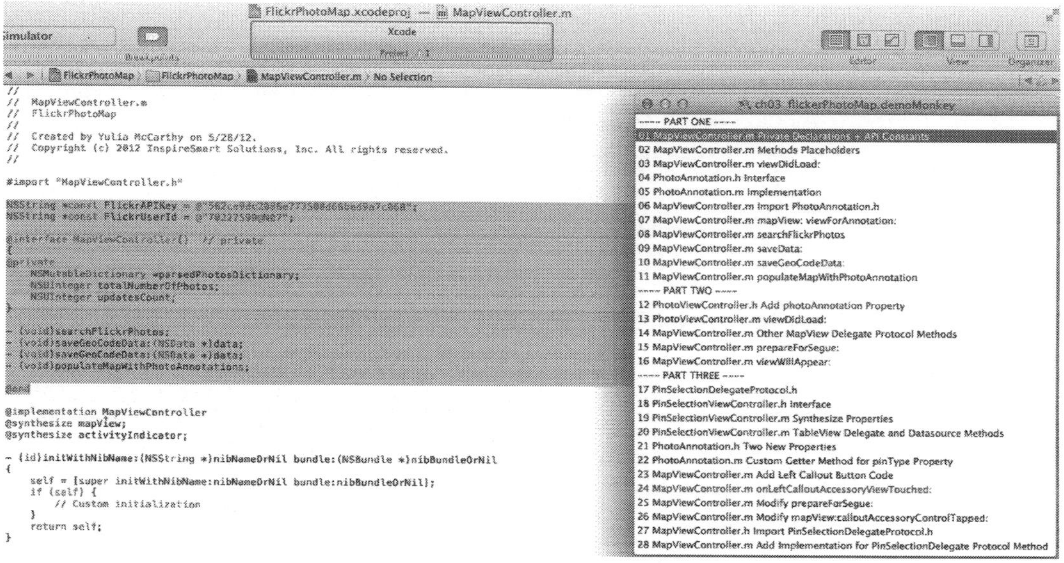

Figure 3-17. *Add private declaration section.*

12. To avoid any unexpected problems, add placeholders for the methods you've just declared. Insert the code shown in Figure 3-18 at the bottom of the file right before @end (DemoMonkey step "02 MapViewController.m Methods Placeholders"). You'll add implementation for these methods as you move along with the project.

```
@implementation MapViewController
@synthesize mapView;
@synthesize activityIndicator;

- (id)initWithNibName:(NSString *)nibNameOrNil bundle:(NSBundle *)nibBundleOrNil
{
    self = [super initWithNibName:nibNameOrNil bundle:nibBundleOrNil];
    if (self) {
        // Custom initialization
    }
    return self;
}

- (void)viewDidLoad
{
    [super viewDidLoad];
    // Do any additional setup after loading the view.
}

- (void)viewDidUnload
{
    [self setMapView:nil];
    [self setActivityIndicator:nil];
    [super viewDidUnload];
    // Release any retained subviews of the main view.
}

- (BOOL)shouldAutorotateToInterfaceOrientation:(UIInterfaceOrientation)interfaceOrientation
{
    return (interfaceOrientation == UIInterfaceOrientationPortrait);
}

#pragma mark - Flickr API Processing

- (void)searchFlickrPhotos
{
}

- (void)saveData:(NSData *)data
{
}

- (void)saveGeoCodeData:(NSData *)data
{
}

- (void)populateMapWithPhotoAnnotations
{
}
@end
```

Figure 3-18. *Add methods placeholders.*

13. Uncomment the viewDidLoad method if it's commented out and insert the code shown in Figure 3-19 at the bottom of the method implementation, right below [super viewDidLoad]; line (DemoMonkey step " 03 MapViewController.m viewDidLoad"). This will tell your MapView to zoom over the specified region and set its delegate property, which will allow your MapViewController to receive standard messages from the MapView during its operation (delegate callbacks). Lastly, in viewDidLoad you'll also initiate the search for geotagged photos on Flickr by evoking the [self searchFlickrPhotos] method call, which you'll be implementing shortly.

```
@implementation MapViewController
@synthesize mapView;
@synthesize activityIndicator;

- (id)initWithNibName:(NSString *)nibNameOrNil bundle:(NSBundle *)nibBundleOrNil
{
    self = [super initWithNibName:nibNameOrNil bundle:nibBundleOrNil];
    if (self) {
        // Custom initialization
    }
    return self;
}

- (void)viewDidLoad
{
    [super viewDidLoad];
    // Do any additional setup after loading the view.
    MKCoordinateRegion region = { {0.0, 0.0}, {0.0, 0.0} };
    region.center.latitude = 38.311491;
    region.center.longitude = -105.24353;
    region.span.longitudeDelta = 1.5f;
    region.span.latitudeDelta = 1.5f;
    [self.mapView setRegion:region animated:YES];
    [self.mapView setDelegate:self];

    [self searchFlickrPhotos];
}

- (void)viewDidUnload
{
    [self setMapView:nil];
    [self setActivityIndicator:nil];
    [super viewDidUnload];
    // Release any retained subviews of the main view.
}
```

----- PART ONE -----
01 MapViewController.m Private Declarations + API Constants
02 MapViewController.m Methods Placeholders
03 MapViewController.m viewDidLoad
04 PhotoAnnotation.h Interface
05 PhotoAnnotation.m Implementation
06 MapViewController.m Import PhotoAnnotation.h
07 MapViewController.m mapView: viewForAnnotation:
08 MapViewController.m searchFlickrPhotos
09 MapViewController.m saveData:
10 MapViewController.m saveGeoCodeData:
11 MapViewController.m populateMapWithPhotoAnnotation
----- PART TWO -----
12 PhotoViewController.h Add photoAnnotation Property
13 PhotoViewController.m viewDidLoad:
14 MapViewController.m Other MapView Delegate Protocol Methods
15 MapViewController.m prepareForSegue:
16 MapViewController.m viewWillAppear:
----- PART THREE -----
17 PinSelectionDelegateProtocol.h
18 PinSelectionViewController.h Interface
19 PinSelectionViewController.m Synthesize Properties
20 PinSelectionViewController.m TableView Delegate and Datasource Methods
21 PhotoAnnotation.h Two New Properties

Figure 3-19. *Add viewDidLoad code in MapViewController.m.*

14. If you didn't leave any steps out, you can run the app, and it will display the map zoomed over the Colorado Springs area as in Figure 3-20.

Figure 3-20. *Run the app to make sure the MapView was connected properly.*

15. Now you're going to create an NSObject<MKAnnotation>
    subclass so you can display custom photo annotations on the
    MapView. Hit ⌘N and select the Objective-C class option. On
    the next screen make sure NSObject is chosen in the "Subclass
    of" section and name it PhotoAnnotation. Save it. Then replace
    all the code in the PhotoAnnotation.h file with that shown in
    Figure 3-21 (you can drag and drop the code from
    DemoMonkey step "04 PhotoAnnotation.h Interface"). Here
    you're declaring several properties—three standard ones
    (coordinate, title, and subtitle) and four custom properties
    that you're going to use specifically for storing information about
    photos represented by the annotations (image, thumbnail,
    imageURL, and thumbnailURL). You'll also declared two methods:
    a custom initializer to create the PhotoAnnotatation objects
    (used to initialize custom properties when annotations are
    created) and the updateSubtitle method, which we'll talk about
    in more detail in the next step.

Figure 3-21. *Select the code you will replace in PhotoAnnotation.h.*

16. Select the `PhotoAnnotation.m` file in the Project Navigator and replace the code in it as shown in Figure 3-22 (DemoMonkey step "05 PhotoAnnotation.m Implementation"). Most of the code here is self-explanatory or has descriptive comments. The method `updateSubtitle` will be called when user touches an annotation on the map. It will update the annotation callout's subtitle to display the name of the place where the photo was taken. It's using the latest iOS 5 feature, reverse geocoder, which is a part of the CoreLocation framework. It provides the easiest way to reverse geocode a location and get the information associated with it, called placemark. You create an instance of `CLGeocoder` and invoke the `reverseGeocodeLocation:completionHandler:` method, from which you get an array of placemarks, with the most relevant one being at index 0. You then extract the information you need from the `CLPlacemark` object using the `placemarkToString:` helper method and update subtitle for that annotation.

```objc
#import "PhotoAnnotation.h"
#import <CoreLocation/CoreLocation.h>

@implementation PhotoAnnotation

@synthesize title, subtitle, coordinate;
@synthesize image, thumbnail;
@synthesize imageURL, thumbnailURL;

- (id)initWithImageURL:(NSURL *)anImageURL thumbnailURL:(NSURL *)aThumbnailURL
                 title:(NSString *)aTitle coordinate:(CLLocationCoordinate2D)aCoordinate
{
    if ((self = [super init])) {
        self.imageURL = anImageURL;
        self.thumbnailURL = aThumbnailURL;
        self.title = aTitle;
        self.coordinate = aCoordinate;
    }
    return self;
}


- (NSString *)title
{
    return title;
}


- (UIImage *)image
{
    // We don't want to have all the images loaded in memory unnecessarily, so we should
    // wait to load the image until we actually want to display it
    if (!image && self.imageURL) {
        NSData *imageData = [NSData dataWithContentsOfURL:self.imageURL];
        self.image = [UIImage imageWithData:imageData];
    }
    return image;
}


- (UIImage *)thumbnail
{
    // We don't want to have all the images loaded in memory unnecessarily, so we should
    // wait to load the image until we actually want to display it
    if (!image && self.thumbnailURL) {
        NSData *imageData = [NSData dataWithContentsOfURL:self.thumbnailURL];
        self.thumbnail = [UIImage imageWithData:imageData];
    }
    return thumbnail;
}

#pragma mark - Reverse geocode subtitle
#pragma mark -

// Returns string of "City, State" format if availbale
- (NSString *)placemarkToString:(CLPlacemark *)placemark
{
    NSMutableString *placemarkString = [[NSMutableString alloc] init];
    if (placemark.locality) {
        [placemarkString appendString:placemark.locality];
    }

    if (placemark.administrativeArea) {
        if (placemarkString.length > 0)
            [placemarkString appendString:@", "];
        [placemarkString appendString:placemark.administrativeArea];
    }

    if (placemarkString.length == 0 && placemark.name)
        [placemarkString appendString:placemark.name];

    return placemarkString;
}


- (void)updateSubtitle
{
    if (self.subtitle != nil)
        return;

    // Reverse geocode the annotation's coordinate
    CLLocation *location = [[CLLocation alloc] initWithLatitude:self.coordinate.latitude
                                                     longitude:self.coordinate.longitude];
    CLGeocoder *geocoder = [[CLGeocoder alloc] init];
    [geocoder reverseGeocodeLocation:location completionHandler:^(NSArray *placemarks, NSError *error) {
        if (placemarks.count > 0) {
            CLPlacemark *placemark = [placemarks objectAtIndex:0];
            self.subtitle = [self placemarkToString:placemark];
        }

    }];
}

@end
```

Figure 3-22. *Replace the code in PhotoAnnotation.m.*

17. Once you have the `PhotoAnnotation` class in place, you can start working on adding annotation to the MapView. First of all, let's make the newly created class visible to the main View Controller. Go to the `MapViewController.m` file and add `#import "PhotoAnnotation.h"` to the imports section at the top (DemoMonkey step "06 MapViewController.m Import PhotoAnnotation.h"). Now you can implement the `MKMapViewDelegate` protocol method in which you'll tell the MapView how your annotations should look like once you add them to the map. Add the implementation for the `mapView:viewForAnnotation:` method to the end of the file right before @end as shown in Figure 3-23 (alternatively you can drag DemoMonkey step "07 MapViewController.m mapView: viewForAnnotation:".

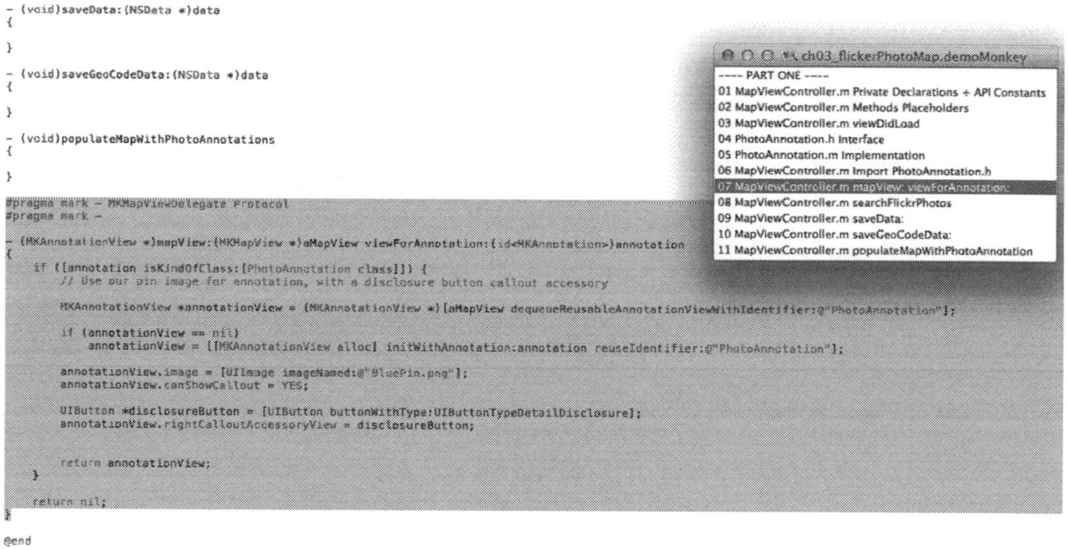

Figure 3-23. *Add implementation for the mapView:viewForAnnotation: method.*

18. In this step you'll add implementation for the searchFlickrPhotos method. Find the empty placeholder for the method, which was added in step 12, and insert code for it as shown in Figure 3-24 (DemoMonkey step "08 MapViewController.m searchFlickrPhotos"). In this method you construct a URL string that will initiate a search request to the Flickr server (the format of the URL request and available parameters are provided in Flickr documentation, at http://flickr.com/services/api/; in our case, we specified the API key, user ID, geotag option, and response format). Note that you're outputting the URL you just built to the console for testing purposes. In the next couple of lines, you create an NSURL object with the constructed string and dispatch synchronous download request for the contents of that URL by calling the dataWithContentsOfURL: static method on NSData. Note that the download request is performed in a background thread—otherwise the UI may become unresponsive to the user. Right before the request is sent, start your Activity Indicator, so you can see the progress. (Upon completion of the data transfer you'll invoke the saveData: selector, in which you parse the JSON data, save it in a usable format, and perform other necessary operations with the fetched data. This step is coming shortly.)

Figure 3-24. *Add searchFlickrPhotos method implementation.*

19. As the result the Flickr server will return a JSON string containing a list of all the photos for the specified user ID that have location information associated with them.

20. By now you should be able to run the app and see the URL string printed in the console window as shown in Figure 3-25.

Figure 3-25. *Run the app to check out the URL string you've constructed.*

21. This step is optional. Select the URL that was printed by the app as shown in Figure 3-26, paste it into your web browser's address bar, and hit Enter. If there were no errors in the URL string, you should get a response from Flickr similar to the one shown in Figure 3-27 (on the left: standard unformatted response, on the right: response in a user-friendly format formatted for you by the JSONView plug-in). What you downloaded from Flickr is JSON data. To be able to use the information stored in it, you must parse it.

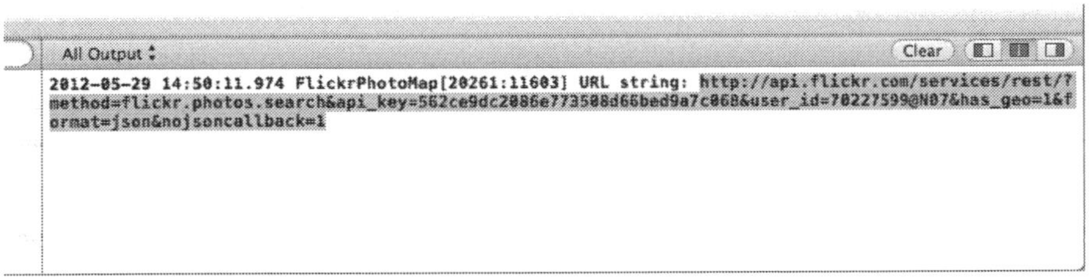

All Output ⬧

2012-05-29 14:50:11.974 FlickrPhotoMap[20261:11603] URL string: http://api.flickr.com/services/rest/?
method=flickr.photos.search&api_key=562ce9dc2086e773508d66bed9a7c068&user_id=70227599@N07&has_geo=1&f
ormat=json&nojsoncallback=1

Figure 3-26. *Copy the URL and paste it into a web browser's address bar.*

22. In the JSON sample in Figure 3-27, you can see that the response from Flickr does not contain the actual image data. To download the images and get their geospatial data, you need to extract the information for each image in the "photo" collection and perform several additional steps. In this case, the most convenient way to accomplish that is to use a new iOS 5 feature: the NSJSONSerialization class. It's a native JSON parser that converts JSON to Foundation objects (usually an NSDictionary or an NSArray based on the structure of your JSON document) and vice versa. The NSJSONSerialization class has a static method called JSONObjectWithData:options:error. You're going to use it to turn your Flickr JSON data into an NSDictionary.

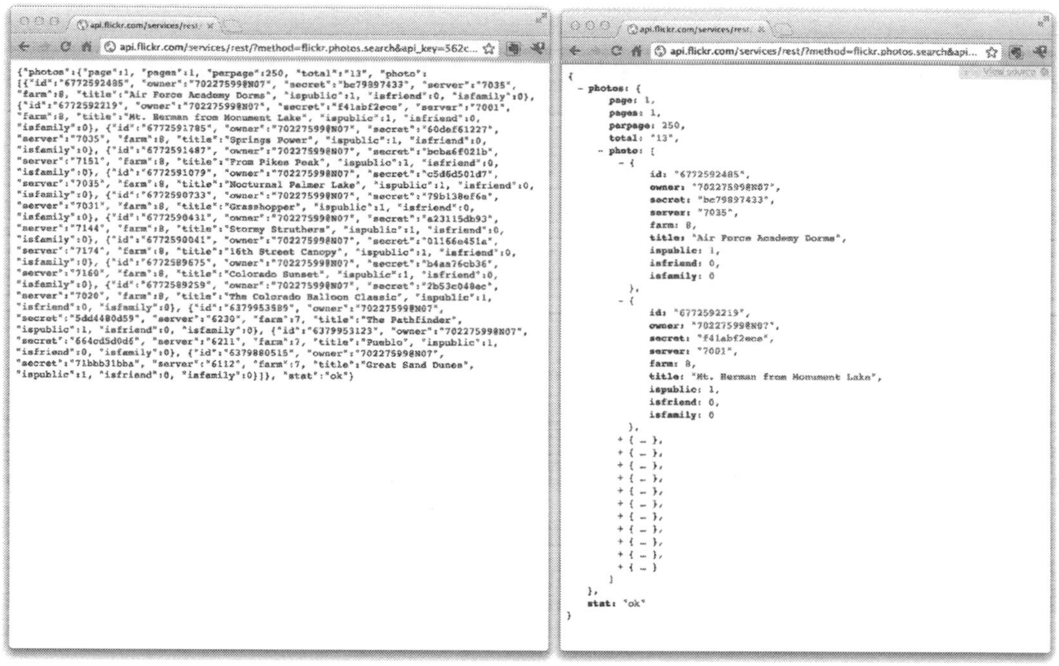

Figure 3-27. *Flickr JSON response displayed in the Chrome browser*

23. Let's add implementation for the `saveData:` method mentioned in step 18. Find its placeholder in the `MapViewController.m` file and insert the code shown in Figure 3-28 (DemoMonkey step "[09 MapViewController.m saveData:").

This method may seem a bit overwhelming at first, but it's actually quite simple. Because you saw the hierarchy of the JSON response in step 19, you know which key in the results dictionary will get you access to the array of photos you're interested in. The following code parses the JSON data into an `NSDictionary` and saves the array of photo info items stored in it under photo key into an `NSArray` for further processing:

```
NSError *error = nil;
NSMutableDictionary *response = [NSJSONSerialization JSONObjectWithData:data
options:NSJSONReadingMutableContainers error:&error];
NSArray *photos = [[response objectForKey:@"photos"] objectForKey:@"photo"];
```

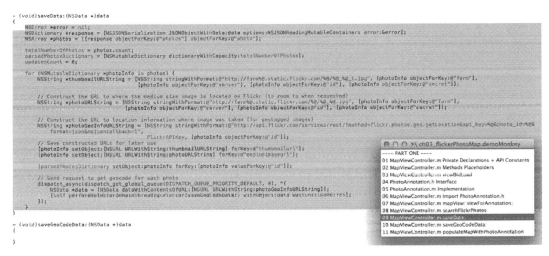

Figure 3-28. *Add the saveData: method implementation.*

24. In this case, the photos array is an array of NSDictionary objects. Each dictionary contains information about the photo, such as ID, farm, server, title, and so forth, from which you can construct the URLs to retrieve the actual image data and image geolocation from Flickr.

Note that we use the NSJSONReadingMutableContainers option for parsing JSON data. We do this to be able to append additional information to the parsed objects (like thumbnail URL, image URL, and geocode).

25. Getting back to the rest of the `saveData:` method code: after
    parsing the JSON data, initialize the variables declared in step
    11 and start enumerating through the array. In this `for` loop you
    simply construct three types of URL strings based on the
    attributes stored in each photo info dictionary. You'll use these
    URLs later to load thumbnail, medium size image, and image
    geo-spatial data for each photo. The rules for constructing
    mentioned URLs are in the Flickr API Documentation at
    `www.flickr.com/services/api/misc.urls.html`. Finally, save the
    dictionaries containing data about each photo into a
    `parsedDataDictionary` variable. Use photo id string as a key so
    later you can update each photo dictionary with geo-spatial
    data by simply retrieving it via photo id. The last code block in
    the method is almost identical to the one from step 18. Because
    the geolocation data of the photos is stored separately on Flickr,
    you have to make another API call using the
    `photoGeoInfoURLString` you've just constructed for each photo
    to retrieve its location data:

```
dispatch_async(dispatch_get_global_queue(DISPATCH_QUEUE_PRIORITY_DEFAULT, 0), ^{
NSData *data = [NSData dataWithContentsOfURL:[NSURL
URLWithString:photoGeoInfoURLString]];
[self performSelectorOnMainThread:@selector(saveGeoCodeData:) withObject:data
waitUntilDone:YES];
});
```

Once the data is fully fetched, it will be parsed and saved by
invoking the `saveGeoCodeData:` method, which you'll implement
next.

26. Find the placeholder for saveGeoCodeData: and insert the code shown in Figure 3-29 (if you're using DemoMonkey, drag step "[10 MapViewController.m saveGeoCodeData:" into the method placeholder). This method is quite similar to the saveData: method discussed in the previous step, except that in this case you only need to retrieve two values from the JSON response (latitude and longitude of where photo was taken). Thus, you parse the JSON data using the same NSJSONSerialization class and, if there were no errors, save the geocode values into the corresponding photo info dictionary retrieved from the parsedPhotosDictionary variable by photo ID key. Note that the parsing options this time are set to kNilOptions constant because you don't need the parsed objects to be modifiable in this case.

Once all objects are updated, stop the progress indicator and call the method that will annotate your photos on the MapView:

```
if (updatesCount == totalNumberOfPhotos) {
    [self.activityIndicator stopAnimating];
    [self populateMapWithPhotoAnnotations];
}
```

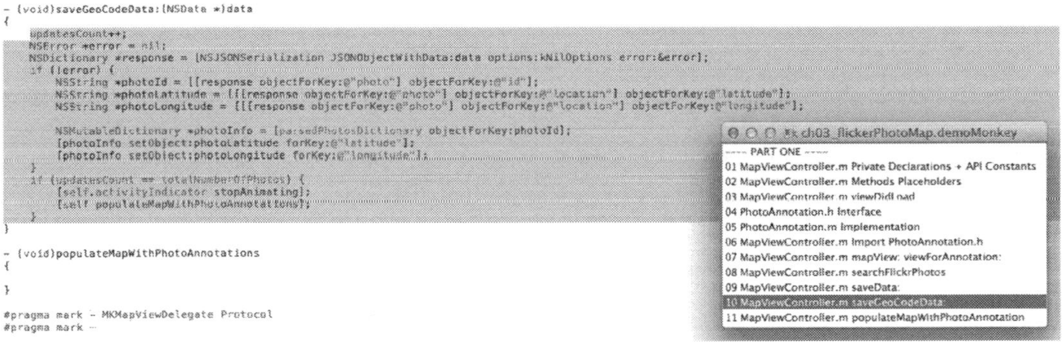

Figure 3-29. *Add the saveGeoCodeData: method implementation.*

27. Find the placeholder for the `populateMapWithPhotoAnnotation` method and insert the code shown in Figure 3-30 (DemoMonkey step "11 MapViewController.m populateMapWithPhotoAnnotation"). In this step you're adding the code to annotate your geotagged photos on the `MapView`. To accomplish that, loop through the objects you saved into `parsedPhotosDictionary`. If `latitude` and `longitude` values aren't nil, you create a `PhotoAnnotation` object for that photo, initialize it with the necessary data from the photo info dictionary (title, geocode, URLs, and so on), and save it into a temporary `NSArray`. Finally you add all created annotations to the MapView. At this point you no longer need the data stored in the `parsedPhotosDictionary` variable, so you free the memory occupied by it simply by setting its value to nil.

Figure 3-30. *Add the populateMapWithPhotoAnnotation method implementation.*

28. You should now be able to see the results of your work as shown in Figure 3-31. If you click any annotation, a callout bubble will show up with the name of the photo the annotation represents.

Figure 3-31. *Build and run the app.*

Step 2: Making a Transition to a Secondary Scene from Annotation Callouts

In the second of your three steps you'll create a secondary scene in Storyboard, which will display a medium-size image represented by a selected MapView annotation and the full image name. You're going to make the app transition to that scene every time the user clicks the selected annotation's callout disclosure button.

1. Chapter 2 showed you how to embed a View Controller into a Navigation Controller using an Xcode menu. This step shows you an alternative way of accomplishing the same task. You can use either, based on your preference. Go the Storyboard file and drag a Navigation Controller from the Object Library onto the canvas. Place it to the left of your `MapViewController` as shown in Figure 3-32.

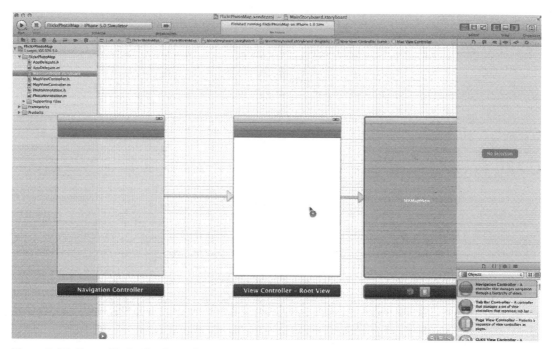

Figure 3-32. *Drag a Navigation Controller onto the Storyboard.*

2. You can get rid of the default Root View Controller that was automatically added to the scene by selecting it and pressing Delete. Additionally, grab the Initial View Controller arrow that's pointing to the MapView Controller and drag it onto the newly added Navigation Controller as shown in Figure 3-33.

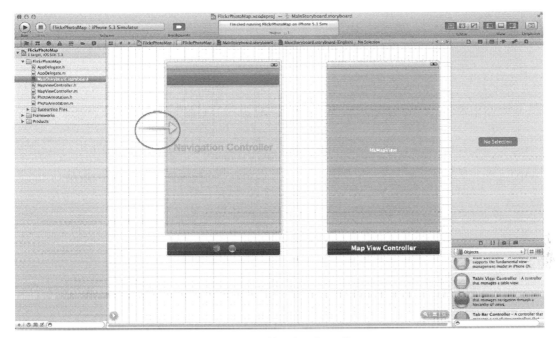

Figure 3-33. *Set the Navigation Controller to be the Initial View Controller.*

3. Create the `rootViewController` relationship between the Navigation Controller and the MapView Controller by Control-dragging from the Navigation Controller to the MapView Controller as shown in Figure 3-34. Let it go and select Relationship – rootViewController from the menu as shown in Figure 3-35.

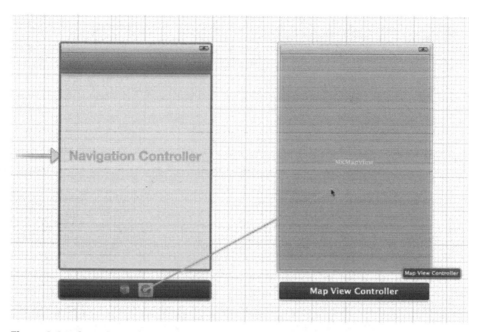

Figure 3-34. *Control-drag from the Navigation Controller to the MapView Controller.*

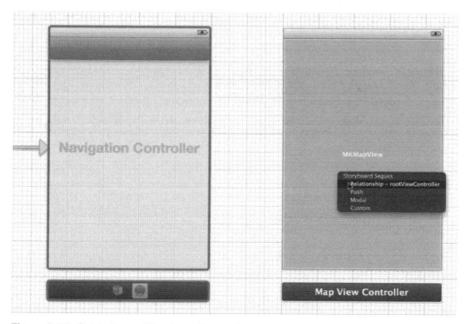

Figure 3-35. *Create the rootViewController relationship.*

4. Select the Navigation Controller and in the Attributes Inspector set its Top Bar to Translucent Black Navigation Bar as shown in Figure 3-36.

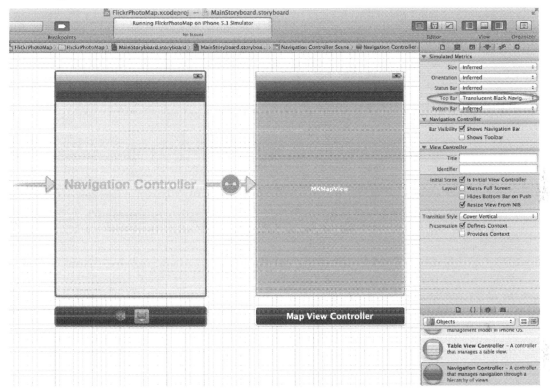

Figure 3-36. *Set the Top Bar property of the Navigation Controller to Translucent Black Navigation Bar.*

5. Drag another View Controller from the Object Library onto the canvas. Place it just to the right of the MapView Controller as shown in Figure 3-37.

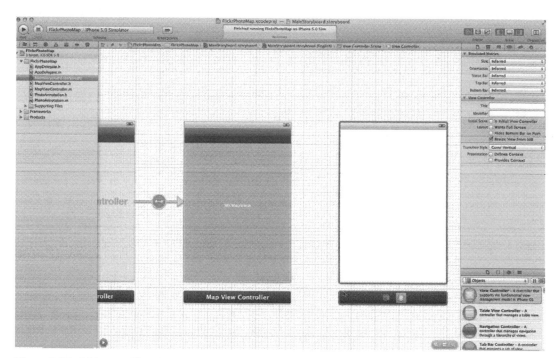

Figure 3-37. *Add a new View Controller to the Storyboard.*

6. Create a Storyboard Segue by Control-dragging from the
    MapView Controller icon to View Controller as shown in Figure
    3-38. Release it and choose Push as the segue type from the
    menu as shown in Figure 3-39. Select the new segue and set its
    Identifier property in the Attributes Inspector to
    ShowFullSizeImageSegue as shown in Figure 3-40. Lastly,
    double-click the View Controller's Navigation Bar and set its title
    to Selected Photo as shown in Figure 3-41.

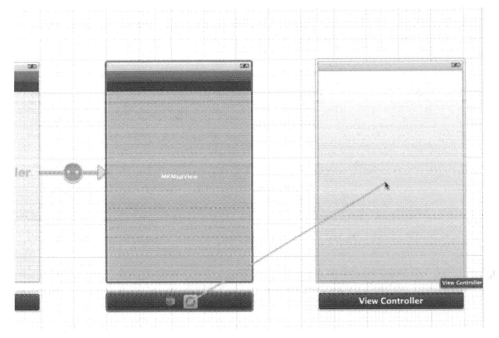

Figure 3-38. *Control-drag from the MapView Controller to the new View Controller.*

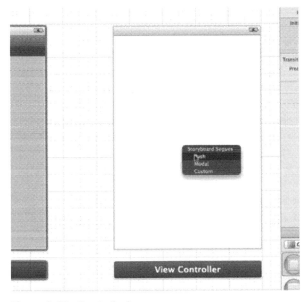

Figure 3-39. *Create Push segue.*

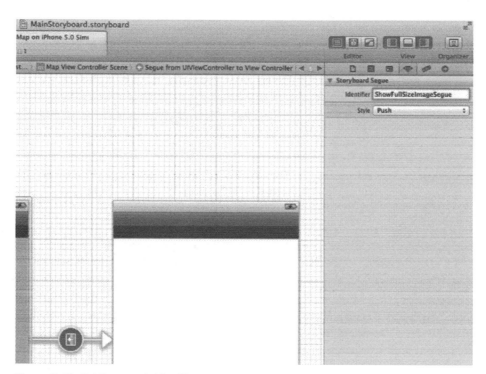

Figure 3-40. *Set the segue's Identifier.*

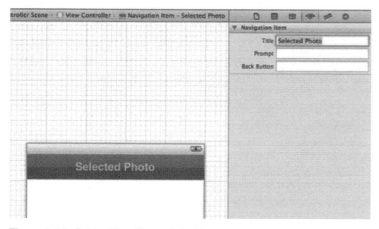

Figure 3-41. *Set the View Controller's title.*

7. You're now ready to add the rest of the elements to your new scene. You're going to need a `UIImageView` to display the downloaded Flickr image and a `UILabel` to show its title. So go ahead and drag an Image View onto the View Controller's view, make it approximately 230 points high and 320 points wide, and position it closer to the top as shown in Figure 3-42.

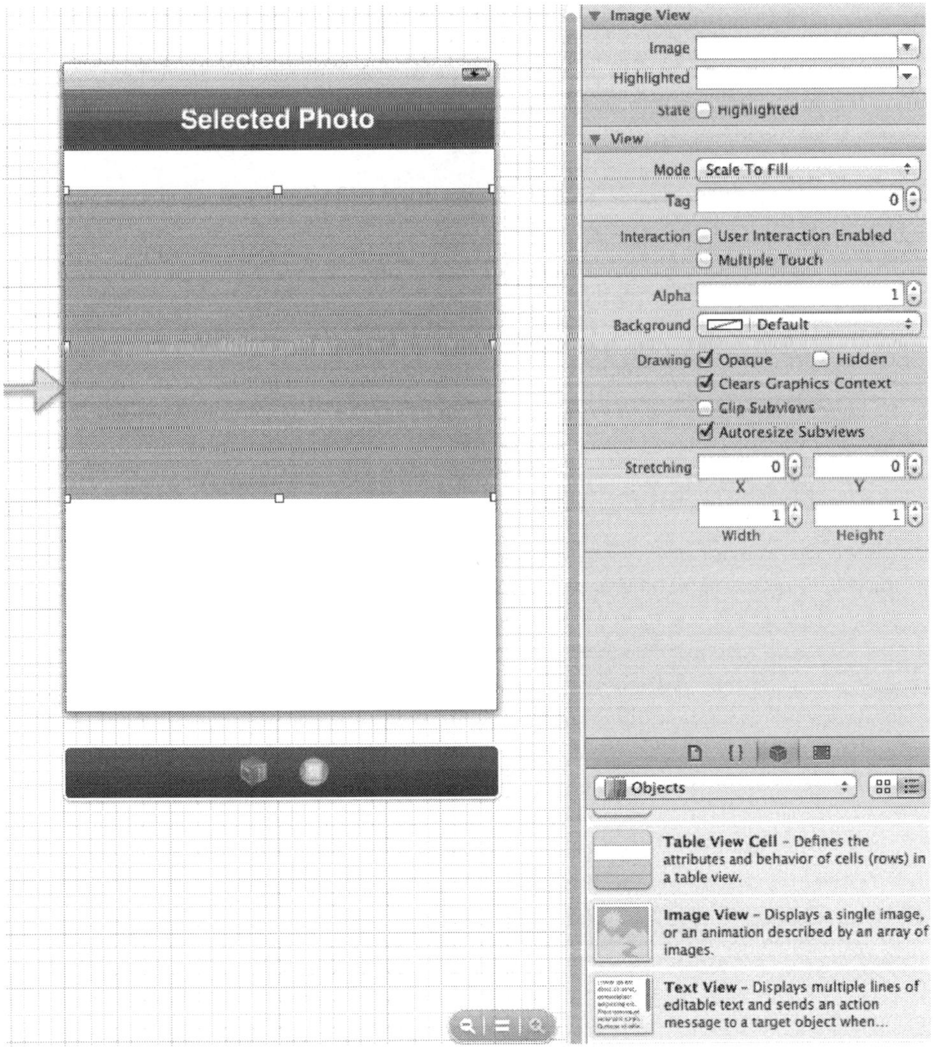

Figure 3-42. *Add an Image View to the scene.*

8. Now find a Label in the Object Library and drag it onto the View
    as well. Adjust its width and position it below the Image View as
    shown in Figure 3-43. You can set its title to Photo Title for
    now, just to keep things organized. It will be changed to the title
    of the actual photo during runtime. Also set Label properties in
    the Attributes Inspector as follows: Font: System Bold of size
    18, Text Color: White Color, Alignment: Center. As you probably
    noticed, the label is no longer visible on the screen. Click
    anywhere inside the main View to select it and change the
    background color to Black in the Attributes Inspector as shown
    in Figure 3-44.

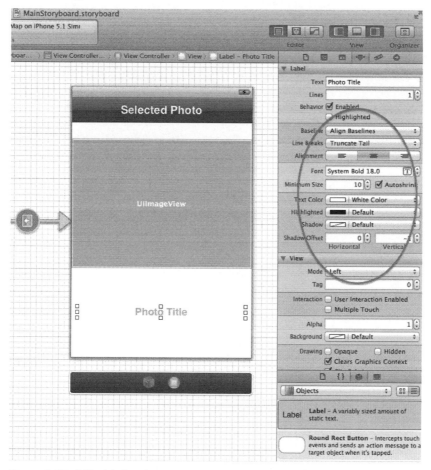

Figure 3-43. *Add a label to the scene and adjust its properties.*

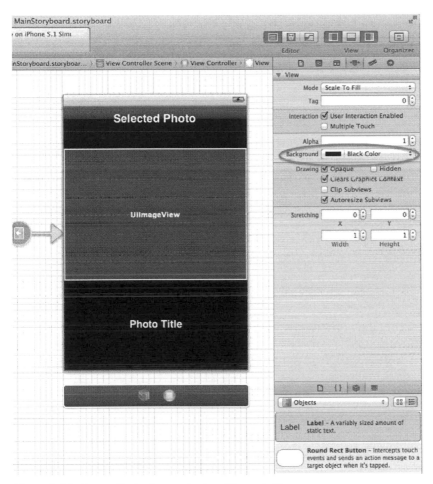

Figure 3-44. *Change the background color of the main View.*

9. In this step you're going to create a new `UIViewController`
    subclass, which will control your secondary scene. Hit ⌘N,
    select the Objective-C class option, and click Next. Make sure
    the `UIViewController` is selected in the "Subclass of" section as
    shown in Figure 3-45. Name the class `PhotoViewController` and
    save it.

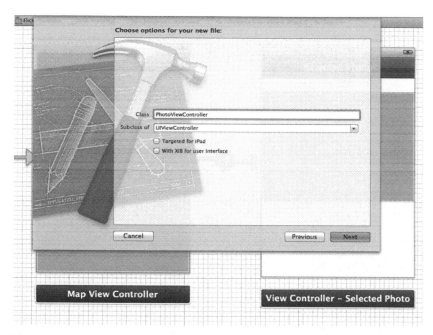

Figure 3-45. *Create a new UIViewController subclass.*

10. In the Storyboard select the second View Controller, and in the Identity Inspector set its class to the newly created PhotoViewController class as shown in Figure 3-46.

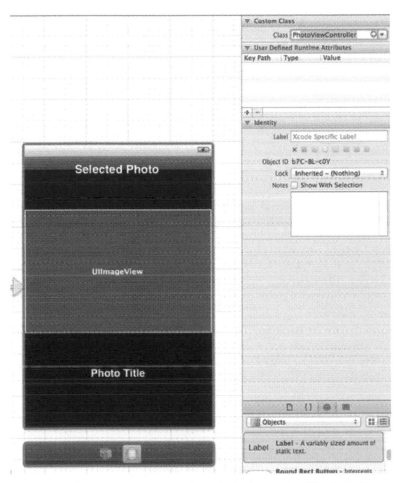

Figure 3-46. *Set the secondary View Controller's class to PhotoViewController.*

11. Click the Assistant icon. If Assistant didn't display the
PhotoViewController.h file automatically, you can select it from
Recent Files submenu under the Related Files Options menu (at
the top of the screen divider). You'll now create and connect
IBOutlets for your PhotoViewController class. Control-drag
from UIImageView into the PhotoViewController.h file and drop
it right before @end as shown in Figure 3-47. Name it
photoImageView. Similarly, Control-drag from the label and name
the property photoTitleLabel.

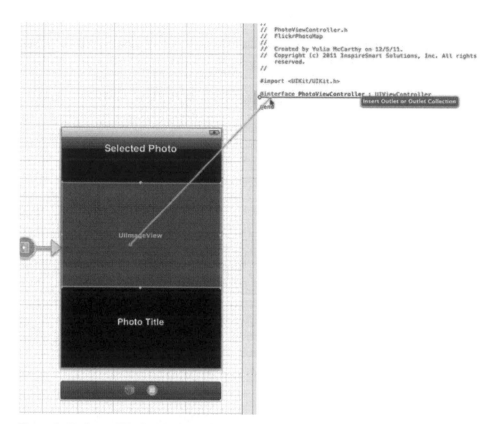

Figure 3-47. *Create IBOutlets for PhotoViewController.*

12. At this point, you're done with the Storyboard. You now need at add a few more lines of code to make everything work. Close the Assistant and navigate to the `PhotoViewController.h` file. Add the forward declaration of the `PhotoAnnotation` class "`@class PhotoAnnotation;`" right before the `@interface` and create another property called `photoAnnotation` as shown in Figure 3-48 (DemoMonkey step "12 PhotoViewController.h Add photoAnnotation Property"). This new property will store a reference to the selected annotation so you can get access to the data necessary to download and display the actual photo. Don't forget to synthesize the new property in `PhotoViewController.m` and make the `PhotoAnnotation` class visible to `PhotoViewController` by adding the following code at the top of the file:

```
#import "PhotoViewController.h"
#import "PhotoAnnotation.h"
@interface PhotoViewController ()
@end
@implementation PhotoViewController
@synthesize photoImageView;
@synthesize photoTitleLabel;
@synthesize photoAnnotation;
...
```

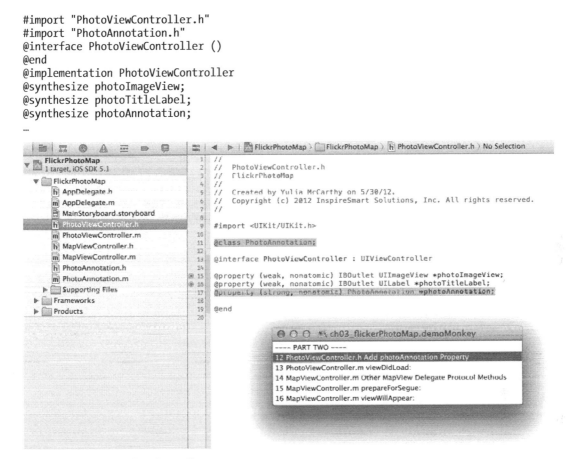

Figure 3-48. *Add the photoAnnotation property.*

13. Here you're going to add implementation for the viewDidLoad method. Find the viewDidLoad method in the PhotoViewController.m file and insert the code shown in Figure 3-49. This code will update the UI so it displays the appropriate image and title for the annotation that will be passed by MapViewController right before the segue is performed.

```
#import "PhotoViewController.h"
#import "PhotoAnnotation.h"

@interface PhotoViewController ()

@end

@implementation PhotoViewController
@synthesize photoImageView;
@synthesize photoTitleLabel;
@synthesize photoAnnotation;

- (id)initWithNibName:(NSString *)nibNameOrNil bundle:(NSBundle *)nibBundleOrNil
{
    self = [super initWithNibName:nibNameOrNil bundle:nibBundleOrNil];
    if (self) {
        // Custom initialization
    }
    return self;
}

- (void)viewDidLoad
{
    [super viewDidLoad];
    // Do any additional setup after loading the view.
    self.navigationController.navigationBarHidden = NO;
    self.photoImageView.contentMode = UIViewContentModeScaleAspectFill;
    self.photoImageView.image = self.photoAnnotation.image;
    self.photoTitleLabel.text = self.photoAnnotation.title;
}

- (void)viewDidUnload
{
    [self setPhotoImageView:nil];
    [self setPhotoTitleLabel:nil];
    [super viewDidUnload];
    // Release any retained subviews of the main view.
}

- (BOOL)shouldAutorotateToInterfaceOrientation:(UIInterfaceOrientation)interfaceOrientation
{
    return (interfaceOrientation == UIInterfaceOrientationPortrait);
}

@end
```

Menu overlay: ch03_flickerPhotoMap.demoMonkey
```
----- PART TWO -----
12 PhotoViewController.h Add photoAnnotation Property
13 PhotoViewController.m viewDidLoad:
14 MapViewController.m Other MapView Delegate Protocol Methods
15 MapViewController.m prepareForSegue:
16 MapViewController.m viewWillAppear:
```

Figure 3-49. *Add the viewDidLoad implementation in PhotoViewController.m.*

14. In this step you'll implement two additional `MKMapViewDelegate` protocol methods, which you need in order to display the secondary scene. First, switch to `MapViewController.m` and import `PhotoViewController.h` to make it visible to this class. Then navigate to the `MKMapViewDelegate` protocol pragma section as shown in Figure 3-50.

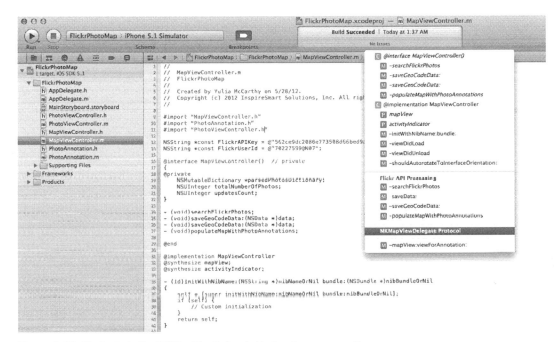

Figure 3-50. *Navigate to the MKMapViewDelegate Protocol pragma section.*

15. Add implementation for the following two methods right before
@end as shown in Figure 3-51 (DemoMonkey step "[14
MapViewController.m Other MapView Delegate Protocol
Methods"):

```
- (void)mapView:(MKMapView *)aMapView annotationView:(MKAnnotationView *)view
calloutAccessoryControlTapped:(UIControl *)control
{ … }
```
and
```
- (void)mapView:(MKMapView *)MapView didSelectAnnotationView:(MKAnnotationView
*)view
{ … }
```

The first of the two MapView callback methods gets called when
the user clicks a callout disclosure button. In that case, you
invoke

```
[self performSegueWithIdentifier:@"ShowFullSizeImageSegue"
sender:photoAnnotation];
```

on your MapView Controller, which will perform the Storyboard Segue created in step 31. This little line of code is all it takes to initiate a secondary scene transition from a MapView callout. In the second delegate callback, which happens when the user selects an annotation on the map, you simply call the updateSubtitle method on the selected annotation so its coordinate is reverse-geocoded and the location name is displayed in the callout subtitle.

```
#pragma mark - MKMapViewDelegate Protocol
#pragma mark -

- (MKAnnotationView *)mapView:(MKMapView *)aMapView viewForAnnotation:(id<MKAnnotation>)annotation
{
    if ([annotation isKindOfClass:[PhotoAnnotation class]]) {
        // Use our pin image for annotation, with a disclosure button callout accessory

        MKAnnotationView *annotationView = (MKAnnotationView *)[aMapView dequeueReusableAnnotationViewWithIdentifier:@"PhotoAnnotation"];

        if (annotationView == nil)
            annotationView = [[MKAnnotationView alloc] initWithAnnotation:annotation reuseIdentifier:@"PhotoAnnotation"];

        annotationView.image = [UIImage imageNamed:@"BluePin.png"];
        annotationView.canShowCallout = YES;

        UIButton *disclosureButton = [UIButton buttonWithType:UIButtonTypeDetailDisclosure];
        annotationView.rightCalloutAccessoryView = disclosureButton;

        return annotationView;
    }

    return nil;
}

- (void)mapView:(MKMapView *)aMapView annotationView:(MKAnnotationView *)view calloutAccessoryControlTapped:(UIControl *)control
{
    if (![view.annotation isKindOfClass:[PhotoAnnotation class]])
        return;

    PhotoAnnotation *photoAnnotation = (PhotoAnnotation *)view.annotation;

    [self performSegueWithIdentifier:@"ShowFullSizeImageSegue" sender:photoAnnotation];
}

- (void)mapView:(MKMapView *)mapView didSelectAnnotationView:(MKAnnotationView *)view
{
    if (![view.annotation isKindOfClass:[PhotoAnnotation class]])
        return;

    // Reverse geocode the annotation if needed
    PhotoAnnotation *photoAnnotation = (PhotoAnnotation *)view.annotation;
    if (!photoAnnotation.subtitle)
        [photoAnnotation updateSubtitle];
}
@end
```

```
O O O    ch03_flickrPhotoMap.demoMonkey
----- PART TWO -----
12 PhotoViewController.h Add photoAnnotation Property
13 PhotoViewController.m viewDidLoad:
14 MapViewController.m Other MapView Delegate Protocol Methods
15 MapViewController.m prepareForSegue:
16 MapViewController.m viewWillAppear:
```

Figure 3-51. *Implement the remaining MKMapViewDelegate protocol methods.*

Finally, you must pass the selected annotation from
MapViewController to the destination PhotoViewController before
the transition takes place. Do this in the prepareForSegue: method.
Scroll up to the #pragma mark - Flickr API Processing section and
insert the code shown in Figure 3-52 right before it (DemoMonkey
step "15 MapViewController.m prepareForSegue:"). Here you check
the Identifier of the invoking segue, and if it matches the desired
one, you simply set the photoAnnotation property of
PhotoViewController (which is the destination View Controller) to
the sender object, for which, as you remember from the previous
step, you passed the selected PhotoAnnotation object. As a minor
cleanup, you should implement the viewWillAppear method
(DemoMonkey step "16 MapViewController.m viewWillAppear:]").
Add the following code right before viewDidUnload:

```
- (void)viewWillAppear:(BOOL)animated {
    [super viewWillAppear:animated];
    self.navigationController.navigationBarHidden = YES;
}
```

Figure 3-52. *Implement the prepareForSegue: method for MapViewController*

In this method you set the navigationBarHidden property of the
Navigation Controller to YES, which insures that once you return
from the secondary scene, the Navigation Bar doesn't cover the
MapView.

16. Build and run the app. You should now be able to click the annotation and see the callout with the photo title and the name of the place where it was taken. If you tap the blue disclosure button, the secondary view displaying the actual photo will appear as demonstrated on Figure 3-53.

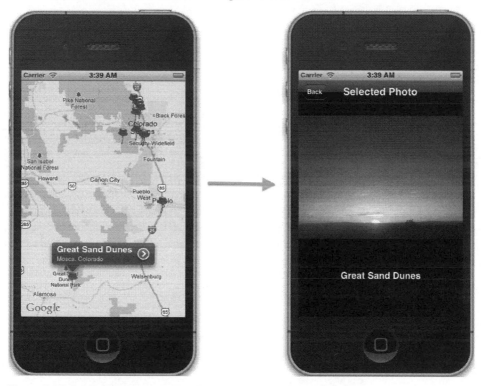

Figure 3-53. *Implement the prepareForSegue: method for MapViewController.*

Step 3: Creating a Modal Scene that Allows the User to Rate Your Photos

In this third step you're going to add some fun to your app and let the user interact with it a bit more. You will create an additional Storyboarding scene, which is going to contain a very simple static TableView fully created in the Storyboard. Once the user clicks a thumbnail, which you're going to add to the Left Callout Accessory View of the annotation callout, you'll present a modal scene with a basic TableView displaying rating choices. When user selects a cell in this TableView, the modal View Controller will be dismissed, and the pin color of the affected annotation will change according to the rating picked.

1. Open the Storyboard. Find a Table View Controller in the Object Library and drag it onto Storyboard canvas right above the Photo View Controller as shown in Figure 3-54.

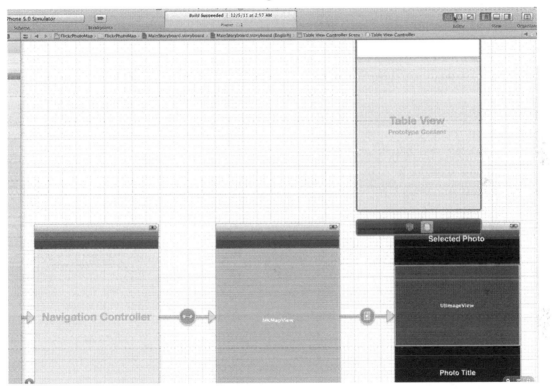

Figure 3-54. *Add a Table View Controller to the Storyboard.*

2. You're now going to use one of the best Storyboarding features—Cell Prototyping. It makes customizing your TableView cells a real breeze.

   First, select the TableView and change the Row Height in the Size Inspector to 64. Then drag an ImageView and a label into the cell as shown in Figure 3-55.

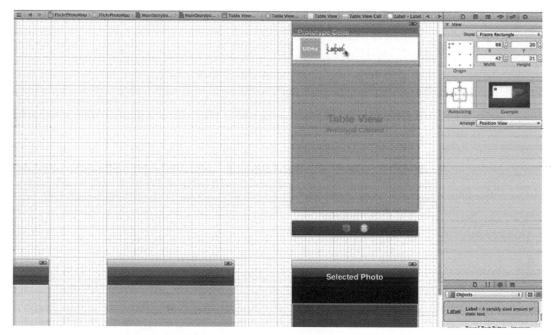

Figure 3-55. *Creating a Prototype Cell.*

3. Select the UIImageView and set its Image property to
   BluePin.png in the Attributes Inspector and then switch to the
   Size Inspector and adjust Image View width and height as
   shown in Figure 3-56. Also make the label wider and set its text
   to "Decide later." Re-align the elements if needed to center
   them inside the cell. You can leave all other properties as
   default.

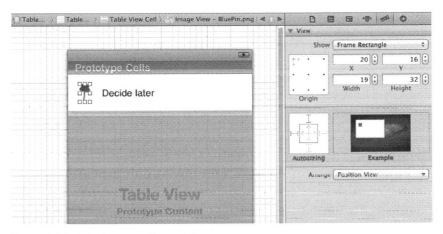

Figure 3-56. *Adjust and position cell elements.*

4. Select the TableView and change its Content type to Static Cells
    and Style to Grouped as shown in Figure 3-57 (if the height of
    the cells shrank back to 44, switch to the Size Inspector and set
    it to 64 again). Select the Table View section by clicking on the
    striped background at the very top of the Table View (you can
    also navigate to it by expanding the Document Outline pane
    located on the left side of the Storyboard canvas). Change the
    Table View Section Rows and Header properties as shown on
    Figure 3-58. Lastly, using the Attribute Inspector, change the
    label text and the image for each cell to match the ones shown
    in Figure 3-59 (use RedPin.png, GreenPin.png, and
    YellowPin.png images respectively).

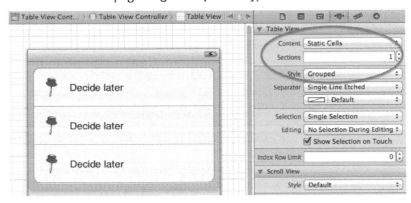

Figure 3-57. *Change Table View properties.*

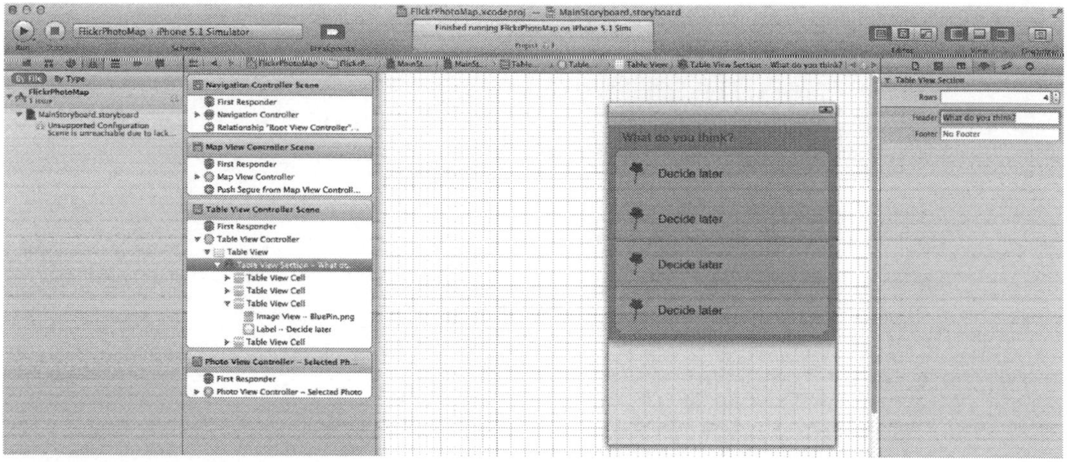

Figure 3-58. *Change Table View Section properties.*

Figure 3-59. *Change images and text for the rest of the static Table View cells.*

5. Create a new segue between the MapView Controller and Table
    View Controller by Control-dragging from the MapView
    Controller icon to the Table View Controller as shown in Figure
    3-60. Release it and select Modal for segue type from the menu.
    Select the new segue, set its Identifier property in the Attributes
    Inspector to ShowPinChoicesSegue, and change its Transition
    type to Flip Horizontal as shown in Figure 3-61.

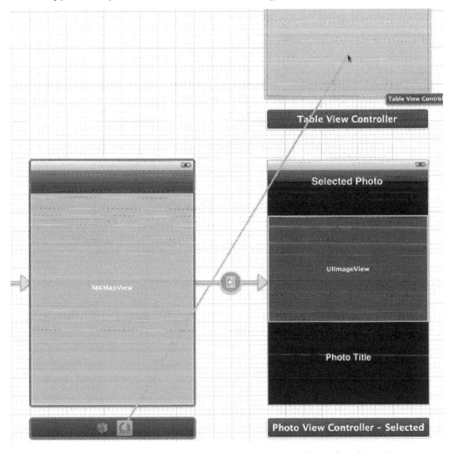

Figure 3-60. *Control-drag from the MapView Controller to the Table View Controller.*

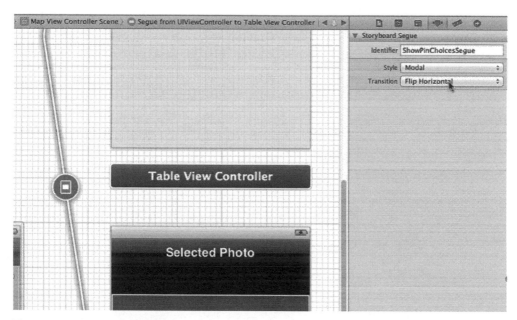

Figure 3-61. *Set segue attributes.*

6. In this step you'll create a new UIViewController subclass, which will control your Table View scene. Hit ⌘N, select the Objective-C class option, and click Next. Make sure UITableViewController is selected as the Subclass option. Name the class PinSelectionViewController and save it.

NOTE: Static TableViews designed in a Storyboard can only be used with a UITableViewController subclass.

---

7. In the Storyboard, select the Table View Controller and in the Identity Inspector set its class to the newly created PinSelectionViewController class as shown in Figure 3-62.

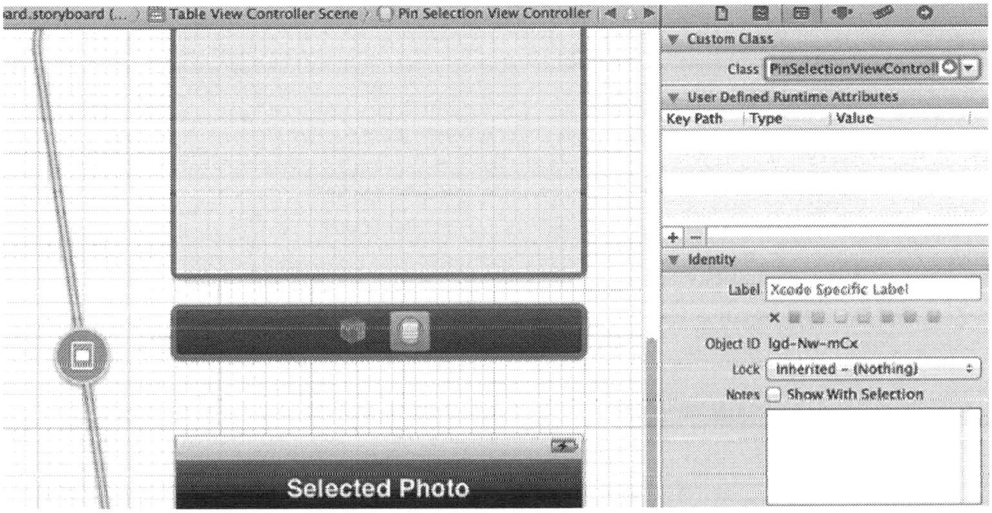

Figure 3-62. *Set the Table View Controller's class to PinSelectionViewController.*

8. Hit ⌘N and select the Objective-C protocol option as shown in Figure 3-63. Click Next, name the file `PinSelectionDelegateProtocol`, and save it.

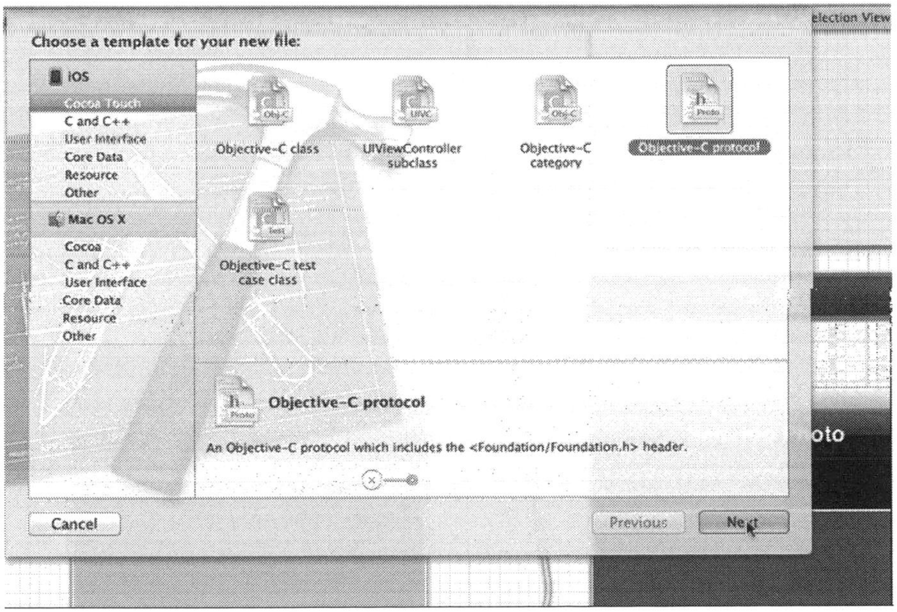

Figure 3-63. *Create an Objective-C protocol.*

9. Open the newly added `PinSelectionDelegateProtocol.h` file and replace the code in it with the one shown in Figure 3-64 (DemoMonkey step "17 PinSelectionDelegateProtocol.h"). Here you define `AnnotationPinType` enum for convenience and a method, which will be implemented by your `MapViewController` class (this method will get called when the user selects the rating cell in the Table View scene).

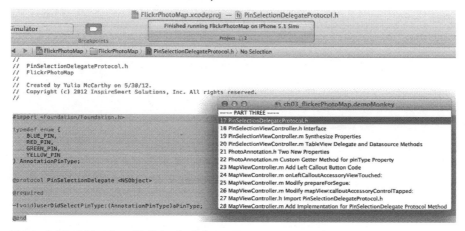

Figure 3-64. *Add code to PinSelectionDelegateProtocol.h*

10. Go to the `PinSelectionViewController.h` file and replace the code in it with that shown in Figure 3-65 (refer to DemoMonkey step "18 PinSelectionViewController.h Interface"). Here you're creating two properties: `delegate` and `currentPinType`. The first one will be used to notify your `MapViewController` about user selection and update its UI. The second one will be used to display the current rating of the photo. As always, go to `PinSelectionViewController.m` and add `@synthesize` statements for both of the properties right below `@implementation` (DemoMonkey step "19 PinSelectionViewController.m Synthesize Properties"):

```
#import " PinSelectionViewController.h"
@interface PinSelectionViewController ()
@end
@implementation PinSelectionViewController
@synthesize delegate;
@synthesize currentPinType;
...
```

```
#import <UIKit/UIKit.h>
#import "PinSelectionDelegateProtocol.h"

@interface PinSelectionViewController : UITableViewController

@property (weak, nonatomic) id<PinSelectionDelegate> delegate;
@property (assign, nonatomic) AnnotationPinType currentPinType;

@end
```

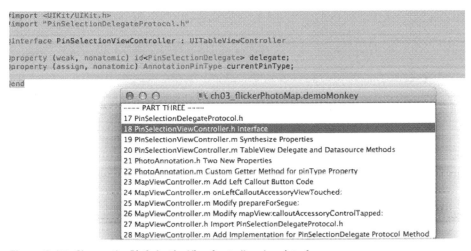

Figure 3-65. *Change the PinSelectionViewController class interface.*

11. Scroll to the #pragma mark - Table view data source section of the code, select everything all the way till @end and replace the selected code with that shown in Figure 3-66 (DemoMonkey step "20 PinSelectionViewController.m TableView Delegate and Datasource Methods") Note that because you're using a static Table View you don't need to implement any standard Table View Data Source methods. The only Data Source method we chose to implement is tableView willDisplayCell:forRowAtIndexPath:. In this method we simply set the accessoryType property of the cell, for which the indexPath.row matches the currentPinType, to checkmark, thus indicating the current rating of the selected photo. In the tableView:didSelectRowAtIndexPath: method you notify the delegate about the row number that was selected by invoking the method you defined in PinSelectionDelegateProtocol. The programming technique used here is one of the most common and most widely used design patterns in iOS development (the delegate pattern).

```
// Uncomment the following line to preserve selection between presentations.
// self.clearsSelectionOnViewWillAppear = NO;

// Uncomment the following line to display an Edit button in the navigation b
// self.navigationItem.rightBarButtonItem = self.editButtonItem;
}

- (void)viewDidUnload
{
    [super viewDidUnload];
    // Release any retained subviews of the main view.
    // e.g. self.myOutlet = nil;
}

- (BOOL)shouldAutorotateToInterfaceOrientation:(UIInterfaceOrientation)interfac
{
    return (interfaceOrientation == UIInterfaceOrientationPortrait);
}

#pragma mark - Table view data source

- (void)tableView:(UITableView *)tableView willDisplayCell:(UITableViewCell *)cell forRowAtIndexPath:(NSIndexPath *)indexPath
{
    if (indexPath.row == currentPinType)
        cell.accessoryType = UITableViewCellAccessoryCheckmark;
}

#pragma mark - Table view delegate

- (void)tableView:(UITableView *)tableView didSelectRowAtIndexPath:(NSIndexPath *)indexPath
{
    [self.delegate userDidSelectPinType:indexPath.row];
}

@end
```

Figure 3-66. *Replace the TableViewDelegate and TableViewDataSource methods.*

12. Go to the PhotoAnnotation.h file. First add #import PinSelectionDelegateProtocol.h right above the @interface. Then create two new properties as shown in Figure 3-67 (DemoMonkey step "21 PhotoAnnotation.h Two New Properties"). In PhotoAnnotation.m add synthesize pinType property only. You don't need to synthesize the annotationViewImageName property here because it's readonly, and you're going to specify a custom getter for it in the next step.

```
//
//  PhotoAnnotation.h
//  FlickrPhotoMap
//
//  Created by Yulia McCarthy on 5/29/12.
//  Copyright (c) 2012 InspireSmart Solutions, Inc. All rights reserved.
//

#import <Foundation/Foundation.h>
#import <MapKit/MapKit.h>
#import "PinSelectionDelegateProtocol.h"

@interface PhotoAnnotation : NSObject <MKAnnotation>

// MKAnnotation properties
@property (nonatomic, copy)     NSString *title;
@property (nonatomic, copy)     NSString *subtitle;
@property (nonatomic, assign)   CLLocationCoordinate2D coordinate;

// Other properties
@property (nonatomic, strong)   UIImage *image;
@property (nonatomic, strong)   UIImage *thumbnail;
@property (nonatomic, strong)   NSURL *imageURL;
@property (nonatomic, strong)   NSURL *thumbnailURL;
@property (nonatomic, assign)   AnnotationPinType pinType;
@property (nonatomic, readonly) NSString *annotationViewImageName;

- (id)initWithImageURL:(NSURL *)anImageURL thumbnailURL:(NSURL *)aThumbnailURL title:(NSString *)aTitle coordinate:(CLLocationCoordinate2D)aCoo
- (void)updateSubtitle;

@end
```

Figure 3-67. *Modify the PhotoAnnotation.h file.*

13. Add the getter method for the `annotationViewImageName` property as shown in Figure 3-68 (refer to DemoMonkey step "22 PhotoAnnotation.m Custom Getter Method for pinType Property"). In this method you define the image name for annotation View based on its type, which will be set when the user rates the photo represented by the annotation. The default image for unrated photos will be `BluePin.png`.

```
#import "PhotoAnnotation.h"
#import <CoreLocation/CoreLocation.h>

@implementation PhotoAnnotation

@synthesize title, subtitle, coordinate;
@synthesize image, thumbnail;
@synthesize imageURL, thumbnailURL;
@synthesize pinType;

- (id)initWithImageURL:(NSURL *)anImageURL thumbnailURL:(NSURL *)aThumbnailURL
                title:(NSString *)aTitle coordinate:(CLLocationCoordinate2D)aCoordinate
{
    if ((self = [super init])) {
        self.imageURL = anImageURL;
        self.thumbnailURL = aThumbnailURL;
        self.title = aTitle;
        self.coordinate = aCoordinate;
    }
    return self;
}
```

```
- (NSString *)annotationViewImageName
{
    switch (self.pinType) {
        case 0:
            return @"BluePin.png";
            break;
        case 1:
            return @"RedPin.png";
            break;
        case 2:
            return @"GreenPin.png";
            break;
        case 3:
            return @"YellowPin.png";
            break;
        default:
            break;
    }
}

- (NSString *)title
{
    return title;
}
```

```
○ ○ ○         ch03_flickerPhotoMap.demoMonkey
───── PART THREE ─────
17 PinSelectionDelegateProtocol.h
18 PinSelectionViewController.h Interface
19 PinSelectionViewController.m Synthesize Properties
20 PinSelectionViewController.m TableView Delegate and Datasource Methods
21 PhotoAnnotation.h Two New Properties
22 PhotoAnnotation.m Custom Getter Method for pinType Property
23 MapViewController.m Add Left Callout Button Code
24 MapViewController.m onLeftCalloutAccessoryViewTouched:
25 MapViewController.m Modify prepareForSegue:
26 MapViewController.m Modify mapView:calloutAccessoryControlTapped:
27 MapViewController.h Import PinSelectionDelegateProtocol.h
28 MapViewController.m Add Implementation for PinSelectionDelegate Protocol Method
```

Figure 3-68. *Add the getter method for the annotationViewImageName property.*

14. You need to modify a few things in the `MapViewController` class. First go to `MapViewController.m` and import `PinSelectionViewController.h` at the top of the file.

15. To add a button with a photo thumbnail, add the code shown in Figure 3-69 at the end of the `mapView:didSelectAnnotationView:` method implementation (use the code from DemoMonkey step "[23 MapViewController.m Add Left Callout Button Code").

```
- (void)mapView:(MKMapView *)aMapView annotationView:(MKAnnotationView *)view calloutAccessoryControlTapped:(UIControl *)control
{
    if (![view.annotation isKindOfClass:[PhotoAnnotation class]])
        return;

    PhotoAnnotation *photoAnnotation = (PhotoAnnotation *)view.annotation;

    [self performSegueWithIdentifier:@"ShowFullSizeImageSegue" sender:photoAnnotation];
}

- (void)mapView:(MKMapView *)mapView didSelectAnnotationView:(MKAnnotationView *)view
{
    if (![view.annotation isKindOfClass:[PhotoAnnotation class]])
        return;

    // Reverse geocode the annotation if needed
    PhotoAnnotation *photoAnnotation = (PhotoAnnotation *)view.annotation;
    if (!photoAnnotation.subtitle)
        [photoAnnotation updateSubtitle];

    if (!view.leftCalloutAccessoryView) {
        UIButton *leftViewButton = [[UIButton alloc] initWithFrame:CGRectMake(0.0, 0.0, 48.0, 32.0)];
        [leftViewButton setBackgroundImage:photoAnnotation.thumbnail forState:UIControlStateNormal];
        [leftViewButton addTarget:self action:@selector(onLeftCalloutAccessoryViewTouched:) forControlEvents:UIControlEventTouchUpInside];
        leftViewButton.tag = 1;
        view.leftCalloutAccessoryView = leftViewButton;
    }
}

@end
```

PART THREE

17 PinSelectionDelegateProtocol.h
18 PinSelectionViewController.h Interface
19 PinSelectionViewController.m Synthesize Properties
20 PinSelectionViewController.m TableView Delegate and Datasource Methods
21 PhotoAnnotation.h Two New Properties
22 PhotoAnnotation.m Custom Getter Method for pinType property
23 MapViewController.m Add Left Callout Button Code
24 MapViewController.m onLeftCalloutAccessoryViewTouched:
25 MapViewController.m Modify prepareForSegue:
26 MapViewController.m Modify mapView:calloutAccessoryControlTapped:
27 MapViewController.h Import PinSelectionDelegateProtocol.h
28 MapViewController.m Add Implementation for PinSelectionDelegate Protocol Method

Figure 3-69. *Modify the mapView:didSelectAnnotationView: method.*

16. When the thumbnail is touched, the
    onLeftCalloutAccessoryViewTouched: method will be called.
    Add implementation for this method as shown in Figure 3-70
    (DemoMonkey step "[24 MapViewController.m
    onLeftCalloutAccessoryViewTouched:"). In this method you
    invoke your second Storyboard Segue with the
    ShowPinChoicesSegue Identifier, which will present a modal Table
    View Controller designed in the Storyboard.

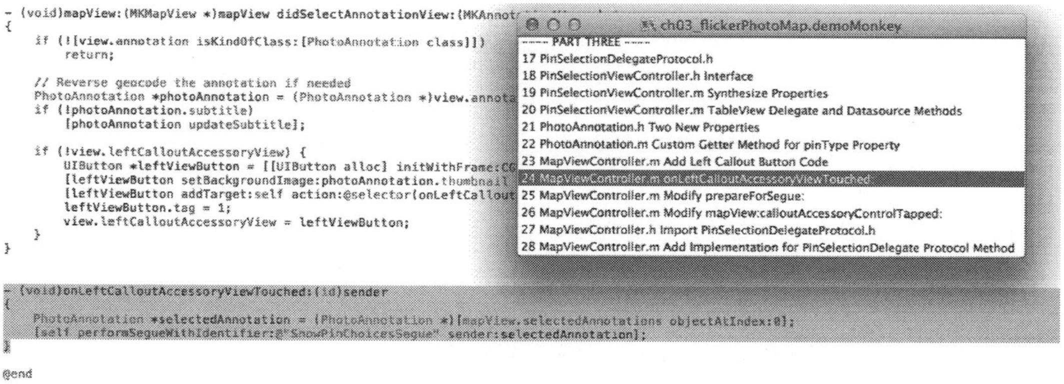

```
- (void)mapView:(MKMapView *)mapView didSelectAnnotationView:(MKAnnotationView *)view
{
    if (![view.annotation isKindOfClass:[PhotoAnnotation class]])
        return;

    // Reverse geocode the annotation if needed
    PhotoAnnotation *photoAnnotation = (PhotoAnnotation *)view.annotation;
    if (!photoAnnotation.subtitle)
        [photoAnnotation updateSubtitle];

    if (!view.leftCalloutAccessoryView) {
        UIButton *leftViewButton = [[UIButton alloc] initWithFrame:CGRectMake(
        [leftViewButton setBackgroundImage:photoAnnotation.thumbnail
        [leftViewButton addTarget:self action:@selector(onLeftCallout
        leftViewButton.tag = 1;
        view.leftCalloutAccessoryView = leftViewButton;
    }
}

- (void)onLeftCalloutAccessoryViewTouched:(id)sender
{
    PhotoAnnotation *selectedAnnotation = (PhotoAnnotation *)[mapView.selectedAnnotations objectAtIndex:0];
    [self performSegueWithIdentifier:@"ShowPinChoicesSegue" sender:selectedAnnotation];
}

@end
```

PART THREE

17 PinSelectionDelegateProtocol.h
18 PinSelectionViewController.h Interface
19 PinSelectionViewController.m Synthesize Properties
20 PinSelectionViewController.m TableView Delegate and Datasource Methods
21 PhotoAnnotation.h Two New Properties
22 PhotoAnnotation.m Custom Getter Method for pinType property
23 MapViewController.m Add Left Callout Button Code
24 MapViewController.m onLeftCalloutAccessoryViewTouched:
25 MapViewController.m Modify prepareForSegue:
26 MapViewController.m Modify mapView:calloutAccessoryControlTapped:
27 MapViewController.h Import PinSelectionDelegateProtocol.h
28 MapViewController.m Add Implementation for PinSelectionDelegate Protocol Method

Figure 3-70. *Add implementation for the onLeftCalloutAccessoryViewTouched: method.*

17. Modify the `prepareForSegue:` method by inserting additional code at the end of the method implementation as shown in Figure 3-71 (use DemoMonkey step "25 MapViewController.m Modify prepareForSegue:"). Here you add a condition for the second segue, where you set the `PinSelectionViewController`'s delegate and pass the current pin type of the selected annotation, so the correct Table View cell is marked.

Figure 3-71. *Modify the prepareForSegue: method.*

18. Scroll to `mapView:viewForAnnotation:` and replace each occurrence of the string `@"PhotoAnnotation"` and `@"BluePin.png"` with the following expression (as shown in Figure 3-72):

`((PhotoAnnotation *)annotation).annotationViewImageName`

There should be a total of three replacements. You're doing this to distinguish the annotations with different ratings. Because the annotation Views are being constantly reused by the MapView, you must specify a unique `reuseIdentifier` for each pin color. In this case the name of the pin image is perfectly suitable to be used as `reuseIdentifier`. Because the default pin type is `BLUE_PIN = 0`, each annotation will display blue by default.

```
#pragma mark - MKMapViewDelegate Protocol
#pragma mark -

- (MKAnnotationView *)mapView:(MKMapView *)aMapView viewForAnnotation:(id<MKAnnotation>)annotation
{
    if ([annotation isKindOfClass:[PhotoAnnotation class]]) {
        // Use our pin image for annotation, with a disclosure button callout accessory

        MKAnnotationView *annotationView = (MKAnnotationView *)[aMapView dequeueReusableAnnotationViewWithIdentifier:((PhotoAnnotation *)annotation).
            annotationViewImageName];

        if (annotationView == nil)
            annotationView = [[MKAnnotationView alloc] initWithAnnotation:annotation reuseIdentifier:((PhotoAnnotation *)annotation).annotationViewImageName];

        annotationView.image = [UIImage imageNamed:((PhotoAnnotation *)annotation).annotationViewImageName];
        annotationView.canShowCallout = YES;

        UIButton *disclosureButton = [UIButton buttonWithType:UIButtonTypeDetailDisclosure];
        annotationView.rightCalloutAccessoryView = disclosureButton;

        return annotationView;
    }
    return nil;
}
```

Figure 3-72. *Modify the mapView:viewForAnnotation: method.*

19. To make sure the right segue gets performed when one or the other Callout Accessory View is touched, replace the last line of code in the `mapView:calloutAccessoryControlTapped:` method with the one shown in Figure 3-73 (DemoMonkey step "[26 MapViewController.m Modify mapView:calloutAccessoryControlTapped:").

```
#pragma mark - MKMapViewDelegate Protocol
#pragma mark -

- (MKAnnotationView *)mapView:(MKMapView *)aMapView viewForAnnotation:(id<MKAnnotation>)annotation
{
    if ([annotation isKindOfClass:[PhotoAnnotation class]]) {
        // Use our pin
```

```
                    ch03_flickerPhotoMap.demoMonkey
        ----- PART THREE -----
        17 PinSelectionDelegateProtocol.h
        18 PinSelectionViewController.h Interface
        19 PinSelectionViewController.m Synthesize Properties
        20 PinSelectionViewController.m TableView Delegate and Datasource Methods
        21 PhotoAnnotation.h Two New Properties
        22 PhotoAnnotation.m Custom Getter Method for pinType property
        23 MapViewController.m Add Left Callout Button Code
        24 MapViewController.m onLeftCalloutAccessoryViewTouched:
        25 MapViewController.m Modify prepareForSegue:
        26 MapViewController.m Modify mapView.calloutAccessoryControlTapped:
        27 MapViewController.h Import PinSelectionDelegateProtocol.h
        28 MapViewController.m Add Implementation for PinSelectionDelegate Protocol Method
```

```
- (void)mapView:(MKMapView *)aMapView annotationView:(MKAnnotationView *)view calloutAccessoryControlTapped:(UIControl *)control
{
    if (![view.annotation isKindOfClass:[PhotoAnnotation class]])
        return;

    PhotoAnnotation *photoAnnotation = (PhotoAnnotation *)view.annotation;

    if (control.tag == 0) {
        [self performSegueWithIdentifier:@"ShowFullSizeImageSegue" sender:photoAnnotation];
    } else {
        [self onLeftCalloutAccessoryViewTouched:control];
    }
}
```

Figure 3-73. *Modify the mapView:calloutAccessoryControlTapped: method.*

20. Now go to the `MapViewController.h` file and add an `import` statement as shown in Figure 3-74. Also add a comma and add `PinSelectionDelegate` in the angle brackets of the class declaration.

```
//
//  MapViewController.h
//  FlickrPhotoMap
//
//  Created by Yulia McCarthy on 5/28/12.
//  Copyright (c) 2012 InspireSmart Solutions, Inc. All rights reserved.
//

#import <UIKit/UIKit.h>
#import <MapKit/MapKit.h>
#import "PinSelectionDelegateProtocol.h"

@interface MapViewController : UIViewController <MKMapViewDelegate, PinSelectionDelegate>

@property (weak, nonatomic) IBOutlet MKMapView *mapView;
@property (weak, nonatomic) IBOutlet UIActivityIndicatorView *activityIndicator;
@end
```

Figure 3-74. *Import PinSelectionDelegateProtocol.h in MapViewController.h.*

21. Finally, implement the `PinSelectionDelegate` Protocol method as shown in Figure 3-75 (drag DemoMonkey step "28 MapViewController.m Add Implementation for PinSelectionDelegate Protocol Method"). This method gets called when user selects a cell in `PinSelectionViewController`'s Table View. Here, you change the pin type based on the received rating, remove the selected annotation from the MapView, and add it back in to force its annotation View to reload. Last, dismiss the modal `PinSelectionViewController`.

```
- (void)populateMapWithPhotoAnnotations
{
    NSMutableArray *photoAnnotations = [[NSMutableArray alloc] init];

    for (NSDictionary *photoDict in [parsedPhotosDictionary allValues])
    {
        // Read the image's metadata
        NSURL *photoURL = [photoDict objectForKey:@"mediumimageurl"];
        NSURL *thumbnailURL = [photoDict objectForKey:@"thumbnailurl"];
        NSString *photoLat = [photoDict objectForKey:@"latitude"];
        NSString *photoLon = [photoDict objectForKey:@"longitude"];

        if (photoLat && photoLon) {
            CLLocationCoordinate2D coord;
            coord.latitude = [photoLat doubleValue];
            coord.longitude = [photoLon doubleValue];

            NSString *fileName = [photoDict objectForK
            PhotoAnnotation *photo = [[PhotoAnnotation
            [photoAnnotations addObject:photo];
        }
    }

    if (photoAnnotations.count > 0) {
        [mapView addAnnotations:photoAnnotations];
    }

    parsedPhotosDictionary = nil;
}
```

---- PART THREE ----
17 PinSelectionDelegateProtocol.h
18 PinSelectionViewController.h Interface
19 PinSelectionViewController.m Synthesize Properties
20 PinSelectionViewController.m TableView Delegate and Datasource Methods
21 PhotoAnnotation.h Two New Properties
22 PhotoAnnotation.m Custom Getter Method for pinType Property
23 MapViewController.m Add Left Callout Button Code
24 MapViewController.m onLeftCalloutAccessoryViewTouched:
25 MapViewController.m Modify prepareForSegue:
26 MapViewController.m Modify mapView:calloutAccessoryControlTapped:
27 MapViewController.h Import PinSelectionDelegateProtocol.h
28 MapViewController.m Add Implementation for PinSelectionDelegate Protocol Method

```
-(void)userDidSelectPinType:(AnnotationPinType)aPinType
{
    PhotoAnnotation *selectedAnnotation = (PhotoAnnotation *)[mapView.selectedAnnotations objectAtIndex:0];
    selectedAnnotation.pinType = aPinType;
    [mapView removeAnnotation:selectedAnnotation];
    [mapView addAnnotation:selectedAnnotation];
    [self.navigationController dismissModalViewControllerAnimated:YES];
}
```

Figure 3-75. *Add the implementation for PinSelectionDelegate Protocol method.*

22. Build and run. Congratulations! You should now be able to see the screens as shown in Figure 3-76 when you click the left or right callout accessory View.

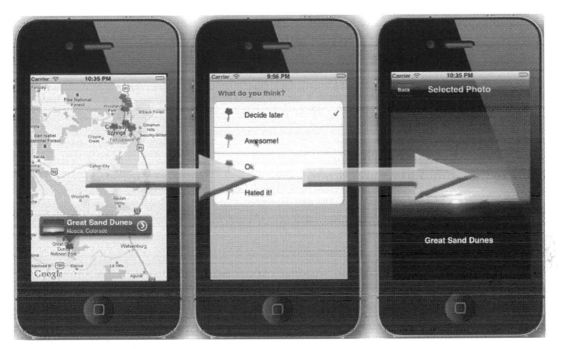

Figure 3-76. *Final look of the app.*

Building a Utility Application

So far in this book you've built two Single View Applications with Storyboards. In Chapter 2 you built AlienView and in Chapter 3 you built FlickrPhotoMap. We are now moving forward, and you're going to build a Utility Application using Storyboards. You typically use Utility Applications when you want to create easy-to-use apps that consist of two pages: a one-page Main View and a second View that comes with a flip animation transition. The Utility Application sets up these two pages with two essential buttons: an Info button and a Done button. The Info button flips the user from the Main View to the Flipside View, and the Done button flips the user back to the Main View.

You may not know it but you're probably very familiar with a Utility application that comes with your iPhone, and that is the Weather app, shown in Figure 4-1. The Weather app is a perfect example of a Utility Application in the sense that it optimizes a simple task that requires a minimal amount of user interaction.

The Utility Application is also one of three special templates in that it, along with the Navigation-Based Application and the Window-Based Application, are the only three project templates that offer the option to automatically include support for Core Data. Furthermore, the Utility Application is one of the most extensive templates in Xcode—it implements a fully working Utility Application right at the get-go.

We introduce the Utility Application with Storyboarding by coding a very cool app that teaches musicians when to select a particular scale for a particular genre or mood. It displays finger notations on both acoustic guitar and electric guitar fretboards, along with accompanying sounds for each scale.

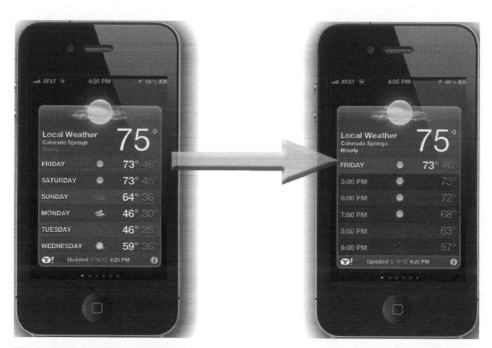

Figure 4–1. *The Weather app that comes along with the iPhone is probably the most famous and most used Utility Application.*

utilityScales: A Utility App

Let's first talk about our utilityScales design decisions: We chose to illustrate the use of the Utility Application template by creating an application with which you can hear various scales on both acoustic and electric guitars. We chose eight musical scales to demonstrate this concept.

We needed to display a list of scales and the genres and moods each scale would be associated with. With this in mind we decided to use the Table View already present in the Flipside View Controller to list the scales. We also selected the Subtitle layout for the table cells so that we could show both the category of each scale as well as its name. We chose the iPad layout because it gave us more room for the scale-fingering images. We created the assets for the program, which consisted of 8 scales each for two guitars, 16 associated scale-fingering diagrams, a smaller image of each guitar for the play buttons, a loading (or Default) screen, an application icon, and more. It meant a total of 16 audio recordings and 23 graphic files in all.

We decided to make the user interface somewhat nonstandard in that we wanted to have play/stop buttons for each guitar type. They both needed to have identical functionality, so we encapsulated their functionality in a dedicated PlayButton class. To incorporate the audio playback functionality—which consists of special configuration and methods to load the files, start and stop playback of each, and so on—we chose to encapsulate this functionality in its own class (an object with its own .h/.m files).

Lastly, we have eight scales, each with two audio files, two images, a title, and a description—all of which we chose to store in instances of a new Scale class (also an object with its own .h/.m files). This lets us have eight initialization statements instead of having to initialize many different arrays with each of these attributes.

In the Storyboard file we set up the initial background of the main display, the Navigation Bar for the display with its custom colors, and a semitransparent "pad" on which we placed the two play buttons programmatically. On the flipside portion of the Storyboard, we configured and named the single dynamic cell template and we configured the title bar coloring and text.

We have divided this project into different phases: one for setting up the project in Xcode, one for setting up the Storyboard, and two for coding. They are as follows:

- *Setup.* Setting up with the template, adjusting the project settings, dragging in the assets, and adding the frameworks.

- *Prepping the Storyboard.* In the Main View and Second View, you'll be tweaking the Navigation Bars, the colors and buttons and so forth, and adding UIImagesViews, UITableViews, and the landing Views.

- *Coding the Main ViewController.* Coding and connecting.

Preliminaries

Similarly to Chapters 2 and 3, we supply you with all the files and code necessary for this chapter at http://bit.ly/sMRvAP as illustrated in Figure 4-2. Again, as always, take the time to clean up your desktop and download all image and audio files to your desktop, and you're ready to roll. If you need more help, go to the forum at http://bit.ly/oLVwpY. In particular, make sure before you start that you've downloaded the DemoMonkey files at http://bit.ly/sMRvAP and unzipped it on your desktop.

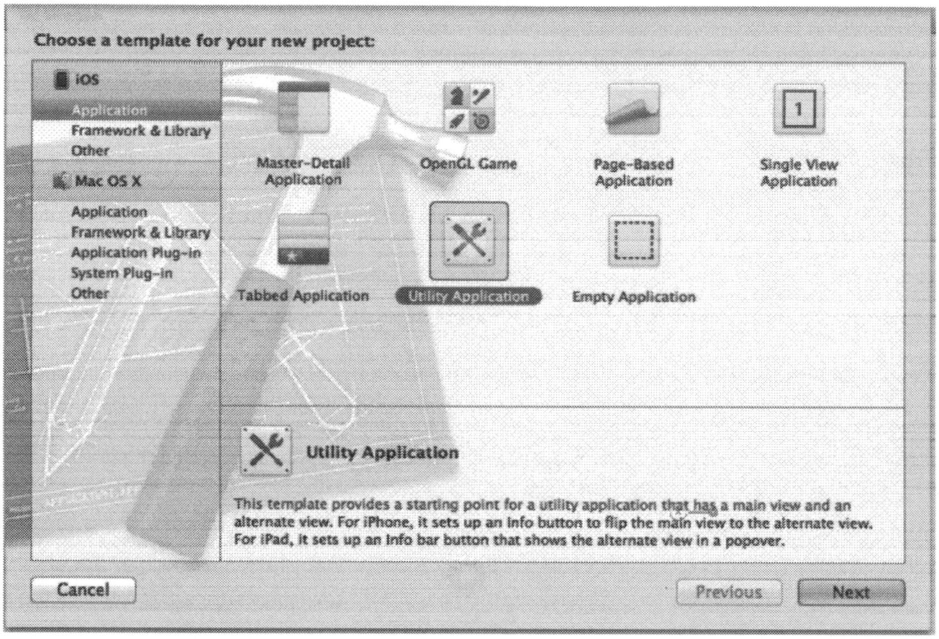

Figure 4-2. *Select Utility Application.*

Step 1: Setup

Setup is the first of the four steps you will follow for this project. You'll create a new iPad Utility Application project, name it utilityScales, and adjust the project settings by deselecting the portrait and upside-down options. Then you'll drag image, class, and audio assets into the project. Finally, you'll add necessary frameworks. With that completed, you'll have set up your project and will be ready to prep the Storyboard in the second step.

1. Open Xcode, press ⌘⇧N (File ➤ New ➤ Project), select the Utility Application template, and click Next.

2. Name the app utilityScales. We've used a Company Identifier called com.apress. You can name yours whatever you like, but if you feel there is a chance you will need to compare your code to ours at any time, go ahead and name it com.apress like ours so there will be less chance of confusion. We won't use a class prefix. Make sure to select iPad and check both Use Storyboard and Use ARC as shown in Figure 4-3. Once created, save it to your desktop.

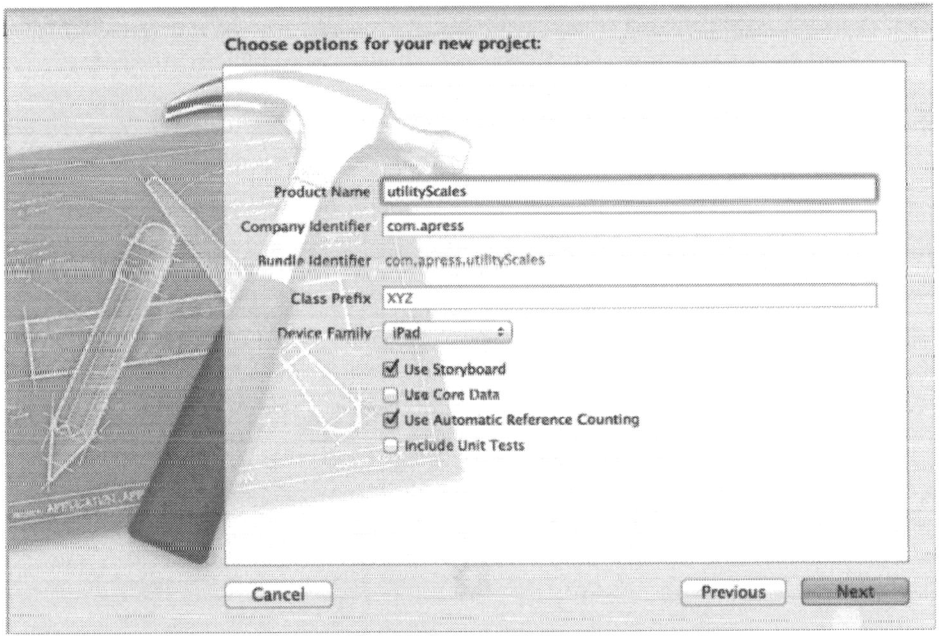

Figure 4-3. *Name the new project utilityScales.*

3. Once you've saved it to your desktop, the Project folder opens. You're only going to use Landscape orientation because it's better for displaying the neck of the guitar. This means you need to deselect the default Portrait and Upside Down orientations. Next, open your utilityScales Assets folder that you downloaded and unzipped onto your desktop from http://bit.ly/sMRvAP. First select the Default-Landscape~ipad.png file and drag the image into the Landscape slot as shown in Figure 4-4.

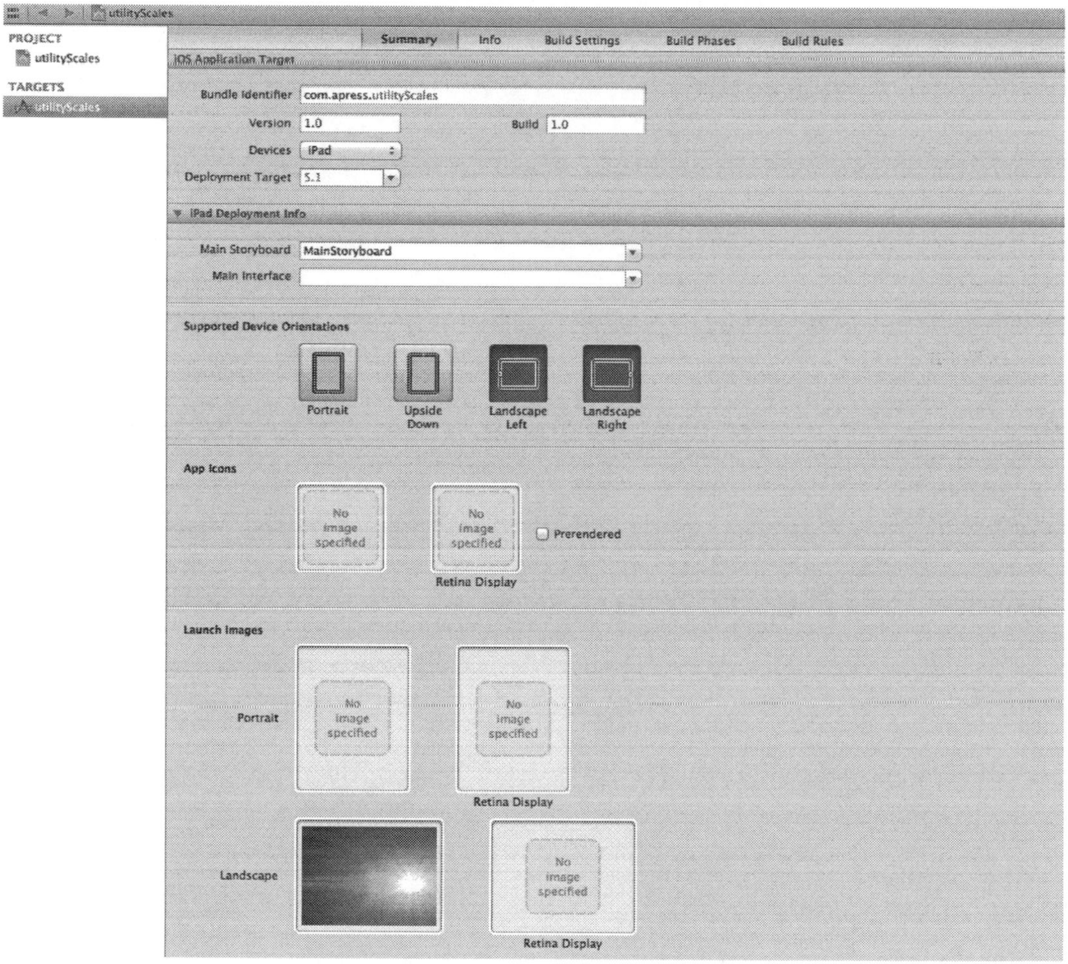

Figure 4-4. *Deselect the Portrait and Upside Down options and drag in Default-Landscape~ipad.png.*

4. You'll perform two tasks in this step. First move the Default-Landscape~ipad.png from the root directory of utilityScales target iOS SDK 5.0 (the blue folder in the upper right-hand corner) to the Supporting Files folder. Then add the Images and Audio Files folders into the Supporting Files folder. To do this, select both the Audio Files folder and the Images folder from inside the UtilityScales Assets folder on your desktop and drag and drop them over to the Supporting Files folder as shown in Figure 4-5.

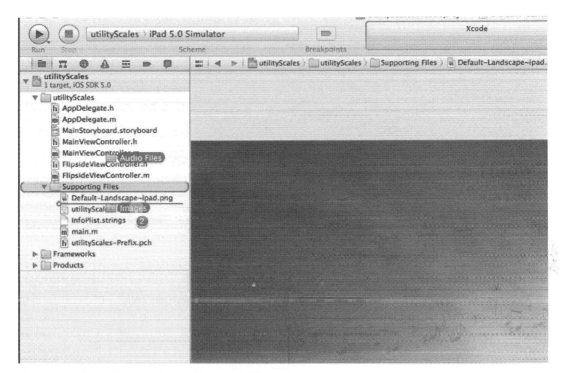

Figure 4-5. *Place all images into the Supporting Files folder.*

5.   The "Choose options for adding these files" dialog opens. Make sure you select the "Copy items into the destination group's folder (if needed)" option. Also select the "Create groups for any added folders" option. Finally make sure you "Add targets" as shown in Figure 4-6. You do this to make sure that it will work on other devices. You can do this only if these images, added folders, and targets are all inherent and encapsulated into your app. Sometimes students send us their homework without selecting these options, which makes the app, upon arrival for grading, void of all the images, folders, audio files, and targets—and of course with these missing, their project does not build.

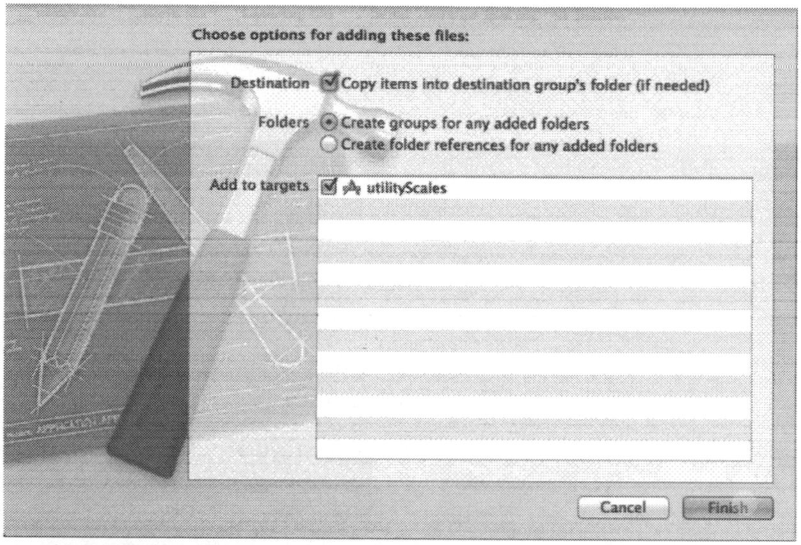

Figure 4-6. *Make sure you select Copy Items and Create Groups to the utilityScales target.*

6. Make sure that your Supporting Files folder looks as our does in Figure 4-7. Because we selected the "groups" option, the Audio Files and Images folders are beautifully instantiated inside the Supporting Files folder. This is good coding and something that tells those who view your code that you have good practices.

Figure 4-7. *A beautiful file structure.*

7. We've created three class files for your convenience because
   we want you to focus on Storyboarding, not creating files: an
   AudioPlayer class (AudioPlayer.h and AudioPlayer.m), a
   PlayButton class (PlayButton.h and PlayButton.m), and a Scale
   class (Scale.h and Scale.m). You want to add this code as well
   to your application. Grab these six files from the utilityScales
   Assets folder and drag them to your utilityScales folder as
   shown in on the upper left-hand image in Figure 4-8. When the
   "Choose options" dialog appears, select "Copy items into
   destination" and check the "Create groups" check boxes. When
   you have done this, click Next as shown on the upper right-
   hand image in Figure 4-8. Finally go to Build Phases, click the
   add button, and select the three implementation files as shown
   on the lower center image in Figure 4-8.

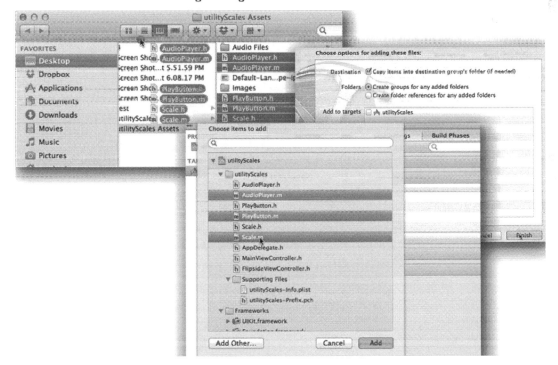

Figure 4-8. *Bring in the class files we've created for you.*

8. Make sure your utilityScales folder looks like ours in Figure 4-9. If for some reason it doesn't have the same files and folders, go back and retrace your steps, making sure that you get to this point with your utilityScales folder looking like ours.

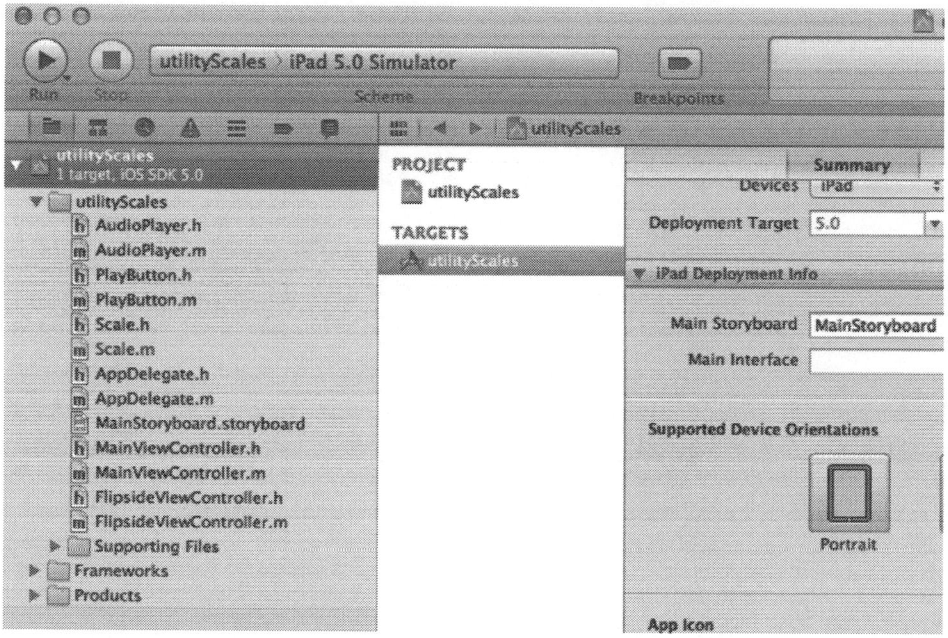

Figure 4-9. *Your utilityScales folder ready to go.*

9. As you already know, you'll be playing audio files in this app. Right now if you tried to build this app (try it if you like, you'll see many errors) you'd have a problem because you don't have any means to play audio files—even though you've defined the class and imported the audio files. You need to add the audio framework. Click the Summary button at the top of the editor, look towards the bottom of the summary page for the section called "Linked Frameworks and Libraries" (you may have to scroll the page to see it). At the bottom of this section, click the [+] button. Now select the AudioToolbox.framework as shown in Figure 4-10.

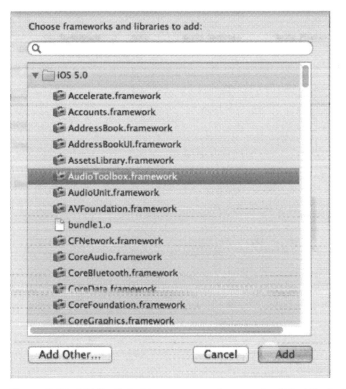

Figure 4-10. *Add the first of two necessary frameworks. Select the AudioToolbox.framework.*

10. Before leaving the frameworks and libraries add dialog, you need to add another framework. You've just added the audio framework, but it seems you also need an Objective-C interface in order to interact with this just included lower-level framework from our code. Therefore, also add the AVFoundation framework, which you call from the code to play audio files. It, in turn, calls the lower level AudioToolbox framework to do the actual file playing. So select the AVFoundation.framework in addition to the AudioToolbox.framework (by Command-clicking on the AVFoundation.framework so that both are selected) as shown in Figure 4-11. Finally, click Add button to add both frameworks to the utilityScales target of the project.

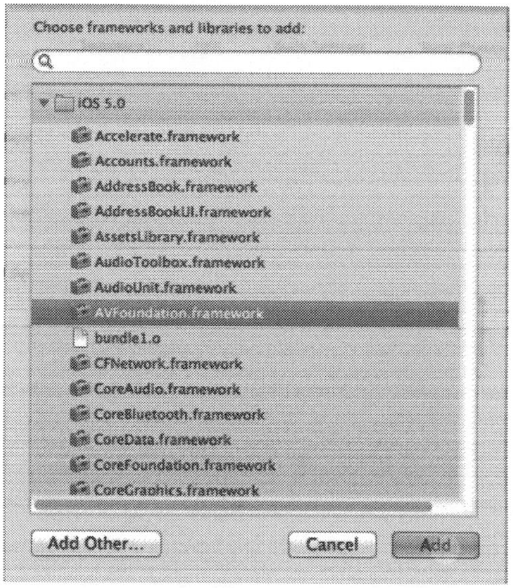

Choose frameworks and libraries to add:

iOS 5.0
- Accelerate.framework
- Accounts.framework
- AddressBook.framework
- AddressBookUI.framework
- AssetsLibrary.framework
- AudioToolbox.framework
- AudioUnit.framework
- AVFoundation.framework
- bundle1.o
- CFNetwork.framework
- CoreAudio.framework
- CoreBluetooth.framework
- CoreData.framework
- CoreFoundation.framework
- CoreGraphics.framework

Add Other...   Cancel   Add

Figure 4-11. *Also add the AVFoundation.framework.*

11. Once you've added your two frameworks, you'll see them located in the root directory of the utilityScales folder. Drag them into your Frameworks folder. Now you should have the three core frameworks of a Utility Application, along with the new AVFoundation and AudioToolbox frameworks, as shown in Figure 4-12.

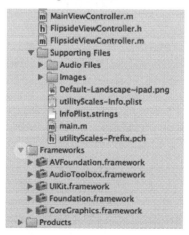

Figure 4-12. *Move your new frameworks to the Frameworks folder.*

Step 2: Prepping the Storyboard

You'll start by prepping the Main View by coloring the Navigation Bar and changing the Info button to Scales. Next you'll add a UIImageView image that doesn't have any user interaction! You'll then add a landing area for your play buttons that, again, won't have any user interaction. Once you do that you'll label the landing area "View - Play button area." This completes the First View.

The Second View will also need prepping—you'll start by coloring and adding a title to the Navigation Bar. Next you'll add a UITableView that will have dynamic cells and be grouped. You'll also set the datasource and delegate to your ViewController.

1. As mentioned earlier, the Utility Application comprises two Views: a Main View and a Flipside View. The user gets to the Flipside View by tapping the Info button found on the right side of the Navigation Bar in the Main View. Let's have a look at this and start setting up the Storyboard. Open the Storyboard and you will indeed see the Main View and the Flipside View as shown in Figure 4-13. You can see that the segue has already been built, and it's all there. Note that in the iPad, the Flipside View is shown as a Popover View.

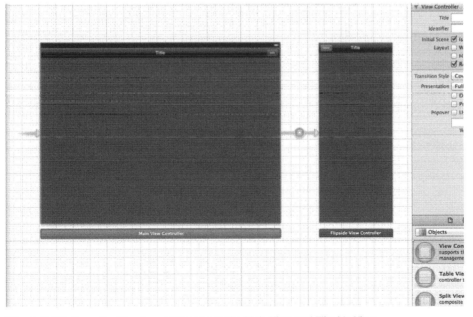

Figure 4-13. *Open the Storyboard file and see the Main View and Flipside View.*

2. Select the Title Bar (Navigation Controller) by clicking it and then use the Attributes Inspector to navigate to the Tint selector. Select the Teal color as shown in Figure 4-14.

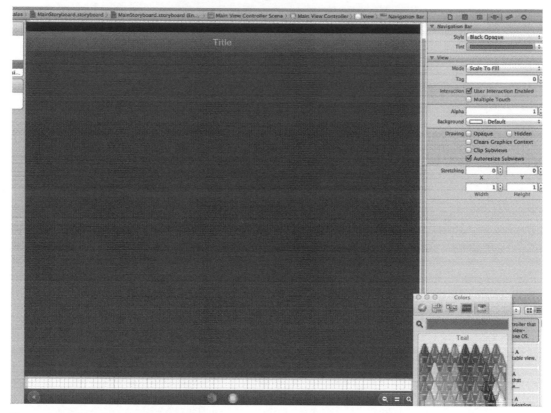

Figure 4-14. *Start by colorizing the Title Bar.*

3. Now you want to customize the Info button. First click the Info button (click twice to get the button itself and not the bar title) and then in the Attribute Inspector go to the Title box in the Bar Item section and change the name to Scales. You also want it to be the same color as the Navigation Bar, so go ahead and change the color to teal as shown in Figure 4-15. Note that you may have programmed another application that has reset the default of Style and Identifier; if this is the case, make sure your selections are like ours in Figure 4-15.

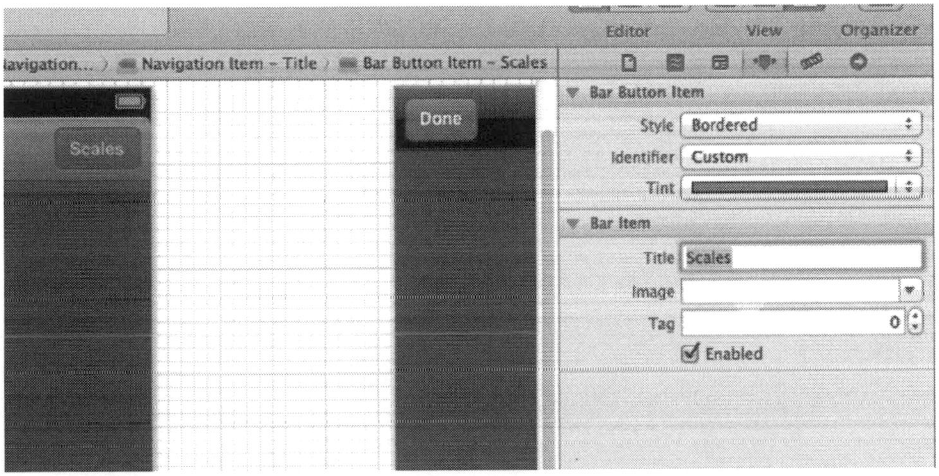

Figure 4-15. *Customize the Info Button.*

4. The main screen will house an image of a guitar fretboard with fingerings on it. This means you need to drag an Image View onto the canvas and allow it to autosize appropriately as shown in Figure 4-16. Depending on the resolution of your display, you may need to first zoom out to do this properly.

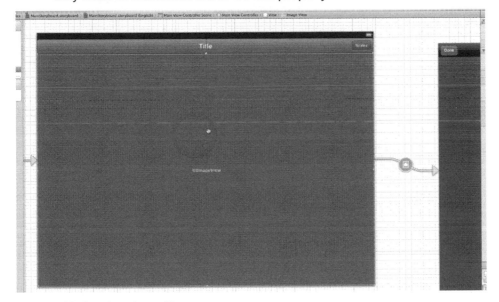

Figure 4-16. *Drag in an Image View.*

5. You'll need a place on the canvas to put your play buttons. (You may want to take a sneak peek and see the play buttons in Figures 4-59 and 4-60.) To do that, drag another view near the top left-hand corner of the existing Image View as shown in Figure 4-17. Note that the view is highlighted with light grey at the bottom of the Library.

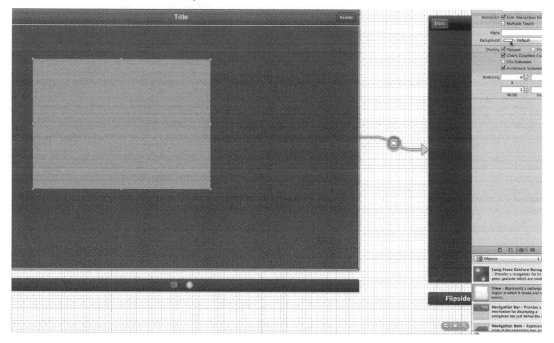

Figure 4-17. *Create a space for the play buttons.*

6. With this new smaller view selected, in the Attributes Inspector change the color to teal. Next go to the Identity Inspector and set the label to "View - Play Button Area" (this allows you to clearly identify this new smaller view in your document outline). Finally, with the new smaller view still selected, and now a teal color, go to the Size Inspector and place the view 20 pixels from the left and 64 pixels from the top. Now make the view have a width of 190 pixels with a height of 110 as shown in Figure 4-18.

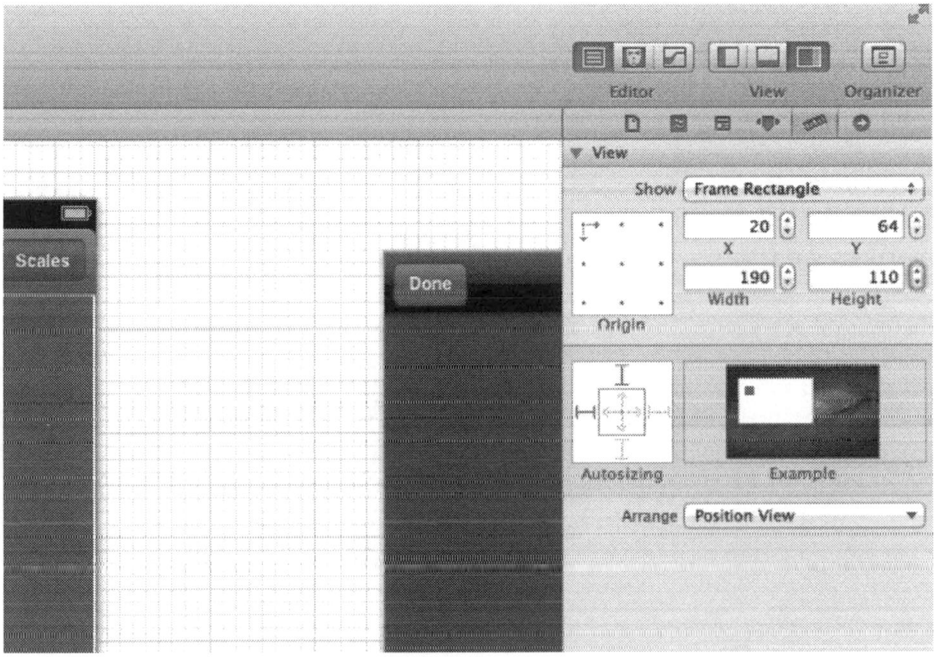

Figure 4-18. *Customize the "play button area" view.*

7. To show the Default image you placed into the Supporting
   Files folder, click the UIImageView in the Main View Controller
   Scene and then in the Attributes Inspector select Default-
   Landscape-ipad.png from the drop-down menu as shown in
   Figure 4-19.

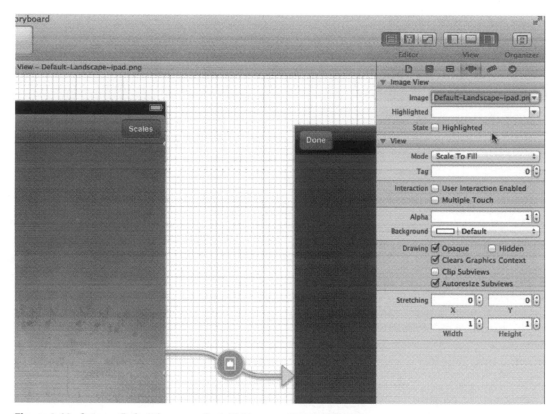

Figure 4-19. *Set your Default image as the initial image within the Main View.*

8. Now go to the Flipside View Controller Scene and select the Navigation Bar Title (in the document outline within the Flipside View Controller Scene, click the "Navigation Item – Title" line). Then in the Attributes Inspector rename the title to Scales as shown in Figure 4-20.

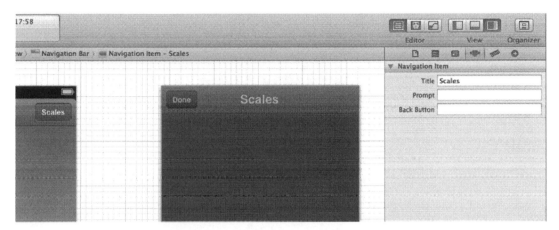

Figure 4-20. *Customize the Flipside View Controller.*

9. You probably want both the Navigation Bar of the Main View and the Navigation Bar of the Flipside View to be the same color, so click the Flipside View's Navigation Bar (in the document outline) and then select teal again in the Attributes Inspector's Tint selector. Now you want to change the Done button to teal, so click it and select teal from the Attributes Inspector. Lastly, think about what you want here in the Flipside View. You want this to be a Table of scales that the user can choose from (refer to Figure 4-58). This means you'll have to drag in a Table View. Once you've dragged in your Table View and allowed it to autosize itself, your Flipside View should look like ours does in Figure 4-21.

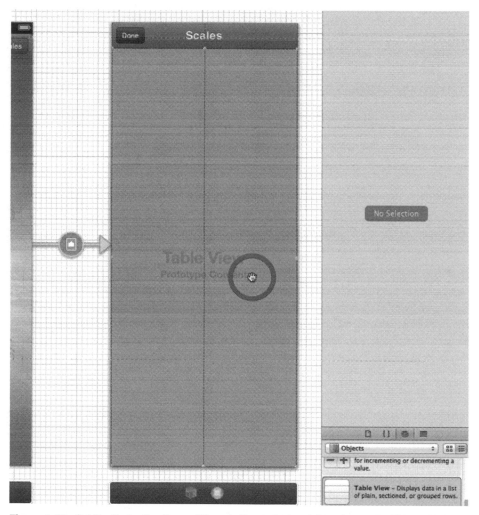

Figure 4-21. *Set the Navigation Bar and Done button to teal and then change the Title and bring in a Table View.*

10. Once your Table View is nicely sized inside your Flipside View,
    with it still selected go to the Attributes Inspector and select
    Dynamic Prototypes as the Type of Content structure in the
    Content drop-down menu. You do this because not only do you
    want a heading in your table, but you also want subtitles.
    Dynamic Prototypes let you adjust the cell style without
    providing cell content. Set the number of Prototype cells to 1
    (from 0). You also want to select the grouped style for your table
    so you can have a header for your group of scale entries in your
    table (refer to Figure 4-58), so in the Style drop-down menu,
    select Grouped. At this point your Table View should look like
    ours in Figure 4-22.

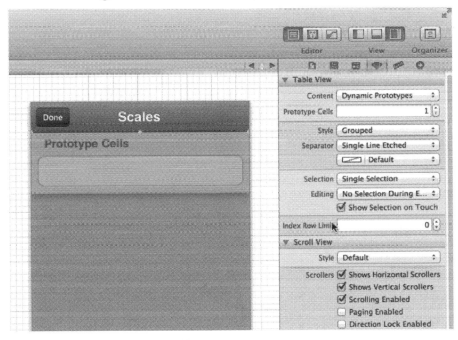

Figure 4-22. *Customizing the Table View.*

11. You'll want to have subtitles in each cell. To do that, click the cell itself to select it and in the Attributes Inspector select Subtitle from the drop-down menu in Style. Also change the default blue color to gray in the Selection drop-down menu. Finally you want to build these cells from code, so you need to name them so you can locate them within the Storyboard file and load them into your code whenever you need them. To do that, name the Identifier in the Attributes Inspector to ScaleCell as shown in Figure 4-23.

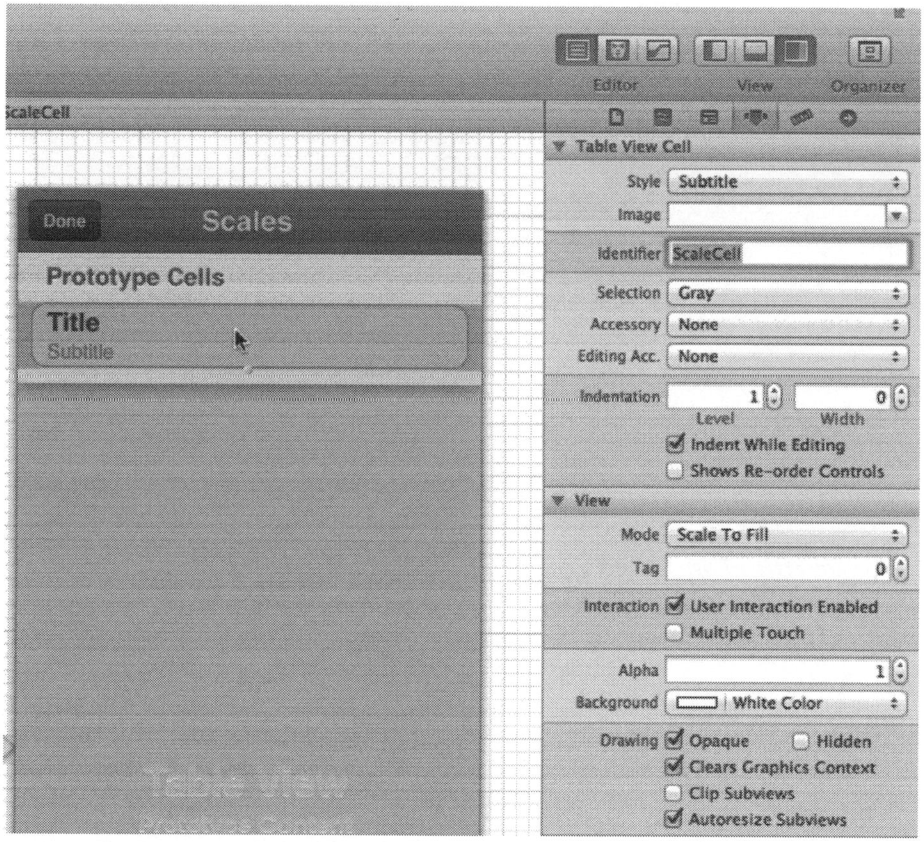

Figure 4-23. *Customizing the cells.*

Step 3: Coding the Flipside View Controller

Keeping it really simple, first you set up the header and implementation files. Then you add ImageView and NavTitle IBOutlets.

1. Start by working on the code that will present the scales to the user—which, as you've seen, are shown on the Flipside View. Do that by going to your desktop, opening your demoMonkey file, and placing it on the right hand side of your screen. You'll probably want to resize your Xcode window to allow you to see your open demoMonkey file on the right-hand side of your screen (Xcode on the left). Now in Xcode open your FlipsideViewController implementation file (.m) as shown in Figure 4-24 by clicking it in the Project Navigator pane on the left-hand of the Xcode window.

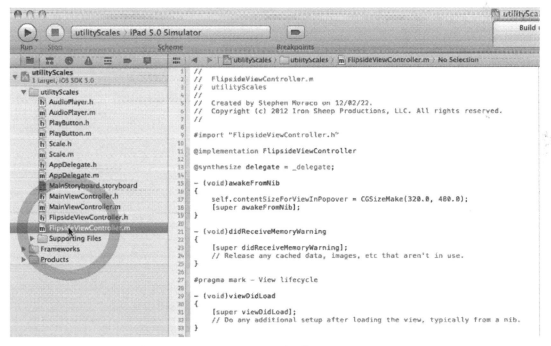

Figure 4-24. *Open the FlipsideViewController implementation file.*

2. You're going to want to code using dual screens of code and Storyboard. To do that, click the Assistant Editor as shown in Figure 4-25. This places your main file of interest on the left and a related file on the right of the editor area in the Xcode window. (For example, when an implementation file is selected, the implementation file is shown on the left and the header file associated with the implementation file is shown on the right.)

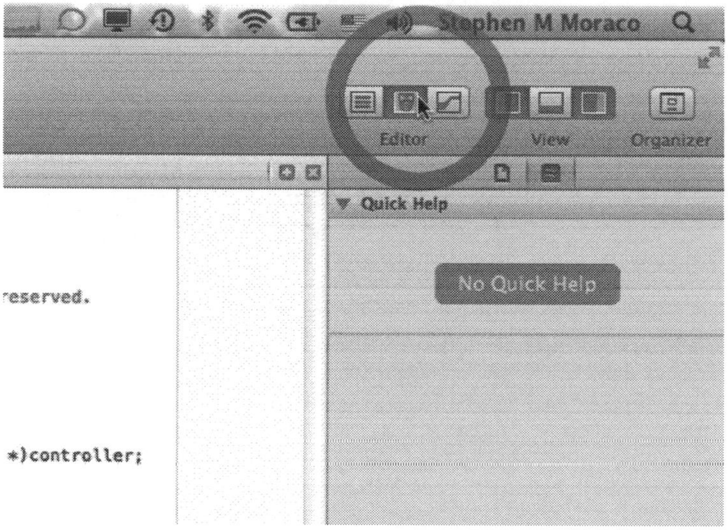

Figure 4-25. *Click the Assistant Editor.*

3. As mentioned, you're building your Flipside View Controller. You do that by dragging in from DemoMonkey the "01 FlipView.h – add include" snippet, which contains the include #import "Scale.h", as this includes the header for the Scale class we built for you. Next drag in the "02 FlipView.h – add protocol message signature" file that adds a little more to the protocol than what you already have, along with comments. Then bring in the "03 FlipView.h – add protocol adheres to," which indicates that the Flipside View adheres to Table View datasource and delegate protocols. Finally drag in "04 FlipView.h – add scaleType property," which remembers/indicates which scale the user selected from the Table View. Now do the drags as shown in the following code and then review Figure 4-26 to ensure that you ended up with the file content looking like the code in the figure.

```objc
#import <UIKit/UIKit.h>
#import "Scale.h"                          01 FlipView.h - add include

@class FlipsideViewController;

@protocol FlipsideViewControllerDelegate
                         02 FlipView.h - add protocol message signature
// report the selection from this view
- (void)flipsideViewController:(FlipsideViewController *)controller
selectedScale:(Scale *)scale;

// report that the user is done with this view
- (void)flipsideViewControllerDidFinish:(FlipsideViewController *)controller;
@end

          03 FlipView.h - add protocols adheres to

@interface FlipsideViewController : UIViewController <UITableViewDataSource,
UITableViewDelegate>    {

}
@property (weak, nonatomic) IBOutlet id <FlipsideViewControllerDelegate>
delegate;
@property (readwrite, atomic) enum eScaleType selectedScaleType;

                         04 FlipView.h - add scaleType property
- (IBAction)done:(id)sender;

@end
```

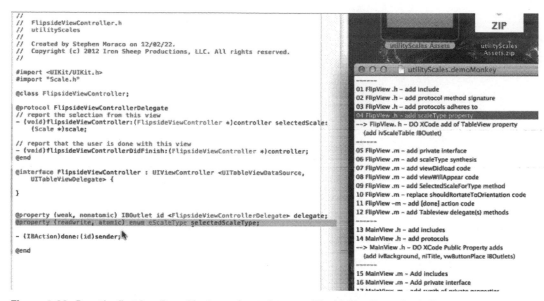

Figure 4-26. *Drag the first four DemoMonkey snippets into your FlipsideViewController.h file.*

4. You're now going to go back to your Storyboard file and hook
    up the Table View. So while still in the dual-screen Assistant
    mode, open up Storyboard as shown in Figure 4-27.

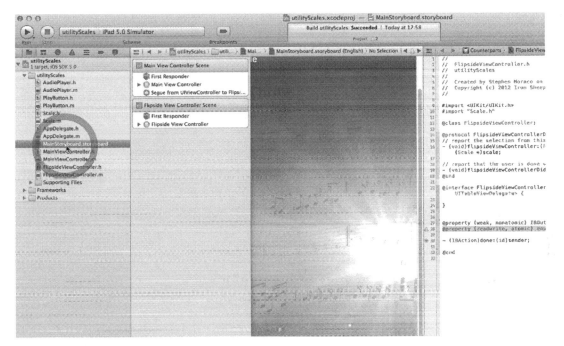

Figure 4-27. *Reopen Storyboard.*

5. You want to add an IBOutlet connecting the TableView to the
    FlipsideViewController. As shown on the left-hand side of
    Figure 4-28, start by locating the Flipside View Controller Scene
    in the document outline. Next open the
    FlipsideViewController, and then the view, and finally when
    you get to the Table View, click to select it and then Control-
    drag from it over to the FlipsideViewController.h file just
    under the second @property as shown in Figure 4.28. Once
    you're there, release it.

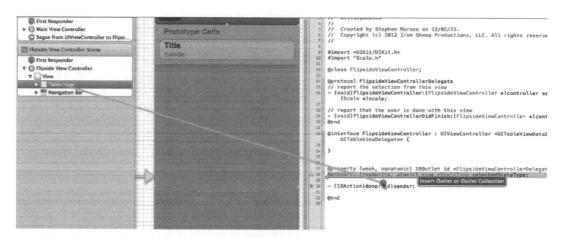

Figure 4-28. *Connect the Table View to the FlipsideViewController.*

6. We'll name it Table View (tv) Scale Table (tvScaleTable). Once
    you've named it, click the Connect button as shown in Figure
    4-29. By using the Control-drag technique, as you already
    know, Xcode has now created the property declaration for you,
    along with the property synthesis and the clearing of the
    property at object deallocation, the last two of which were
    modifications it made in the class implementation file.

```
 5   //  Created by Stephen Moraco on 12/02/22.
 6   //  Copyright (c) 2012 Iron Sheep Productions, LLC. All rights rese
 7   //
 8
 9   #import <UIKit/UIKit.h>
10   #import "Scale.h"
11
12   @class FlipsideViewController;
13
14   @protocol FlipsideViewControllerDelegate
15   // report the selection from this view
16   - (void)flipsideViewController:(FlipsideViewController *)controller
        (Scale *)scale;
17
18   // report that the user is done with this view
19   - (void)flipsideViewControllerDidFinish:(FlipsideViewController *)c
20   @end
21
22   @interface FlipsideViewController : UIViewController <UITableViewDa
        UITableViewDelegate> {

     }

     @property (weak, nonatomic) IBOutlet id <FlipsideViewControllerDele

     @property (weak, nonatomic) IBOutlet UITableView *tvScaleTable;

     - (IBAction)done:(id)sender;

     @end
```

Connection: Outlet
Object: Flipside View Contr...
Name: tvScaleTable
Type: UITableView
Storage: Weak
Cancel   Connect

Figure 4-29. *Name the IBOulet tvScaleTable.*

7. It's a good habit to make sure that when you Control-drag into code, you always check that the connection was correctly made. This is easy to see if you look for it. Looking at Figure 4-30, you see two dots, one showing that the @property has a connection with a Storyboard object and the second indicating that the IBAction has a connection. Now, if you move your mouse pointer over the dot next to the new @property, you'll see the Table View highlight in the Storyboard View, indicating that the connection has been established. Nice, right? Now go hover over the IBAction dot to see what's connected to the action! (Hint: it should be the Done button.) You've completed adding code to the FlipsideViewController.h (header file). Now move on to its implementation file.

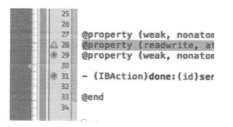

Figure 4-30. *Make sure the IBOutlet connected.*

8. The open implementation file should look as shown in
    Figure 4-31.

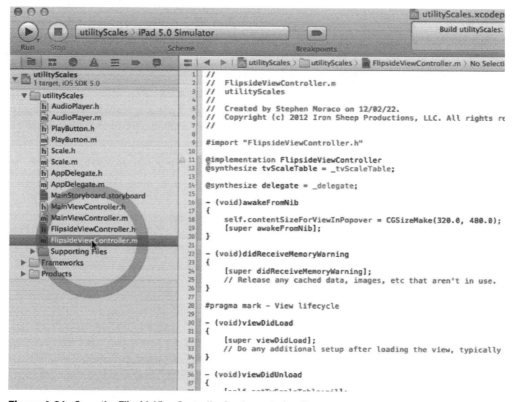

Figure 4-31. *Open the FlipsideViewController implementation file.*

9. The `FlipsideViewController` has a method and an instance variable that do not need to be referenced publicly (that is, from outside the class itself.) Therefore, we choose to declare them as private at the top of this implementation file. We have a mutable array of musical scales and we're going to have a property in which we record the scale that's been selected by the user. Drag the "05 FlipView.m – add private interface" snippet from DemoMonkey into your implementation immediately to the right of the `@interface FlipsideViewController ()` line of code. You should end up with the code looking like Figure 4-32.

Figure 4-32. *Create the private interface.*

> **NOTE:** Private instance variables, methods, and properties are declared most often by placing them in the unnamed category at the top of the implementation file. You'll notice that the latest templates generated by Xcode already have this private interface declared for you at the top of generated implementation files. This serves to remind you where to put these items as you're adding code to these generated files.

You now want to synthesize the scale type that you created, so drag in "06 FlipView.m – add scaleType synthesis" from DemoMonkey and place it under the @synthesize tvScaleTable = _tvScaleTable; line as shown in the following code:

```
@implementation FlipsideViewController

@synthesize delegate = _delegate;
@synthesize tvScaleTable = _tvScaleTable;
@synthesize selectedScaleType;
```
                                              06FlipView.m – add scaleType synthesis

10. Now that you've synthesized the set/get methods for the scale type property, you want to load the scales into memory the first time you load the app. Drag in "07 FlipView.m – add viewDidload code" and place it directly under [super viewDidLoad]; inside your viewDidLoad. Here you can see that we have created eight Scale objects and added them to our array, as shown in Figure 4-33.

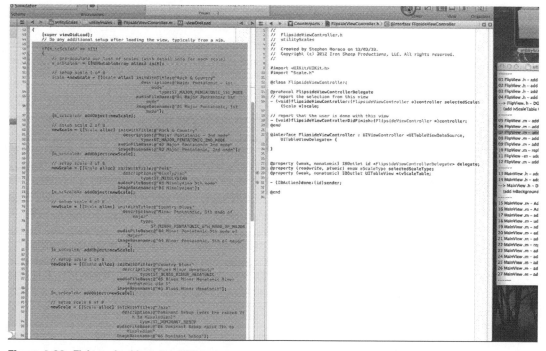

Figure 4-33. *Eight scale objects to add to our array.*

11. When the view first appears, you have a responsibility to show
    what scale was viewed the last time. Or, if no scale has been
    selected yet—as in the first time that the app is used—you'll
    show the first scale. To do this, drag in the code in "08
    FlipView.m – add viewWillAppear code" and place it directly
    after the close of the viewDidLoad method as shown in
    Figure 4-34.

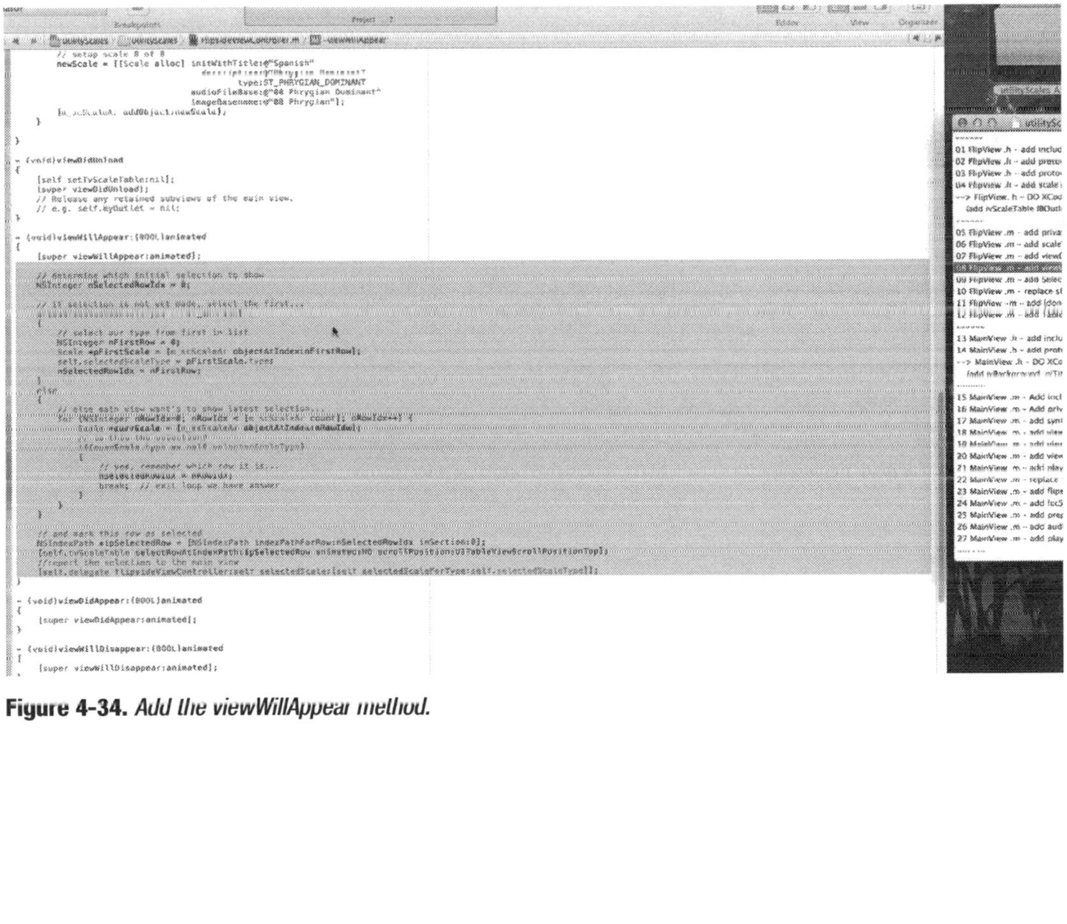

Figure 4-34. Add the viewWillAppear method.

12. In this step you'll drag in four snippets of code from DemoMonkey. First set a method that will set up the scale for type by dragging in the "09 FlipView.m – add SelectedScaleforType method" just before the -(BOOL)shouldAutorotateToInterfaceOrientation line. Next replace the code inside the -(BOOL)shouldAutorotateToInterfaceOrientation:, which would normally determine the view of the rotation. In this case you'll only use Landscape (to show the guitar neck). Select the return YES; statement and delete it. Place new code inside the squiggly brackets by dragging in "10 FlipView.m – replace shouldRotateOrientation code," which invokes a macro that determines whether the passed-in rotation is one of the two accepted Landscape orientations and returns yes if it's one of the two. Now, *if the user has pressed the Done button*, you want to grab the musical scale and tell the Main View what was selected and then tell the Main View to tear down this View. So grab "11 FlipView.m – add [done] action code" and place it inside the - (IBAction)done:(id)sender squiggly brackets in front of the line that's already there. The last of our four snippets, shown in shown in Figure 4-35, comprises the code in "12 FlipView.m – add Tableview delegate(s) methods." Place it right before the @end of the code. This is the UITableView delegate code, which actually responds to the selection of a scale by the user. Here you will see we added the UITableViewDataSource protocol methods and the UITableViewDelegate protocol methods.

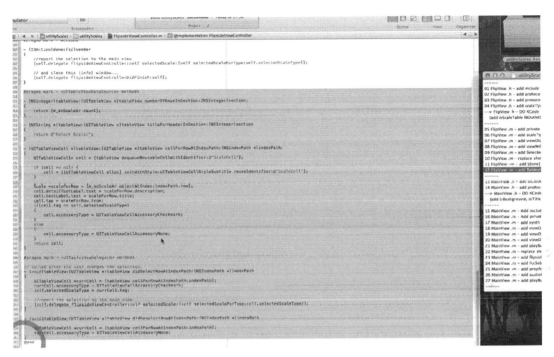

Figure 4-35. *Our implementation file after adding the fourth snippet.*

13. Now that you've taken care of the Flipside View, let's move on to the controller! Open up the `MainViewController`'s header file as shown in Figure 4-36. Also, let's move out of the Assistant editor for a little bit and work in the Standard editor. Click the button to the left of the Assistant editor (shown back in Figure 4-25) to return the editor portion of the Xcode window to a single editor pane.

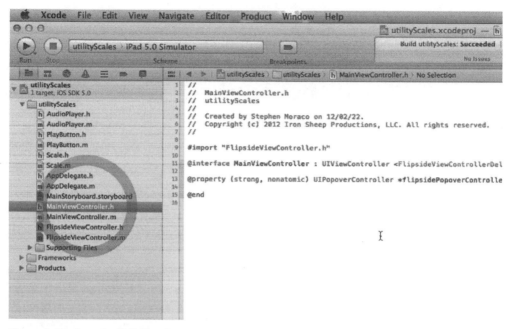

Figure 4-36. *Open the MainViewController.*

14. Start by adding two includes (#import "AudioPlayer.h" and
#import "PlayButton.h") located in the "13 MainView.h – add
includes." You do this because you need to get the information
from the audio and play button header files. Next, make sure
that this object supports the FlipsideViewControllerDelegate,
UIPopoverControllerDelegate, and AudioPlayer protocols. Do
that by dragging in "14 MainView.h – add protocols" as shown
in Figure 4-37.

Figure 4-37. *Start customizing the mainView interface file.*

15. Now you need to add some properties for some objects in the Main View, which means you need to get back into the Storyboard file. Also, select the Assistant editor so you can see the interface code in one screen and the Storyboard in the other. Reopen your Storyboard file as shown in Figure 4-38.

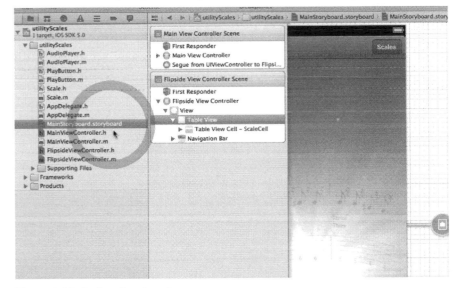

Figure 4-38. *Back to Storyboard.*

16. You're going to create IBOutlets again, but before you can Control-drag from the Storyboard objects into the MainViewController.h, you need to make sure that the second screen is indeed displaying the MainViewController.h file. In the document outline, click the MainViewController in the MainViewController scene. If the right side is still configured correctly, it will now be showing MainViewController.h. If it's not showing your .h file, you need to reselect automatic as shown in Figure 4-39. If automatic is selected, then the interface file will be shown for the currently selected scene.

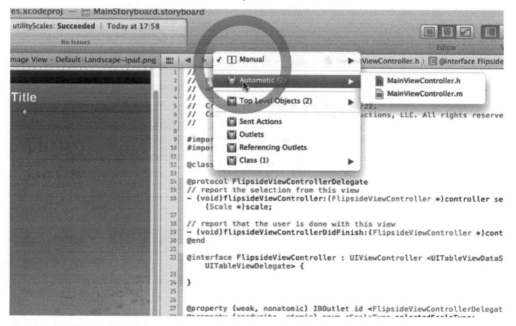

Figure 4-39. *Make sure your second screen is displaying the MainViewController.h file.*

17. Control-drag from the Image View in the document outline to the MainViewController.h file, just under the @property as shown in Figure 4-40.

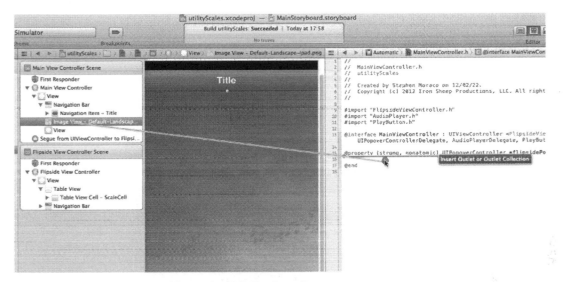

Figure 4-40. *Connect the Image View to the MainViewController.*

18. This is an Image View (iv) which you want to be showing your background image, so name it ivBackground as shown in Figure 4-41. After entering the name, click Connect.

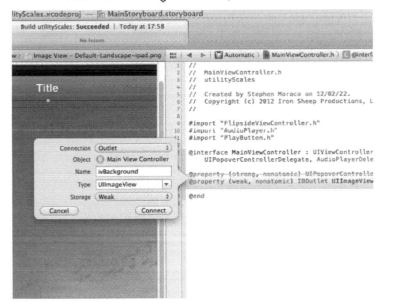

Figure 4-41. *Name the property ivBackground.*

19. Now let's hook up the "Play Button Area" View. Select it in the document outline and Control-drag from it to under the @property you added in the previous step. This is illustrated in Figure 4-42.

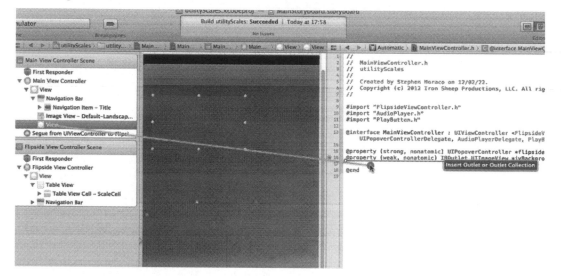

Figure 4-42. *Now you hook up the button.*

20. This is just a View (vw) and is the button's place, so name it vwButtonPlace. Once entered, click Connect as shown in Figure 4-43.

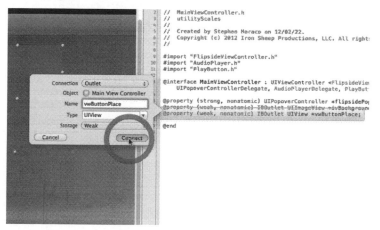

Figure 4-43. *Name the property vwButtonPlace.*

21. Because you want to set the title from code, you'll also need to hook up the Navigation Bar Title to the `MainViewController`. So Control-drag from the Navigation Item - Title to below the previous @properties as shown in Figure 4-44.

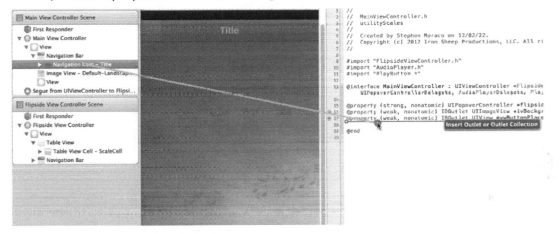

Figure 4-44. *Hook up the Navigation Bar Title.*

22. This is a navigation item (ni) and it's the title, so name it `niTitle` as shown in Figure 4-45.

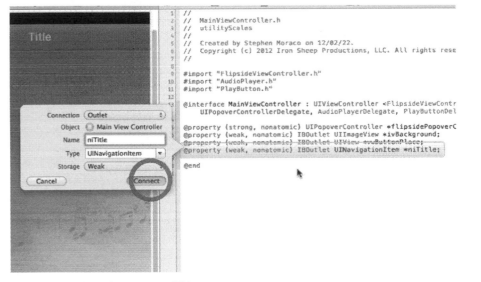

Figure 4-45. *Name the property niTitle.*

23. While you're here, you need to set the datasource and delegate for the table to the `FlipsideViewController`. We forgot about this in the video, and the book follows directly along with the code generated by the video. Right-click the `Table View` cells and connect the datasource to the `FlipsideViewController` as shown in Figure 4-46.

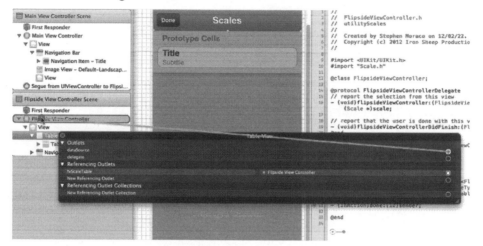

Figure 4-46. *Start setting the datasets and delegates for the flipside.*

24. Connect the delegate as shown in Figure 4-47.

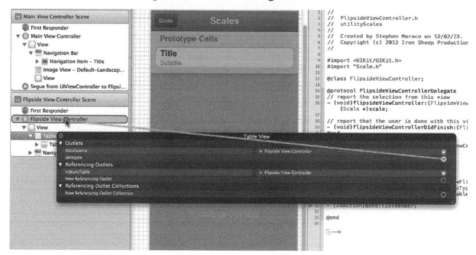

Figure 4-47. *Now connect the delegate.*

25. Open up the `MainViewController`'s implementation file as
    shown in Figure 4-48.

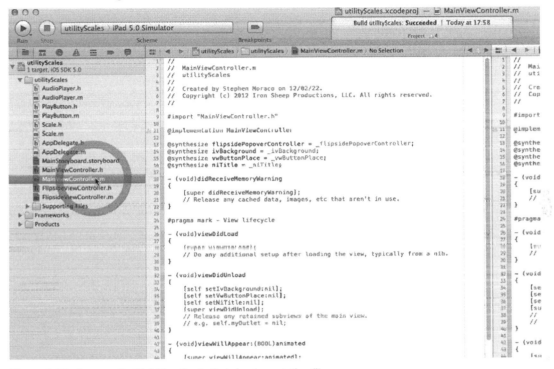

Figure 4-48. *Open up the MainViewController's implementation file.*

26. Leaving the Assistant editor mode and going back to the
    Standard Editor mode (one screen), drag in two DemoMonkey
    snippets. First add in the includes: `#import "Scale.h"` and
    `#import "PlayButton.h"` with "15 MainView.m – add includes."
    The `MainView` also has a private interface, so also drag in "16
    MainView.m – add private interface." In this case you have
    instance variables for the selected scale, the audio player, and a
    reference to the last play button pressed. You also have two
    private properties that contain references to your two play
    buttons, and last, you have some methods that are invoked
    when the electric guitar or acoustic guitar play buttons are
    pressed. This is illustrated in Figure 4-49.

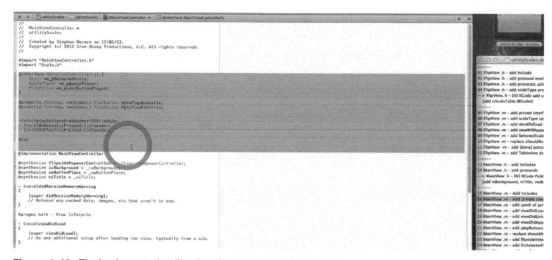

Figure 4-49. *The implementation file after the next two code additions.*

27. You now need to synthesize the private properties, so drag in "17 MainView.m – add synth of private buttons" as shown in Figure 4-50.

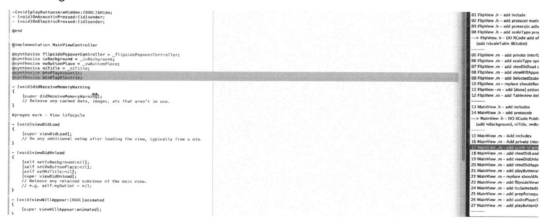

Figure 4-50. *More synthesis is necessary for acoustic and electric guitar play buttons.*

28. Remember that when the view loads the first time you want to continue setting up the application, so within the `viewDidLoad` method you set up details of the audio player and keep track of the last button that was played. Also round the corners of the buttons themselves, as well as the corners of the button place View you've just had. You also need to hide the buttons when you start. Drag in "18 MainView.m – add viewDidLoad code" and place it under the comment of the super `viewDidLoad` (`// Do any additional setup after loading the view, typically from a nib`) as shown in Figure 4-51.

Figure 4-51. *Customize the viewDidLoad method.*

29. In `viewDidUnload`, you need to remove your two private buttons from the view and remove references to them. Here you'll need to drag in "19 MainView.m – add viewDidUnload code" and place it in the `viewDidUnload` method as shown in Figure 4-52.

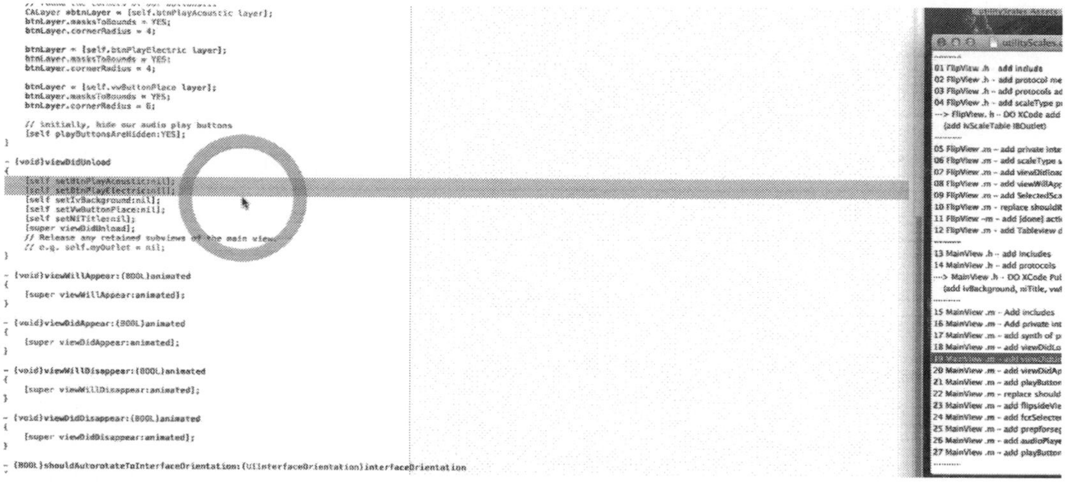

Figure 4-52. *Customize the viewDidUnload method.*

30. When the view first appears, you're going to set up the title so that the user is told to go ahead and select a scale for the first time. Drag in "20 add viewWillAppear code," placing it immediately after the `viewDidUnload` method you just modified. Drag in "21 MainView.m – add playButtonsAreHidden method" and place it right after the closing parenthesis of - `(void)viewWillAppear` as shown in Figure 4-53. You'll do the same thing with orientation left and right. Drag in "22 MainView.m – replace shouldAutoRotate code" and after deleting the existing autorotate code (`return YES;`), place this in its place. You also want to hide the buttons when you start so that the user will be prompted to first choose a scale. Drag in the "23 MainView.m – add flipsideViewControllerDidFinish" code as the new first line of that method.

Figure 4-53. *After the second of your four code additions.*

31. You also want to set a method that will identify the scale that was selected by the View Controller. Drag in "24 MainView.m – add fccSelctedScalemethod" and place this after flipsideViewControllerDidFinish as shown in Figure 4-54. And you need to tell the view what scale is selected so that it will show itself. Drag in "25 MainView.m – add prepforsegue code."

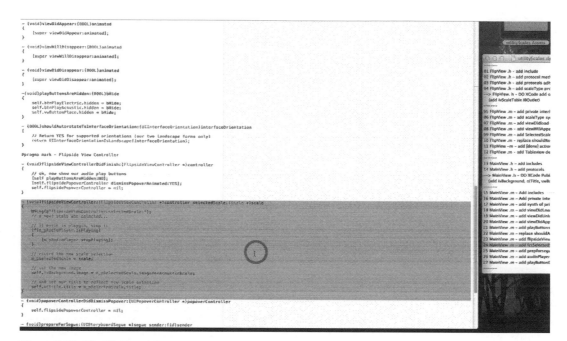

Figure 4-54. *Identify the scale.*

32. You need to add an audio player delegate. Drag "26 MainView.m – add audioPlayerDelegate methods" and place it right before the @end as shown in Figure 4-55.

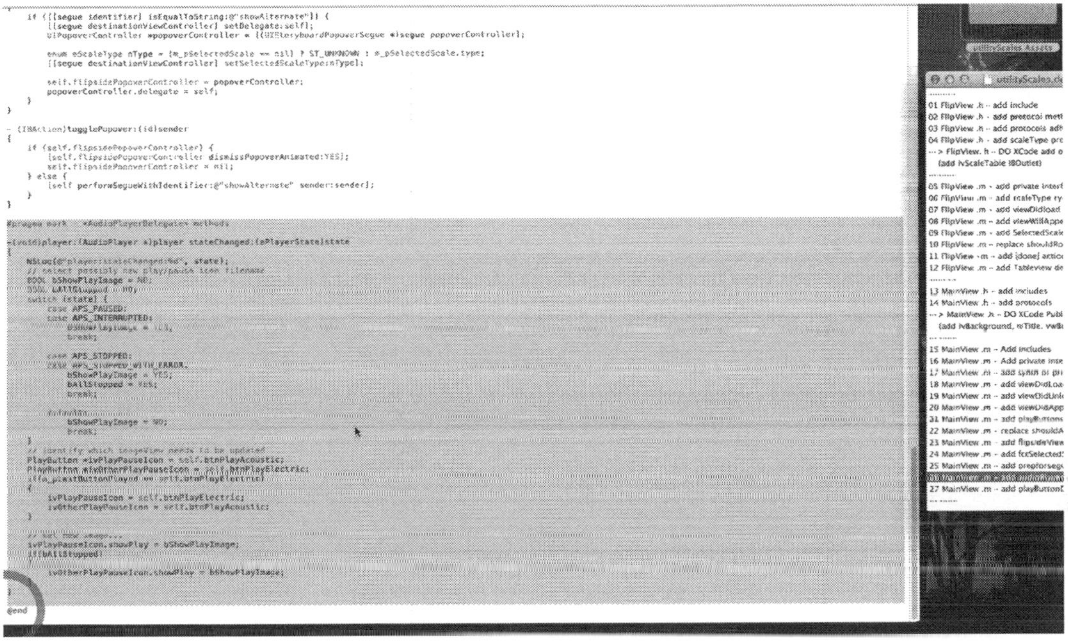

Figure 4-55. *Add the audio player delegate method.*

33. Finally you need to add the methods in support of the play
button delegate protocol. Drag in "27 MainView.m – add
playButtonDelegate methods" and place it right before the @end
as shown in Figure 4-56. And that is it! Click Run and see your
beautiful app run.

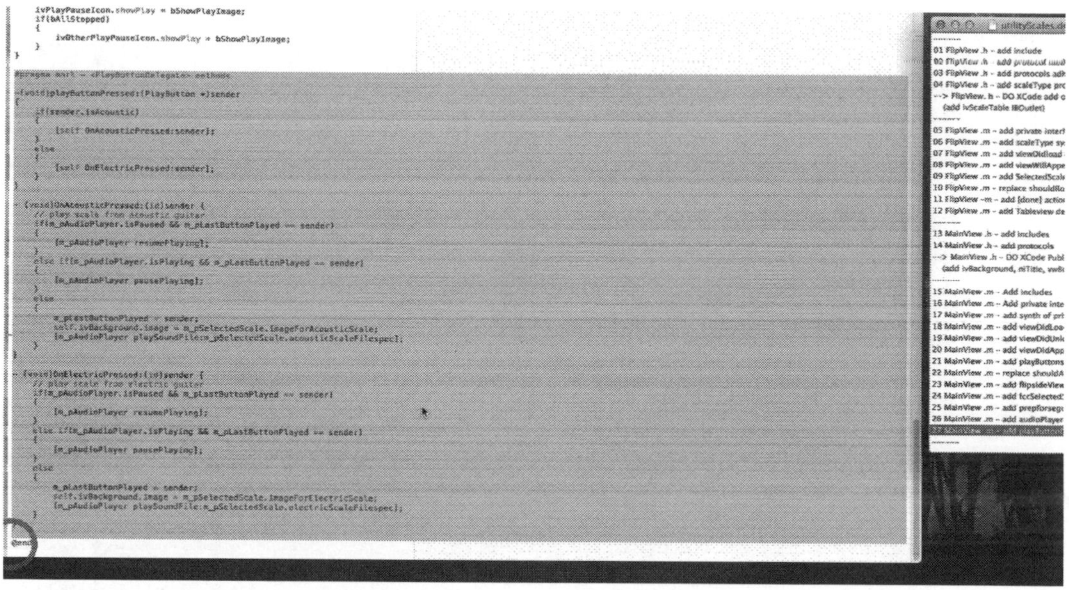

Figure 4-56. *Add the PlayButtonDelegate methods.*

34. It starts up and asks you to select a scale; when you select a
scale, the first image appears. In this case, we first selected
Major Pentatonic and then, as shown in Figure 4-57, we're
about to choose a new scale. When the new scale is selected,
the image changes dynamically. Figure 4-58 illustrates how the
button appears when you say Done. Figure 4-59 shows how
you can switch between looking at the scales on an acoustic
guitar and an electric guitar.

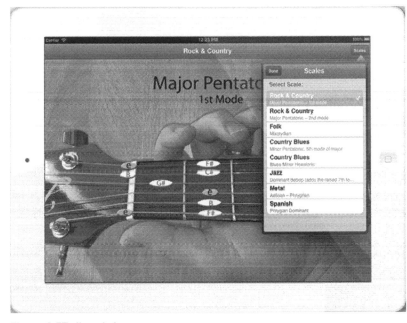

Figure 4-57. *It works!*

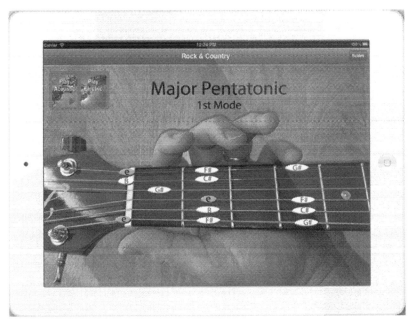

Figure 4-58. *Now when we say Done … the button appears.*

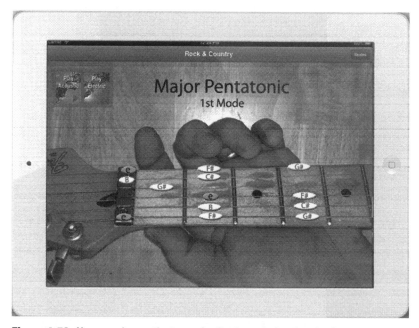

Figure 4-59. *You can change the type of guitar by pressing the play buttons.*

5

Storyboarding a Page-Based App

Our fourth Storyboarding app is a pretty zany endeavor to say the least. You'll be building a Page-Based Application that will house a dynamic, electronic brochure that actually consists of 4 mini-brochures. The fun thing is that your "client" is a time travel agency that has the ability to travel forward and backwards in time! We're calling this the futureTravel application, and you will learn many cool tools and methods as you use it to move forward in your Storyboarding skills.

Note that apps 1 through 3 were based on standard Storyboarding skills with an emphasis on the code. Apps 4 through 7 will focus on advanced Storyboarding features and methods that build on the theoretical code covered in earlier sections.

FutureTravel encapsulates four brochures in one. This means that as the user lands on the second page of four, the user may choose one of the four possible destinations. After this choice is made, the remaining two pages are then automatically customized to the user's choice of destination. If the user decides that she wants to explore the other three destinations, futureTravel allows her to simply page back and select a different destination and then page forward again with new dynamic pages associated with the new choice of destination.

Using the Page-Based Application template is all about replacing the built-in data model with your own. The page navigation simply lets you view the pages generated from this underlying model. You'll use the iPad layout as it gives you more room for text on the pages of your travel flyer. You'll replace the built-in model with your own set of pages, with an image for the page and the page number. You'll encapsulate this page data in its own class (object with own .h/.m files). And you'll build the array of pages data at runtime in the ModelController startup methods. In the Storyboard file you adjust the UI to your liking.

futureTravel: A Page-Based App

We divide this project into five steps. First you create the project from a template and then you prep the Storyboard. Steps 3 through 5 consist of coding the `ModelController`, `DataViewController`, and `RootViewController`. This project will become quite hierarchical in nature, so you may want to note the general outline of our coding strategy:

1. *Create from Template.* First we start a new Page-Based Application called futureTravel, with com.apress, iPad, and using ARC. Then we adjust project settings by deselecting portrait and upside-down capabilities. Next we drag in assets such as the `Default-Lanscape*~ipad.png` and the `ModelPageData` class files (`.h` & `.m`) to the futureTravel group. To test that it's all working, we build the project.

2. *Prep Storyboard.* Two parts to think about here: the Root View and the Data View. For the Root View we color the view background: RGB(254,196,37), the color of Apress yellow. The Data view is a little more complex. Here we also color the view background: RGB(253,224,145), a lighter version of Apress yellow we used earlier, but we need to do more here. We remove subordinate view and add a `UIImageView` in its place, which will be the same as our load image (20,20 984x679). This will not have any user interaction. With this done, we adjust all four edges and autosize in both directions. We also adjust the placement and configuration of the label and place it correctly. Finally we change the text to right-aligned and its color to Dark Gray Color.

3. Code `ModelController`.

4. Code `DataViewController`.

5. Code `RootViewController`.

Preliminaries

We created the assets for the program, which consist of a launch image and the first two images (travel introduction and destination selection), and then we created two images for each of the four destinations. We generated @2x versions of all these files, which will automatically be used if we run this application on the new iPad (Retina display version). We also created a special image, used to mark the client's destination selection. This leaves us with a total of 23 images generated for this project. You can download the images, assets, extras, and DemoMonkey files here: `http://www.rorylewis.com/xCode/ StoryBoarding%20in%20Xcode/Chapter05_futureTravel%20Assets.zip`. You can download the source code we programmed while filming the video here: `http://www.rorylewis.com/xCode/StoryBoarding%20in%20Xcode/Chapter05_futu reTravel.zip`. As always, we suggest that you clean up your desktop, download all the images, and open up your DemoMonkey tile before you begin.

Step 1: Create from Template

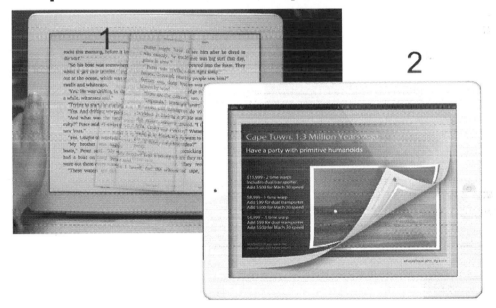

Figure 5-1. *iBooks and our app, the Page-Based Application.*

1. Before proceeding too far let's make sure you understand when you'd want to use a Page-Based Application. After Apple released the iBook app in the App Store, there was an immediate demand to code the cool page-curling effect. In response, Apple introduced a new template called Page-Based Application in Xcode 4. The Page-Based Application uses a single View Controller that dynamically replaces content based on each page the user navigates to. It's somewhat strange for

Apple to provide the one and only instance where Xcode provides a template that is so far beyond the stripped-down, basic foundation it usually provides. With the Page-Based Application, Apple actually provides a sample application. However, we will go over some cool tricks and hidden traps very carefully in this chapter.

> **NOTE:** You will want to use the Page-Based Application template when you want to create a project containing an application designed to display a page for each new view.

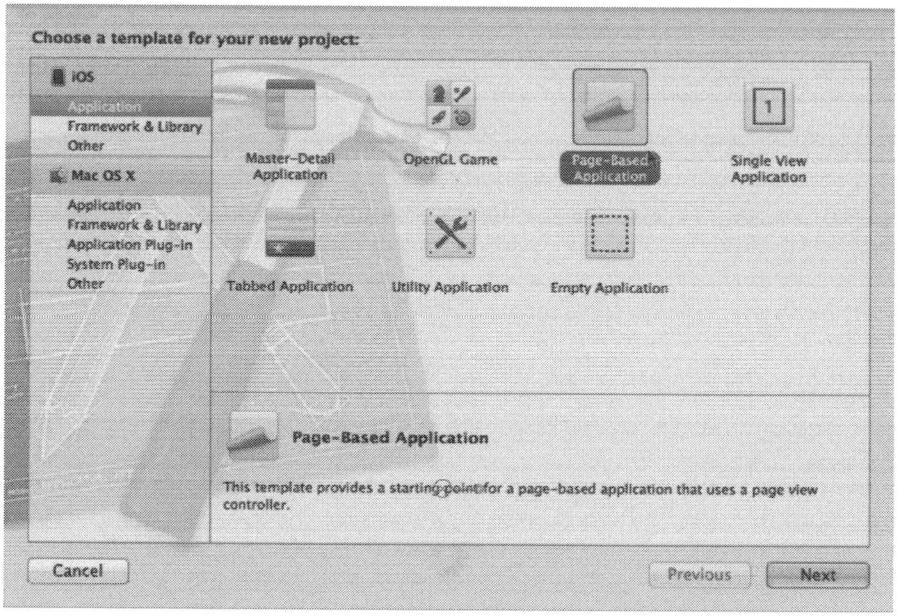

Figure 5-2. *Start a new Page-Based Application project in Xcode.*

2. Open Xcode, press ⌘+⇧+N, select a Page-Based Application, and click Next as shown in Figure 5-2.

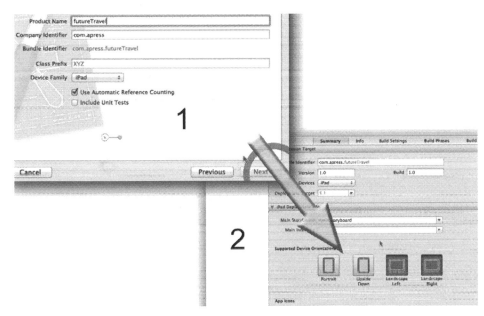

Figure 5-3. *Name the app futureTravel and then deselect Portrait and Upside Down.*

3. Enter com.apress as the Company Identifier. We won't use a
    class prefix. Make sure to select iPad and check Use
    Automated Reference Counting. Do not check Include Unit
    Tests (Figure 5-2). Once created, save it onto your desktop. You
    will see the new futureTravel project open up. As mentioned,
    we're making this app for the iPad only—we'll also make it
    Landscape only for the text images that we will be using. They
    have text orientated in Landscape orientation, so uncheck
    Portrait and Upside Down as shown in Figure 5-3. Interesting to
    see what is missing here … can you see it? Notice there's no
    option of not using the Storyboard with this Page-Based App.

> **NOTE:** When using the Page-Based model template, you have one goal: to go in and
> replace the model for the page content with your own model for the page content.
> You will now start this by adding your own data object and reworking the existing
> object to use the new data object.

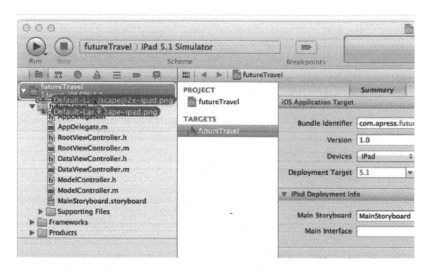

Figure 5-4. *Drag the startup images into your root directory.*

1. Open up your futureTravel Assets folder you downloaded from
   http://www.rorylewis.com/xCode/StoryBoarding%20in%20Xcode
   /Chapter05_futureTravel%20Assets.zip and unzip it onto your
   desktop. Select both of the startup images `Default-`
   `Landscape@2x~ipad.png` and `Default-Landscape~ipad.png` and
   drag them over to the root directory. Notice that you also have
   images for the new iPad (the Retina iPad), if you choose to
   compile this app directly onto the Retina iPad, as shown in
   Figure 5-4.

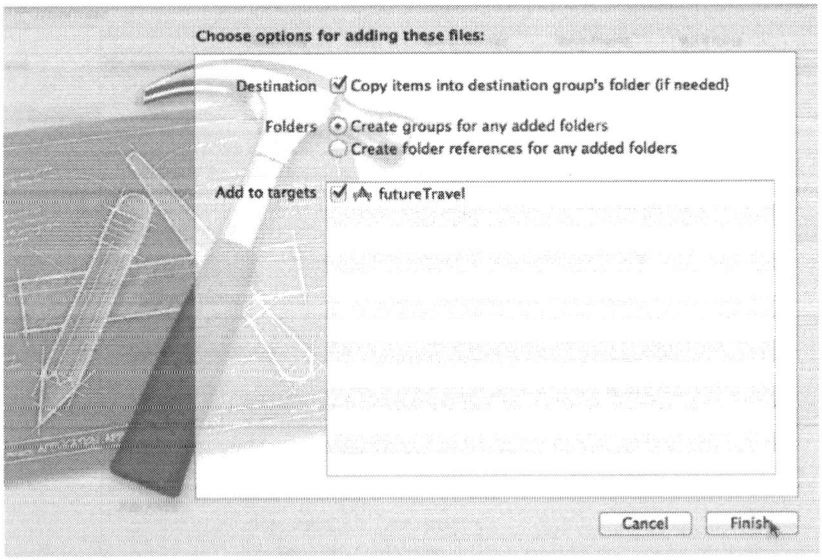

Figure 5-5. *Make sure you copy the startup images into your project.*

2. When the "Choose options for adding these files" dialog pops up, check "Copy items into destination group's folder." Also check "Create groups for any added folders." Make sure your target is futureTravel and that it is checked (Figure 5-5).

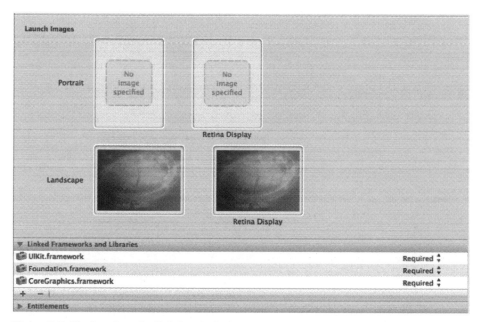

Figure 5-6. *Xcode automatically brings in the images.*

3. Notice that Xcode detects that these images are for the
    Landscape and the Retina display and automatically drops them
    into the appropriate Launch Image boxes as shown in
    Figure 5-6.

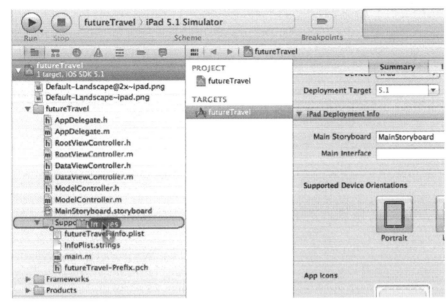

Figure 5-7. *Drag the Images folder into the Supporting Files folder.*

4. Now select the entire Images folder and drag it into the
    Supporting Files folder as shown in Figure 5-7.

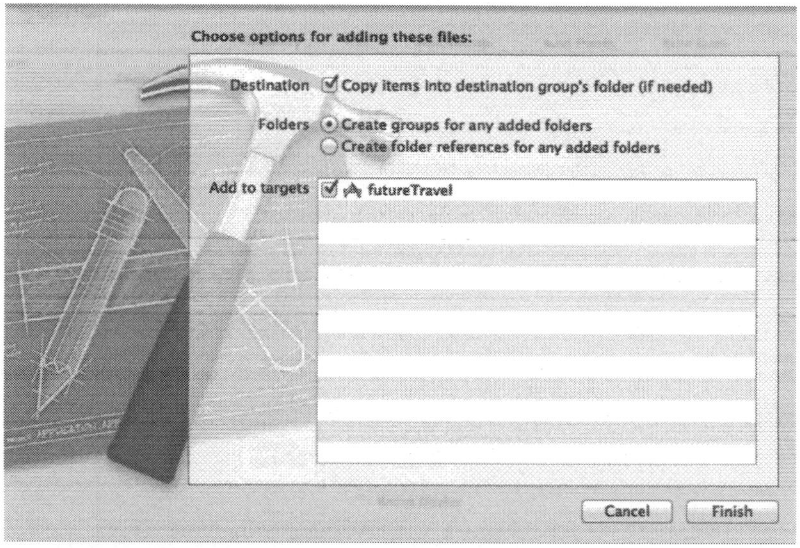

Figure 5-8. *Copy the startup images folder into your project.*

5. As in step 5, when the "Choose options for adding these files" dialog pops up, check "Copy items into destination group's folder" and "Create groups for any added folders." Make sure your target is futureTravel and that it is checked as shown in Figure 5-8.

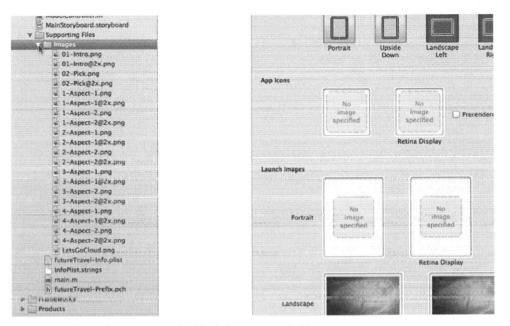

Figure 5-9. *Notice the new group that Xcode has now created for you.*

6. Xcode instantiates a brand new group inside the Supporting
   Files folder as shown in Figure 5-9.

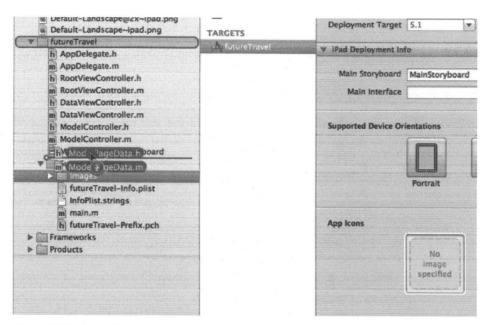

Figure 5-10. *Drag in the Data class.*

7.   Because we're focusing on the Storyboard aspect, we decided
     to create the data model code for you. We describe this code in
     detail later in the chapter, but for now just select both the
     ModelPageData.h and the ModelPageData.m files and drag them
     into your project as shown in Figure 5-10. If you have one of the
     older versions of Xcode, you may have to instruct Xcode to
     build these new files. (By the time this book comes out, this may
     be fixed.) Step 12 shows you how to tell XCode to build these
     new files.

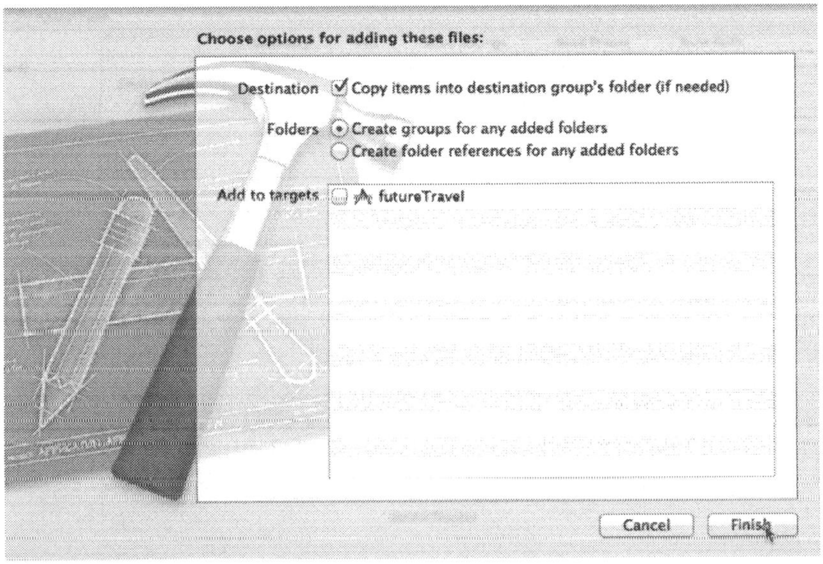

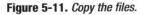

Figure 5-11. *Copy the files.*

    8.   Again check all the proper boxes as shown in Figure 5-11.

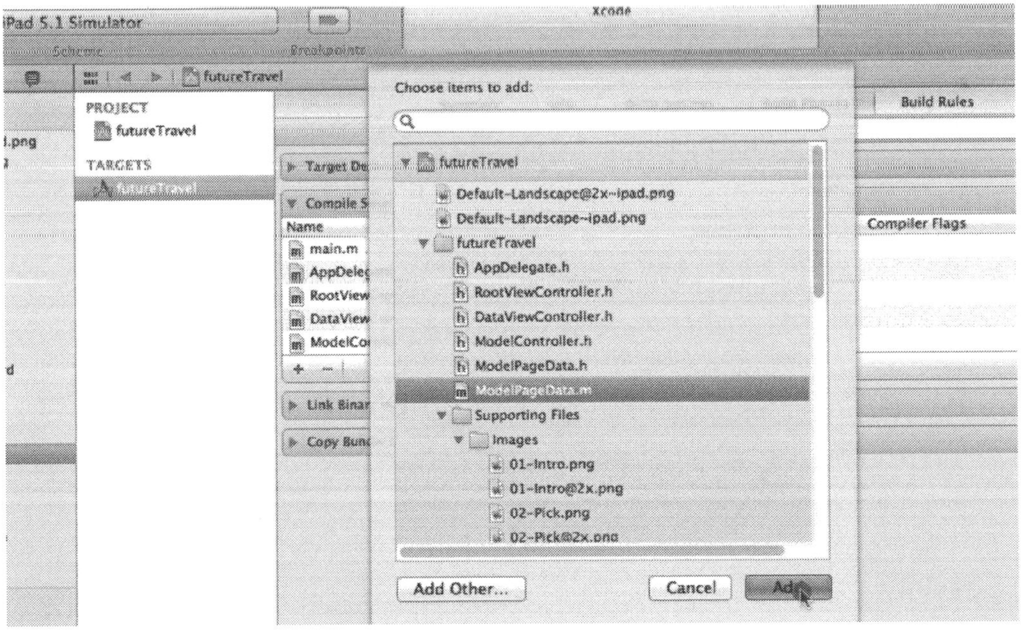

Figure 5-12. *Manually add the new file to be built, if not already there.*

9. Click `futureTravel` at the root of the Navigation tree. In Target settings on the left, pick the Build Phases tab at the top. Now expand the Compile Sources section. If you don't see the `ModelPageData.m` file in this list, click the + (plus) button, select the `ModelPageData.m` implementation file, and click Add as shown in Figure 5-12. This will add `ModelPageData.m` to the project. In case the desired files aren't shown in the "Choose items to add" list, click the Add Other button and find the files you want to add in your directory structure.

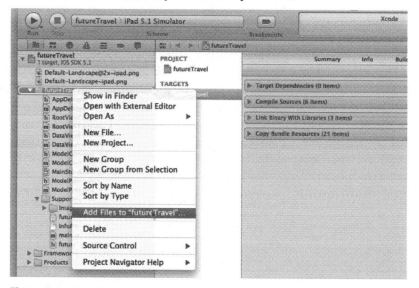

Figure 5-13. *Another way to do this...*

10. This is not the only way to do this if, by the time you read this, Apple has not fixed it. If you go to your `futureTravel` folder, right-click it, and select Add Files to futureTravel, as shown in Figure 5-13, and then go out to your folder on your desktop and select the files, it automatically adds the sources to the compile list. This way you have two different ways to get around this minor bug with the new Xcode working in Lion.

Step 2: Prep Storyboard

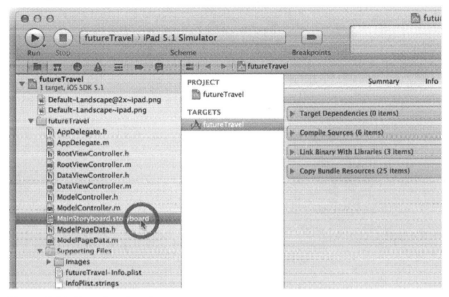

Figure 5-14. *Open Storyboard.*

1. We're going to work on the real thing now: the Storyboard.
    Let's open your Storyboard! Go to the Project Navigator and
    click your Storyboard file as shown in Figure 5-14.

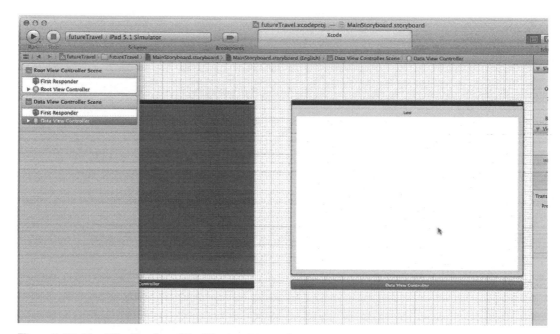

Figure 5-15. *Wow! The Storyboard itself is already set up!*

2.   When you open the Storyboard, you will probably be amazed
how the Page-Based Application template has instantiated a
fully working paging app! You see two scenes, the Root View
Controller and the Data View Controller, as shown in Figure
5-15. Remember that the Root View Controller is the frame that
shows the pages. The Data View Controller shows you an
instance of a page. It's sometimes difficult for students to get it
that all the pages will be procured through each instance of the
Data View Controller. You don't get to add a whole lot of other
UI elements into this, but you can tweak it.

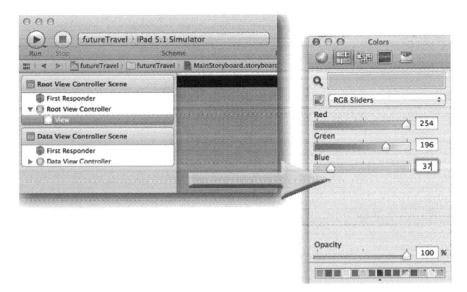

Figure 5 16. *Change the color of the Root View Controller to Apress Yellow*

3. You're going to change the background color of the Root View
   Controller from the default brown color to the Apress yellow.
   Start by clicking the Root View Controller. You can see that in
   the View being highlighted on the left side of Figure 5-16. The
   Apress colors are Red@254, Green@196 and Blue@37. Change
   the three primary colors in the Colors dialog as shown in the
   right image in Figure 5-16.

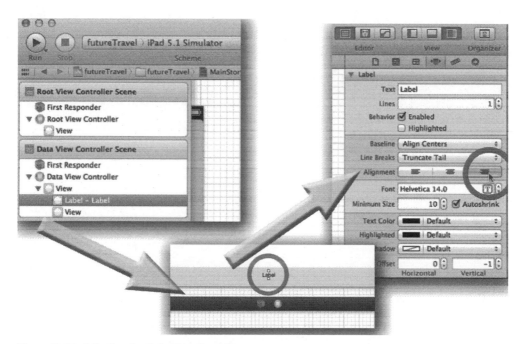

Figure 5-17. *Adjusting the Data View Controller.*

4. We do like the frame Apple gave us here, but we will arrange some of the other default attributes as follows. We want to keep the label but we want it to be at the bottom. Simply grab it and move it down to the bottom by selecting it in the Document Outline as shown on the left side in Figure 5-17. Or simply click the actual label itself and drag it down. Use the guideline to center it as needed. Open the Attributes Inspector tab and make the text align to the right as shown on the right side in Figure 5-17. Lastly, change the Text Color property to Dark Grey Color as shown in Figure 5-18. Also move the internal content View up a little, so it doesn't intersect with the Label—you can either drag it up using the mouse or select it, going to the Size Inspector pane on the right and changing the Frame Rectangle's Y attribute to 20.

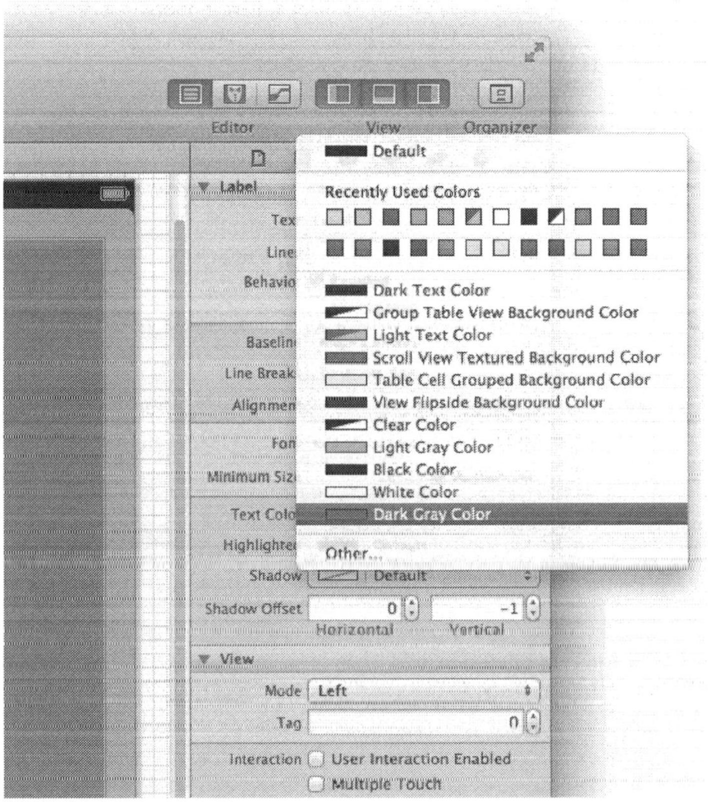

Figure 5-18. *Set the font color.*

5. You need to house images in the scene, so drag an Image View
    from the Library and place it inside the current View in the
    center of the scene.

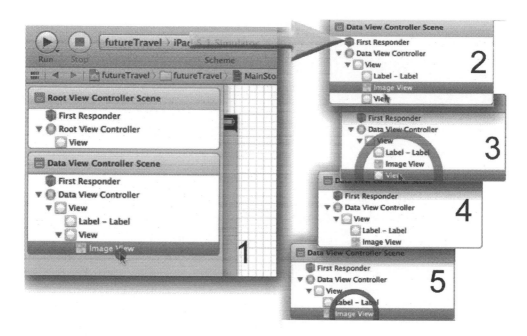

Figure 5-19. *Replace and delete the old view.*

6. If you didn't care about the amount of objects you have, then you could leave the nesting of layers as they are—but there is a lesson here. What you want to do is develop good practices, so what we want you to do is replace the View with the Image View. Look at Figure 5-19: in 1 you select the Image View. In 2 you drag it above the View and below the Label - Label. In 3 you select the old View. In 4 you delete this old View you just selected. In 5 you select the Image View so you can bring it back to position on the Storyboard in the next step.

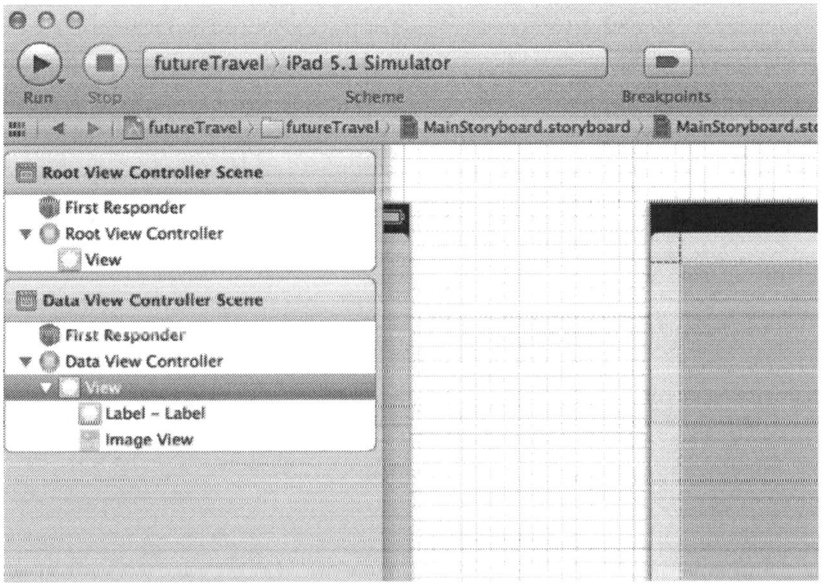

Figure 5-20. *Move the View to its correct position.*

7. Move the main View until you see the square dotted lines on both the left and right upper sides of the Data View Controller as shown in Figure 5-20.

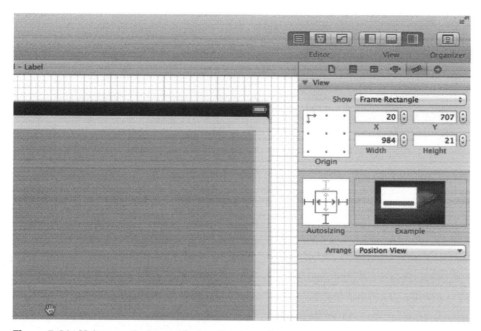

Figure 5-21. *Make sure the Image View scales correctly.*

8.   Click the Image View and then go to the View in Size Inspector and see that the red rectangle in the Example scales appropriately. It will look like it stretches with the window, and this is correct. But the label needs to be grounded, so click the label and in the Autosizing box select the bottom, left, and horizontal middle red anchors. Deselect the top one. Your label should be grounded as shown in Figure 5-21. This means that as the View that contains the label changes its size, the label maintains its proper position and size. The property you've just set visually by selecting appropriate anchor points is called autoResizingMask. Every UIView subclass has it. In fact, it's a very handy attribute, especially when you're developing an app that supports multiple device orientations.

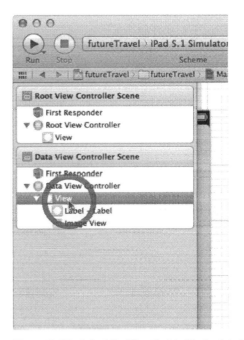

Figure 5-22. *Select the View that holds the label and Image View for a final edit.*

9. We have one more adjustment to make to the main View. Select
    the main View that holds the Label - Label and the Image View
    as shown in Figure 5-22.

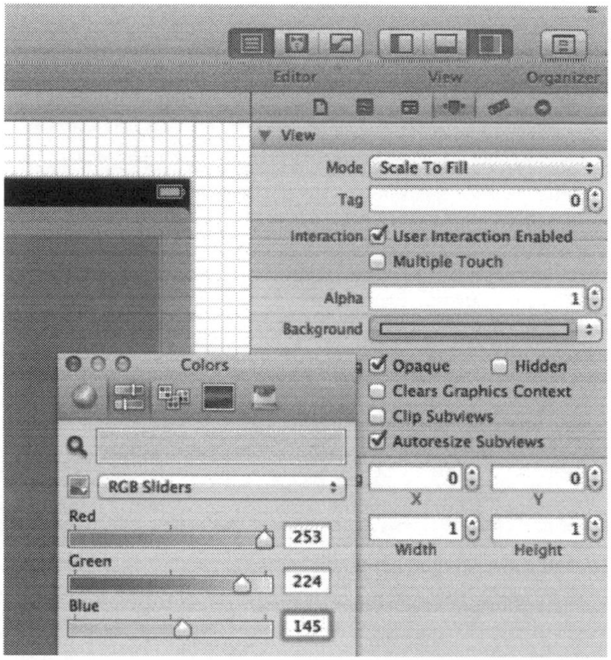

Figure 5-23. *Change the color of the View to Apress yellow.*

10. Once you've selected the View, in the Attributes Inspector open the Colors dialog by clicking the Background color swatch. Open the RGB selection from the drop-down menu and set Red@253, Green@224, and Blue@145 as shown in Figure 5-23. Close it. You now can run the app and see what you have.

Figure 5-24. *A beautiful launch image starts the app.*

11. Sure enough, once the app builds and runs, it begins with the
    beautiful launch image you inserted that displays while the
    application finishes starting up. Notice how it automatically
    starts in Landscape regardless of how you're holding it. The
    image also fits beautifully onto the page as shown in
    Figure 5-24.

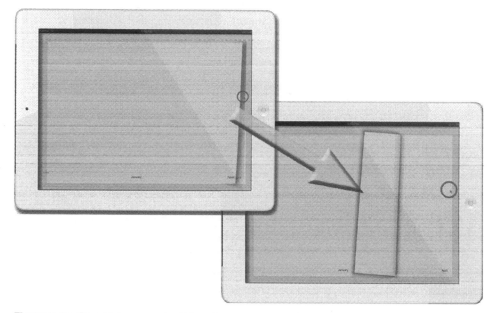

Figure 5-25. *Beautiful page curls all done for you.*

12. As mentioned at the beginning of this chapter, it's unprecedented for Apple to provide such a turnkey Xcode framework. Once the launch image is completed, you go immediately to the first page and see the Apress yellow, the grey font, and the placement of the labels—all of which you took care of in the Storyboard. Then, selecting the page to turn on the very right hand side of the page, as shown in Figure 5-25, you see a beautiful page curl appear, all without coding a single line. Wow! The only thing missing now is your page content, which is what we do in step 3 of 5. So let's get to it!

Step 3: Code: ModelController

Before you start coding, we'd like to take a minute to recap, look around, and view the forest as well as the trees. You have three steps left. The first was setting up the project. The second was adjusting your Storyboard. Now you will code step 3, the ModelController, step 4, the DataViewController, and step 5, the RootViewController. There is a good reason for these three steps, because the Page-Based Application provides exactly these three classes:

RootViewController, ModelController, and DataViewController. You will now spend the rest of this chapter coding these three classes.

> **NOTE:** We strongly suggest that when you use the Page-Based Application template for your own projects, you *too* divide your project into five steps: first, preliminary files allocation; second, Storyboard adjusting; and lastly coding the three provided classes.

An easy way to remember these classes in the Page-Based Apps is as follows:

- The DataViewController manages the actual data and Views you want your user to see.

- RootViewController keeps track of current and new Views (pages) requested by your user.

- ModelController receives and creates new Views (pages) requested from RootViewController.

So now that you have a refresher on where we've been, where we're at, and where we're going, let's start coding.

> **NOTE:** We're going to go a little out of order and start with the ModelController first. The reason for this is that if you start building the code in order, DataViewController to RootViewController to ModelController, then it will be difficult to test whether the code is building correctly. Alternatively, building it in the reverse order as we are coding, you can literally press ⌘+B at the end of every section, and if there are no compile errors or warnings you know you're doing it correctly. Essentially, we're going backwards so that we can test by building as we go.

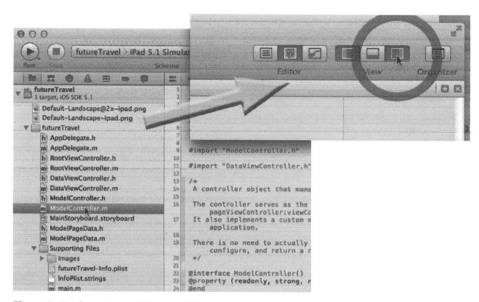

Figure 5-26. *Open the* ModelController.m *and set the stage.*

1. You need to first reorganize the Xcode windows for coding. First select the ModelController.m implementation file and then, looking at the right-hand image In Figure 5-26, if your Standard editor is on, deselect it by selecting the Assistant editor. Keep the Navigator on, close the Debug area, and deselect the Utilities pane as shown in Figure 5-26.

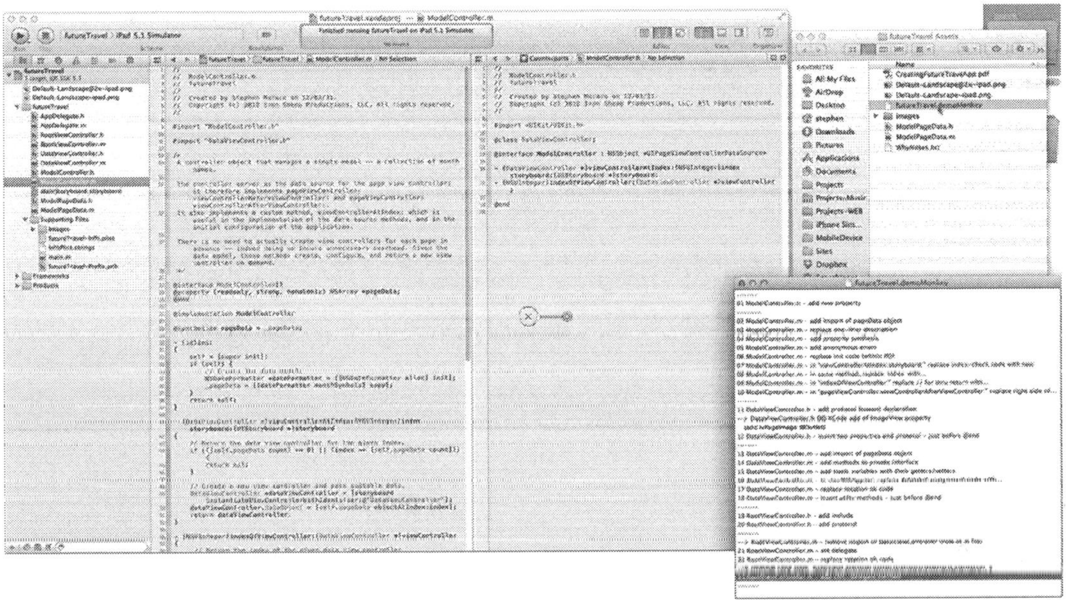

Figure 5-27. *Your Xcode canvas for coding and following along with us.*

2. Once you've set the Xcode stage with the `ModelController` implementation file on your left pane and its header file on your right pane, open up DemoMonkey and, depending upon the size of your screen, place it at about the same position shown in Figure 5-27.

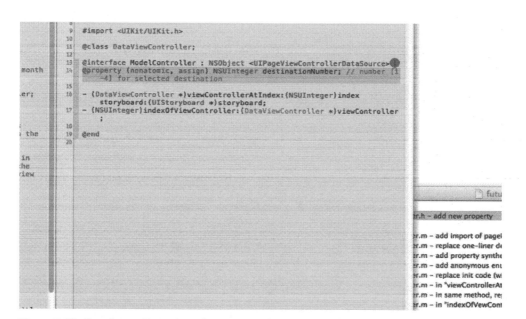

Figure 5-28. *Drag in your first snippet from DemoMonkey.*

3. We want to add a new property called destinationNumber
    because in the travel flyer you're making, you have four possible
    destinations that you want to see as you're paging through the
    flyer. As we move forward we will dig deeper into this property.
    For now, start by dragging the "01 ModelController.h – add new
    property" snippet from demoMonkey into the header file
    immediately under the @interface ModelController line of code
    as shown in Figure 5-28.

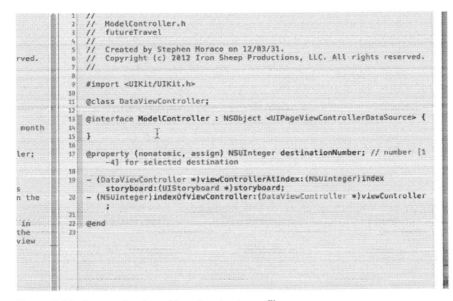

Figure 5-29. *A general review of how to set out your files.*

4. Before you go too far dragging snippets onto the
    ModelController.h file, let's quickly go over the format we use
    in setting up each page, which is the format we strongly suggest
    that you adhere to. From the top, our public interface, a section
    for instance variables, properties, and then our instance
    methods at the end. We will call these sections as we guide you
    to where you should place your DemoMonkey snippets as shown
    in Figure 5-29. This view, however, is with the Assistant editor.
    We'll be switching back and forth between the Assistant editor
    and the Standard editor as shown in Figure 5-30.

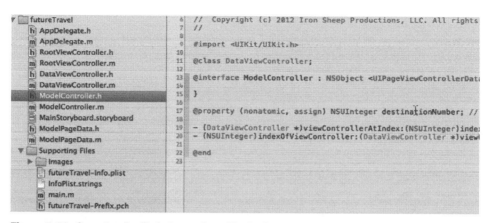

Figure 5-30. *Same header file but now viewed in the Standard editor.*

5. The reason we're going over this is because, as you know, these screen shots are directly from the video, and because we switch between the Assistant and Standard editors constantly, you need to be able to recognize them. For example, Figure 5-30 shows the same header file shown in Figure 5-29, except we've switched off the Assistant editor and clicked the Standard editor.

```
9   #import "ModelController.h"
10
11  #import "DataViewController.h"
12  #import "ModelPageData.h"
13
14  /*
15   A controller object that manages a simple model -- a collection of ModelPageData o
16
17   The controller serves as the data source for the page view controller; it therefore
        pageViewController:viewControllerAfterViewController:.
18   It also implements a custom method, viewControllerAtIndex: which is useful in the in
        configuration of the application.
19
20   There is no need to actually create view controllers for each page in advance -- in
        methods create, configure, and return a new view controller on demand.
21  */
22
23  @interface ModelController() {
24
25  }
26
27  @property (readonly, strong, nonatomic) NSArray *pageData;
28
29  @end
30
31
32  @implementation ModelController
33
34  @synthesize pageData = _pageData;
35  @synthesize destinationNumber = m_nDestinationNumber; // [1-4]
```

Figure 5-31. *Open the ModelController implementation file and drag the first of the three snippets into the implementation file.*

6. Open the ModelController.m. You will drag in three snippets.

      ▓ First drag in the "02 ModelController.m – add import of pageData object" snippet, which connects the implementation file with the class you brought into the project in Figure 5-10. We will dig deeper into why we connect it and what the class does, but for now just import it as seen on line 12 in Figure 5-31.

      ▓ Now looking at line 14, right after the /*, delete the first line of text and replace it with "03 ModelController.m – replace one-liner description" just to remind yourself that this is a controller object that manages an array, or collection of data objects.

      ▓ This model was originally written to support the number of elements in an array, but that's no longer true for us. We have a fixed value for max pages, so what you will do is after adding the property synthesis for the new property you've added is simply add a definition for the number of pages.

> **NOTE:** Another way you could have done this would be to make a property getter override with a property for the number of pages that would always return the same value.

The reason we chose our method to change the array with destinationNumber = m_nDestinationNumber; rather than the option described in the nearby gray box is because our method is fun and teaches you a couple of really cool techniques to use with Storyboarding:

      ▓ We have an anonymous enumeration enum that's not given any name.

```
enum {
    MAX_PAGES = 4
};
```

      ▓ We also work with no instance variables tied to this enumeration. Our method abides strictly to the value that we can now use by name.

■ It's similar in a way to creating a #define directive but it's not treated as a text substitution by the compiler. Instead, this mechanism creates a constant integer value for each name within the enum, which means we're showing you a cool way to create a number of unrelated named integer constants without using an array and then use them should your application require. In our case, we will use only MAX_PAGES. But for you, this way frees you and opens the door to using this method for your specific purposes in any other future applications.

Now go back and do what we've outlined with the bullets. Start off by adding the property synthesis. Drag in the "04 ModelController.m – add property synthesis" snippet and place it directly under @synthesize pageData = _pageData; as shown in Figure 5-31.

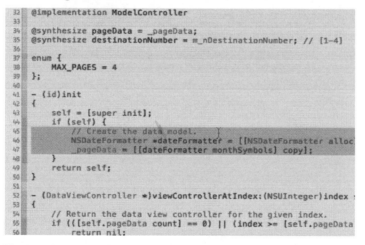

Figure 5-32. *Add a definition for the number of pages and then delete the date formatting for the old data model.*

7. You need to have a definition for the number of pages your array will be working with. Drag in the "05 ModelController.m – add anonymous enum" snippet and place it underneath the synthesis you just placed as shown in Figure 5-32. Now you need to take out the generation of the older model, because as mentioned you're not going to use dates anymore, and substitute it with our own data. So select the three lines of code as shown in Figure 5-32 and delete them.

```
32  @implementation ModelController
33
34  @synthesize pageData = _pageData;
35  @synthesize destinationNumber = m_nDestinationNumber; // [1-4]
36
37  enum {
38      MAX_PAGES = 4
39  };
40
41  - (id)init
42  {
43      self = [super init];
44      if (self) {
45          // Create the data model...
46
47          // - set starting page
48          self.destinationNumber = 1;   // set our default destinatio
49
50          // - create the pages
51          NSMutableArray *mpdPagesAr = [NSMutableArray array];
52
53          ModelPageData *newPageDescription = [[ModelPageData alloc]
54          [mpdPagesAr addObject:newPageDescription];
55
56          newPageDescription = [[ModelPageData alloc] initWithImageFi
```

Figure 5-33. *Replace the old data model with your data model.*

8. Drag in the "06 ModelController.m – replace init code (within if
   {})"_snippet and place it exactly in place of the code you deleted
   in Figure 5-33 inside the if statement as shown in Figure 5-34.
   You can see that we preset our destination Page 1 with
   self.destinationNumber = 1;. You also need to set up an array
   of pages, but because we don't just have 4 pages in our flyer
   but 4 flyers integrated into one, you end up with an 8-pack of
   pages plus 2 front pages, which make a total of 10 pages—
   whereas the max number of pages for any one trip through the
   flyers is 4. Here's what we're going to do:

   ▨ Always reserve "01-Intro.png" for slot 1 in the array

   ▨ Always reserve "02-Pick.png" for slot 2 in the array

Now we have only 2 slots left in our array and we need to stuff 8
pages into it. Solutions:

   ▨ newPageDescription "n-Aspect-ni.png" for slot 3 in the
   array

   ▨ newPageDescription "n-Aspect-ni+1.png" for slot 4 in
   the array

Expanding this a little more:

```
ModelPageData …."01-Intro.png" andPageNbr:1ofMax:MAX_PAGES];…;
newPageDescription …"02-Pick.png" andPageNbr:2ofMax:MAX_PAGES];…;
newPageDescription …"1-Aspect-1.png" andPageNbr:3ofMax:MAX_ PAGES];…;
newPageDescription …"1-Aspect -2.png" andPageNbr:4ofMax:MAX_ PAGES];…;


newPageDescription …"4-Aspect-1.png" andPageNbr:3ofMax:MAX_ PAGES];…;
newPageDescription …"4-Aspect-2.png" andPageNbr:4ofMax:MAX_ PAGES];…;
```

What we've done here is overcome the obstacle of keeping an array of 4 to handle 10 pages. But you need to adjust your `DataViewController` for this to work. If you understand this well, move onto step 35 and Figure 5-35. If you 're still not quite clear, then check out Figure 5-34.

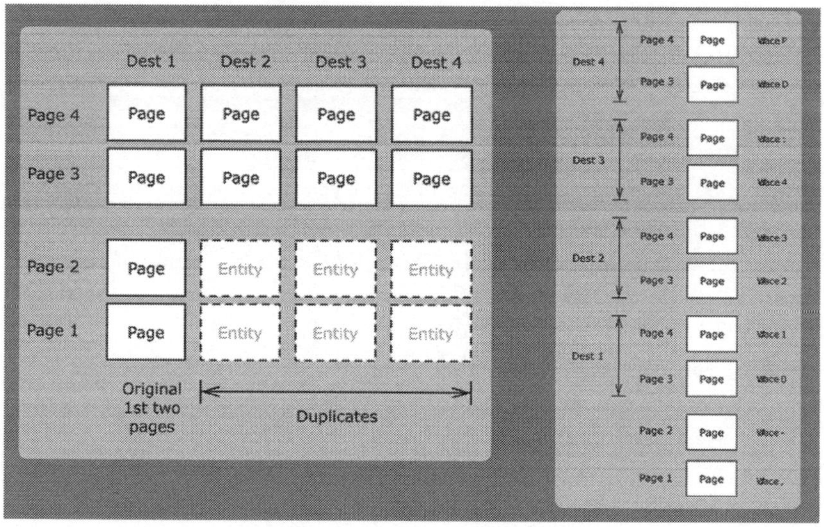

Figure 5-34. *Two diagrams to help illustrate how our pages are stored in the 10 position array.*

9. Figure 5-34 comprises two images that help illustrate the non-trivial method we're using to organize our array. The left side of Figure 5-34 shows our Storyboard pages as four sets of destinations with our original first two pages, but arranged in a way that we end up with duplicates. To solve this problem we instead layout the non-duplicate pages into a list of 10, as illustrated on the right-hand side of Figure 5-34 and described in detail in step 34.

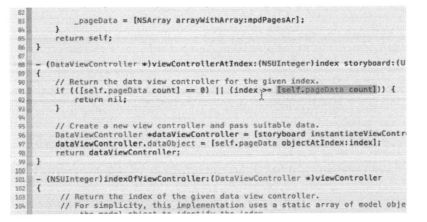

```
82
83        _pageData = [NSArray arrayWithArray:mpdPagesAr];
84      }
85      return self;
86    }
87
88  - (DataViewController *)viewControllerAtIndex:(NSUInteger)index storyboard:(U
89    {
90      // Return the data view controller for the given index.
91      if (([self.pageData count] == 0) || (index >= [self.pageData count])) {
92        return nil;
93      }
94
95      // Create a new view controller and pass suitable data.
96      DataViewController *dataViewController = [storyboard instantiateViewContr
97      dataViewController.dataObject = [self.pageData objectAtIndex:index];
98      return dataViewController;
99    }
100
101  - (NSUInteger)indexOfViewController:(DataViewController *)viewController
102    {
103      // Return the index of the given data view controller.
104      // For simplicity, this implementation uses a static array of model obje
```

Figure 5-35. *Take out the code pointing to the original array.*

10. As mentioned, you need to adjust your DataViewController for this method of organizing the array to work. Find the viewControllerAtIndex:storyboard: method. Remember that, as evident in Figure 5-34, you can't use the array count [self.pageData count] as shown and done for you on line 90 in Figure 5-35. You need to change this as follows:

... if (([self.pageData count] == 0) || (index >= **[self.pageData count]**)) {
        return nil;...

we change to:

... if (([self.pageData count] == 0) || (index >= **MAX_PAGES**)) {
        return nil;...

So select lines those 4 lines and delete them as shown in Figure 5-35.

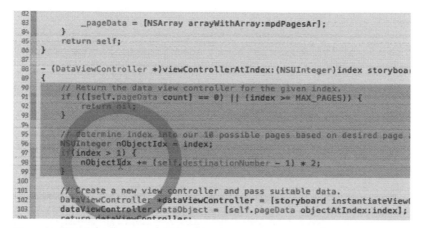

Figure 5-36. *Insert the new code that interacts with the new array.*

11. Drag in the "07 ModelController.m – In "ViewControllerAtIndex: Storyboard:" replace index-check code with new" snippet and drop it into the exact spot where you deleted your code in Figure 5-35, as shown in Figure 5-36. Note that nObjectIdx += (self.destinationNumber - 1) * 2; is how you take care of your new index, which returns a value of 0 thru 9 based on the destination. But you have a problem, because it's still grabbing objects based on the old index (line 103 of Figure 5-36). You need to change this in the next step.

```
88    - (DataViewController *)viewControllerAtIndex:(NSUInteger)index storyboard:(UIStoryboard
89    {
90        // Return the data view controller for the given index.
91        if (([self.pageData count] == 0) || (index >= MAX_PAGES)) {
92            return nil;
93        }
94
95        // determine index into our 10 possible pages based on desired page and desired desti
96        NSUInteger nObjectIdx = index;
97        if(index > 1) {
98            nObjectIdx += (self.destinationNumber - 1) * 2;
99        }
100
101        // Create a new view controller and pass suitable data.
102        DataViewController *dataViewController = [storyboard instantiateViewControllerWithIde
103        dataViewController.dataObject = [self.pageData objectAtIndex:index];
104        return dataViewController;
105    }
106
107    - (NSUInteger)indexOfViewController:(DataViewController *)viewController
108    {
109        // Return the index of the given data view controller.
110        // For simplicity, this implementation uses a static array of model objects and the
                the model object to identify the index.
111        return [self.pageData indexOfObject:viewController.dataObject];
112    }
```

Figure 5-37. *Copy the new nObjectIdx.*

12. All you have to do here is replace the old index index

```
dataViewController.dataObject = [self.pageData objectAtIndex:index];
```

with the new index nObjectIdx

```
if(index > 1) {
    nObjectIdx+= (self.destinationNumber - 1) * 2;
}
```

Select it as shown in Figure 5-37 and copy it.

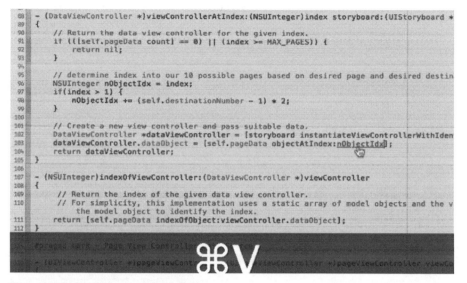

Figure 5-38. *Paste the new nObjectIdx.*

13. Paste the new index as shown in Figure 5-38. This now finishes the changes to this method. Now you're getting the DataViewController for a given page index to go to the next page, and the next page, up to 4. This will calculate the right location within this array.

NOTE: You could have used "08 ModelController.m – in same method, replace 'index' with ..." but most of you will copy and paste as we have done.

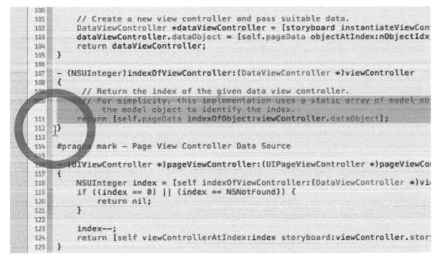

Figure 5-39. *Looking at the reverse calculation.*

14. Up to this point you've been dealing with the forward calculation for positions on the array. Now you need to deal with the reverse calculations. You need to replace three lines from indexOfViewController as shown in Figure 5-39. Select and delete them.

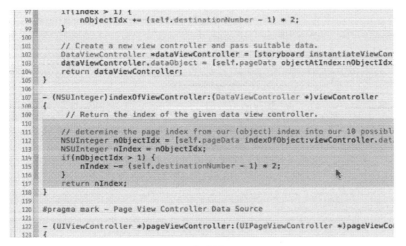

Figure 5-40. *Insert the new reverse calculations.*

15. Drag in the "09 ModelController.m –in "indexOfViewController" replace // for thru return with..." snippet and drop it into the spot you deleted in Figure 5-39. This is shown in Figure 5-40.

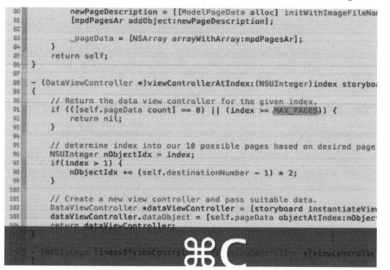

Figure 5-41. *Select MAX_PAGES.*

16. You need to make sure that our idea of using MAX_PAGES as an array count will work, so you need to associate it with the pageViewController. Copy it as shown in Figure 5-41.

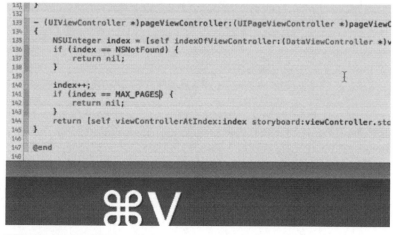

Figure 5-42. *Paste MAX_PAGES.*

17. Once you've copied `MAX_PAGES`, scroll down to the line `if
    (index == [self.pageData count])` and paste it over the
    `[self.pageData count]` as shown here:

```
index++;
if (index == [self.pageData count]) {
    return nil;
}
```

Replace `self.pageData.count` with

```
index++;
if (index == MAX_PAGES) {
    return nil;
}
```

This is shown in Figure 5-42.

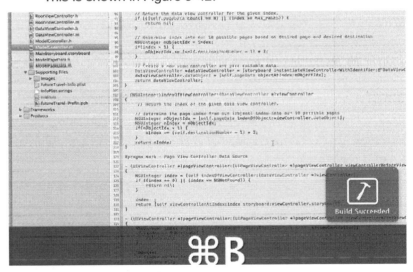

Figure 5-43. *Before moving on, make sure it builds.*

18. Before moving on to step 4 of 5, let's make sure that everything
    builds as expected. Press ⌘+B and make sure it all builds
    correctly as shown in Figure 5-43.

> **NOTE:** You could have used "10 ModelController.m – in
> viewControllerAfterViewController: replace right side of final equals with…" but most
> of you will copy and paste the `MAX_PAGES` as we have done.

Step 4: Code: DataViewController

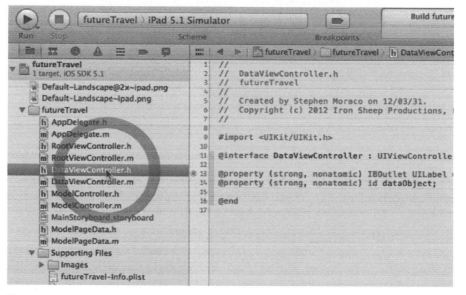

Figure 5-44. *Open the DataViewController.*

1. First, keep in mind that the DataViewController is the guy that manages the views you want your user to see and interact with, along with the RootViewController and ModelController, which present the pages. So open up the DataViewController as shown in Figure 5-44.

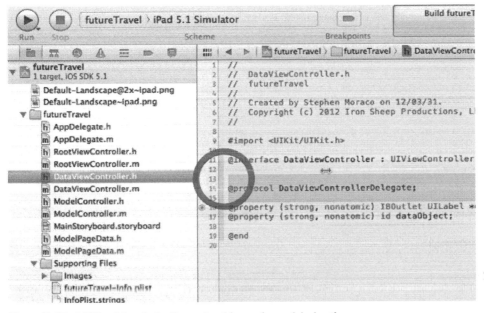

Figure 5-45. *Add the delegate for the protocol for our forward declaration.*

2. You need to first add a protocol forward declaration. Drag in the "11 DataViewController.h –add protocol forward declaration" snippet and drop it right before the @interface as shown in Figure 5-45. The reason you need the @protocol DataViewControllerDelegate; forward declaration is that you'll need to declare a property that is a delegate which conforms to this protocol (meaning that the methods defined by the protocol will be implemented by the delegate class). Then when your user selects a destination, this DataViewController is going to tell whatever is listening (the delegate) the number of the destination that was selected via a method in this protocol. You'll see this in an upcoming step.

    Next, DataViewController needs a new property. You do have your data label *dataLabel, but you created a new image view in Storyboard and right now you *don't* have a means to display images in it. So you need to jump back into Storyboard and add it. Let's quickly take care of that.

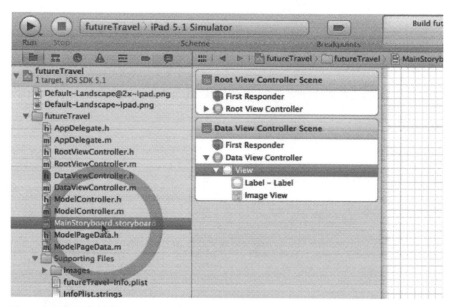

Figure 5-46. *Open Storyboard.*

3.   Open Storyboard as shown in Figure 5-46, but make sure you also click the Assistant editor, which is not shown in Figure 5-46.

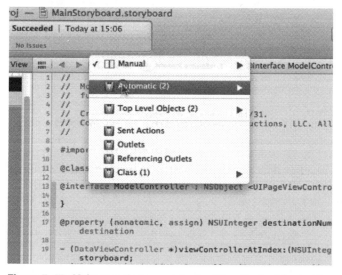

Figure 5-47. *Make sure that your default settings for Assistant editor are on Automatic.*

4. Make sure your default settings for the Assistant editor are on Automatic. Ours were on Manual from earlier, and so might yours be. Click the label saying either Automatic or Manual just to the right of the two forward and back arrows as shown in Figure 5-47.

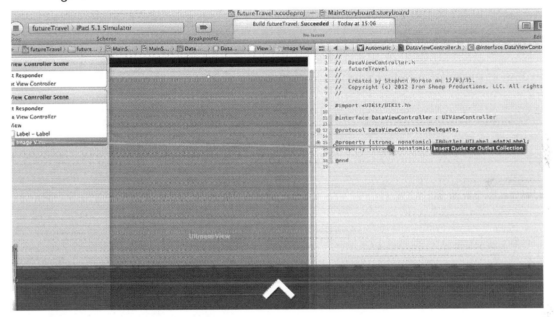

Figure 5-48. *Control-drag to the header file.*

5. Once you've selected the Assistant editor, and it's on Automatic, Control-drag from the UIImageView out to the DataViewController.h file next to your existing properties as shown in Figure 5-48.

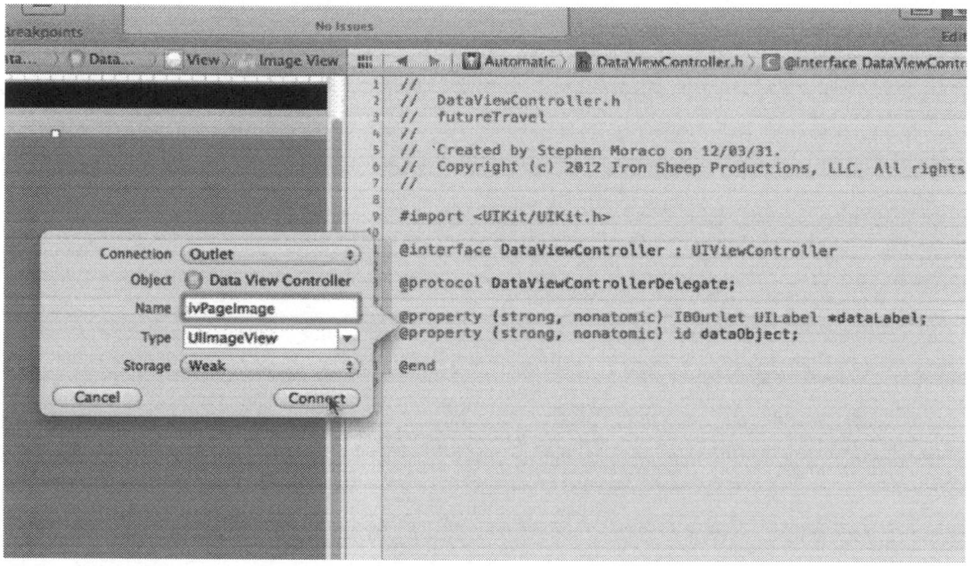

Figure 5-49. *Name the UIImageView data type.*

6. Xcode knows that this is a `UIImageView` data type, so you don't have to change that once the dialog appears. You do need to give it a name, though. This is your page image variable (iv), so preface the name "`PageImage`" with "`iv`" (we use data type names so we can remember what type each variable refers to). Name it `ivPageImage` as shown in Figure 5-49. Okay, you're done doing what we forgot to do in Storyboard in the first place, so let's go back to the `DataViewController` header file (you can switch off the Assistant editor and go back to the Standard editor).

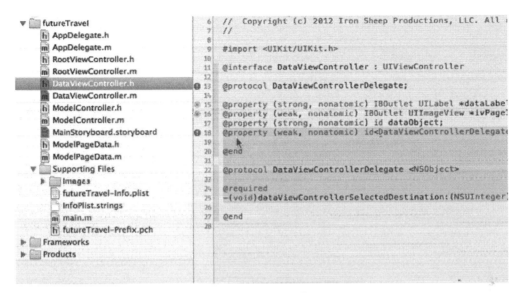

```
 6   // Copyright (c) 2012 Iron Sheep Productions, LLC. All
 7   //
 8
 9   #import <UIKit/UIKit.h>
10
11   @interface DataViewController : UIViewController
12
13   @protocol DataViewControllerDelegate;
14
15   @property (strong, nonatomic) IBOutlet UILabel *dataLabe
16   @property (weak, nonatomic) IBOutlet UIImageView *ivPage
17   @property (strong, nonatomic) id dataObject;
18   @property (weak, nonatomic) id<DataViewControllerDelegat
19
20   @end
21
22   @protocol DataViewControllerDelegate <NSObject>
23
24   @required
25   -(void)dataViewControllerSelectedDestination:(NSInteger
26
27   @end
28
```

Figuro 5 50. *Add tho now dolegato proporty into the header filc.*

7.   Drag in the "12 DataViewController.h -insert two properties and
     protocol - just before the @end" snippet and insert it right
     before the @end. Here wo inserted the now delegate property
     and the definition of the protocol we forward-declared in step
     44. As you can see in Figure 5-50, you have a couple of
     warnings because you don't have the implementation done yet,
     which is normal. Let's get to the implementation file and get
     things working correctly!

Figure 5-51. *Open the implementation file and import the page data objects.*

8. Notice that because you did the drag-and-drop for ivPageImage
    through the Storyboard, Xcode added the necessary
    implementation code for you as well: @synthesis and the
    ivPageImage in the viewDidUnload is set to nil. Now you need
    to import the interface for the pageData object. Drag in the "13
    DataViewController.m – add import and pageData object
    (#import "ModelPageData.h")" snippet and insert it under the
    #import "DataViewController.h".

    You also need to add some methods to the private interface.
    Drag in the "14 DataViewController.m – add methods to private
    interface" snippet and insert it alongside, not under, the
    @interface DataViewController as shown Figure 5-51.

    The private method declarations added to the
    DataViewController.m file are as follows:

```
-(void)onButtonPress:(UIButton*)sender;
-(void)showHideImageSelectionIndicator:(NSInteger)imageNbr;
-(void)placeImageSelectorButtonAtLocation:(CGPoint)location tag:(NSInteger)tag;
-(void)placeSelectionIndicatorAtLocation:(CGPoint)location
label:(NSString*)text;
```

Figure 5-52. *Bring in the setter overrides.*

Note that as of yet you don't have your delegate property synthesized. There's a reason for this, and you're just about to see it. You're *not* going to synthesize the delegate setter and getter. Rather, you're going to add an explicit setter and getter pair. This is a little bit sneaky because you're going to communicate with the delegate and the selected page by referencing a single variable from all instances of this class. You do this by using your static class variables (s_pDelegate and s_nSelectedDestinationNumber) rather than instance variables. This way every instance has the same value for these guys once they are set. (Instance variables have separate values for each instance of a class. Class variables have a single shared value for all instances of a class.)

Drag in the "15 DataViewController.m – add static variables and their getters/setters" snippet and drop it in below the @synthesize dataObject = _dataObject; as shown in Figure 5-52.

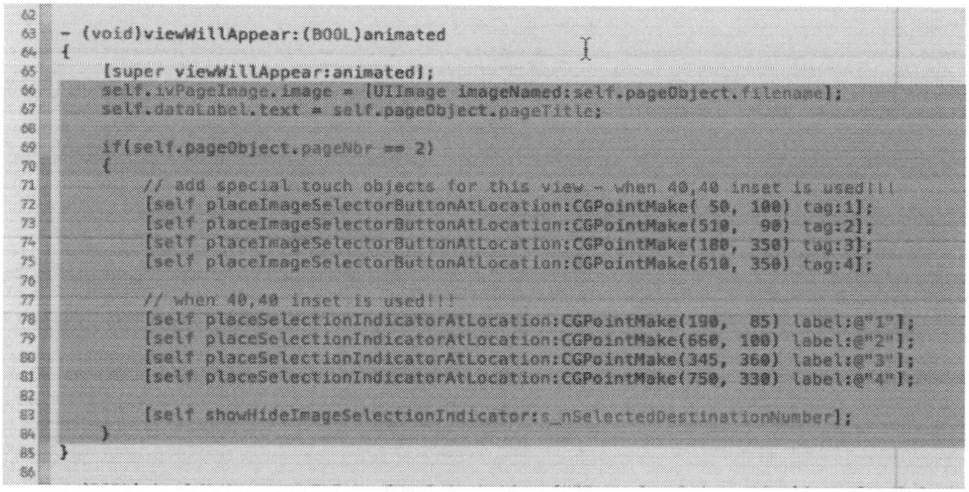

Figure 5-53. *Make* `viewWillAppear` *adhere to our own text.*

9. You may notice in `viewWillAppear` that it's actually setting a label text `self.dataLabel.text` with a description of the data object `[self.dataObject description]`, which turns out to be the month object.

```
- (void)viewWillAppear:(BOOL)animated
{
    [super viewWillAppear:animated];
    self.datalabel.text = [self.dataObject description];
}
```

As you know by now, this is the default "app" that Apple, for our convenience, randomly chose to use for the generic Page-Based App sample. However, you are doing a travel flyer, so you need to change this by dragging in "16 DataViewController.m – in viewWill Appear: replace datalabel assignment code with …" and inserting it under `[super viewWillAppear:animated];` (making sure you remove the line that's currently underneath it).

This now sets out the tasks that you want to execute just before the view appears. Specifically, you want to set the image and the new label text to the ones stored in the current `pageObject`:

```
self.ivPageImage.image = [UIImage imageNamed:self.pageObject.filename];
self.dataLabel.text = self.pageObject.pageTitle;
```

Now, once you open up the brochure and are on the second page, you put transparent buttons over the images:

```
[self placeImageSelectorButtonAtLocation:CGPointMake( 50, 100) tag:1];
[self placeImageSelectorButtonAtLocation:CGPointMake(510,  90) tag:2];
[self placeImageSelectorButtonAtLocation:CGPointMake(180, 350) tag:3];
[self placeImageSelectorButtonAtLocation:CGPointMake(610, 350) tag:4];
```

Then put a set of markers on the images to indicate user selection (these will be displayed one at a time):

```
[self placeSelectionIndicatorAtLocation:CGPointMake(190,  85) label:@"1"];
[self placeSelectionIndicatorAtLocation:CGPointMake(660, 100) label:@"2"];
[self placeSelectionIndicatorAtLocation:CGPointMake(345, 360) label:@"3"];
[self placeSelectionIndicatorAtLocation:CGPointMake(750, 330) label:@"4"];
```

You're also choosing to show and hide the markers here:

```
[self showHideImageSelectionIndicator:s_nSelectedDestinationNumber];
```

This is shown in Figure 5-53.

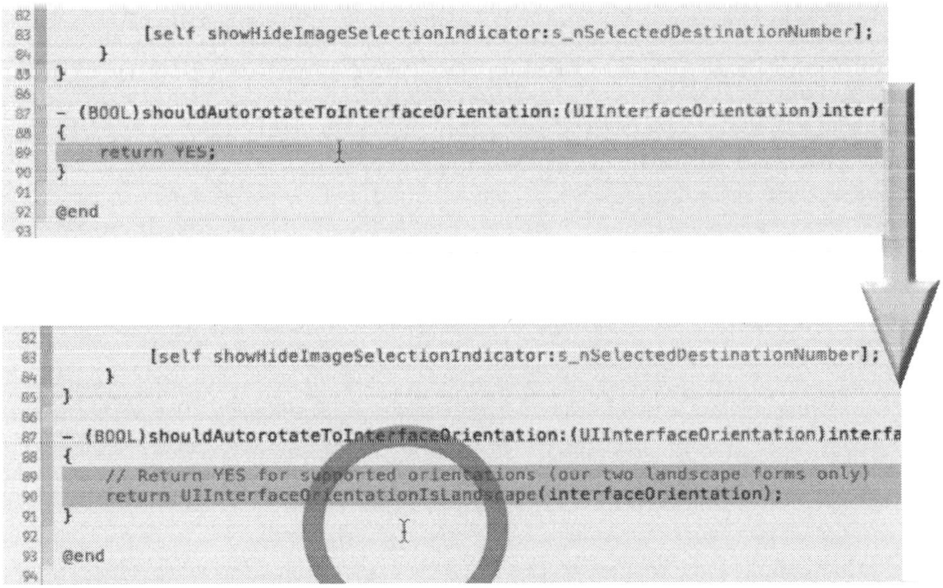

Figure 5-54. *Change to Landscape only.*

10. The default template app is designed for both Landscape and Portrait orientations, but yours is Landscape only. You need to change this by modifying `shouldAutorotateToInterfaceOrientation:` : to return true only for Landscape. Drag in "17 DataViewController.m –replace rotation ok code" and insert in place of the `return YES;` code as shown in Figure 5-54.

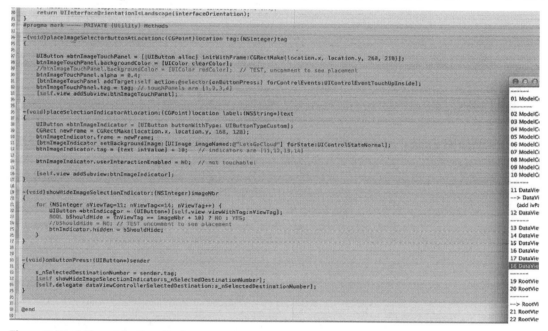

Figure 5-55. *Add our private methods.:*

11. You now need to implement all the private methods we've been talking about. Drag in "18 DataViewController.m – insert utility methods - just before @end" and insert it right before the @end.

    Here you implement the private methods that create and position the hidden buttons and markers (see Figure 5-54):

`placeImageSelectorButtonAtLocation` and `placeSelectionIndicatorAtLocation`

    Looking at the implementation of `placeSelectionIndicatorAtLocation:` method, note that it simply creates a `UIButton` instance, sets its position and background image, and adds the marker button to the view:

```
[btnImageIndicator setBackgroundImage:[UIImage imageNamed:@"LetsGoCloud"]
forState:UIControlStateNormal];
```

You also define a tag for each button so you can later show only the one that's currently selected by the user, as well as make it non-touchable:

```
btnImageIndicator.tag = [text intValue] + 10;
btnImageIndicator.userInteractionEnabled = NO;  // not touchable!
```

We also have coded our buttons so that if your user taps on any of the four hidden buttons, an action method gets called:

```
-(void)onButtonPress:(UIButton*)sender
{
    s_nSelectedDestinationNumber = sender.tag;
    [self showHideImageSelectionIndicator:s_nSelectedDestinationNumber];
    [self.delegate
dataViewControllerSelectedDestination:s_nSelectedDestinationNumber];
}
```

When it's called it invokes the delegate method [self.delegate dataViewControllerSelectedDestination:s_nSelectedDestinationNumber]; which in turn tells your RootViewController which page set to load.

This is shown in Figure 5-55.

12. You're now ready to Build and see if it all works. If you didn't miss anything, you should see a "Build Succeeded" message.

Step 5: Code: RootViewController

Figure 5-56. *Let's code the RootViewController to handle the communication it will be receiving.*

1. Open up the `RootViewController.h` file. Drag in "19 RootViewController.h – add include" and insert it right after the `#import <UIKit/UIKit.h>` as shown in Figure 5-56. You do this because you need make the `DataViewControllerDelegate` protocol visible to the `RootViewController`, because you're going to make it conform to this new protocol. But it's not there yet, so let's add it in. Remove the closing angle bracket at the end of `@interface` line, drag in "20 RootViewController.h – add protocol," and insert it right alongside `UIPageViewControllerDelegate`, as shown here:

```
#import <UIKit/UIKit.h>
#import "DataViewController.h"

@interface RootViewController : UIViewController <UIPageViewControllerDelegate,
DataViewControllerDelegate> {
}

@property (strong, nonatomic) UIPageViewController *pageViewController;
@end
```

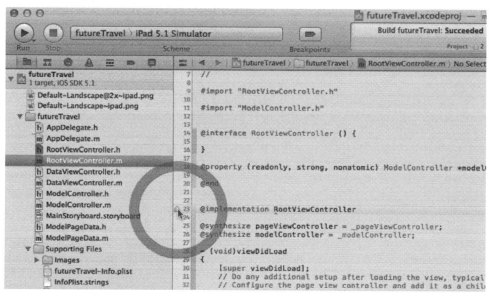

Figure 5-57. *Finish the implementation.*

2. You're done with the header. It's time to finish the implementation. Navigate to RootViewController.m. The first thing you want to take care of is that you no longer need #import "DataViewController.h" because it's in your header file, so delete it. Note the warning on line 23 in Figure 5-57. That's there because your protocol method isn't implemented yet. So first set the delegate. Find the viewDidLoad method implementation, drag in "21 RootViewController.m – set delegate (startingViewController.delegate = self;)," and insert it right after the DataViewController *startingViewController instantiation and before NSArray *viewControllers as shown here:

```
DataViewController *startingViewController = [self.modelController
viewControllerAtIndex:0 storyboard:self.storyboard];
startingViewController.delegate = self;  // tell object we want to hear from it
    NSArray *viewControllers = [NSArray arrayWithObject:startingViewController];
```

You have to do this because you, not Apple, support this delegate, so you need to insert code to actually set the delegate. The RootViewController will now receive the messages from the DataViewController.

```
59   - (void)viewDidUnload
60   {
61       [super viewDidUnload];
62       // Release any retained subviews of the main view.
63   }
64
65   - (BOOL)shouldAutorotateToInterfaceOrientation:(UIInterfaceOrientation)inter
66   {
67       // Return YES for supported orientations (our two landscape forms only)
68       return UIInterfaceOrientationIsLandscape(interfaceOrientation);
69   }
70
71   - (ModelController *)modelController
72   {
73       // Return the model controller object, creating it if necessary.
74       // In more complex implementations, the model controller may be passed
75       if (!_modelController) {
76           _modelController = [[ModelController alloc] init];
77       }
78       return _modelController;
79   }
80
```

Figure 5-58. *Support Landscape only.*

3. Again you need to show that you support Landscape only. Go to shouldAutorotateToInterfaceOrientation:, delete the return YES; line of code, drag in "22 RootViewController.m – replace rotation ok code," and insert it as shown in Figure 5-58.

```
75
76   #pragma mark – UIPageViewController delegate methods
77
78   /*
79   - (void)pageViewController:(UIPageViewController *)pageViewController didFinishAnimating:(BOOL)finished
80   {
81
82   }
83   */
84
85   - (UIPageViewControllerSpineLocation)pageViewController:(UIPageViewController *)pageViewController spine
86   {
87       if (UIInterfaceOrientationIsPortrait(orientation)) {
88           // In portrait orientation: Set the spine position to "min" and the page view controller's view
                  'UIPageViewControllerSpineLocationMid' in landscape orientation sets the doubleSided propert
89           UIViewController *currentViewController = [self.pageViewController.viewControllers objectAtIndex
90           NSArray *viewControllers = [NSArray arrayWithObject:currentViewController];
91           [self.pageViewController setViewControllers:viewControllers direction:UIPageViewControllerNaviga
92
93           self.pageViewController.doubleSided = NO;
94           return UIPageViewControllerSpineLocationMin;
95       }
96
97       // In landscape orientation: Set set the spine location to "mid" and the page view controller's view
                  the current and next view controllers; if it is odd, set the array to contain the previous and
98       DataViewController *currentViewController = [self.pageViewController.viewControllers objectAtIndex:
99       NSArray *viewControllers = nil;
100
101      NSUInteger indexOfCurrentViewController = [self.modelController indexOfViewController:currentViewCon
102      if (indexOfCurrentViewController == 0 || indexOfCurrentViewController % 2 == 0) {
103          UIViewController *nextViewController = [self.modelController pageViewController:self.pageViewCon
104          viewControllers = [NSArray arrayWithObjects:currentViewController, nextViewController, nil];
105      } else {
106          UIViewController *previousViewController = [self.modelController pageViewController:self.pageVie
107          viewControllers = [NSArray arrayWithObjects:previousViewController, currentViewController, nil];
108      }
109      [self.pageViewController setViewControllers:viewControllers direction:UIPageViewControllerNavigatio
110
111
112      return UIPageViewControllerSpineLocationMid;
113  }
114
115  @end
```

Figure 5-59. *Adjust the PageViewController.*

4. You need to adjust the PageViewController now, considering that with an iPad, if you're in Portrait it will be a single presentation. If you're in Landscape, it goes to a dual page presentation with left and right pages by default. You're not going to do this. You're going to use the Portrait-only option (although displaying the app in Landscape mode). So find the pageViewController:spineLocationForInterfaceOrientation: method, select the bottom portion of its code that's related to the Landscape option (it starts with the // In landscape orientation... comment), and delete it as shown in Figure 5-59. Lastly, remove the surrounding if (UIInterfaceOrientationIsPortrait(orientation)) {} statement, so only the code inside the if-statement is left in the implementation.

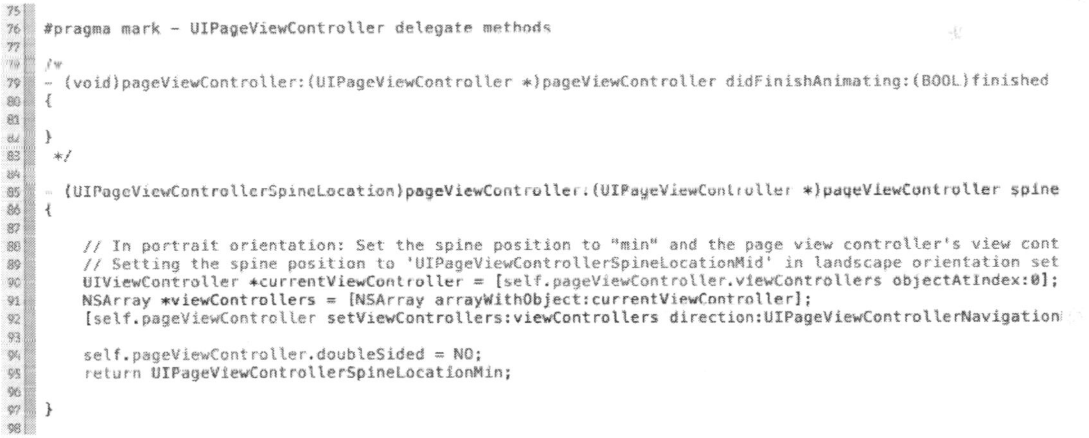

```
75
76    #pragma mark - UIPageViewController delegate methods
77
78    /*
79    - (void)pageViewController:(UIPageViewController *)pageViewController didFinishAnimating:(BOOL)finished
80    {
81
82    }
83    */
84
85    - (UIPageViewControllerSpineLocation)pageViewController:(UIPageViewController *)pageViewController spine
86    {
87
88        // In portrait orientation: Set the spine position to "min" and the page view controller's view cont
89        // Setting the spine position to 'UIPageViewControllerSpineLocationMid' in landscape orientation set
90        UIViewController *currentViewController = [self.pageViewController.viewControllers objectAtIndex:0];
91        NSArray *viewControllers = [NSArray arrayWithObject:currentViewController];
92        [self.pageViewController setViewControllers:viewControllers direction:UIPageViewControllerNavigation
93
94        self.pageViewController.doubleSided = NO;
95        return UIPageViewControllerSpineLocationMin;
96
97    }
98
```

Figure 5-60. *Final view of the pageViewController*

5. Figure 5-60 is a final view of the deleting we did in the previous step. It doesn't fit in the figure so we've placed it here in smaller font for your convenience:

```
- (void)pageViewController:(UIPageViewController *)pageViewController
didFinishAnimating:(BOOL)finished previousViewControllers:(NSArray
*)previousViewControllers transitionCompleted:(BOOL)completed
{}
 */
- (UIPageViewControllerSpineLocation)pageViewController:(UIPageViewController
*)pageViewController
spineLocationForInterfaceOrientation:(UIInterfaceOrientation)orientation
```

```
{
    // In portrait orientation: Set the spine position to "min" and the page view
    controller's view controllers array to contain just one view controller. Setting
    the spine position to 'UIPageViewControllerSpineLocationMid' in landscape
    orientation sets the doubleSided property to YES, so set it to NO here.
    UIViewController *currentViewController =
[self.pageViewController.viewControllers objectAtIndex:0];
    NSArray *viewControllers = [NSArray arrayWithObject:currentViewController];
    [self.pageViewController setViewControllers:viewControllers
direction:UIPageViewControllerNavigationDirectionForward animated:YES
completion:NULL];
    self.pageViewController.doubleSided = NO;
    return UIPageViewControllerSpineLocationMin;
}
@end
```

Figure 5-61. *Insert the delegate response methods and run it.*

6. Insert the delegate response methods by dragging in "23
    RootViewController.m – add DVC - delegate method" and
    inserting it right before the @end as shown in Figure 5-61. We
    know you've been waiting for this for a while. Go ahead and Run
    it!

Figure 5-62. *Initial splash*

7. The initial splash screen to the four-page flyer is shown in Figure 5-62, with the red circle showing from where to swipe (or tap) to turn the page.

Figure 5-63. *The page navigation*

8. Once the user enters the flyer they see that we have four destinations. As the user taps on them, they see that they are clickable. The "Let's go here" indicator appears on the one the user has tapped and is immediately hidden on the one the user last tapped. You want to make sure that whatever image the user selects correctly selects the expected next page when they tap to go to the next page as shown in the right-hand picture in Figure 5-63. Sure enough, the trip to Los Angeles 2 million years ago appears. Similarly, Figure 5-64 shows Cape Town, 1.3 million years ago. Wow!

Figure 5-64. *More views*

Mastering Table Views with Storyboarding: Core Data Setup

The last two apps you'll work on in this book are more complex and professional. Accordingly, we are dividing each one into three chapters. The Master-Detail Application: bookManager app is covered in Chapters 6, 7, and 8. The final app, Single View #3: wanderBoard, is covered in Chapters 9, 10, and 11.

In this chapter, you'll begin to develop a fairly intricate book manager application that will demonstrate how Storyboarding simplifies the building of apps that extensively utilize Table Views. Before diving in to this project, appreciating a little bit about the iOS history behind the Master-Detail Application will help you decide whether to use this template in the future. Remember how in Chapter 4 you used the Utility Application template to make an iPad Split View (see that chapter's Figure 4-57)? You created a Main View by coding a `MainViewController` and then created a Secondary View by coding a `FlipSideViewController`.

Well, that wasn't always so easy. When we first began coding for the iPad with the iOS SDK 3.2, it took a whole lot of work to create a Split View. Now in iOS 5 Apple has integrated the Split View-based Application template into the Navigation-based Application template and called it the Master-Detail Application template. Simply put, when you use the Master-Detail Application template and a user runs your app on an iPhone, it acts like it was programmed with a Navigation-based Application template. When a user runs your app on an iPhone, it acts like it was programmed with a Split View-based Application template.

On the Internet, most Master-Detail Application "tutorials" show instructions for coding the Split View Controller, *not* using Storyboard but still doing things the old-fashioned way—by going back to xibs. That method ignores the reason why Apple created the Master-Detail Application template. Remember to use the Master-Detail Application template when you know you'll be working with lists, databases, and tables—particularly if you want to let the user drill down through your data in a hierarchical manner.

In this app, you'll learn Storyboarding for lists and tables using the Master-Detail Application template. You'll also learn how to connect this data dynamically to a SQLite database. We've included the database component because it's certainly a game changer when you can say you know how to hook up data to a database. Finding Xcoders who have any experience at all with SQL is difficult for employers. As if that weren't enough, we will also introduce you to MagicalRecord, an open source library available on GitHub and used by many of the coders. MagicalRecord is a very efficient and amazingly easy-to-use framework created by MagicalPanda Software specifically for interacting with Core Data.

We explain all that later in the chapter. For now, feel good that you are about to embark on learning how to encapsulate the following:

- SQLite

- GitHub (a repository for software development projects using the git revision control system)

- Core Data into a Master-Detail Application template!

Awesome!

bookManager: A Master-Detail App

The bookManager app keeps track of a select group of Apress books, including their categories, titles, and authors. It also provides the ability to add, edit, and delete books in the SQLite database.

The top of the hierarchical tree is the My Library node, which has two categories, Books and Authors, as shown in the left-hand image in Figure 6-0A. Tapping Books drills down to the Categories node, where the user can choose a category of Apress books, edit them, or go back to My Library as shown in the center image in Figure 6-0A. Tapping Authors in the left-hand image leads to the

Authors node, where the user can select an Apress author, edit the authors, or go back to My Library as shown in the right-hand image in Figure 6-0A.

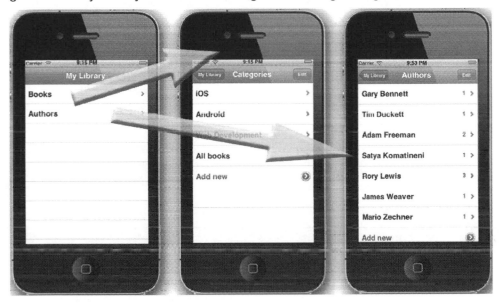

Figure 6-0A. *The bookManager app's My Library at the root level.*

The bookManager app has three views in which one can see the Apress books. First, as illustrated in Figure 6-0B, when the user taps Books from the Author selection; second, when the user taps Books from the Categories selection; and third, when the user wants to edit, delete, or add a book. The bookManager app also provides two distinct dialog boxes for adding a new category or a new author, illustrated in Figure 6-0C.

Figure 6-0B. *Books from Authors, from Categories, and editing from Categories*

Figure 6-0C. *Adding a Category and adding an Author*

The project is divided into three chapters. In this chapter, you set up the files, images, Core Data, and data model. In Chapter 7, you design the entire app using only Storyboard. And in Chapter 8, you insert the code behind the Storyboard elements and tweak a couple of Storyboard necessities.

Preliminaries

This chapter is the most challenging yet. We provide a substantial set of assets to help you in case you get stuck along the way. Again, as in all the chapters, we supply you with all the files and code necessary at `http://bit.ly/sMRvAP` and on the book's page at apress.com. You can also download the final version of the app here at `http://www.rorylewis.com/xCode/StoryBoarding%20in%20Xcode/Chapter06_bookManager.zip` but just downloading the final version won't really help you learn how to use GitHub, MagicalRecord, or SQLite, so we suggest downloading the assets folder now and taking note of the following: when you download the assets zip file from at `http://www.rorylewis.com/xCode/StoryBoarding%20in%20Xcode/Chapter06_bookManager%20Assets.zip` you will see two files, `bookdata.plist` and `chapter6.demoMonkey`, together with two folders, `images` and `MagicalRecord`.

You will be using the plist file for database creation, the DemoMonkey file for the code, and the `images` folder for your images. If you can't get your head wrapped around GitHub and MagicalRecord, don't worry. We also provide the entire folder `MagicalRecord`, which is what you end up with after going through the GitHub exercise, so you can drag it entirely into your project and continue following along. We suggest using MagicalRecord and exploring GitHub. It will certainly elevate you into an elite set of coders if you can say that you have GitHub and Core Data experience.

Clear out your desktop, download `http://www.rorylewis.com/xCode/StoryBoarding%20in%20Xcode/Chapter06_bookManager%20Assets.zip` unzip the folder, and let's get going.

Step 1 of 3: Set Up files, Images, Core Data and Data Model

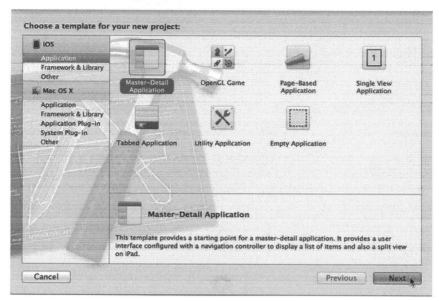

Figure 6-1. *Start a Master-Detail Application.*

1. Open Xcode, press ⌘+⇧+N, and select Master-Detail Application as shown in Figure 6-1.

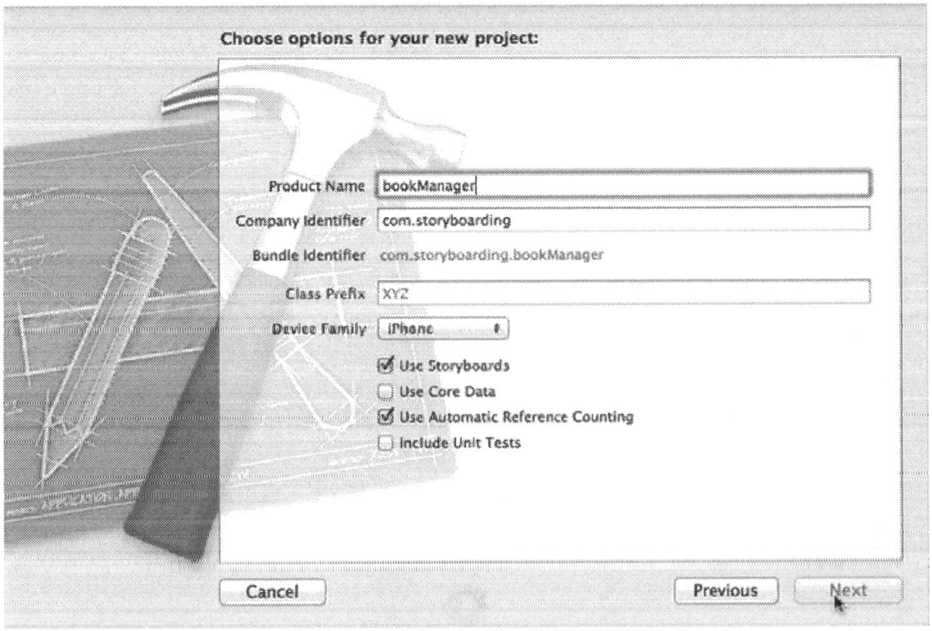

Figure 6-2. *Select the options for the bookManager app.*

2. For Product Name, enter bookManager, and for the Company
   Identifier enter com.storyboarding. We won't use a class prefix.
   Make sure to select iPhone and put a check mark next to Use
   Storyboards and Use Automatic Reference Counting as shown
   in Figure 6-2. Leave Use Core Data and Include Unit Tests
   unchecked. Save the project to your desktop.

> **NOTE:** We left Use Core Data option unchecked for this project template only to
> prevent Xcode from generating CoreData setup code for us. Since we are going to
> use MagicalRecord in this app the above-mentioned code is already integrated into it.

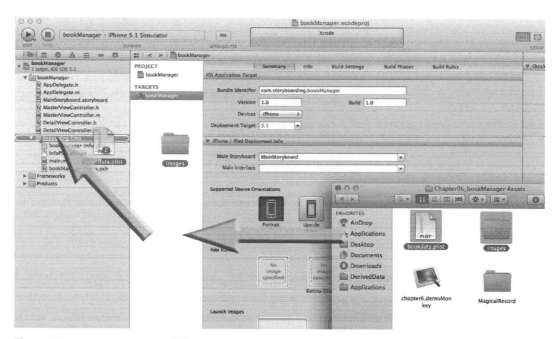

Figure 6-3. *Open up your assets folder.*

3.   You'll now drag assets into your project. If you have not
     downloaded the assets folder from http://www.rorylewis.com/
     xCode/StoryBoarding%20in%20Xcode/Chapter06_bookManager%20
     Assets.zip, do it now. After saving it to you desktop, unzip it.
     Select the images folder and bookdata.plist as shown in Figure
     6-3. Drag both items over into the Supporting Files folder inside
     the bookManager folder as indicated by the arrows in Figure 6-3.
     Your Supporting Files folder should look similar to our
     Supporting Files folder shown in Figure 6-3.

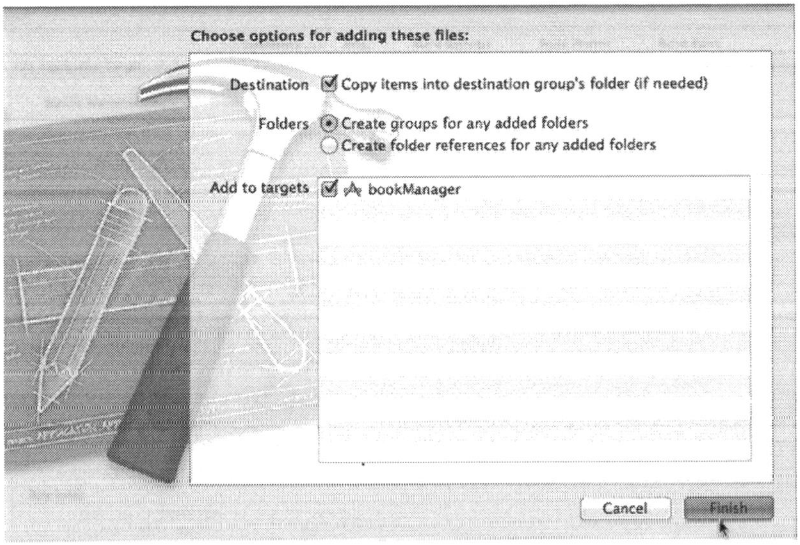

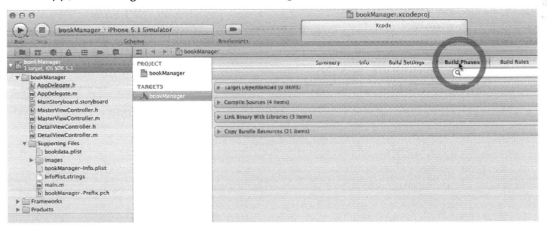

Figure 6-4. *Copy items into destination group's folder.*

4. You need to make sure that the actual contents of the file and the plist are inherent in the app, so make sure you select "Copy items into destination group's folder (if needed)" and "Create groups for any added folders" and that your target will be this app, bookManager. This is illustrated in Figure 6-4.

Figure 6-5. *Add the CoreData frameworks to the project.*

5. You'll be using a database quite extensively in this app—this is part of the Core Data framework. Coding a database from scratch would take a huge amount of resources, time, and effort. Core Data provides pre-built classes and tools for data management, and it's done in a way that you simply build your custom code on top of the basic functionality provided in Core Data. To set this up, select the main project file in the Project Navigator, select bookManager under Targets, and click the Build Phases tab as shown in Figure 6-5.

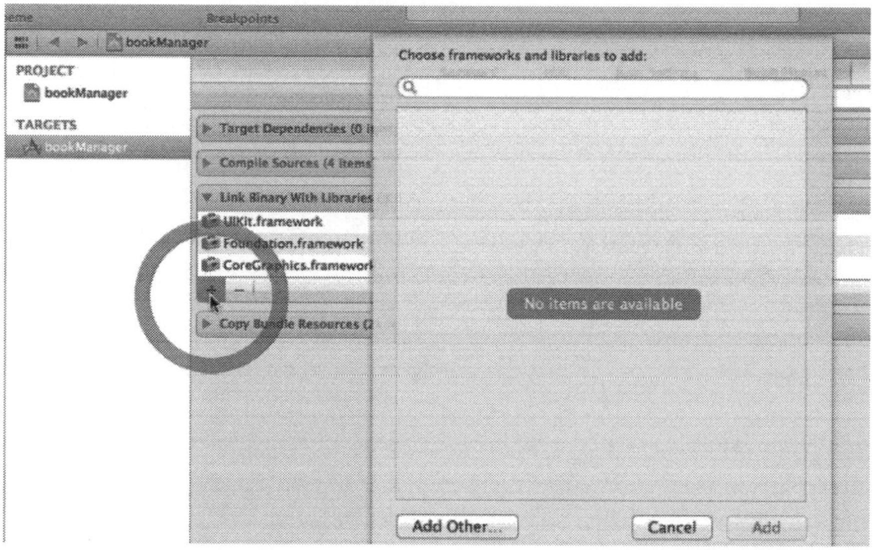

Figure 6-6. *Click the add button.*

6. Once the Build Phases tab is open go to the Link Binary with Libraries section and expand it. To add Core Data framework to this list, click the add (+) button as shown in Figure 6-6.

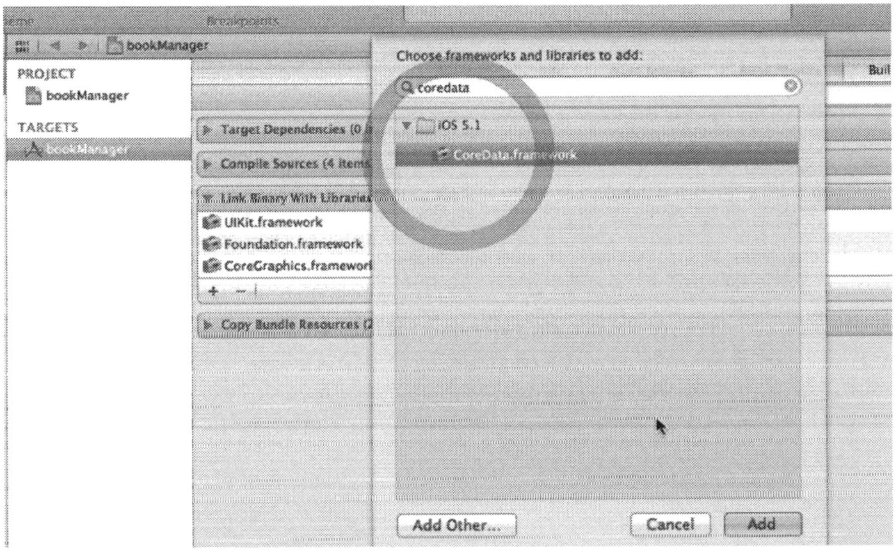

Figure 6-7. *Search for and then select CoreData framework.*

7. After you click +, enter *coredata* Into the search field. This will yield the `CoreData.framework` icon. Select it as shown in Figure 6-7 and then click Add.

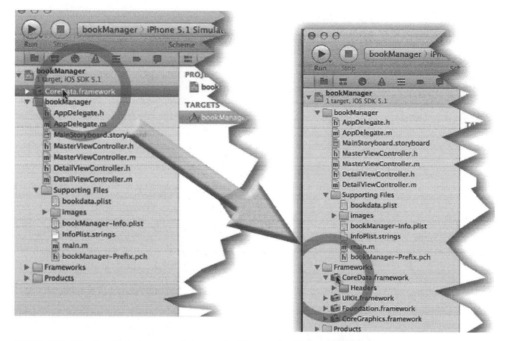

Figure 6-8. *The CoreData.framework is now inside your bookManager target.*

8. Once you've added the CoreData.framework, it will appear
    inside your bookManager target as shown in the left-hand image
    in Figure 6-8. Move it to the Frameworks folder as shown in the
    right-hand image in Figure 6-8.

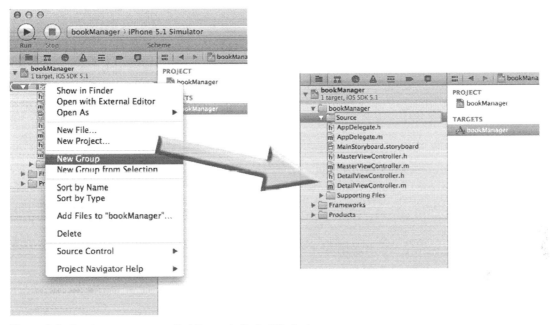

Figure 6-9. *Create a new group called Source in Project Navigator.*

9. While in the Project Navigator, go ahead and create a new subgroup inside the bookManger group called Source as shown in Figure 6-9. You'll use this in a moment.

MAGICALRECORD

Core Data is not the emphasis of this book, so we won't go too deeply into all its details. To make life easier, though, we'll bring in an open source helper that's being used extensively by many highly respected Xcoders—including our students who are now working at Apple. This open source framework makes working with Core Data incredibly easy. It's called MagicalRecord, and it's available on GitHub at https://github.com/magicalpanda/MagicalRecord. To download the zip file directly, you can use https://github.com/magicalpanda/MagicalRecord/zipball/master or you can get it from the assets folder you downloaded earlier for this chapter. Take our advice, though, and explore GitHub. If you don't already have a GitHub account, you can go ahead and get one. It's free!

> **NOTE:** Here's a resource for getting yourself familiar with MagicalRecord's setup:
> http://yannickloriot.com/2012/03/magicalrecord-how-to-make-
> programming-with-core-data-pleasant/.

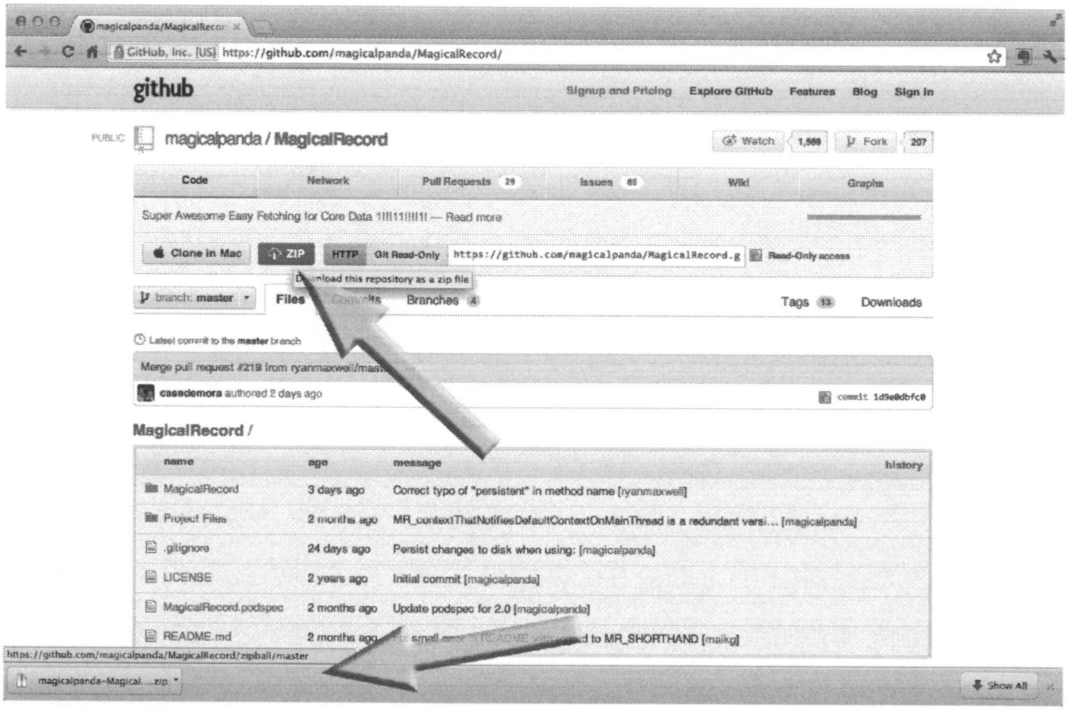

Figure 6-10. *Download MagicalRecord.*

10. Once you're inside GitHub, you can search for *MagicalRecord* or
MagicalPanda and you should arrive at `https://github.com/`
`magicalpanda/MagicalRecord`. Click the Zip button, and the
download will begin as indicated by the arrows in Figure 6-10.

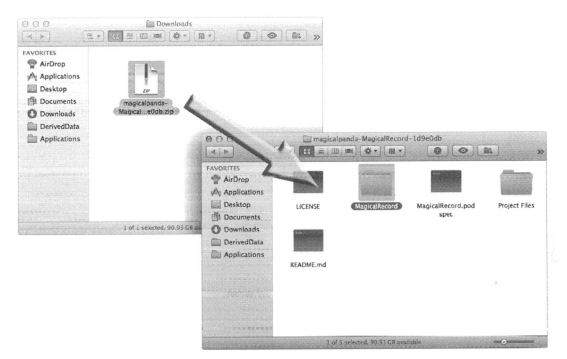

Figure 6-11. *Unzip and navigate to the MagicalRecord folder.*

11. Once you have successfully downloaded the `magicalpanda-MagicalRecord` zip file to your desktop, unzip it and navigate your way to the `MagicalRecord` folder. Select the folder as shown in Figure 6-11.

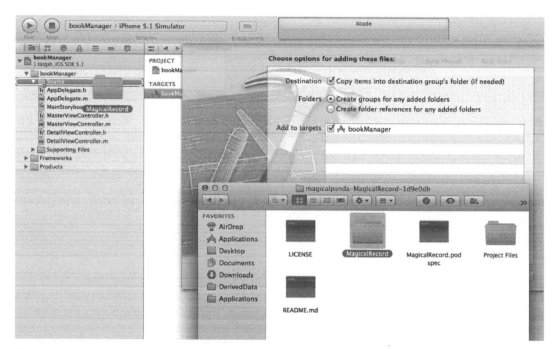

Figure 6-12. *Drag the MagicalRecord folder into your project.*

12. Drag the MagicalRecord folder into your project inside the
    Source folder you created in step 9, as shown in Figure 6-12,
    and select the same saving protocols that you did a few steps
    ago back in Figure 6-2.

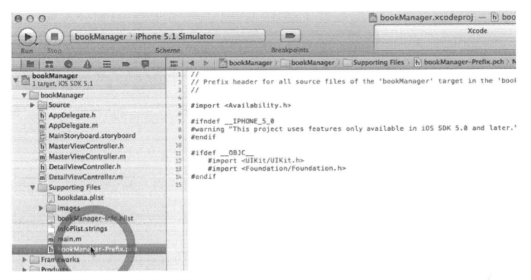

Figure 6-13. *Open the project's .pch file.*

13. Now that you've added the MagicalRecord source code to your project, you need to make it visible to your project so you can enjoy all the various extensions to Core Data that it provides. Essentially, MagicalRecord is a collection of categories that extend main Core Data functionality and simplify its usage. All the important header files necessary for it to function properly are listed in the CoreData+MagicalRecord.h file. You can make MagicalRecord visible to the entire project by simply putting this header file into the bookManager-Prefix.pch file. Navigate to the Supporting Files folder and click the .pch (pre-compile header) file to open it as shown in Figure 6-13.

> **NOTE:** Xcode has a high-level command called ProcessPCH that informs the compiler which header files it needs to precompile and include into the project based on information in .pch file. These pre-compiled headers are kept in a subdirectory of /Library/Caches and then automatically included in every file during compilation. The files included into prefix header are usually the files that rarely change, which can speed up the compilation process. This lets you include a file without adding an import statement to every file that uses it, thus making it globally "visible" throughout the entire project.

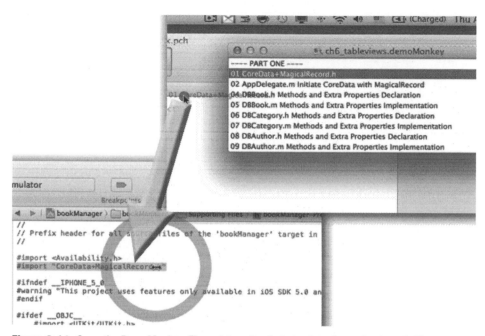

Figure 6-14. *Open the DemoMonkey file and drag the first step into the project's .pch file.*

14. Open the .demoMonkey file supplied with this chapter and keep it in a handy place on your desktop. Start by dragging the "01 CoreData + MagicalRecord.h" snippet from DemoMonkey into the bookManager - Prefix.pch file, immediately under the #import <Availability.h> line of code as shown in Figure 6-14 and as follows:

```
#import <Availability.h>
#import "CoreData+MagicalRecord.h
```

This header now makes the MagicalRecord framework available throughout the project without the need to import any additional files.

15. When adding a new library/framework to your project, it's good practice to immediately run or at least build it to check your work, as this is a critical juncture, and errors need to be immediately corrected before you continue to code. Click Run and make sure your project compiles successfully. Sometimes things change pretty quickly in the open source community, and fact is of course beyond our control. In this book we're using MagicalRecord-2.0.3-12-g1d9e0db. If you followed all the steps carefully, and your project doesn't compile at this point, check your version of MagicalRecord—if it doesn't match ours, replace your MagicalRecord source folder with the one provided in the Assets bundle for this chapter and try again.

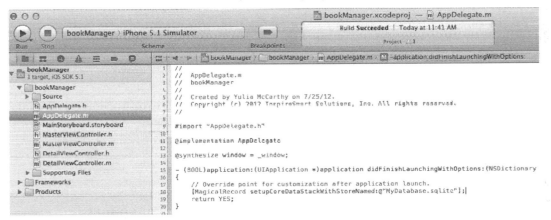

Figure 6-15. *Initialize the SQLite database.*

16. You're now going to embark on a task that frustrates many computer science students and is a huge obstacle for many Xcoders out there: connecting a database to Xcode. In this case you're going to set up a SQLite database using the MagicalRecord API, and you're going to love it! Open the AppDelegate.m file and drag the "02 AppDelegate.m initiate CoreData with MagicalRecord 1" snippet from DemoMonkey right before the return YES, as shown in Figure 6-15 and as follows:

```
#import "AppDelegate.h"
@implementation AppDelegate
@synthesize window = _window;
```

```
- (BOOL)application:(UIApplication *)application didFinishLaunching
...*)launchOptions
{
    // Override point for customization after application launch.
    [MagicalRecord setupCoreDataStackWithStoreNamed:@"MyDatabase.sqlite"];
    return YES; ...
```

> **NOTE:** With MagicalRecord you can initialize the entire SQLite database with a single line of code! It's not difficult—it just requires you to focus on exactly what you're doing and why you're doing it. So let's do it!

```
- (void)applicationWillEnterForeground:(UIApplication *)application
{
    // Called as part of the transition from the background to the inactive state; here you can undo many of the
        changes made on entering the background.
}

- (void)applicationDidBecomeActive:(UIApplication *)application
{
    // Restart any tasks that were paused (or not yet started) while the application was inactive. If the application
        was previously in the background, optionally refresh the user interface.
}

- (void)applicationWillTerminate:(UIApplication *)application
{
    // Called when the application is about to terminate. Save data if appropriate. See also
        applicationDidEnterBackground:.
    [MagicalRecord cleanUp];
}

@end
```

Figure 6-16. *Clean the persistence store.*

17. You also need to clean your persistence store in the applicationWillTerminate method. Do that by dragging the "03 AppDelegate.m initiate CoreData with Magic Record 2" snippet from DemoMonkey and placing it as shown in Figure 6-16.

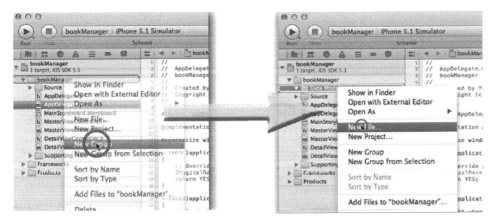

Figure 6-17. *Creating Data Model*

18. To create your data model, create data files inside a new group
    called Data Model. Starting with creating the group, right-click
    the bookManager folder and select New Group as shown on the
    left in Figure 6-17. Once the new group is created, a folder
    called New Group appears. Rename it Data Model. Right-click the
    Data Model folder and select New File as shown on the right in
    Figure 6-17.

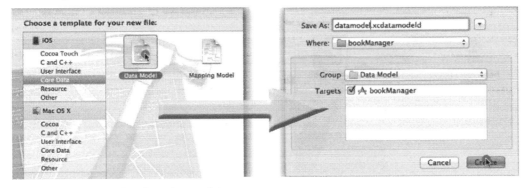

Figure 6-18. *Create a Core Data data model.*

19. A dialog box asks you to choose a template for your new file. By
    default the Cocoa Touch selection under iOS in the left-hand
    pane is selected. Ignore this and choose the Core Data ➤ Data
    Model template as shown on the left in Figure 6-18. A new
    dialog box asks you whether you would like to save the data
    model. Replace the default `Model.xcdatamodeld` with
    `datamodel.xcdatamodeld` as shown on the right in Figure 6-18.

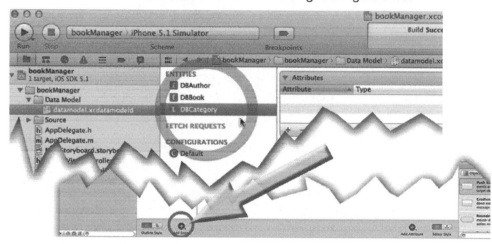

Figure 6-19. *Create your SQLite entities.*

20. Your database will hold a selection of Apress books that you'll
    define in terms of three *tables* (also called *entities*):

    ▓ The author

    ▓ The book

    ▓ The book's category (such as iOS, Android, web, and so
      on)

    You need to tell the SQLite database about that. Click the + icon
    at the bottom of the data model canvas and name the first entity
    `DBAuthor`. Repeat this two more times, naming the two new
    entities `DBBook` and `DBCategory` respectively, as illustrated in
    Figure 6-19.

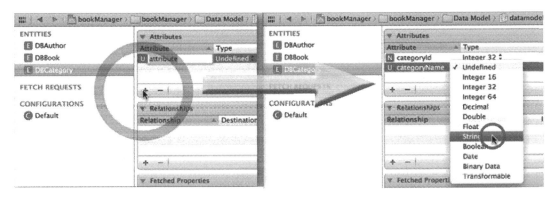

Figure 6-20. *Create the attributes for the Category records.*

21. After your three entities are created, you need to create the attributes for each entity. We'll go through the creation of the Category entity in detail and then assign the remaining two for you to do on your own with less help. With the DBCategory entity selected, click the + button as shown on the left in Figure 6-20. When you first add an attribute, the default name will simply be attribute. You need a way to give each category (such as iOS, Android, or web) a name and an ID. So, name the first attribute categoryId. Click the + button again and name the next attribute categoryName. Click the selection button to the right of the Type column on the categoryId row and choose Integer 32. Then click the selection button on the categoryName row and select String as shown on the right in Figure 6-20.

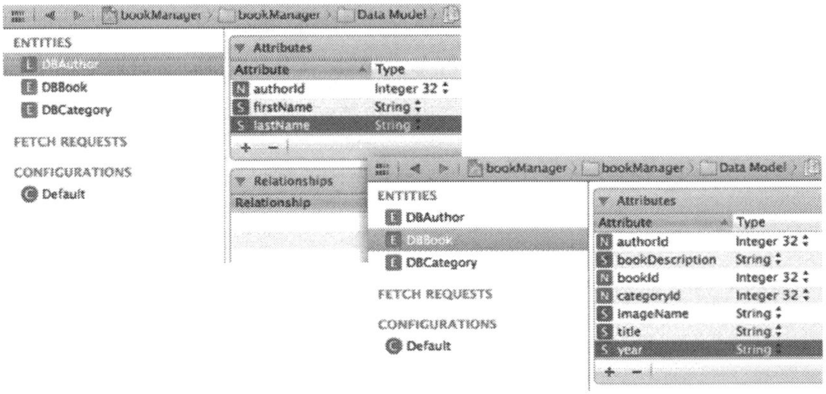

Figure 6-21. *Finish the attributes for DBAuthor and DBBook.*

22. Now you have to repeat the process for the author and book entities. For your Author entity, you only need an authorId, firstName, and lastName set of attributes. Make the authorId be Integer 32 and the first and last names String. For the Book entity you need seven attributes (of course, you could have many more, but for this exercise seven will suffice). You'll bring in the authorId and categoryId from DBAuthor and DBCategory as foreign keys, so you find a corresponding author and category for each book. You also need a unique bookId. And you need four more attributes describing each book: a short description, an image name associated with each book that you'll later link to the cover image of each book, the book title, and the book's publishing year. With that said, make authorId, bookId, and categoryId all as type Integer 32. Make bookDescription, imageName, title, and year all be type String as shown in Figure 6-21.

> **NOTE:** A *foreign key* points to another entity in the database and is a way to link different entities together. For example, you're linking a book to its author and its category using foreign keys.

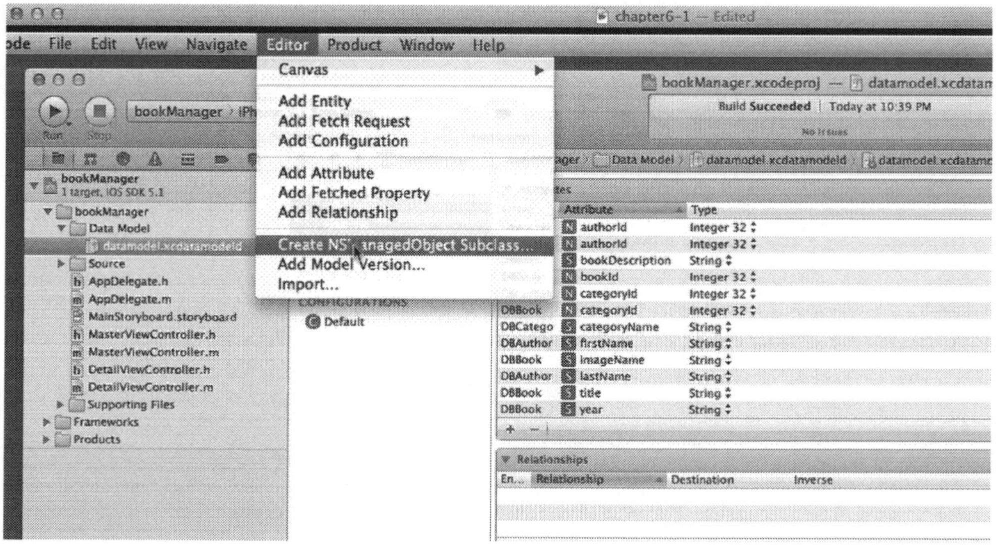

Figure 6-22. *Generate classes for all the entities.*

23. Now that you've defined the necessary tables and fields, you need to generate classes for all the entities so you can manipulate them from code. Select all three attributes DBAuthor, DBBook, and DBCategory by selecting the first one, holding down the Shift key, and clicking the last one. Click Editor and choose Create NSManagedObject Subclass as shown in Figure 6-22. An options dialog box will appear—press Enter or click the Create button, keeping the default settings.

Figure 6-23. *Success!*

24. You'll know you've been successful when you see header and implementation files for all your entities neatly lined up inside your Data Model folder. This may not seem like a big deal now, but when you have a few hundred entities in you database, having Xcode automatically create these is a miracle of sorts. You can now add custom methods to each of these entities. Make sure your Data Model folder, entities, and attributes look exactly like ours in Figure 6-23 before moving on.

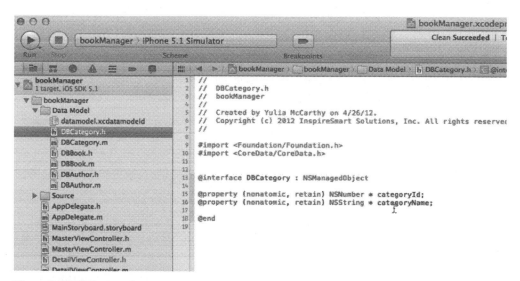

Figure 6-24. *Before moving on …*

25. Also before moving on, you should check a couple of things so you're aware of what you've created so far. Click the DBCategory.h file. As you can see in Figure 6-24, Xcode has generated all the properties for you based on the data fields you've specified in your data model over the last few steps. What you'll be doing over the next few steps is adding methods to these properties so that you can retrieve the data.

> **NOTE:** Over the next six steps, all the methods you'll be adding essentially do the same thing: they either create or delete a new entity with the values provided in a dictionary or they allow you to retrieve other data based on foreign key relationships, such as books wanting authors' names and authors wanting category names.

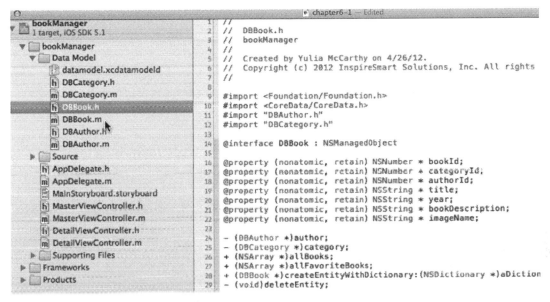

Figure 6-25. *Setting up the DBBook.h file*

26. Select DBBook.h in the Project Navigator. Drag in the "04
    DBBook.h Methods and Extra Properties Declaration" snippet
    from DemoMonkey and place it right before the @end. Then type
    in two #imports, for DBAuthor.h and DBCategory.h, as shown in
    Figure 6-25 and as follows:

```
#import <Foundation/Foundation.h>
#import <CoreData/CoreData.h>
#import "DBAuthor.h"
#import "DBCategory.h"

@interface DBBook : NSManagedObject
...
@property (nonatomic, retain) NSString * imageName;
- (DBAuthor *)author;
- (DBCategory *)category;
...
- (void)deleteEntity;
@end
```

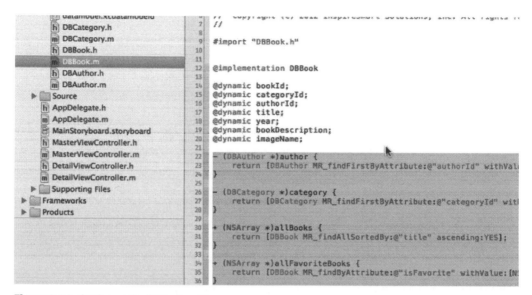

Figure 6-26. *Setting up the DBBook.m file*

27. Navigate to DBBook.m. Drag in the "05 DBBook.m Methods and Extra Properties Implementation" snippet from DemoMonkey and place it right before the @end as shown in Figure 6-26.

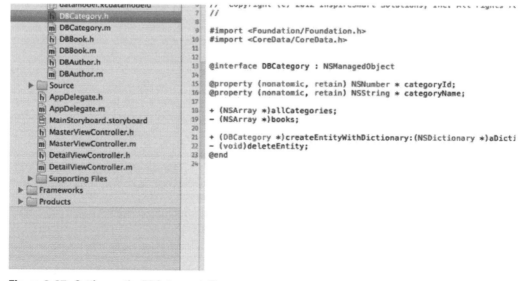

Figure 6-27. *Setting up the DBCategory.h file*

28. Open DBCategory.h and drag in the "06 DBCategory.h Methods and Extra Properties Declaration" snippet from DemoMonkey. Place it between the last @property and the @end as shown in Figure 6-27.

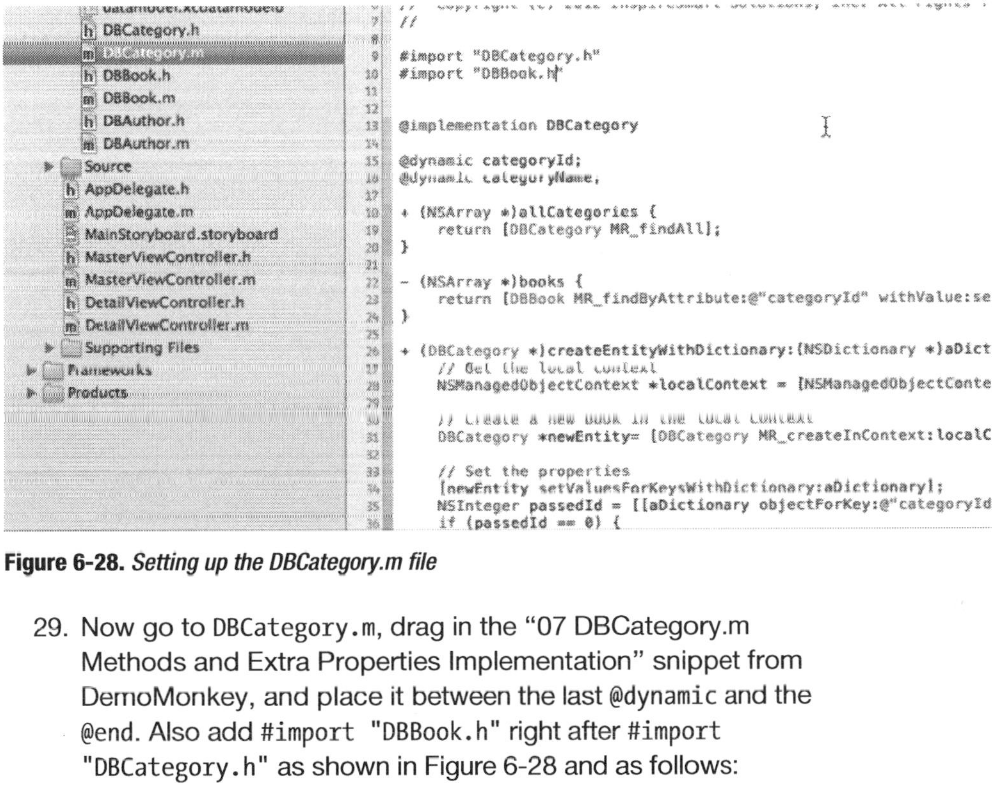

Figure 6-28. *Setting up the DBCategory.m file*

29. Now go to DBCategory.m, drag in the "07 DBCategory.m Methods and Extra Properties Implementation" snippet from DemoMonkey, and place it between the last @dynamic and the @end. Also add #import "DBBook.h" right after #import "DBCategory.h" as shown in Figure 6-28 and as follows:

```
#import "DBCategory.h"
#import "DBBook.h"
```

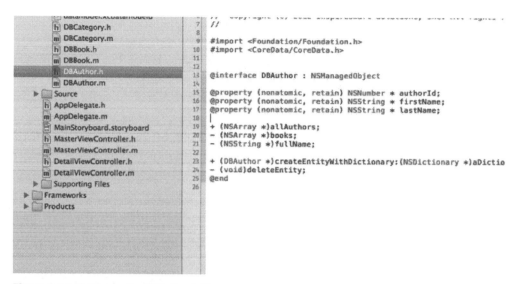

Figure 6-29. *Setting up the DBAuthor.h file*

30. Open DBAuthor.h and drag in the "08 DBAuthor.h Methods and
Extra Properties Declaration" snippet from DemoMonkey. Place
it between the last @property and the @end as shown in
Figure 6-29.

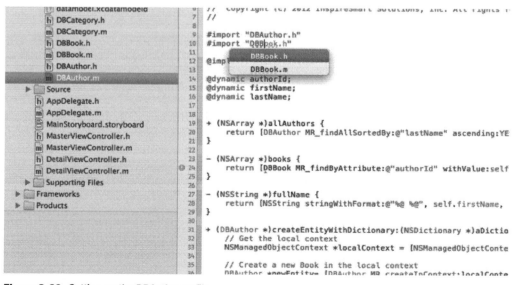

Figure 6-30. *Setting up the DBAuthor.m file*

31. Navigate to DBAuthor.m. Drag in the "09 DBAuthor.m Methods and Extra Properties Implementation" snippet from DemoMonkey and place it between the last @dynamic and the @end. Also add #import "DBBook.h" right after the #import "DBAuthor.h" as shown in Figure 6-30 and as follows:

```
#import "DBAuthor.h"
#import "DBBook.h"
```

That's it! You've got through the setup and are ready to get on with designing the app using Storyboarding in Chapter 7.

Mastering Table Views with Storyboarding: Designing the Flow

You've finished setting up the foundation for the bookManager Master-Detail Application (in step 1 of 3, Chapter 6) and are ready to move on to step 2 of the app in this chapter. You've brought in all the images and the info about the books and set up the SQLite database. Cool! Well, if you think *that* was cool, wait until you see what we have in store for you as we lay out the entire app's workflow in the Storyboard. Here in Chapter 7 you'll be routing and connecting elements with such ease it will amaze you—particularly if you ever tried that sans Storyboard.

Step 2: Storyboarding the App

Okay—let's go.

Configuring the Master Scene

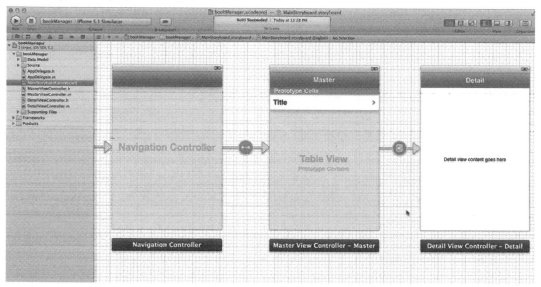

Figure 7-1. *Open the Storyboard.*

1. Now that you've set up your data model, you can start designing your interface. Open the Storyboard. You will immediately see that Xcode has already created a basic hierarchy of the Master-Detail Application for you. A basic Navigation Controller is connected to a Master View Controller that segues to a Detail View Controller as shown in Figure 7-1. You'll be using this template to fulfill your requirements.

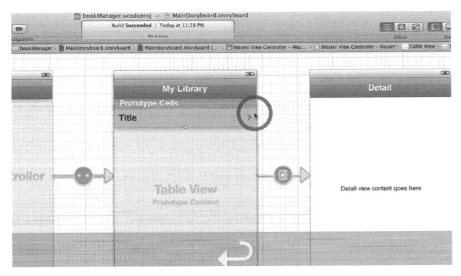

Figure 7-2. *Rename the title to My Library.*

2. Double-click the title Master on the header of the Master View Controller, rename it My Library, and then click once on the prototype cell to select it as shown in Figure 7-2.

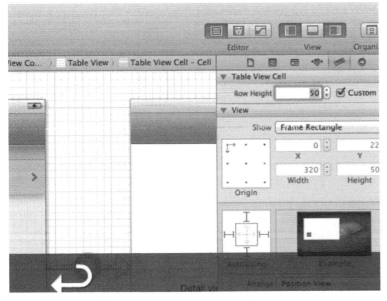

Figure 7-3. *Change the Row Height of the cell to 50.*

3. Select the Utilities View and click the Size Inspector. Enter *50* for the Row Height attribute as shown in Figure 7-3 and press Enter.

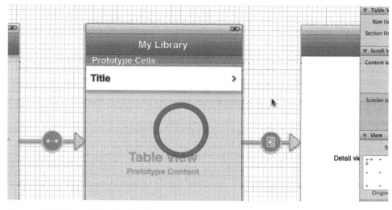

Figure 7-4. *Select the Table View.*

4. The scene you're working on is going to be the first view in your app. In this case, it will let the user choose between the two top hierarchies of your library: Books and Authors. So, you know exactly how many cells you're going to display in your Table View: two cells. That makes it a great candidate for being a Static Table View—a wonderful new feature only available with Storyboarding that allows you to lay out the content of your Table View statically in Storyboard, display it at the runtime, and even transition to other views when user selects a cell, all without writing any code at all! Let's convert the Table View to static format: select the Table View by clicking below the prototype cell as shown in Figure 7-4.

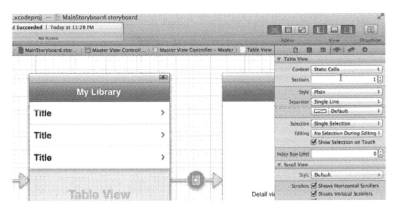

Figure 7-5. *Change the Table View Content type.*

5. Select the Attributes Inspector and change the Content type from Dynamic Prototypes to Static Cells. You'll see three identical cells appear as shown in Figure 7-5.

NOTE: Dynamic Table Views display dynamic content, and in that case Table View is a large (and sometimes unbounded) number of rows. Dynamic Table Views use reusable Dynamic Cell Prototypes to display quite large data sets very efficiently. Static Table Views are basically "what you see is what you get." With static content, the number of rows in a Table View is a known and fixed number, so you can design all rows in the Interface Builder. Note that Static Table Views can only be created using Storyboards and must be controlled by a Table View Controller subclass.

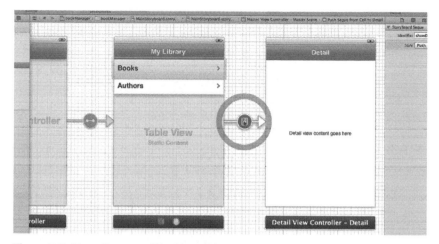

Figure 7-6. *Name the roots of the hierarchical tree.*

6. Click one of the three cells and delete it so that only two remain. Now let's think about things. You'll have two trees of data, flowing from looking at the database in terms of Books, or looking at the database in terms of Authors. This means your root node has two choices: Books and Authors. Change the label text of the two cells from Title to Books and Authors as shown in Figure 7-6. Now you're going to delete the segue connecting the Master View Controller to the Detail View Controller: click the segue, as shown in Figure 7-6, to select it and then delete it.

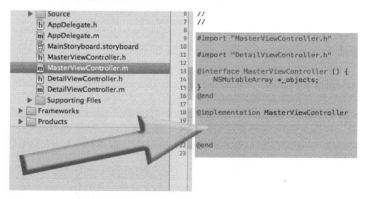

Figure 7-7. *Delete the code between @end and @implementation in MasterViewController.m—the arrow indicates the place where the code used to be.*

7. Before moving on to the next step, there's one last thing you must do for your Static Table View to display properly. You need to delete some of the existing code for the Master View Controller. Xcode created some code for you in `MasterViewController.m` as part of the Master-Detail Application template. This code implements the `UITableViewDelegate` and `UITableViewDataSource` protocol methods, which will override the Static Table View content you defined in the Storyboard if they are present. So click the `MasterViewController.m` file in the Project Navigator, select all the code between `@implementation` and `@end`, and remove it as shown in Figure 7-7.

> **NOTE:** Because this is a static table it doesn't require any additional code. Later you'll create segues from each of the static cells Books and Authors to their respective View Controllers you want them to transition to. That's why for now you won't have a segue connecting the Master View Controller to the Detail View Controller.

Designing the Top Level Views: Categories Scene

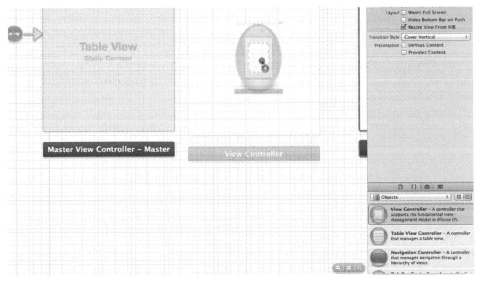

Figure 7-8. *Drag in a new View Controller.*

1. According to the app's flow, you want to display a list of available categories when the user taps the Books cell. Thus you'll need an additional View Controller that will display the various categories for the books. Now you'll move the current Detail View Controller, which you disconnected from the Master View Controller in the previous step, over to the right. You can just see the left-hand side of it on the right in Figure 7-8. You're doing this to make space for the new View Controller you're going to drag in. Once you have enough space, drag in a new View Controller from your Object Library as shown in Figure 7-8.

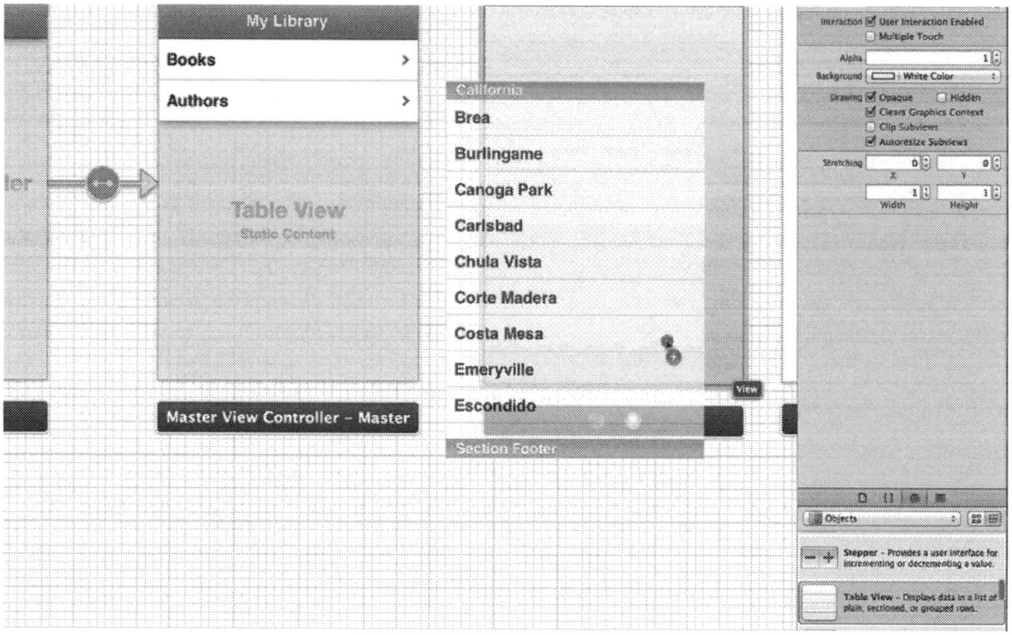

Figure 7-9. *Drag in a Table View.*

2. Find a Table View in the Object Library and drag it onto your new View Controller as shown in Figure 7-9.

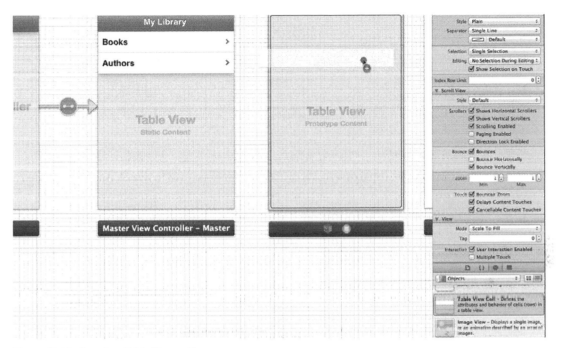

Figure 7-10. *Drag in a Table View cell.*

3. Now drag a Table View cell into your new Table View as shown
    in Figure 7-10.

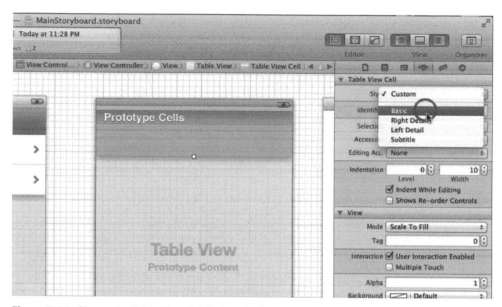

Figure 7-11. *Change the Table View Cell Style to Basic.*

4. For this Table View you'll use Dynamic Prototypes. In fact, your Table View will display three different types of cells. One will be a basic style that will just display a label with a category name for each category you have in your database. There will be as many cells of this kind in the Table View as you have categories in your database. A second type of cell will display the "All books" label that when the user taps the cell shows all the books in the database regardless of category. This cell will be displayed at all times at the end of the list of categories. The third type of cell will be an "Add new" cell that gives the user an ability to add new category to the database. This cell will also be displayed all the time and is always the very last cell of the Table View. Modify your Table View Prototype content to achieve this. First, click the cell you've already added and change its style to Basic as shown in Figure 7-11.

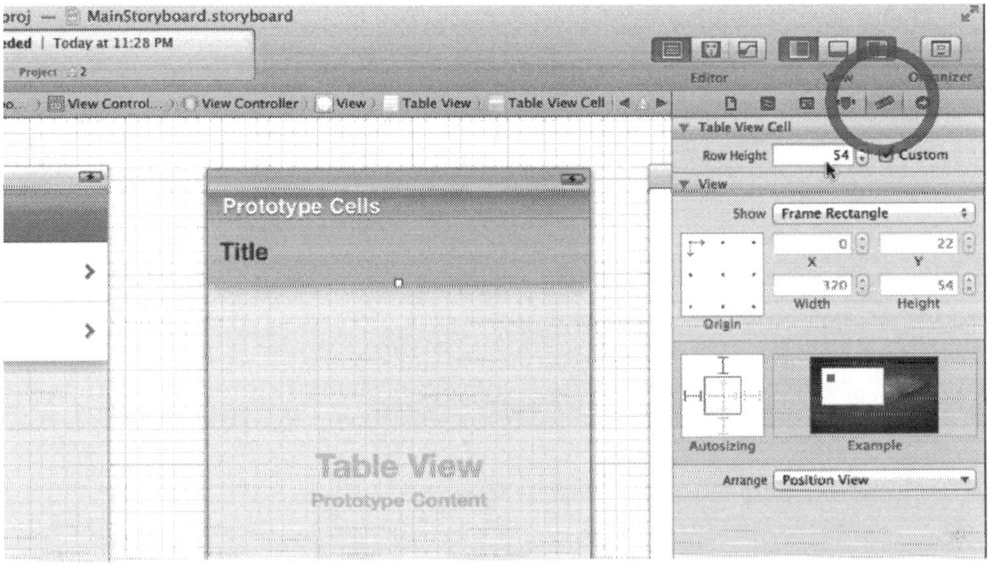

Figure 7-12. *Change Cell's Row Height.*

5. Click the Size Inspector as shown in Figure 7-12 and then change the Row Height from whatever your height is to 50 (we had manually adjusted ours to 54, but change whatever height you have in your case to 50).

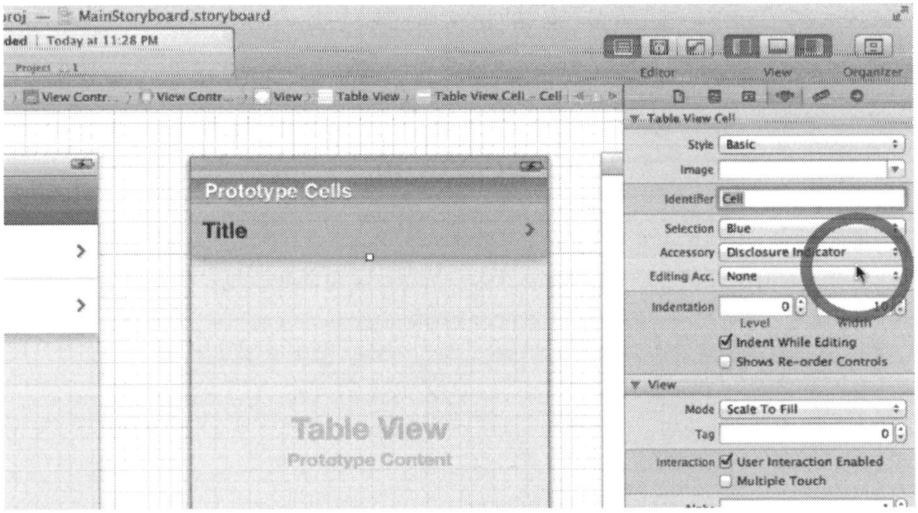

Figure 7-13. *Change the Identifier and Accessory attributes.*

6. Go back to the Attributes Inspector and change the Identifier to a name that will mean something in your code—let's call it *Cell*, because this is the standard cell prototype you'll be reusing to display your categories. Now click the Accessory option and from the drop-down menu select Disclosure Indicator as shown in Figure 7-13. Double-click the Title label inside the Table View Cell prototype and rename it "Category name." Then make sure the cell you just configured is selected (highlighted blue) and press ⌘+C to copy it.

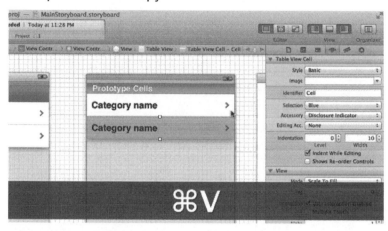

Figure 7-14. *Duplicate the first cell.*

7. Press ⌘+V and paste the duplicated "Category name" cell as shown in Figure 7-14. Double-click the new cell you just pasted and change its name to "All books," because this cell takes the user to a page containing all the Apress books. The regular "Category name" cell takes the user to books that belong to iOS, Android, or any other category you may choose. Once you've changed the name to "All books," change its Identifier (which is still showing up as Cell from the paste you made of the first cell) to *AllCell*. Once your identifier shows AllCell, continue to the next step.

> **NOTE:** As you've now seen, the Storyboard makes it incredibly easy to copy cells and modify them to your needs as you create prototypes. It's key that you wrap your head around this concept and use it as much as you can. We still see experienced coders coding this by hand because they just haven't "gotten it"—how Storyboarding makes it so easy to create new prototypes.

Figure 7-15. *Create the "Add new" cell.*

8. You need to make one more cell. This new cell will be the one that allows the user to add a new category that that can be anything the user wants. Think about this for a second: you're going to create a cell that in the future, without you or the user doing any coding, can be named Best Apress Books, Monkey, or anything else—amazing! Do what you did in Figure 7-14: click either of the two cells you already have to select it and press ⌘+C to copy it. Press ⌘+V and rename the cell's label to "Add new." To make it look different, let's have some fun and change a few properties. Set the Accessory type to Detail Disclosure as shown in Figure 7-15. You'll have to rename the Identifier to something unique, because this is a special cell, so change it to *AddCell*.

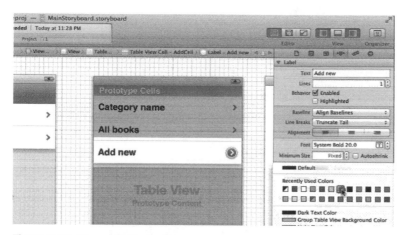

Figure 7-16. *Change the text color.*

9. Change the color of the "Add new" text so that the user can easily see that "Add new" is different from the other options. Click once on the text "Add new" and change the color to blue as shown in Figure 7-16.

NOTE: Make sure you're saving your work as you go along!

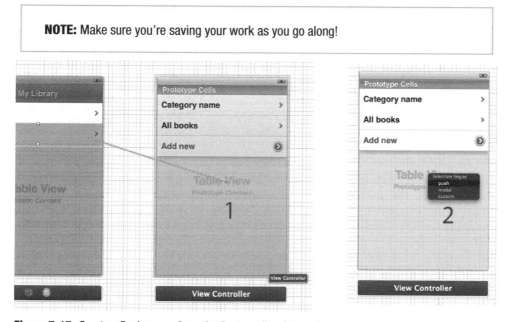

Figure 7-17. *Create a Push segue from the Books cell to Categories.*

10. We are now ready to create a Push segue from the Books cell of the Master View Controller to the scene you've just set up. Because you have a Static Table View in the Master, you can initiate segues right from the cell itself. So click the Books cell in Master and Control-drag from it to the View Controller (see 1 in Figure 7-17) that will display our categories, release it, and choose Push (see 2 in Figure 7-17) from the pop-up.

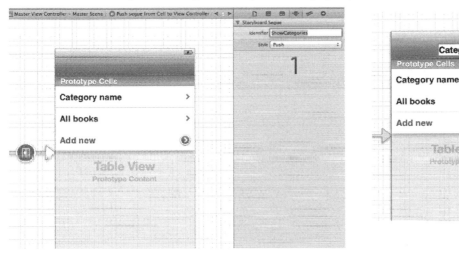

Figure 7-18. *Set the segue Identifier and change the destination view's title.*

11. Select the new segue and set its Identifier option in the Attributes Inspector to *ShowCategories* (see 1 in Figure 7-18). Also double-click the destination View Controller's Navigation Bar and set its title to *Categories* (see 2 in Figure 7-18).

> **NOTE:** An *identifier* is a string that your application uses to distinguish one segue from another. You assign different identifiers to each segue so that the prepareForSegue:sender: method in your Source View Controller can tell them apart and prepare each segue appropriately. You always assign identifiers to your segues.

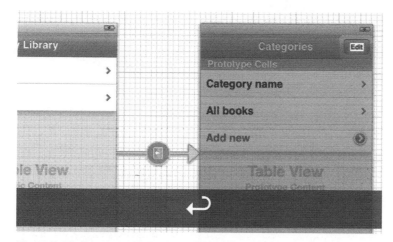

Figure 7-19. *Create an Edit Bar button item.*

12. As mentioned, you're going to let the user edit the Table View and remove cells. This means you need a button on the Navigation Bar to switch the Table View into editing mode. Drag a Bar button item from your Object Library onto the right side of your Navigation Bar. Double-click its default title *Item* and change the text to *Edit* as shown in Figure 7-19.

Designing the Top Level Views: Authors Scene

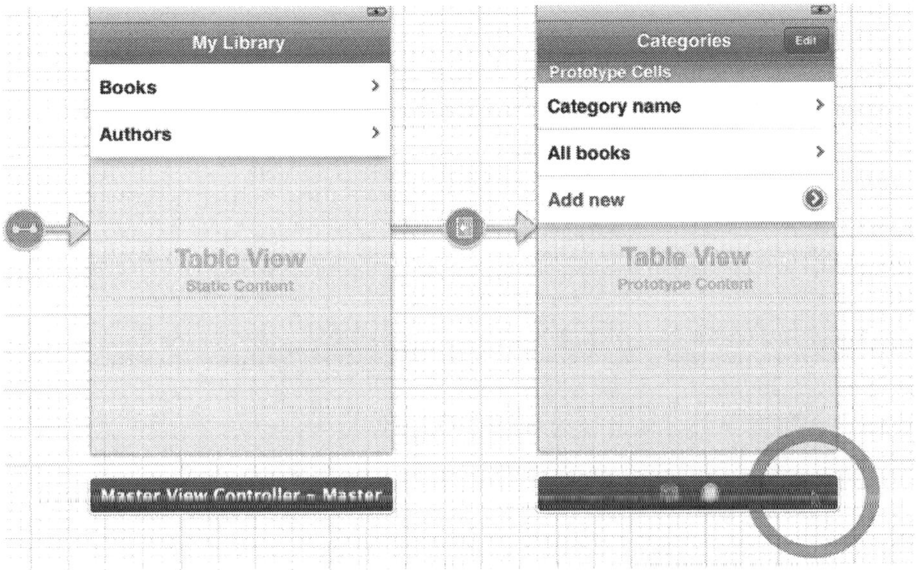

Figure 7-20. *Select the Categories Scene and copy it.*

1. You're finished with the first of your two Root Views: Books that leads to Categories. The next view you need is Authors. That view will be very similar to the Categories View you just made. To save time you can simply copy this scene and paste it into your Storyboard by clicking the scene as shown in Figure 7-20 and pressing ⌘+C.

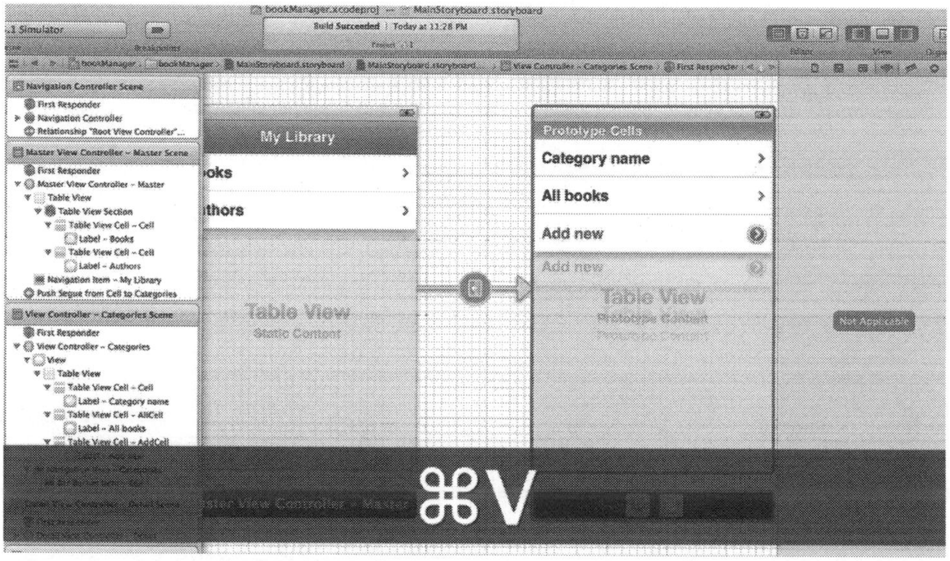

Figure 7-21. *Paste the new scene.*

2. Click once on the Storyboard background (indicated by the blue graph paper look) and press ⌘+V as shown in Figure 7-21.

> **NOTE:** It will look like nothing happened at first because it's been pasted right on top of the original scene.

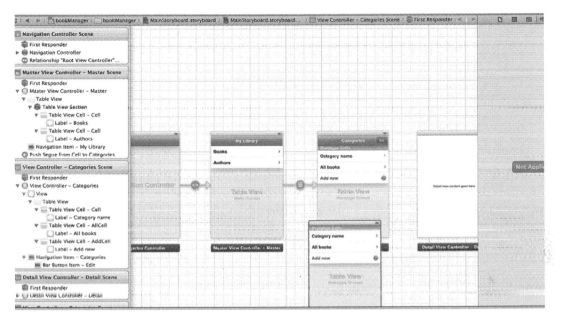

Figure 7-22. *Zoom out and reorganize.*

3. You need to drag the new scene you created, which is currently
    residing on top of the Categories Scene. First zoom out and
    then drag the new scene as shown in Figure 7-22 to a position
    directly below the Categories Scene.

> **NOTE:** Strictly speaking, it's correct to call it the [YourName] View Controller Scene.
> However, in various Xcode communities some have chosen to shorten the name to
> either View or Scene. Hence, even within Apple, there are arguments on this matter.
> Xcode books, blogs, and conference proceedings also don't yet agree. We refer to
> them using both terms in order to get you used to people referring to it either way.

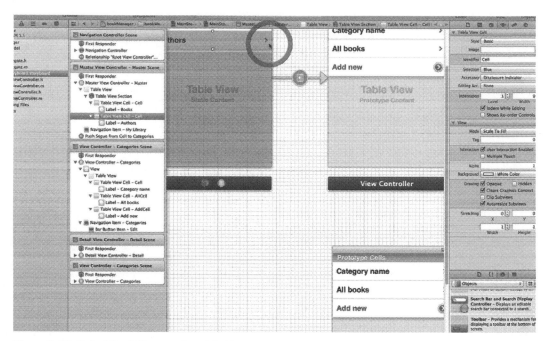

Figure 7-23. *Select the Authors static cell in Master.*

4. Zoom back in, click the Authors cell in the Master View Controller as shown in Figure 7-23, and begin to Control-drag toward the newly added scene.

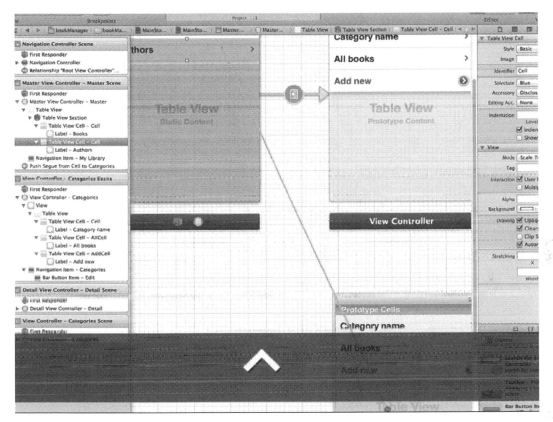

Figure 7-24. *Connect the Authors cell of Master View Controller to the Authors Scene.*

5. Continue Control-dragging from the Master View Controller and
   release it when you get to the Table View of the Authors Scene
   as shown In Figure 7-24.

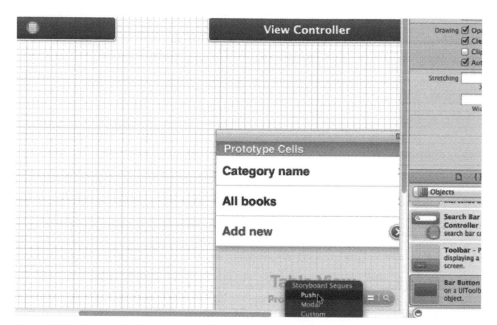

Figure 7-25. *Create a Push segue.*

6. When you release, select the Push option from the Storyboard Segues menu as shown in Figure 7-25. Select the segue and set its Identifier property to *ShowAuthors* in the Attributes Inspector as you did for the ShowCategories segue in step 17.

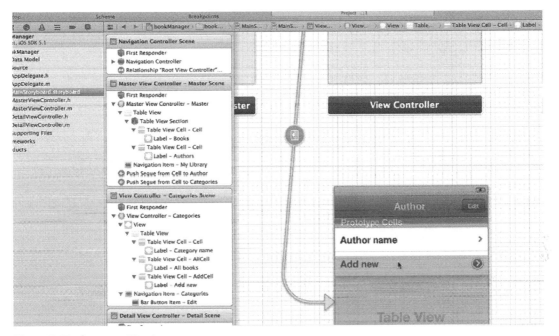

Figure 7-26. *Some modifications*

7. Change the Categories title on the Navigation Bar to Authors, and the "Category name" label of the top prototype cell to "Author name." Also, because we don't need the "All Books" cell here, delete it. Your Authors Scene should now look just like the one shown in Figure 7-26.

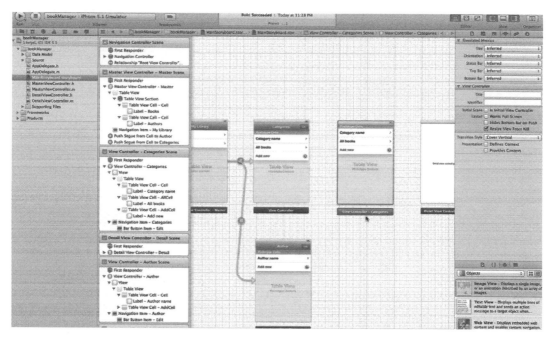

Figure 7-27. *Create another View Controller.*

8. The next view is the one to display a list of books, belonging either to a category or author that the user selects. This means you have to create another View Controller. It's going to be very similar to the one you just copied for the Authors Scene—you can use it again as a basis for this new View Controller. You still have a copy of the Categories Scene in your clipboard unless you've copied something else since, so just click anywhere on the blue Storyboard canvas and press ⌘+V to paste it again (otherwise copy the Categories Scene to the clipboard again and paste it onto the Storyboard canvas). Zoom out, moving the Detail View Controller over to the right-hand side to make enough room to position the new View Controller just to the left of it as shown in Figure 7-27.

Laying Out the Main Book List View: Books Scene

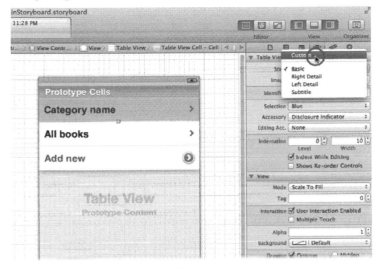

Figure 7-28. *Create the Custom cell.*

1. In this view users see a list of books in which each row displays the title and a thumbnail of the book cover. You dragged in some book images in Chapter 6. What we need to do here is change the "Category name" cell, which is now a Basic cell, to a Custom cell you can add custom UI elements to. Click the cell and in the Attributes Inspector change the Style from Basic to Custom as shown in Figure 7-28.

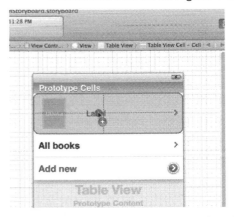

Figure 7-29. *Drag one UIImageView and three labels into the Custom cell.*

2. With the top cell selected, open the Size Inspector and change the row height to 87 to accommodate the height of the book cover images. You also need a `UIImageView` to hold the book image, so drag a `UIImageView` into the cell. Make the Image View width 50 and the Image View height 66 (using either the Size Inspector or your mouse). You also need to display three information labels for the book cover: title, publishing year, and author. Drag a label to the right of the Image View and, after configuring it, copy and paste it twice. Figure 7-29 shows the first label being dragged onto the cell.

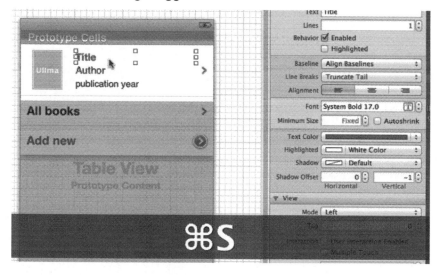

Figure 7-30. *Copy and paste the first label.*

3. Copy and paste the first labels two times and align the labels under each other nicely. Drag the right side of each label over so that it fills the majority of the cell—or make them all 200 points in width using the Size Inspector. With the top label selected, go back to the Attributes Inspector, uncheck the Autoshrink option, change the font to System Bold 17.0, and change its color to blue. Then change the text of each label to "Title," "Author." and "publication year" respectively as shown in Figure 7-30. We also changed the font size of *publication year* to be System 15.0 because it just looked a little too big. Save your work.

NOTE: You're adding text to prototype cells solely to help the design process. Because it's a prototype cell, all the label titles will be assigned dynamically during the runtime, but adding placeholder data to our elements helps guide you through the layout and customization process.

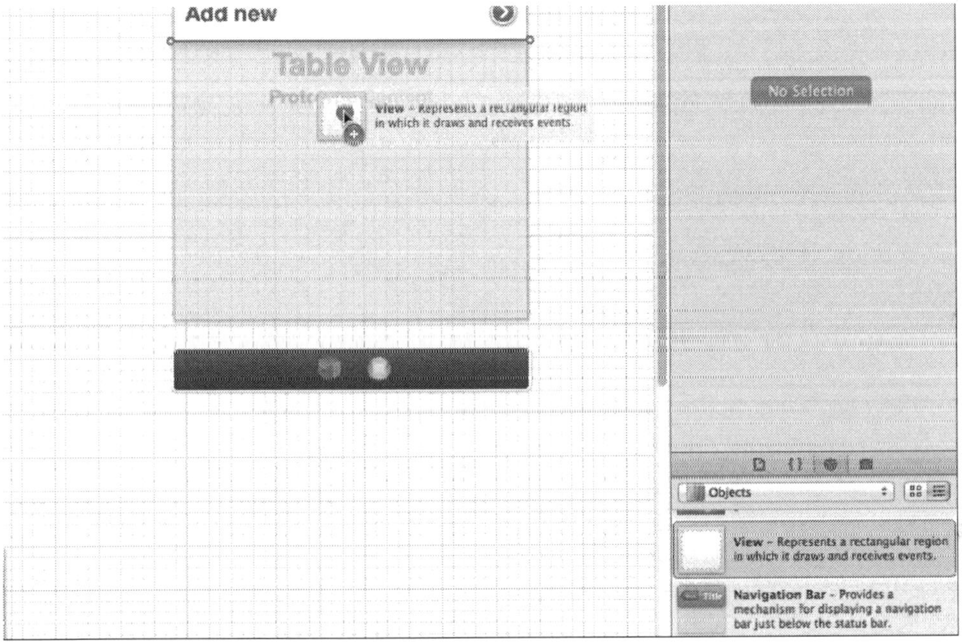

Figure 7-31. *Adding a subview*

4. You also want the ability to show, at all times, a total count of the books you have in any category. You can easily achieve that by placing an arbitrary UIView at the bottom of our Table View contents, underneath the prototype cells. Drag a basic UIView from the Object Library into the Table View as shown in Figure 7-31.

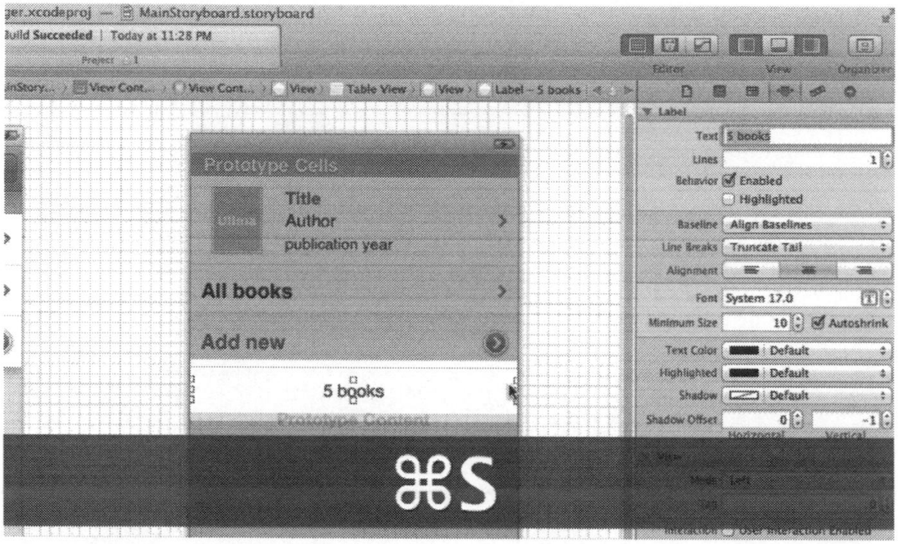

Figure 7-32. *Enter temporary text into the label.*

5. You also need to add a text label to tell the user what the count is, so drag a UILabel from the Object Library and place it inside the UIView you added in the previous step. Pull the handles out on each side to cover the entire view, center the text, and enter the temporary text "5 books" as shown in Figure 7-32. (You may then want to change the text color to Dark Gray Color and the font to System Bold 15.)

NOTE: This footer view can contain anything, such as an image, a button, a text view, a map—whatever the application needs. Using Storyboards makes it easy to lay out diverse application UIs without having to code much behind the Storyboard.

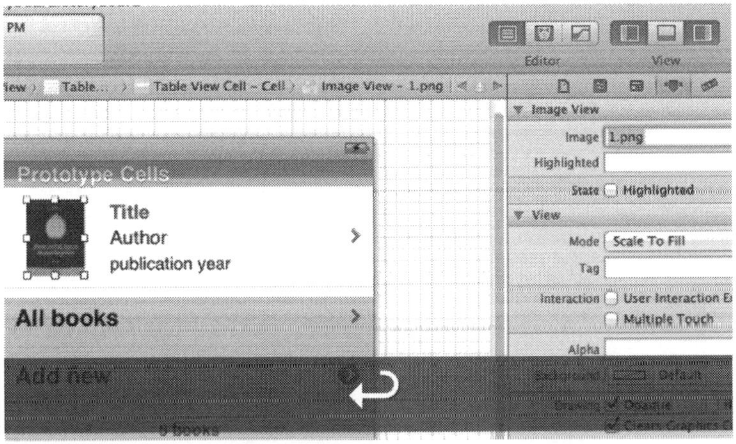

Figure 7-33. *See what an image will look like.*

6. To get even better visual overview of the appearance of your custom cell at runtime, check out an example book cover image. When the app is running, it will retrieve the images for each book based on data stored in the SQLite database. But for now, click the blank Image View, locate the Image property in the Attributes Inspector, and enter *1.png* or choose any other image filename from your Supporting Files images folder. If you do select the 1.png file, then it should look similar to what's shown in Figure 7-33. While you're in the Attributes Inspector, also change the Background color of the Image View to Light Gray, just so it stays visible in case you don't have an image to display for some of the books.

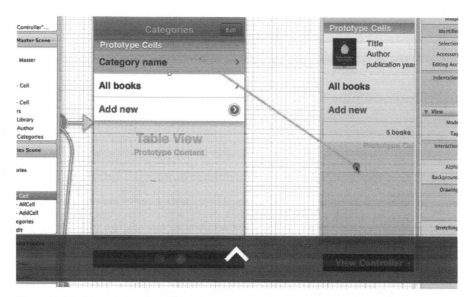

Figure 7-34. *Connect the "Category name" prototype cell to the newly created scene.*

7. You want the book list to display a specific list of books whenever a user taps a cell in the parent View Controller (the "Category name," "All books," and "Author name" cells). This means you still need to make segues from each of the three parent cells to your newly created View Controller Scene. Select "Category name" prototype cell and Control-drag to the newly created View Controller as shown in Figure 7-34. When you release the segue connector, choose Push from the Storyboard Segues menu.

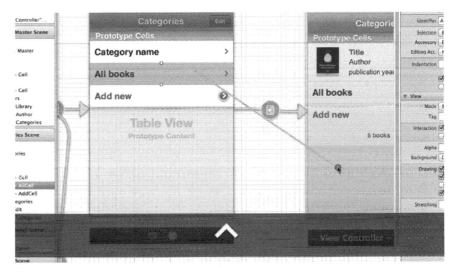

Figure 7-35. *Connect the "All books" cell to the newly created scene.*

8. Select the "All books" cell and Control-drag to the same View
    Controller as in the previous step, which is shown in Figure
    7-35. Make it a Push segue as well.

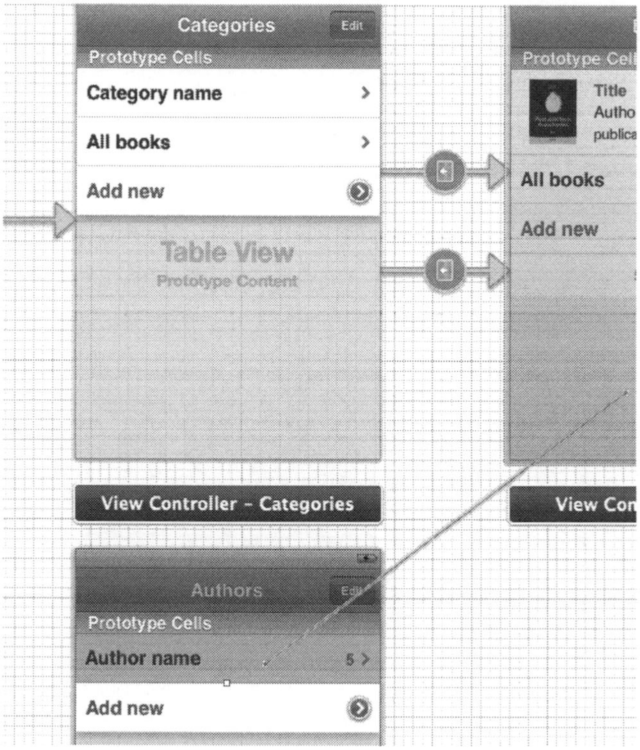

Figure 7-36. *Connect the "Author name" prototype cell to the newly created scene.*

9. Scroll down to the Authors Scene, select the "Author name" cell, and Control-drag up to the newly created View Controller as shown in Figure 7-36. When you release the segue connector, choose the Push option from the Storyboard Segues menu.

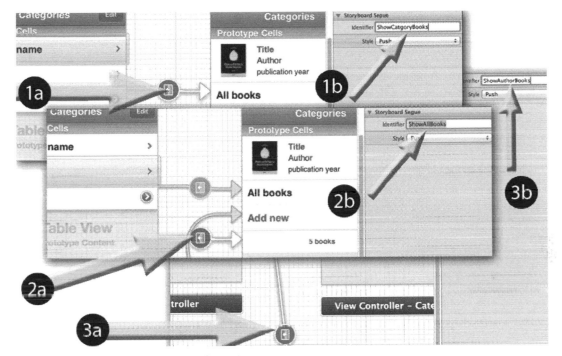

Figure 7-37. *Specify unique identifiers for each segue.*

10. Now that you've connected the segues, you need to do one
    more step because you have to pass additional data to the book
    list View Controller. You need to specify an identifier for each
    segue so you can access them later when you code. Select the
    "Category name" cell segue (1a in Figure 7-37) and in the
    Attributes Inspector, enter *ShowCategoryBooks* as its Identifier
    property (1b in Figure 7-37). Select the "All books" cell segue
    (2a in Figure 7-37) and set its Identifier to *ShowAllBooks* (2b in
    Figure 7-37). Select the "Author name" cell segue (3a in Figure
    7-37) and set the Identifier property to *ShowAuthorBooks* (3b in
    Figure 7-37).

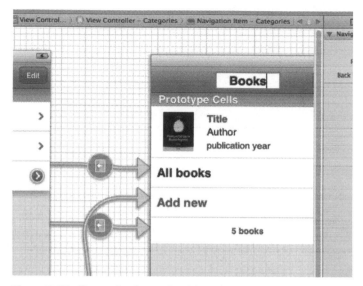

Figure 7-38. *Change the Categories title to Books.*

11. As you may have noticed, your book list view still displays the
title Categories because you created it by copying the
Categories scene and modifying it. Let's change it to match its
contents. Double-click the text and replace it with *Books* as
shown in Figure 7-38. You may also get rid of the "All books"
cell prototype, as it doesn't apply to this View Controller
(although it won't cause any problems if you leave it as is; that
cell will just never get used for this Table View).

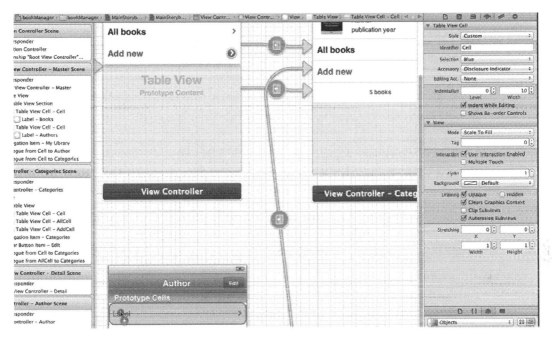

Figure 7-39. *Modifying the "Author name" cell*

12. Let's make the Authors Scene a bit more interesting by making each author's cell display a count, at the end of the cell, of how many books by this author are in the database. (In real life you may create, for example, an inventory app wherein your client can immediately see the tally of items in stock. This data will be calculated on the back end and displayed inside each cell. This step is a perfect example to teach you how to do that.) So, modify the "Author name" cell. Select it and in the Attributes Inspector change the Style property from Basic to Custom. Also drag a label onto the cell, placing it on its left-hand side as shown in Figure 7-39.

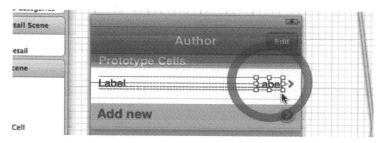

Figure 7-40. *Adjust the two labels.*

13. Drag a second label (this one will hold the count) onto the right-hand side of the cell as shown in Figure 7-40. With it still selected, in the Attributes Inspector set its Text attribute to any number, so you can remember its role later. We gave ours the number 5. Also, align the text to the right, make it System Bold 16.0 font, and change the font color to blue.

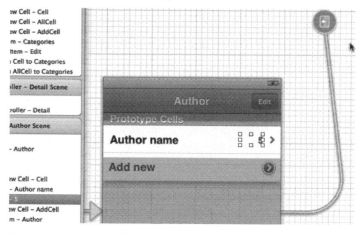

Figure 7-41. *Change Label to Author.*

14. Now select the first label you brought in, make it wide enough to take all the space up to the beginning of the count label, set its font to System Bold 20, and change its text to *Author name* as shown in Figure 7-41.

Storyboarding the Detail View: Book Detail Scene

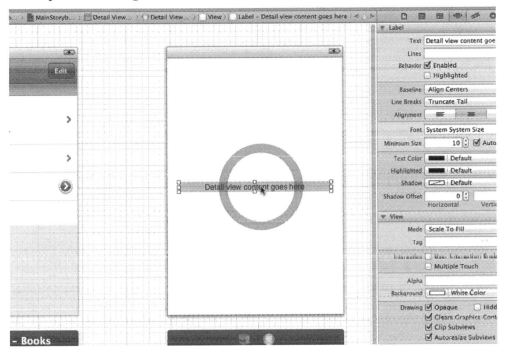

Figure 7-42. *Start editing the Detail Scene for the selected book.*

1. You'll now start designing your Detail View Controller. You first have to navigate your way to the very right-hand side of the canvas. Click the "Detail view content goes here" label and delete it as shown in Figure 7-42.

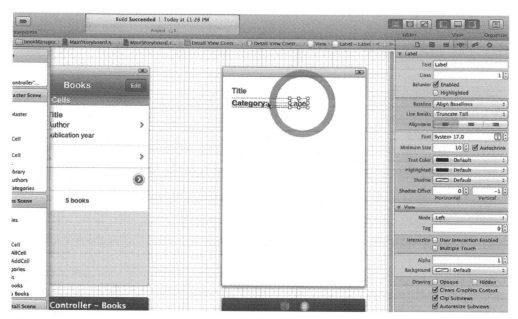

Figure 7-43. *Start bringing in the labels.*

2. Jump ahead to Figure 7-46 just for a minute—you'll see that you need a Title and three lines of text, each of which includes two labels. What you'll do is bring on a label for the Title, stretch it over the width of the view, format it, bring in two labels for the first of the three lines, format them as well, and then copy and paste them both twice. So, drag in your first label and change the text to *Title*. Make it almost as wide as the view itself, center it, set the font to System Bold 16.0, and change the text color to blue. Drag in another label and place it left-aligned, directly under Title. Change the text to *Category:* and set the font to System Bold 17.0. Then pull it to the right to stretch it just enough to accommodate the text. Now bring in another label and place it to the right of the one you just added as shown in Figure 7-43. Drag the right-hand handle of the label out almost to the right-hand edge of the canvas and change its text to *Category Label*.

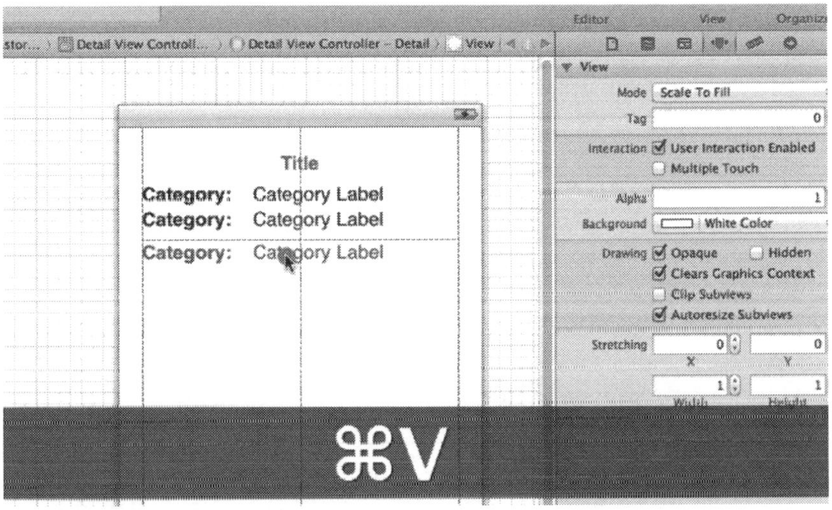

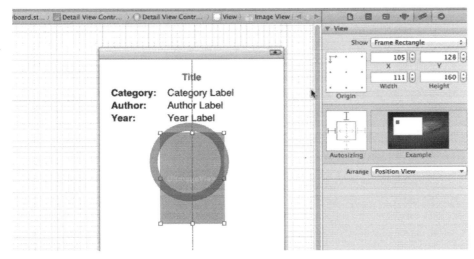

Figure 7-44. *Paste and align two more lines.*

3. Select the Title label and set its Alignment in the Attributes Inspector to center the text. Now select both Category: and Category Label, press ⌘+C to copy them both, and then press ⌘+V twice. Now start to align them as shown in Figure 7-44. Once you have them nicely aligned—perfectly under one another—move on to the next step.

Figure 7-45. *Rename and drag in a UIImageView for the book cover.*

4. Rename the two lines you just pasted to *Author:* with *Author Label* and *Year:* with *Year Label*. Now drag in a `UIImageView` from the Library to accommodate an image of the book's cover. Go to the Size Inspector and set the dimensions to 111 x 160. Then center the image as shown in Figure 7-45.

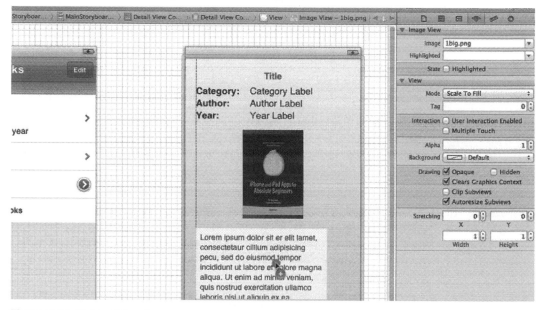

Figure 7-46. *Finish off the view.*

5. Two last things you'll do is associate the Image View to the temporary larger image `1big.png` and drag in a Text View, as shown in Figure 7-46, that will accommodate the short book description we've provided for you. The text for Text View is selected from the database along with the appropriate name of the image.

Figure 7-47. *Align and rename the text of the Text View.*

6. Once you place the Text View onto the canvas, center it. In the Attributes Inspector uncheck the Editable option and enter *Description* in the Text box as shown in Figure 7-47. Please keep saving each step as you move along.

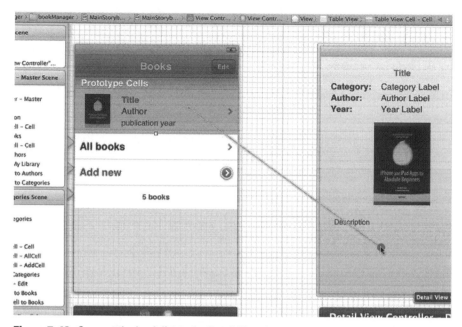

Figure 7-48. *Connect the book list to the Detail View Controller.*

7. This view will appear when the user taps any of the books in the list, so let's arrange this navigation in the Storyboard. Select the top cell in the Books Scene and Control-drag over to the Detail View Controller as shown in Figure 7-48. When you release the segue connector, choose the Push option from the Storyboard Segue menu.

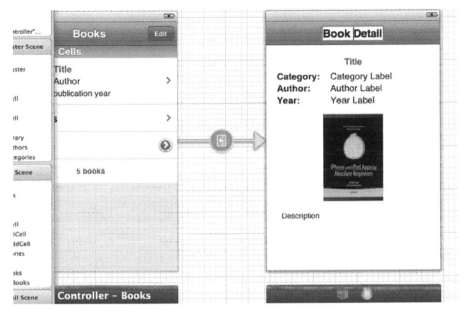

Figure 7-49. *Rename the View title to Book Detail.*

8   Once you connect your segue, you'll see the Navigation Bar
    appear in the Detail View. Double-click the title text and rename
    it to *Book Detail* as shown in Figure 7-49.

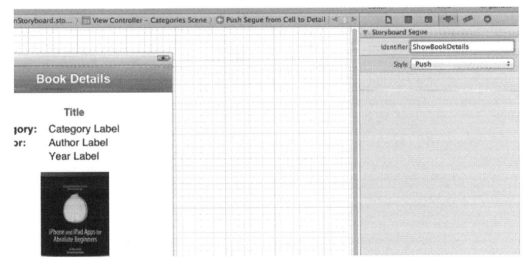

Figure 7-50. *Assign the identifier*

9. You need to assign a unique identifier to the new segue, so click the segue going to the Detail View Controller. Once you have it selected, switch to the Attributes Inspector and name the Identifier for this segue *ShowBookDetails* as shown in Figure 7-50.

Creating the UI for Entering and Saving New Data: Add Book Scene

One of the cool things about your app is that it will allow the user to do something that used to be very difficult to program: add new content into the app and save it. Storyboarding has made this task a lot easier—furthermore, it's an incredible skill to have.

Figure 7-51. *Creating the Add Book Scene*

1. You'll now start designing a new scene that will display a simple form where the user can enter basic information about a book and save it into the database. Because you know what kind of data you need to capture for a book, it makes sense to make a Static Table View for it. To create a Static Table in Storyboards

you must use a Table View Controller. Drag out a Table View Controller from the Object Library onto your Storyboard canvas as shown in Figure 7-51.

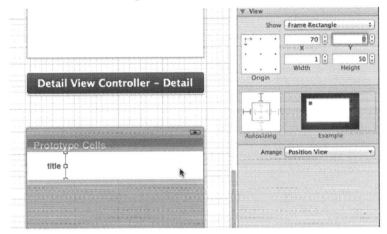

Figure 7-52. *Edit the Table View cell of the Static Table View.*

2. Click the top cell and in the Size Inspector set the Row Height to 50. Because you don't need this cell to be highlighted on touch, with the cell still selected switch to the Attributes Inspector and change the Selection property from Blue to None. Drag out a label and place it on the left-hand side of the cell. Then in the Attributes Inspector change Text to *title*, set the font to System Bold 14.0, and make it any color you choose (we picked a grey-blue color from the standard palette). Also change the text from being left-aligned to right-aligned. Now for a pretty cool trick, use an Image View as a separator to sit between the field's header and the information the user will be entering. Bring in a UIImage View and place it in the cell. In the Attributes Inspector set the Background color to Light Grey. Back in the Size Inspector, set the width to 1 and the height to 50 so it looks just like thin grey line separator. Finally, set the Y value to 0 as shown in Figure 7-52.

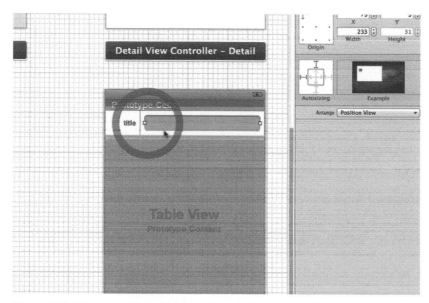

Figure 7-53. *Drag in the Text Field.*

3. To be able to add new content into a SQLite database from the app, you need to be able to type data into the app. You'll need to use a Text Field for this. Drag a Text Field from the Object Library into your cell and expand it until it reaches about 233 points as shown in Figure 7-53. In the Attributes Inspector set the Border Style of the Text Field to be invisible. That's the first button to the left.

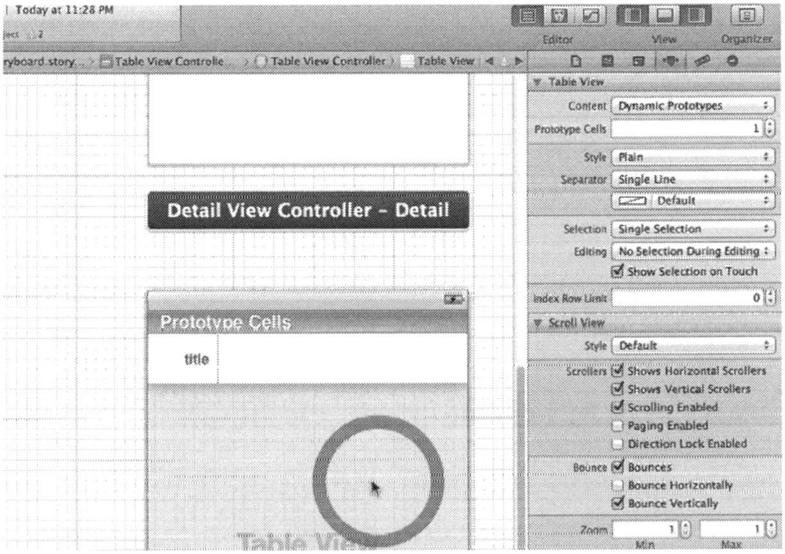

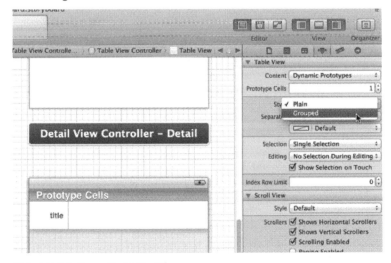

Figure 7-54. *Select the Table View for further edits.*

4. You want to set your Table View to Grouped so you can provide sections for it. Make sure as you go through the next steps that the Table View is selected. You can click anywhere inside the Table View below the prototype cell to select it as shown in Figure 7-54.

Figure 7-55. *Group the Table View.*

5. With the Table View selected, in the Attributes Inspector change the Style from Plain to Grouped as shown in Figure 7-55.

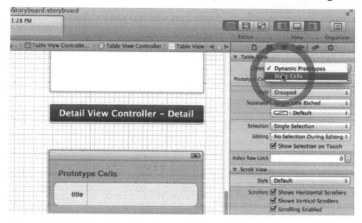

Figure 7-56. *Change the Table Content type.*

6. Change the Content type from Dynamic Prototypes to Static Cells as shown in Figure 7-56. After that you will see three static cells appear. You only need two. Select one and delete it.

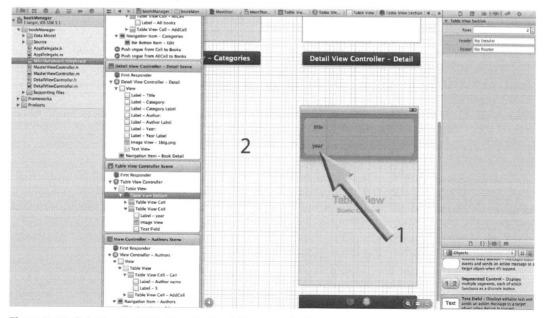

Figure 7-57. *Selecting the Table View Section in Document Outline.*

7. Change the left label's text of the bottom cell to *year* (see 1 in Figure 7-57). Now click carefully anywhere on the striped grouped Table View background (see 2 in Figure 7-57) and make sure you don't select one of the cells or the Table View itself. You can open the Document Outline pane and select the Table View Section as shown on the right in Figure 7-57.

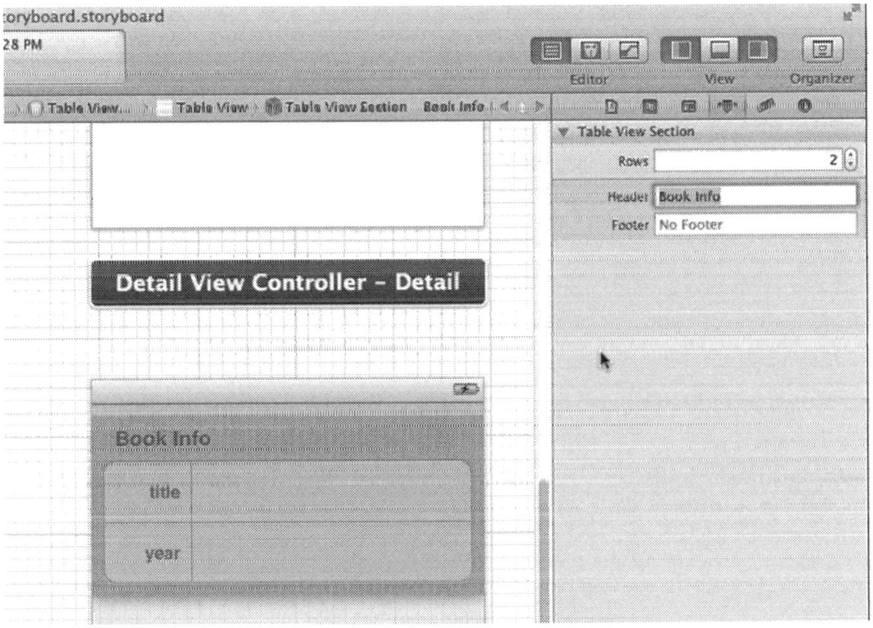

Figure 7-58. *Set the Header to Book Info.*

8. With the Table View Section selected, in the Attributes Inspector enter *Book Info* as the Header attribute of the Table View Section as shown in Figure 7-58.

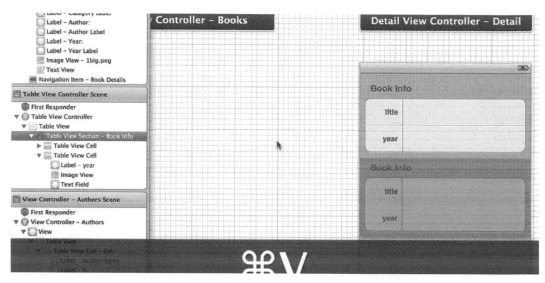

Figure 7-59. *Create another section*

9.   Now you can simply copy the first section and paste it. Make sure you click Table View Section – Book Info in the Document Outline again to select it—otherwise these instructions may not produce the desired results. With the section selected, press ⌘+C and then immediately press ⌘+V as shown in Figure 7-59.

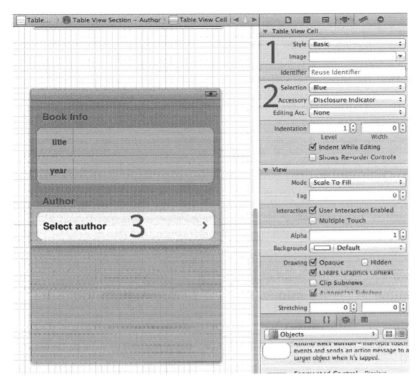

Figure 7-60. *Modify the new section.*

10. You'll let the user do something really cool here. Rather than have users remember an author's name, you'll let them select a name from a list. Double-click the header of the new section you just pasted and change its text from *Book Info* to *Author*. You also have too many cells in this section—delete one cell so only one remains. Select the cell and in the Attributes Inspector change the following properties: set Style to Basic (see 1 in Figure 7-60), Selection to Blue, and Accessory to Disclosure Indicator (see 2 in Figure 7-60). Double-click the Title label that appeared after you changed the cell's style and change its text to *Select author* (see 3 in Figure 7-60) so users know they're now going to select from one of Apress's authors. The final look of this section is shown in Figure 7-60.

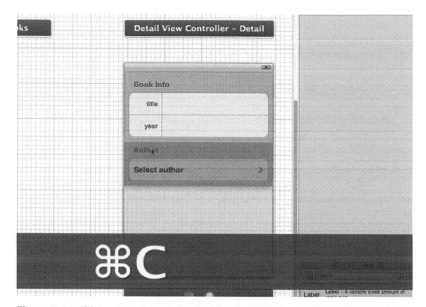

Figure 7-61. *Click once on the Author header to select the section and press ⌘+C.*

11. Unlike the copying in the first section, where you used
Document Outline to help select the right section object, your
sections are now clearly identified by headers. You can easily
select the second section in the view canvas itself to copy and
paste it. Click the Author header text to highlight it, press ⌘+C
to copy it as shown in Figure 7-61, and immediately press ⌘+V
to paste it.

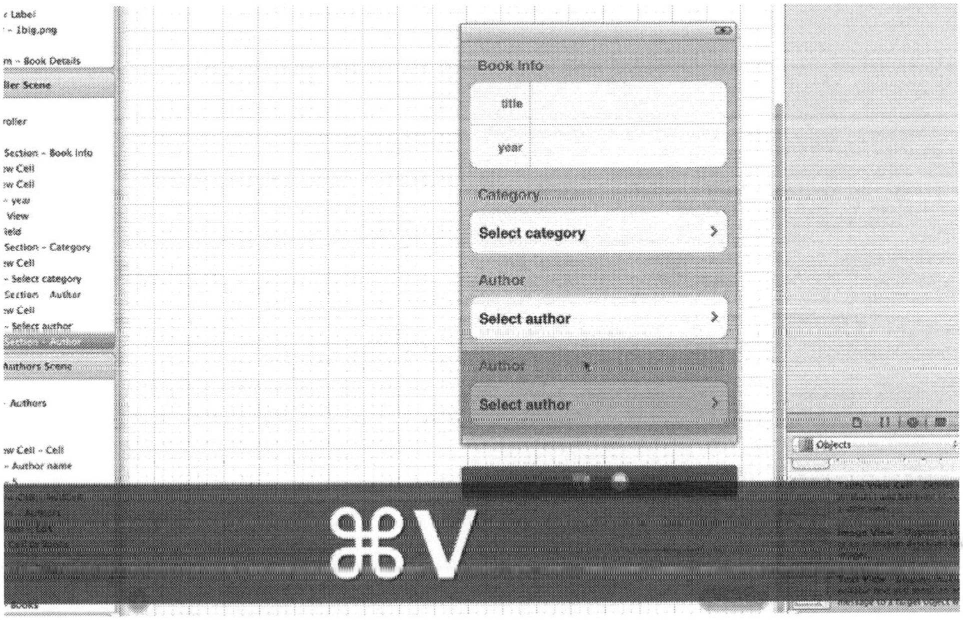

Figure 7-62. *Making another section*

12. You should now see the third section appear at the bottom of the Table View, which is identical to the one right above it, as shown in Figure 7-62. Double-click the header and change its text to *Category*.

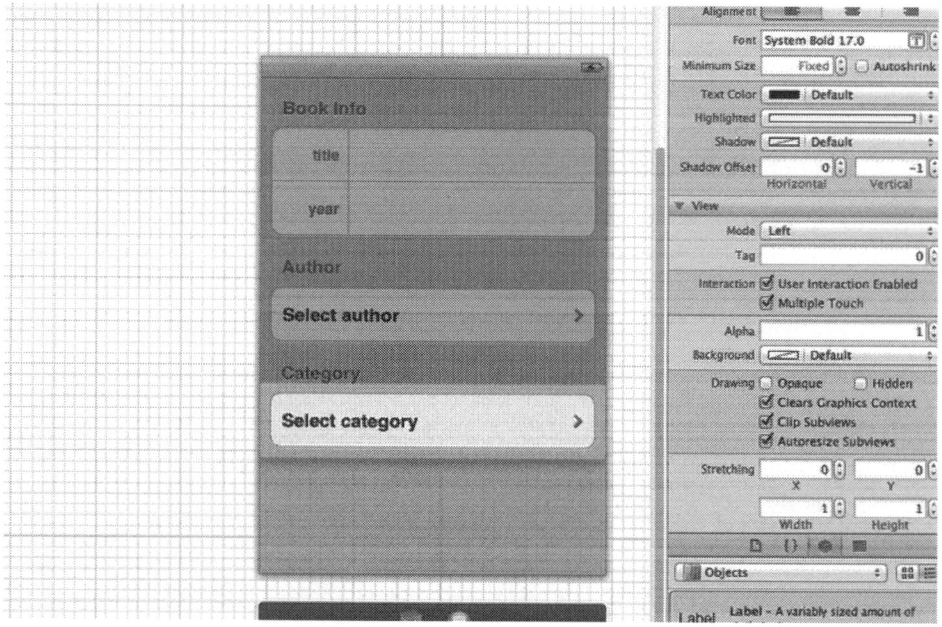

Figure 7-63. *Edit the third section.*

13. Also change the "Select author" label's text to *Select category*. The final look of the section is shown in Figure 7-63.

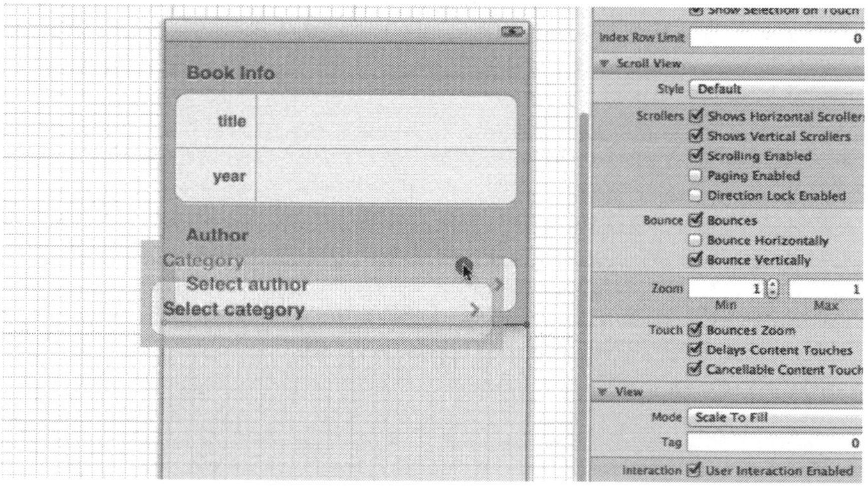

Figure 7-64. *Rearrange sections exercise*

14. It's important that you know how easy it is to create and rearrange sections in Storyboards when you're programming your own app because you or your client may want to change the order of these sections. So, pretend that you want to move the Category section above the Author section. Simply click it once and drag it up as shown in Figure 7-64.

15. You want to allow the user to add Book info, Category, Author, and Description data for a book just as you have it in your SQLite database. To do that, you need to add one more section. Copy and paste the Author section again, just as in step 60. Yup, it's now that easy once you get past that first section!

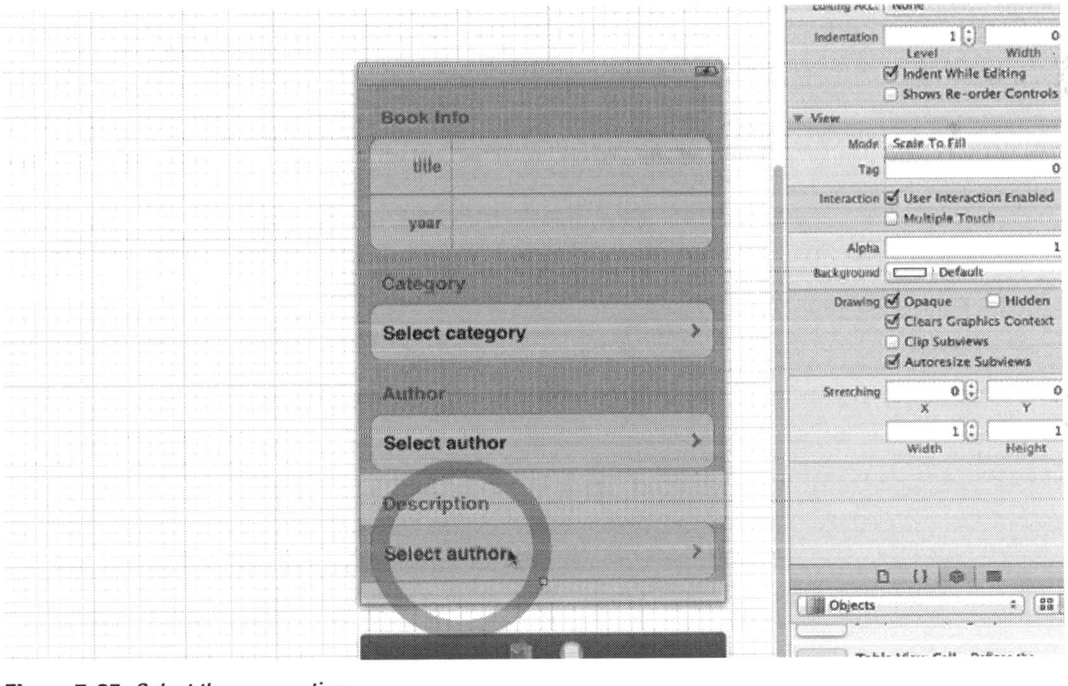

Figure 7-65. *Select the new section.*

16. Click the header and change its title from *Author* to *Description*. Then select the last cell by clicking it once as shown in Figure 7-65.

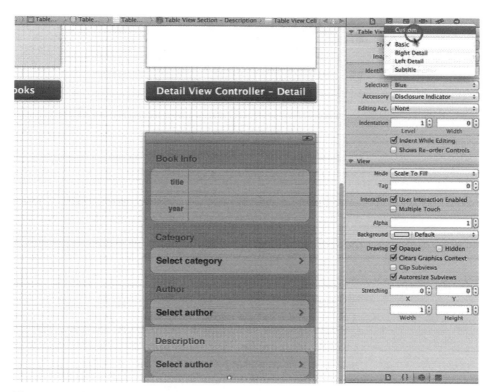

Figure 7-66. *Changing the cell's Style*

17. The Description section is where users can add their own description. You need to modify what you just pasted to accommodate this basic need. In the Attributes Inspector change the style from Basic to Custom as shown in Figure 7-66. Also change Selection from Blue to None. There's no need for the disclosure icon in this cell, so also change Accessory from Disclosure Indicator to None.

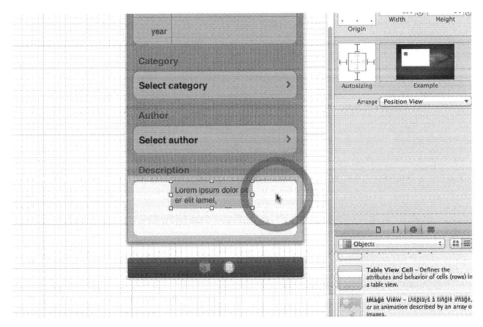

Figure 7-67. *Adding Text View to the cell*

18. You'll need the cell to have enough height to accommodate the lines of text the user will enter to describe the book being added. You'll also need to have a Text View. With the cell selected, in the Size Inspector change the cell height to 100. This will give users enough room to see a few rows of the text they're entering (it's difficult to type text when you can only read one or two lines). The next thing you need to do is add a Text View as shown in Figure 7-67. Drag the handles so that it fills the cell nicely. We made ours 281 points wide and 88 points high.

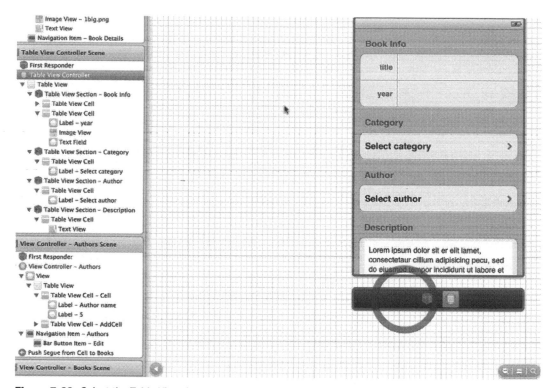

Figure 7-68. *Select the Table View Controller for embedding.*

19. This scene is going to be a Modal Scene, so you need to embed it into a Navigation Controller to be able to use the Navigation Bar in this view. To do that, select the Table View Controller as shown in Figure 7-68. Note that the Document Outline on the left of Figure 7-68 shows that the Table View Controller is selected inside the Table View Controller Scene. Make sure this is the case with your project before you start to embed—you won't be happy if it's not, because you'll have to start all over.

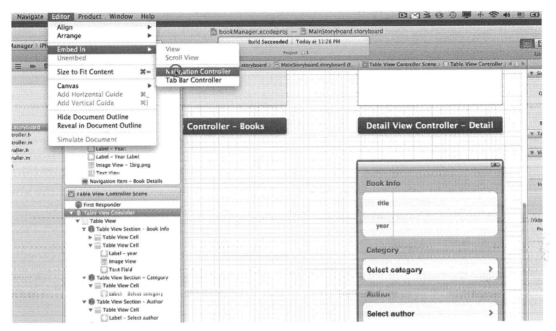

Figure 7-69. *Embed the Table View Controller into a Navigation Controller.*

20. With the Table View Controller selected, choose Editor ➤
Embed In ➤ Navigation Controller as shown in Figure 7-69.

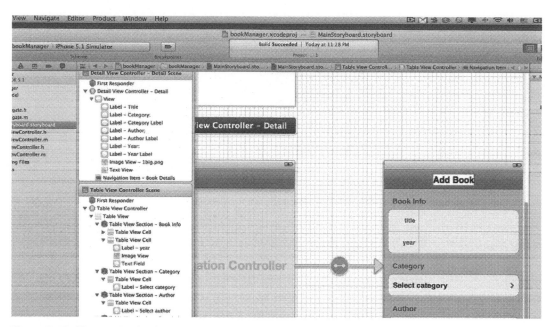

Figure 7-70. *The new Navigation Controller is created.*

21. A beautiful, brand spanking new Navigation Controller is created
    with a Root View Controller relationship to what you'll now name
    the Add Book View. Double-click the view title and name it *Add
    Book* as shown in Figure 7-70.

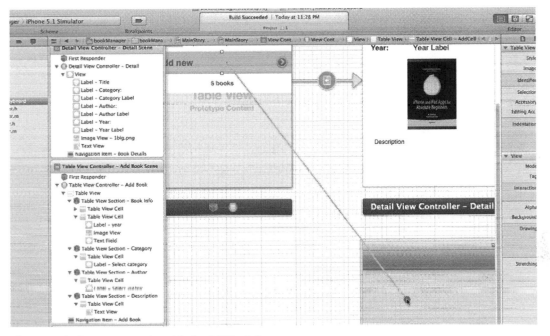

Figure 7-71. *Create a segue to get to the Add Book Scene.*

22. Now you need to do a little thinking. In order to get to this scene, the user needs to tap the Add New cell in the Books View. Right now, nothing connects these scenes, so you need to create a new segue. Click the Add New cell and Control-drag over to the Navigation Controller as shown in Figure 7-71. Because this is a Modal Scene—which is only presented to enter data—this time, rather than do a Push segue that makes the next view slide in, you'll do a Flip segue that makes the next view flip in. This time when you release the segue connector, select the Modal option from the Storyboard Segues menu.

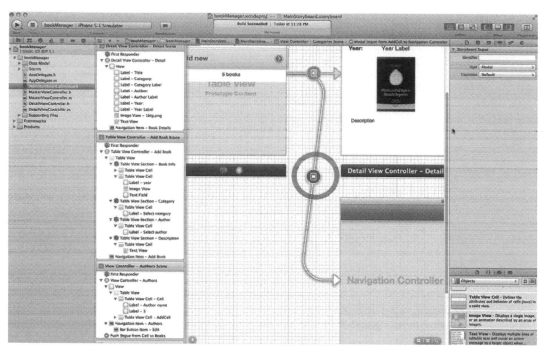

Figure 7-72. *Select the new segue.*

23. Ahh… a beautiful new segue is created. Let's tweak it a little bit. Select it as shown in Figure 7-72.

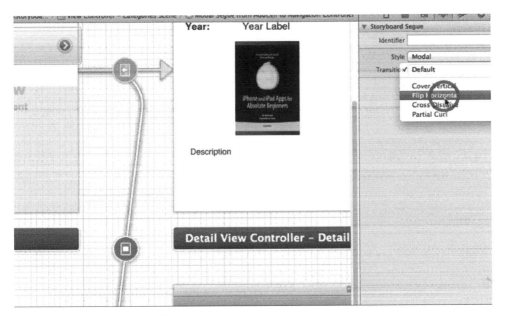

Figure 7-73. *Change the Transition type.*

24. With the new segue selected, change the Transition type to Flip Transition using the Attributes Inspector as shown in Figure 7-73—because as mentioned earlier, it's nice to experiment with different transition types so that you become familiar with them. Also set the segue's Identifier attribute to *AddNewBook*.

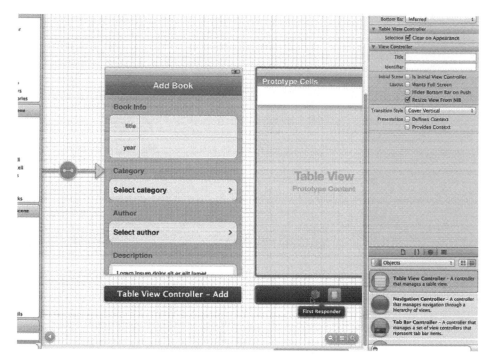

Figure 7-74. *Last thing: create a new Table View Controller*

25. The last thing you need to do is allow the user to select a
category or author that's available. To do that, make a really
basic Table View Controller. But here's something fun: rather
than make two Table View Controllers, one for Authors and one
for Categories, we'll show you how Storyboarding lets you use
the same Table View for both needs! Drag out another Table
View Controller and place it in the right-hand side of the Add
Book Scene as shown in Figure 7-74.

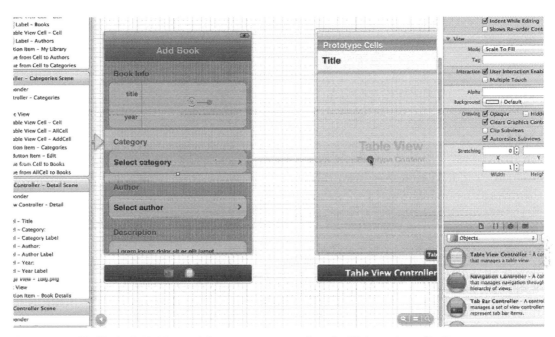

Figure 7-75. *Modify the Table View and then connect a segue from the "Select category" cell.*

26. This new Table View, as mentioned, will be a very basic—no frills. Select the Prototype cell that was automatically added to the Table View for you, in the Attributes Inspector set its Style to Basic, and enter *Cell* for the Identifier property. This cell will eventually hold either the name of the Category or the name of the Apress Author in it. Now step back and think about how your user is going to get to this scene. Your user must select either the "Select category" cell or the "Select author" cell. This means you'll need two segues, one from each of those cells. First select the "Select category" cell and Control-drag over to the Table View Controller as shown in Figure 7-75. When you release the segue connector, select the Push option from the Storyboard Segues menu. Enter *SelectCategory* as the Identifier to the segue in the Attributes Inspector, as you've done multiple times throughout the chapter.

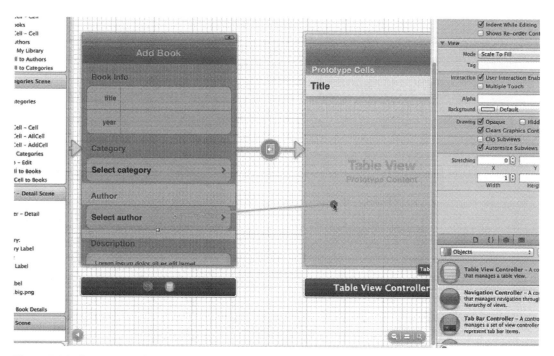

Figure 7-76. *Connect the "Select author" cell in the same way.*

27. Now select the "Select author" cell and Control-drag over to the Table View Controller as shown in Figure 7-76. When you release the segue connector, choose Push from the Storyboard Segues menu. Enter *SelectAuthor* as the Identifier to the segue in the Attributes Inspector as usual.

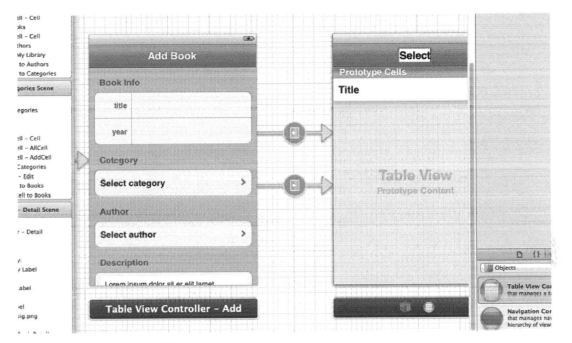

Figure 7-77. *Modify the View Title.*

28. Double-click the View Title and change it to *Select* as shown in Figure 7-77.

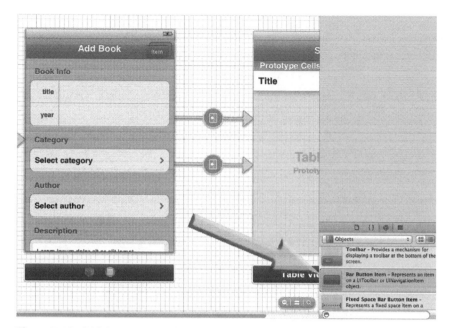

Figure 7-78. *Add the buttons to the Modal Scene.*

29. Because the Add Book Scene is a Modal Scene, you need to have two Bar button items. One will be to save the entry that the user has just created, and the other will let the user cancel out of the situation and return back to the previous View Controller. Drag in your first Bar button item from the Object Library as shown in Figure 7-78.

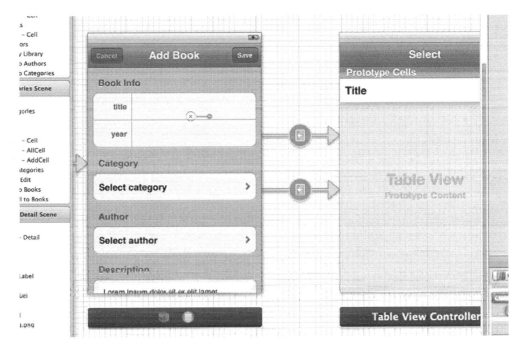

Figure 7-79. *Add two Bar button items.*

30. Drag the first Bar button item onto the right side of the header
    and name it *Save*. Then drag another out to the right side of the
    header and name that one *Cancel* as shown in Figure 7-79.

Making Final Tweaks

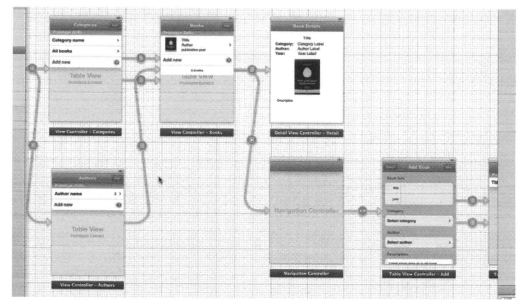

Figure 7-80. *App's story flow so far.*

1. Figure 7-80 shows the Storyboard so far. Looking pretty good! It tells you the entire app's story and logical flow. You can see how the parts of your app fit together without even thinking about writing any code at all. Isn't that exciting? Finally, you can make one more minor improvement to your data flow. Consider a situation in which the author only has one book, meaning there's no need to go to a list of books (Books Scene). In that case, it makes more sense to just jump right to the Book Details Scene (to the right of the Books Scene). To implement this, you need to modify a couple things.

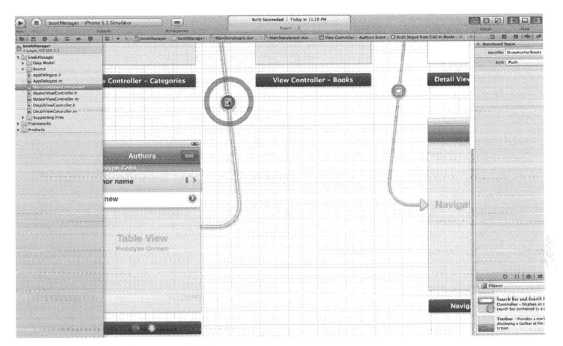

Figure 7-81. *Delete the ShowAuthorBooks segue.*

2. Select the segue going from the Authors Scene to Books Scene
   (the one that has the ShowAuthorBooks Identifier assigned to it)
   as shown in Figure 7-81 and delete it.

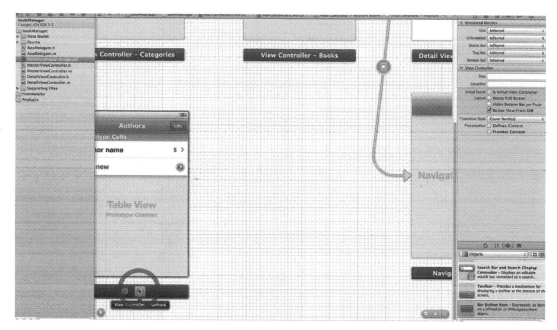

Figure 7-82. *Create a new segue from the actual View Controller.*

3. Now, instead of going from the "Author name" cell to the list of books, you'll create a segue from the View Controller itself. Select the Authors Scene by clicking its Dock (the black bar at the bottom). Then choose the View Controller as shown in Figure 7-82.

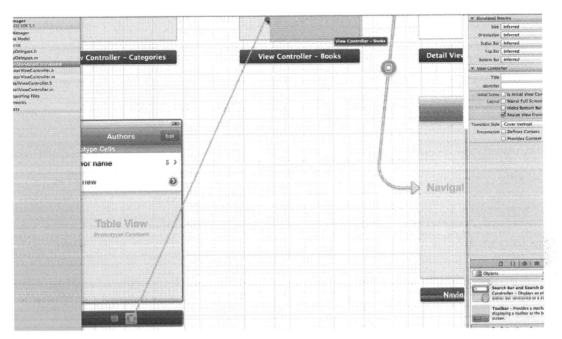

Figure 7-83. *Control-drag to the Books Scene.*

4. Control-drag from the View Controller out to the Books Scene
   as shown in Figure 7-83. When you release the segue
   connector, choose Push from the Storyboard Segues menu.
   Assign the ShowAuthorBooks Identifier to it, just as you
   previously had it set up.

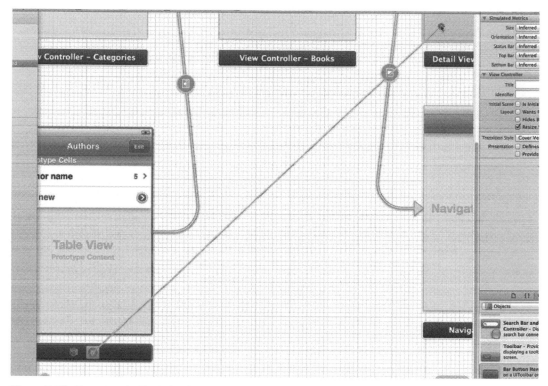

Figure 7-84. *Repeat to the Book Detail Scene.*

5. You'll do the exact same thing for the Detail View Controller as shown in Figure 7-84—except that when segue is created, make sure to assign a different Identifier to it.

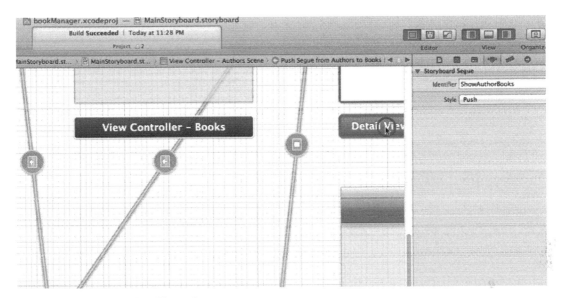

Figure 7-85. *Assign the identifier to the new segue.*

6. Name this one *ShowAuthorBookDetail* (shown in Figure 7-85). The trick with creating the segues from the View Controller is that you can manually perform those segues from the code when certain conditions are met. In this case, you'll determine which one of the two segues to perform when user taps the Table View Cell based on the number of books the particular author has.

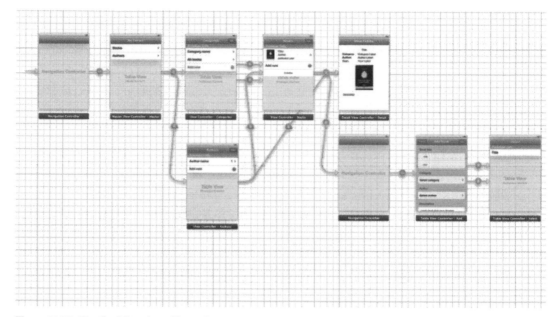

Figure 7-86. *The final Storyboard layout!*

7. At this point, your final Storyboard should look just like Figure 7-86. It's time to run your app and see what you have!

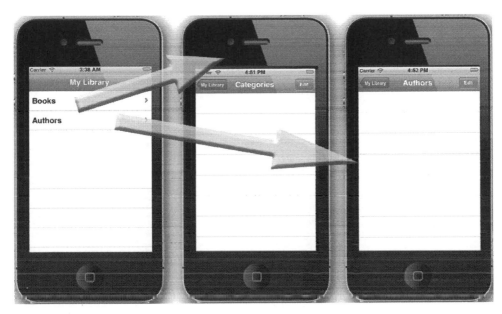

Figure 7-87. *It works!*

8. As can be seen from Figure 7-87, the app actually works and
    navigates from the Root View to Categories and Authors
    Scenes—except, when you compare it to Figures 6-0A and 6-
    0B (the final look of the app), you can see that the lists aren't
    populated. This is because even though the Storyboard is
    functional, there's no code underneath it that would connect the
    views and tables to the SQLite database. That's the part you're
    going to tackle in the next chapter.

Mastering Table Views with Storyboarding: Coding the Back End

So far, without writing any code, you've designed a pretty complex inventory system that will keep track of items—in this case, Apress books—and add items to the database from the app itself. As you saw in Chapter 7's Figure 7-87, it all works except that you don't have any data linked to the app.

Here in Chapter 8, in step 3 of 3 for the app, you'll be writing code that will connect your SQLite database to each of the View Controllers you created in Chapter 7.

Step 3: Insert the Code Behind the Storyboard Elements and Tweak a Couple Storyboard Necessities

Let's start this third step by creating a custom `UITableViewCell` subclass.

Creating a Custom UITableViewCell subclass

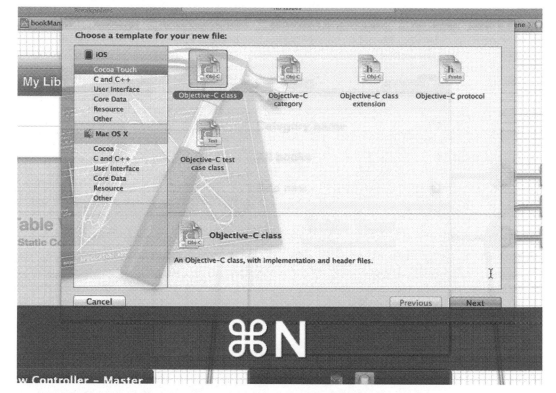

Figure 8-1. *Create a new class to connect to your custom cell prototypes.*

1. The `UITableViewCell` located at the root of the Storyboard you created in Figure 7-29 is a good place to start because most of the connections lead out from there. However, you'll first need to create a subclass of `UITableViewCell` that will provide you with all the necessary outlets to connect the elements in your custom cell prototypes. Press ⌘+N to create a new class and, after selecting the Objective-C class, click Next as shown in Figure 8-1.

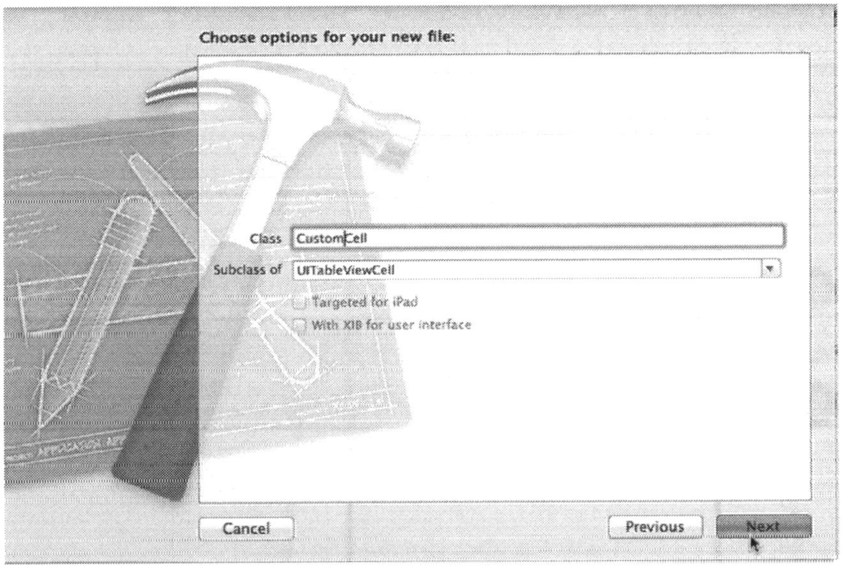

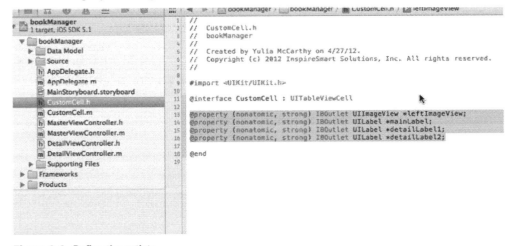

Figure 8-2. *Make sure it's a subclass of UITableViewCell.*

2. Typically, you go screaming past this dialog box, but please
   slow down and make sure that this is a subclass of
   UITableViewCell. You'll call this class CustomCell. Click Next as
   shown in Figure 8-2. Use the default save settings in the next
   dialog by clicking Create.

Figure 8-3. *Define the outlets.*

3. By default, Xcode will open the implementation file but we want you to first open the header file. Go to CustomCell.h in the Project Navigator and open it. The first thing you'll do here is define the outlets you'll need for your interface. Start by dragging the "10 CustomCell.h IBOutlets" snippet from DemoMonkey, which is the first snippet in PART THREE. Place it where you always define outlets, before the @end. You are defining four outlets here: leftImageView, mainLabel, detailLabel1, and detailLabel2, as shown in Figure 8-3 and as follows:

```
#import <UIKit/UIKit.h>

@interface CustomCell : UITableViewCell

@property (nonatomic, strong) IBOutlet UIImageView *leftImageView;
@property (nonatomic, strong) IBOutlet UILabel *mainLabel;
@property (nonatomic, strong) IBOutlet UILabel *detailLabel1;
@property (nonatomic, strong) IBOutlet UILabel *detailLabel2;

@end
```

All the properties here are pretty self-explanatory. You'll learn what roles they play soon, when you connect them to your UI in the Storyboard. Save the header file, and let's add a few things to its implementation.

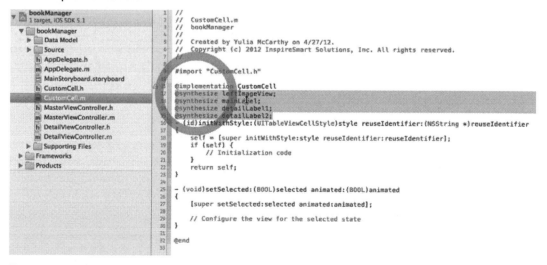

Figure 8-4. *Synthesize the four outlets.*

4. Jump over to the CustomCell.m implementation file and synthesize the four IBOutlets you just defined. Drag in the "11 CustomCell.m @synthesize" snippet from DemoMonkey and place it right after the @implementation CustomCell as shown in Figure 8-4 and as follows:

```
#import "CustomCell.h"

@implementation CustomCell
@synthesize leftImageView;
@synthesize mainLabel;
@synthesize detailLabel1;
@synthesize detailLabel2;
```

Modifying the Detail View Controller

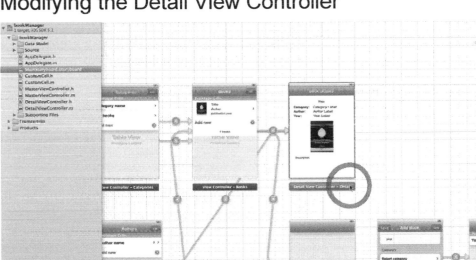

Figure 8-5. *Select the Book Details Scene.*

1. In Chapter 7 you already created connections from Table View cells located at the root of your Storyboard. Now you'll go backwards from the leaves of each branch of the Storyboard toward the root and add the code for all these scenes. Start with the Detail View Controller. Click the Storyboard, open it up, and then select the Book Details Scene as shown in Figure 8-5.

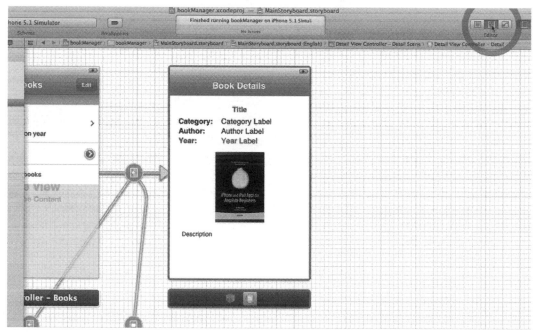

Figure 8-6. *Open the Assistant editor.*

2. You'll be dragging connections from the Storyboard over to your code, so as you've done in the past, you'll need to have Storyboard open on the left and the code on the right. Open up the Assistant editor as shown in Figure 8-6.

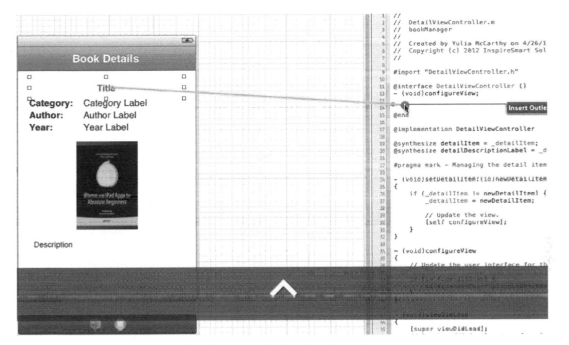

Figure 8-7. *Control-drag from the Title label over to the DetailViewController.m.*

3. Looking at the Book Details, before getting immersed in the
    code, think about this: you have UI elements that you want to
    connect to the SQLite database, so they can display data, right?
    You need outlets that your code can use to do this. So you need
    outlets for each of the elements you have here. You'll go a step
    further than simply creating them—you'll also make them
    private interfaces, because you don't need to access them from
    outside this class. You have the Assistant open, but make sure
    it has the DetailViewController.m file open. If not, switch to it
    using the drop-down right above the code. We added a couple
    spaces after the -(void)configureView so there would be some
    room. Now Control-drag from the Title over to the code as
    shown in Figure 8-7.

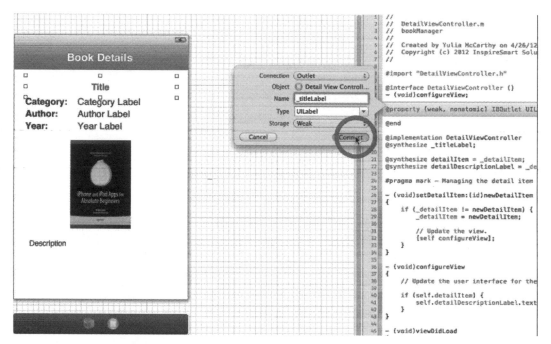

Figure 8-8. *Creating the Outlet connection.*

4. Release the Control-drag and leave all the defaults in the pop-up that will configure the Outlet connection. All you need to do is give it a name. Let's call it _titleLabel, as shown in Figure 8-8 and as follows:

```
#import "DetailViewController.h"
#import "DBBook.h"

@interface DetailViewController ()
- (void)configureView;

@property (weak, nonatomic) IBOutlet UILabel *_titleLabel;

@end
```

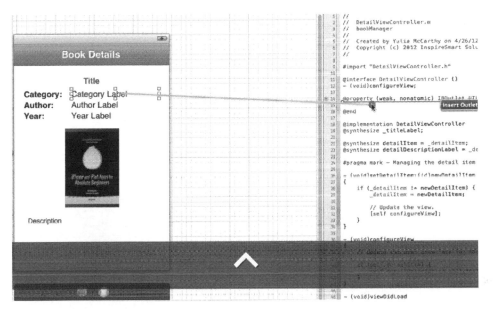

Figure 8-9. *Repeat for the next three of five elements.*

5. You now need to repeat the process of Figures 8-7 and 8-8 five
    more times, one for each of the three right-hand labels: the
    Category Label, Author Label, and Year Label. Control-drag
    from Category Label to the implementation file as shown in
    Figure 8-9 and name it _categoryLabel just as you named Title
    _titleLabel in Figure 8-8. Repeat two more times: Control-drag
    from Author Label to the implementation file and name it
    _authorLabel; Control-drag from Year Label to the
    implementation file and name it _yearLabel.

The three labels are shown here:

```
#import "DetailViewController.h"
#import "DBBook.h"

@interface DetailViewController ()
- (void)configureView;

@property (weak, nonatomic) IBOutlet UILabel *_titleLabel;
@property (weak, nonatomic) IBOutlet UILabel *_categoryLabel;
@property (weak, nonatomic) IBOutlet UILabel *_authorLabel;
@property (weak, nonatomic) IBOutlet UILabel *_yearLabel;

@end
```

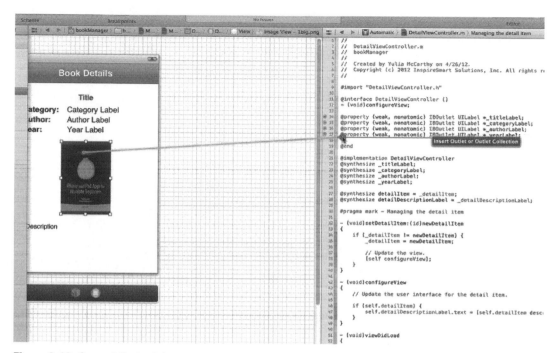

Figure 8-10. *Connect the book image.*

6. Click the image of the book as shown in Figure 8-10, Control-drag from it to the implementation file, and name the outlet _bookImage as shown here:

```
#import "DetailViewController.h"
#import "DBBook.h"

@interface DetailViewController ()
- (void)configureView;

@property (weak, nonatomic) IBOutlet UILabel *_titleLabel;
@property (weak, nonatomic) IBOutlet UILabel *_categoryLabel;
@property (weak, nonatomic) IBOutlet UILabel *_authorLabel;
@property (weak, nonatomic) IBOutlet UILabel *_yearLabel;
@property (weak, nonatomic) IBOutlet UIImageView *_bookImage;

@end
```

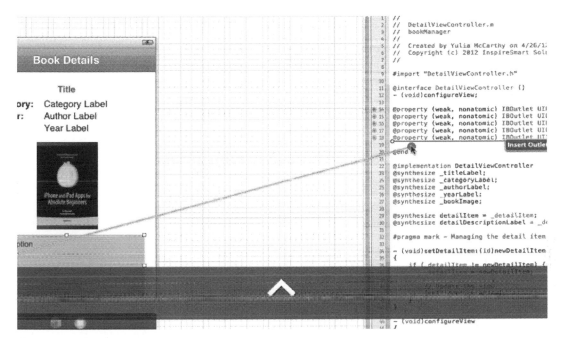

Figure 8-11. *Connect the Description.*

7. Lastly, click once directly under Description and Control-drag from the highlighted box to the implementation file as shown in Figure 8-11. Name the outlet _descriptionTextView as shown here:

```
#import "DetailViewController.h"
#import "DBBook.h"

@interface DetailViewController ()
- (void)configureView;

@property (weak, nonatomic) IBOutlet UILabel *_titleLabel;
@property (weak, nonatomic) IBOutlet UILabel *_categoryLabel;
@property (weak, nonatomic) IBOutlet UILabel *_authorLabel;
@property (weak, nonatomic) IBOutlet UILabel *_yearLabel;
@property (weak, nonatomic) IBOutlet UIImageView *_bookImage;
@property (weak, nonatomic) IBOutlet UITextView *_descriptionTextView;

@end
```

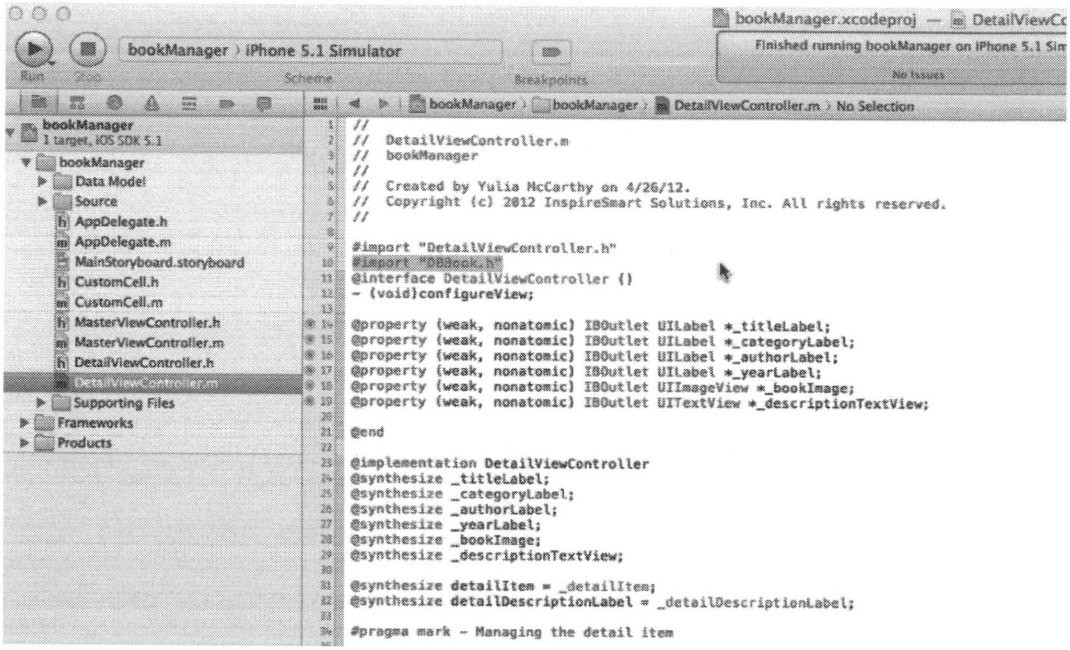

Figure 8-12. *Edit the DetailViewController.m file.*

8.   Now that you've hooked up elements from the Storyboard over
      to the DetailViewController.m file, you need to add a few more
      snippets of code. Particularly, you need to import the DBBook.h
      file so you can access the interface for this class. Open up the
      DetailViewController implementation file, drag in the "--
      DetailViewController.m Imports" snippet from DemoMonkey,
      and place it right after the #import "DetailViewController" as
      shown in Figure 8-12 and as follows:

```
#import "DetailViewController.h"
#import "DBBook.h"

@interface DetailViewController ()
- (void)configureView;

@property (weak, nonatomic) IBOutlet UILabel *_titleLabel;
```

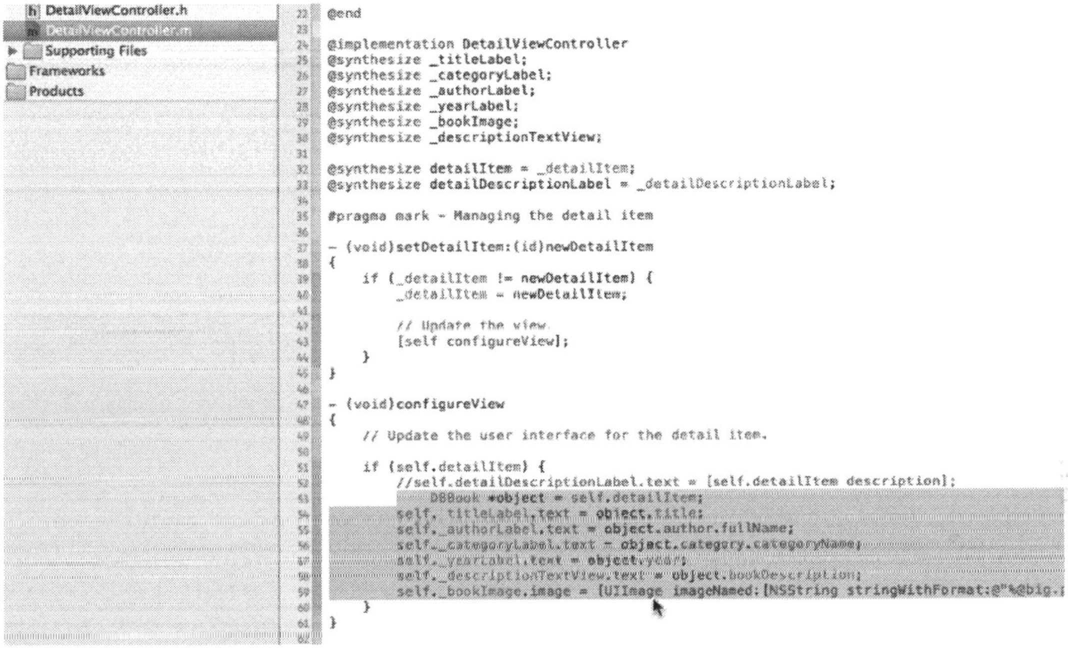

Figure 8-13. *Add in code for the configureView method.*

9. You need to update UI for the Book Details Scene with data
    from the SQLite database comprising all these essential details
    of whatever book the user selects. To do this, you edit and
    tweak the configureView method. We've written out these
    additional elements for configureView for you in a way that you
    can always use it as a template. First of all, comment out the
    line of code that's currently there:

```
//self.detailDescriptionLabel.text = [self.detailItem description];
```

Drag in the "12 DetailViewController.m configureView" snippet
from DemoMonkey and place it inside the configureView
method implementation, right below the commented-out line as
shown in Figure 8-13 and as follows:

```
- (void)configureView
{
    // Update the user interface for the detail item.

    if (self.detailItem) {
        //self.detailDescriptionLabel.text = [self.detailItem description];
        DBBook *object = self.detailItem;
```

```
    self._titleLabel.text = object.title;
    self._authorLabel.text = object.author.fullName;
    self._categoryLabel.text = object.category.categoryName;
    self._yearLabel.text = object.year;
    self._descriptionTextView.text = object.bookDescription;
    self._bookImage.image = [UIImage imageNamed:[NSString
stringWithFormat:@"%@big.png", object.imageName]];
  }
}
```

In DBBook object = self.detailItem, you get the detailItem passed to you during the segue. Then for the next six lines, beginning with the self.*, you assign all the properties for the text and image outlets you created in Figures 8-7–8-11.

> **NOTE:** You may want to navigate to your Data Model folder and open the DBBook.h file to understand why you created the bookId, categoryId, authorId, title, year, and bookDescription in Chapter 6. You can see how the DetailViewController is going to use those attributes to display the data stored in the database entity.

This ends what you need to add in the DetailViewController. You'll now move onto creating another ViewController class, the SelectionViewController.

Creating the SelectionViewController

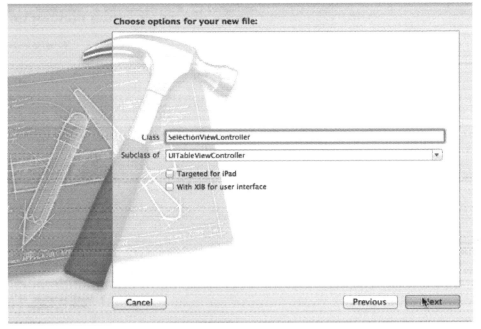

Figure 8-14. *Create the SelectionViewController.*

1. Another "leaf" scene in your Storyboard is the one that allows users to choose the author or the category when they are creating a new book. Press ⌘+N to create a new subclass and after selecting the Objective-C class, click Next just as you did in Figure 8-1. Call this class the `SelectionViewController`, make sure it's a subclass of `UITableViewController`, and then click Next as shown in Figure 8-14.

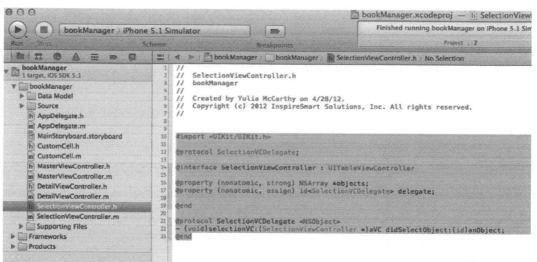

Figure 8-15. *Replace the code in SelectionViewController.h.*

2. You're going to radically change the SelectionViewController's header file, so to save time you'll simply replace the entire code for reasons that'll be explained as you go along. First, select all the original code in SelectionViewController.h and delete it. Drag in the "13 SelectionViewController.h interface + Protocol" snippet from DemoMonkey and place it at the bottom of the file as shown in Figure 8-15 and in the rest of this step.

First, you have set out an array that will be passed to the View Controller during the segue. It will contain a collection of DBAuthor or DBCategory objects, based on which cell the user taps. You do this with the following:

```
@property (nonatomic, strong) NSArray *objects;
```

Then you need to return the book or category selection the user makes. That means you need a delegate object you'll be passing the selection back to. You do this with the following:

```
@property (nonatomic, assign) id<SelectionVCDelegate> delegate;
```

Lastly, you define a protocol with the selectionViewController:didSelectObject: method, which you'll use to pass that selection back to the delegate:

```
@protocol SelectionVCDelegate <NSObject>
```

```
- (void)selectionVC:(SelectionViewController *)aVC didSelectObject:(id)anObject;
```

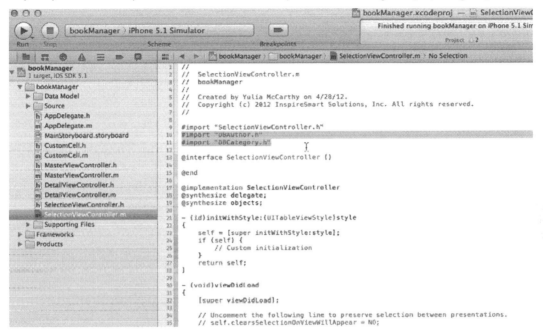

Figure 8-16. *Synthesize and import what you added into the header file.*

3. You now need to synthesize the `delegate` and `objects` properties
    you created in your header file. Open the
    `SelectionViewController.m` file. You haven't made a
    DemoMonkey step for this, so just type *@synthesize delegate;*
    and *@synthesize objects;* under @implementation
    SelectionViewController. You also need to import the header
    files for the database entities of Author and Category because
    you need to have access to their attributes. Drag in the "--
    SelectionViewController.m imports" snippet from DemoMonkey
    and place it under #import "SelectionViewController.h" as
    shown in Figure 8-16 and as follows:

```
#import "SelectionViewController.h"
#import "DBAuthor.h"
#import "DBCategory.h"

@interface SelectionViewController ()

@end
```

```
@implementation SelectionViewController
@synthesize delegate;
@synthesize objects;

- (id)initWithStyle:(UITableViewStyle)style
```

Figure 8-17. *Replace the UITableViewDataSource protocol methods.*

4.   You'll now add the code for your Table View. You'll replace the
     TableViewDataSource protocol methods that Xcode has already
     inserted for you with your own to make things less confusing.
     Scroll down from where you've just been working. Go to the end
     of shouldAutorotateToInterfaceOrientation, select everything
     from there to just before the @end, and delete it. Drag in the "14
     SelectionViewController.m TableView Datasource and Delegate"
     snippet from DemoMonkey and put it right before the @end as
     shown in Figure 8-17.

Because you're using this Table View Controller for both
Categories and Authors, in the
cellForRowAtIndexPath:(NSIndexPath *)indexPath method
check the class of the object you have in the array and then
display the category name from the database if it's a Category.

```
if ([object isKindOfClass:[DBCategory class]]) {
    cell.textLabel.text = ((DBCategory *)object).categoryName;
}
```

... or the author's name from the database if it's an Author:

```
if ([object isKindOfClass:[DBAuthor class]]) {
    cell.textLabel.text = ((DBAuthor *)object).fullName;
}
```

Then, when the user selects a choice, make a call back to the delegate to pass the object the user selected:

```
if ([self.delegate respondsToSelector:@selector(selectionVC:didSelectObject:)])
{
    [self.delegate selectionVC:self didSelectObject:[objects
objectAtIndex:indexPath.row]];
    }
```

Save it now because you need to go back into Storyboard to assign this `ViewController` class to the corresponding scene.

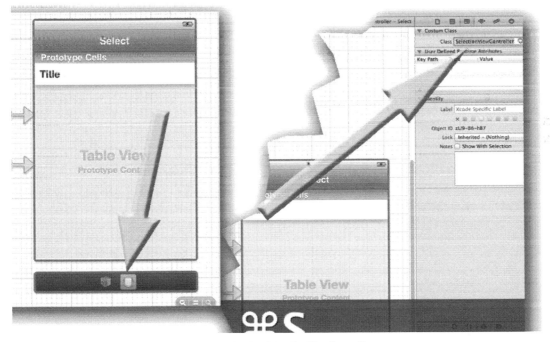

Figure 8-18. *Click Select Scene and associate it with SelectionViewController.*

5. Open up Storyboard and go to the Table View Controller, which is directly to the right of Add Book Scene (refer back to Figure 7-77). Click the Table View Controller icon once as indicated by the left arrow in Figure 8-18. With the View Controller selected, go to your Identity Inspector and make its Class adhere to what you just coded: `SelectionViewController`, shown by the right arrow in Figure 8-18. Select the Prototype cell, switch to the Attributes Inspector, and make sure its Identifier property is set to *Cell*.

Coding the Add Book View Controller

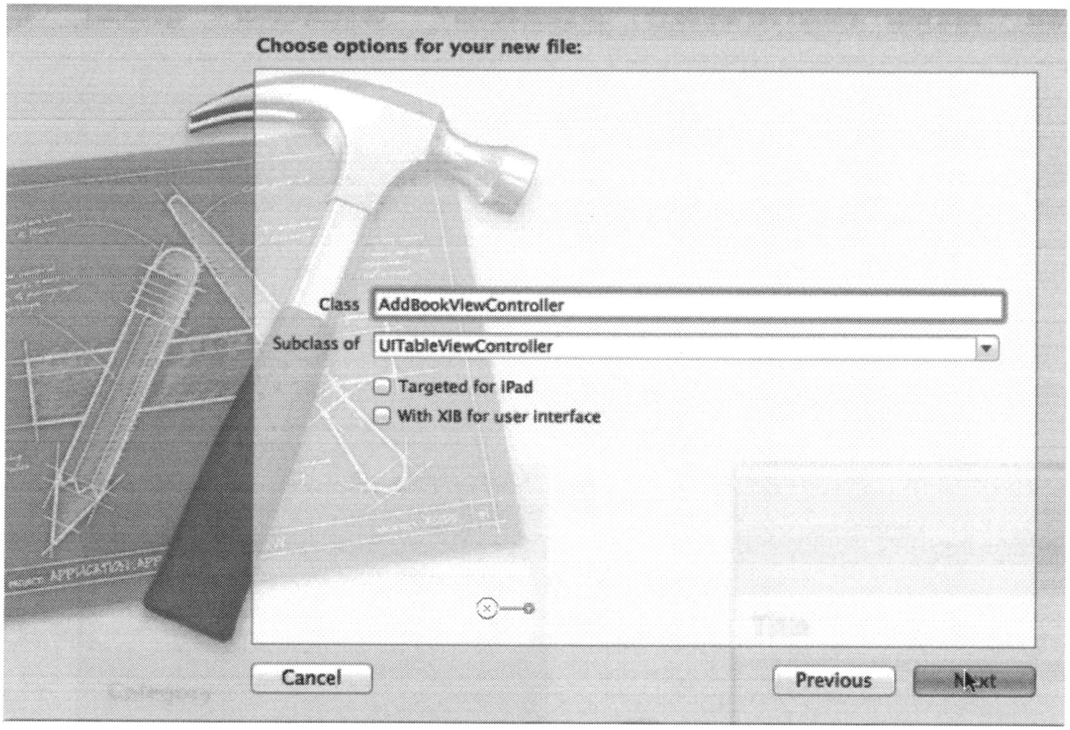

Figure 8-19. *Create the next class, AddBookViewController.*

1. Press ⌘+N to create a new subclass and, after selecting the Objective-C class, click Next. Name it `AddBookViewController` and make it a subclass of `UITableViewController` as shown in

Figure 8-19. Once saved, you'll first want to add outlets to it, so let's go back to Storyboard.

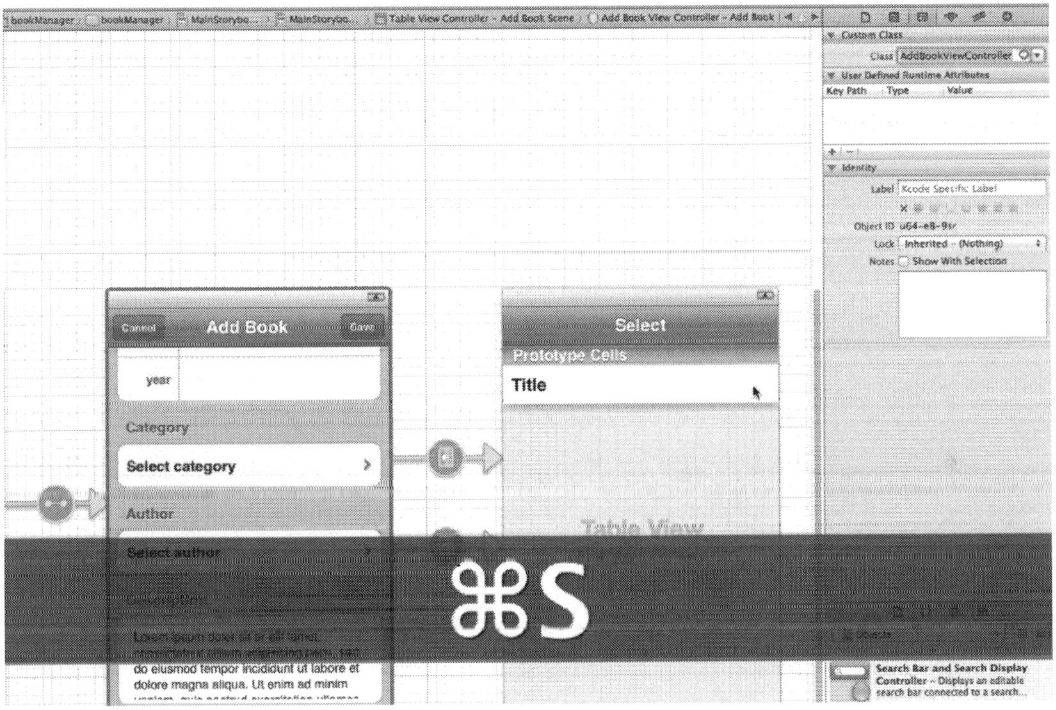

Figure 8-20. *Add Outlets to AddBookViewController.*

2. Open up Storyboard and select the Add Book Table View Controller just as you selected the Selection View Controller in Figure 8-18. With the Table View Controller selected, go to the Identity Inspector and make the Class adhere to what you just created, the AddBookViewController as shown in Figure 8-20.

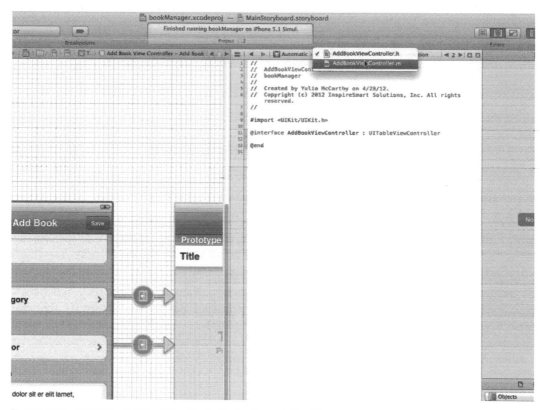

Figure 8-21. *Select the AddBookViewController implementation file.*

3. Switch to the Assistant editor mode. In the right-hand pane
   you'll see that by default Xcode brings up the header file. You
   want to work in the implementation file, so in the selection
   ribbon above the code of the header file select the
   implementation file as shown in Figure 8-21.

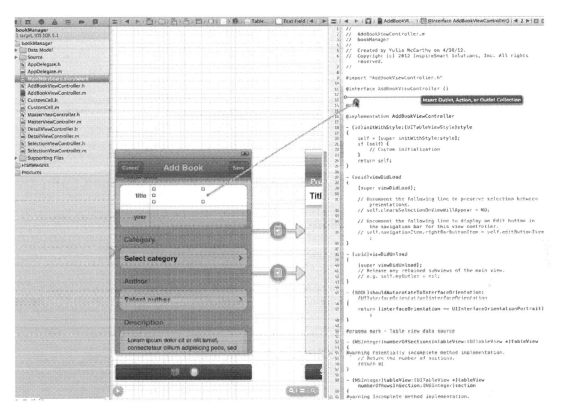

Figure 8-22. *Create outlets for the title and year attributes.*

4. You want to make outlets for the title of the book and the year
    of the book first. Click once on the title text field area to the right
    of the title label and Control-drag over to the implementation file
    below the @interface as shown in Figure 8-22. Name it
    _titleTextField in the pop-up dialog. Repeat the same for the
    year text field and name it _yearTextField. Your outlet code
    should now look like the following:

```
#import "AddBookViewController.h"

@interface AddBookViewController () {
  NSMutableDictionary *_bookDict;
}

@property (weak, nonatomic) IBOutlet UITextField *_titleTextField;
@property (weak, nonatomic) IBOutlet UITextField *_yearTextField;
...
```

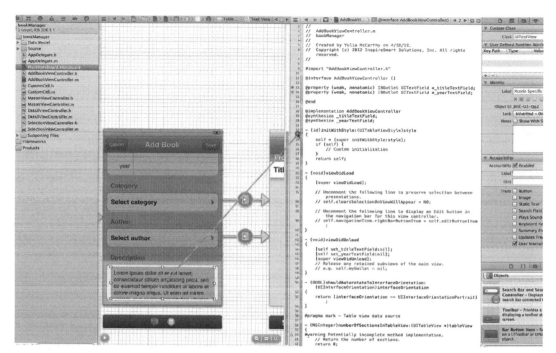

Figure 8-23. *Create an outlet for the Description text.*

5. You need to make one more IBOutlet here. The tricky part is to
    make sure to only click the text as shown in Figure 8-23 and
    that you only click it once. Once correctly selected, Control-
    drag over to the implementation file and name the outlet
    _descriptionTextView as shown here:

```
#import "AddBookViewController.h"

@interface AddBookViewController () {
  NSMutableDictionary *_bookDict;
}

@property (weak, nonatomic) IBOutlet UITextField *_titleTextField;
@property (weak, nonatomic) IBOutlet UITextField *_yearTextField;
@property (weak, nonatomic) IBOutlet UITextView *_descriptionTextView;
...
```

While focused on this Text View, you can really empty the text out
of here because users will be entering data into it when they create
a new book. So, with the text View still selected, go to the
Attributes Inspector and delete all the text in the text box.

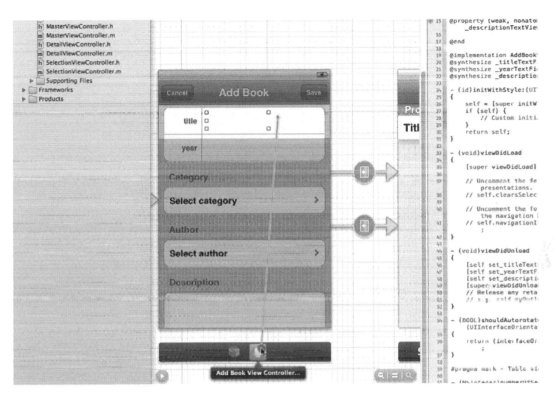

Figure 8-24. *Set up the delegate for your text fields.*

6. You need to set the delegate of your text fields to be the Add
    Book View Controller so you can save the data that the user
    types into them. Control-drag from the title text field to the
    Table View Controller icon in the Dock as shown in Figure 8-24.
    Another dialog connection window appears with options,
    divided under two sections: Storyboard Segues and Outlets.
    You want this to be an outlet, so select delegate, nested inside
    the Outlets option. Repeat the exact same procedure with the
    year text field.

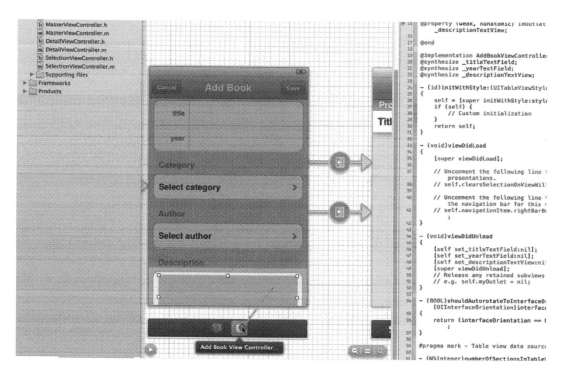

Figure 8-25. *Set up the delegate for Description Text View.*

7. You now need to set up the delegate for your Description Text
    View. Control-drag from the Text View as shown in Figure 8-25.
    Again, you want this to be an outlet, so select delegate nested
    inside the Outlets option.

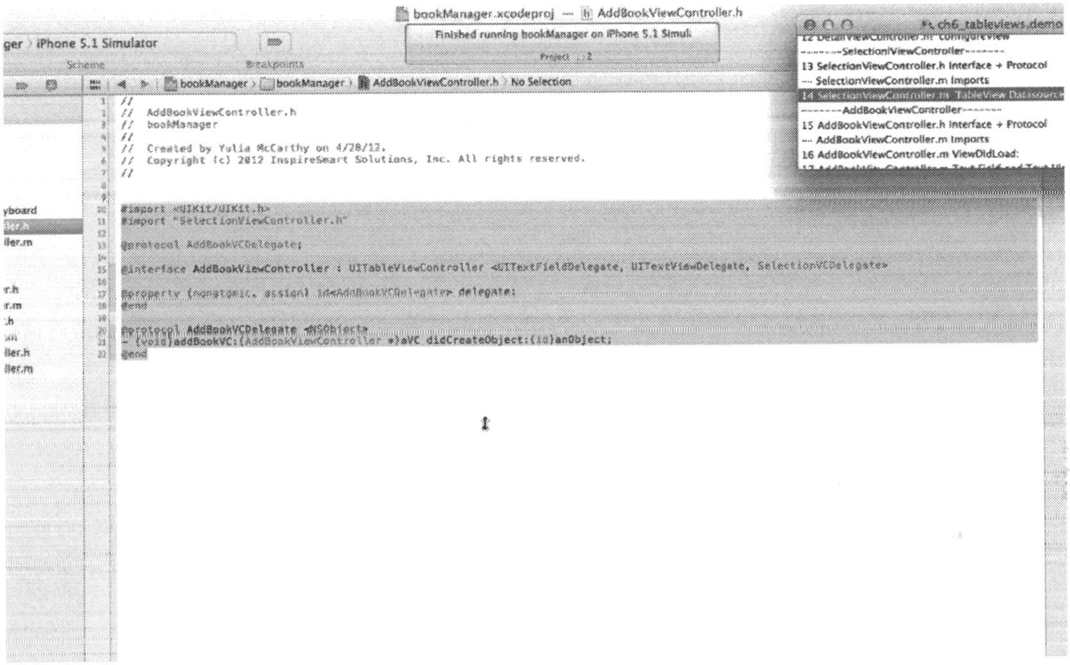

Figure 8-26. *Editing the new interface*

8. Close the Assistant and open the Standard editor. Open the
    `AddBookViewController.h` header file so you can modify the
    interface. Delete the three lines of code that appear by default
    and replace them with the next snippet you saved in
    DemoMonkey. Drag in the "15 AddBookViewController.h
    interface and protocol" snippet from DemoMonkey and place it
    where you just deleted the original header text. This is shown in
    Figure 8-26.

    The `delegate` property and `AddBookVCDelegate` protocol you
    included in the header file

```
@property (nonatomic, assign) id<AddBookVCDelegate> delegate;
```

    is what you'll use to notify the parent View Controller when the
    new database entity has been created, which will be passed up
    to the implementation file so it can be displayed as follows:

```
- (void)addBookVC:(AddBookViewController *)aVC didCreateObject:(id)anObject;
```

    Before you forget, let's synthesize the delegate.

Figure 8-27. *Synthesize the delegate.*

9. Open up the AddBookViewController.m file and synthesize the
delegate as shown in Figure 8-27 and as follows:

```
@interface AddBookViewController () {
…
…
@end

@implementation AddBookViewController
@synthesize _titleTextField;
@synthesize _yearTextField;
@synthesize _descriptionTextView;
@synthesize delegate;

…
```

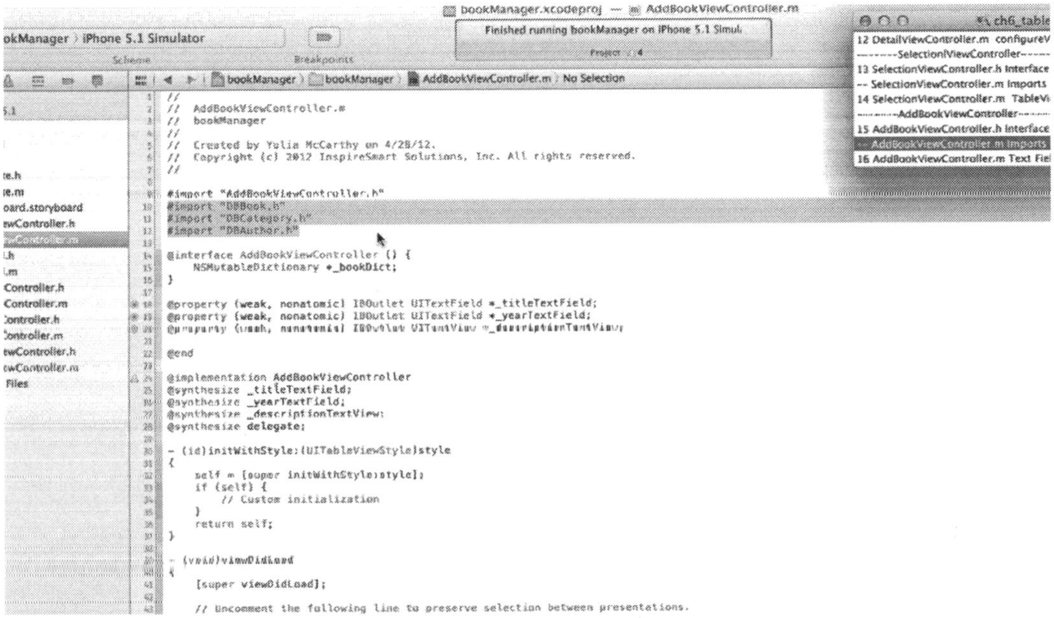

Figure 8-28. *Add mutable dictionary and #import your database entities.*

10. While the user is entering the information about the new book, such as title, year and book description, you need a place to safely and temporarily store the data until they tap Save. You could do this in many ways: one of them is to use a mutable dictionary. That means you need an `NSMutableDictionary` instance variable, from which you'll create a new entity later. Call it `_bookDict`. Declare it inside a set of curly braces right under the `@interface` in the private declarations section, as shown in the following code. You need to import all your database entities. Drag in the "-- AddBookViewController.m Imports" snippet from DemoMonkey and place it under the `#import` as shown in Figure 8-28 and as follows.

```
#import "AddBookViewController.h"
#import "DBBook.h"
#import "DBCategory.h"
#import "DBAuthor.h"

@interface AddBookViewController () {
  NSMutableDictionary *_bookDict;
}
```

```
@property (weak, nonatomic) IBOutlet UITextField *_titleTextField;
...
...
```

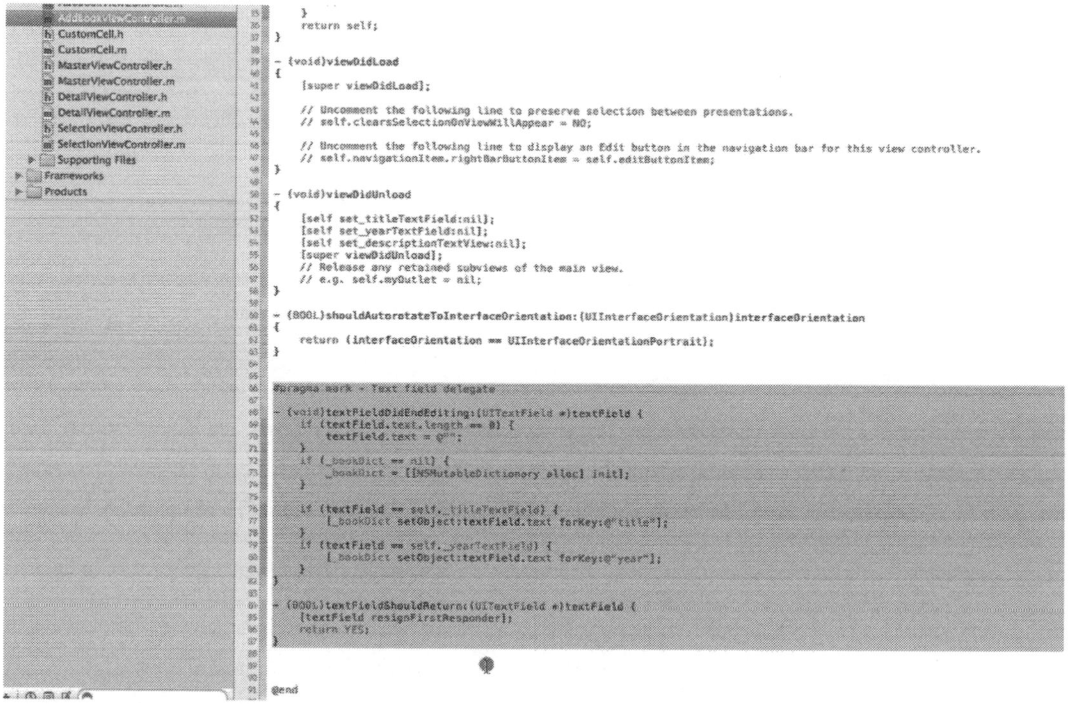

Figure 8-29. *Bring in the text field delegate methods.*

11. Because this is a Static Table View, you don't need to
    implement dataSources or delegate methods, so delete
    everything between the end of the
    shouldAutorotateToInterface rotation method to just before the
    @end. In its place bring in things you do need, such as the text
    field delegate methods and the Text View delegate methods,
    which will help you save the data as the user enters the
    information. Starting with the text field delegate methods, drag
    in the "16 AddBookViewController.m Text Field Delegate
    Methods" snippet from DemoMonkey and place it before the
    @end. It should look like what's shown in Figure 8-29.

Figure 8-30. *Bring in the text view delegate methods.*

12. Continuing with the text view delegate methods, drag in the "17 AddBookViewController.m Text View Delegate Methods" snippet from DemoMonkey and place it between the @end and the text field delegate method you placed in Figure 8-29. This is illustrated in Figure 8-30.

NOTE: The delegate methods you added in the last two steps are part of the standard UITextFieldDelegate and UITextViewDelegate protocols declared in the UIKit framework. These methods are the most common way to pass notifications from your text fields and Text Views about changes in their editing state. In your case, simply save the data typed by the user into the _bookDict dictionary object once each UITextField (or UITextView) notifies your AddBookViewController, which you assigned to be the delegate, that the user finished editing. The latter is achieved via textFieldDidEndEditing: (textViewDidEndEditing:) method callbacks, which get invoked every time a text field (Text View) loses focus or programmatically resigns First Responder after a Return key is pressed. The data collected into the _bookDict dictionary will eventually be saved into the database once the editing is complete and the Save button is pressed.

```
                l_booubic sctobject.textrietu.text lorney.@ yeo! ];
        }
    }
- (BOOL)textFieldShouldReturn:(UITextField *)textField {
    [textField resignFirstResponder];
    return YES;
}


#pragma mark - Text view delegate

- (void)textViewDidEndEditing:(UITextView *)textView {
    if (textView.text.length == 0) {
        textView.text = @"";
    }
    if (_bookDict == nil) {
        _bookDict = [[NSMutableDictionary alloc] init];
    }
    if (textView == self._descriptionTextView) {
        [_bookDict setObject:textView.text forKey:@"bookDescription"];
    }
}

- (BOOL)textViewShouldReturn:(UITextView *)textView {
    [textView resignFirstResponder];
    return YES;
}
```

```
- (void)prepareForSegue:(UIStoryboardSegue *)segue sender:(id)sender
{
    if ([[segue identifier] isEqualToString:@"SelectCategory"]) {
        [(SelectionViewController *)[segue destinationViewController] setObjects:[DBCategory allCategories]];
        [(SelectionViewController *)[segue destinationViewController] setDelegate:self];
    }
    if ([[segue identifier] isEqualToString:@"SelectAuthor"]) {
        [(SelectionViewController *)[segue destinationViewController] setObjects:[DBAuthor allAuthors]];
        [(SelectionViewController *)[segue destinationViewController] setDelegate:self];
    }
}
@end
```

Figure 8-31. *Implement the prepareForSegue: method.*

13. Still in the AddBookViewController.m file, implement the
    prepareForSegue: method. Drag in the "18
    AddBookViewController.m prepareForSegue" snippet from
    DemoMonkey and place it just before the @end as shown in
    Figure 8-31.

    In this method you first check for the segue identifier

```
if ([[segue identifier] isEqualToString:@"SelectCategory"]) {
...
```

    or

```
if ([[segue identifier] isEqualToString:@"SelectAuthor"]) {
...
```

    and then you pass the array of categories

```
[(SelectionViewController *)[segue destinationViewController]
setObjects:[DBCategory allCategories]];
```

    or the array of authors

```
[(SelectionViewController *)[segue destinationViewController]
setObjects:[DBAuthor allAuthors]];
```

to the destination View Controller, which is the
SelectionViewController in both cases.

Finally, you set the delegate of the SelectionViewController to
your AddViewController so that once the user selects an author
or a category, you can save that selection into your _bookDict
dictionary:

```
[(SelectionViewController *)[segue destinationViewController]
setDelegate:self];
```

Figure 8-32. *Implement the delegate method to choose category or author.*

14. Continuing to focus on the code users will need as they enter a new book, author, and category, you still have a couple more chores to fulfill. Once the user selects the category or the author, you want to receive a delegate callback from the `SelectionViewController`, so you need to implement this delegate method. Drag in the "19 AddBookViewController.m Choose Category of Author" snippet from DemoMonkey and place it just before the @end as shown in Figure 8-32.

You defined this delegate method in the `SelectionViewController.h` file:

```
- (void)selectionVC:(SelectionViewController *)aVC
didSelectObject:(id)anObject;
```

Here, based on what kind of class the received object is,

```
if ([anObject isKindOfClass:[DBCategory class]]) {
```

you'll either save the category ID

```
[_bookDict setObject:((DBCategory *)anObject).categoryId forKey:@"categoryId"];
```

or the author ID

```
[_bookDict setObject:((DBAuthor *)anObject).authorId forKey:@"authorId"];
```

and display the category name

```
cell.textLabel.text = ((DBCategory *)anObject).categoryName;
```

or display the author name

```
cell.textLabel.text = ((DBAuthor *)anObject).fullName;
```

in the corresponding cell. After all that's done, you'll pop the View Controller off the stack

```
[self.navigationController popViewControllerAnimated:YES];
```

so the user can return back to the `AddBookViewController` and continue editing book info.

Figure 8-33. *Implement two IBActions for the Save and Cancel buttons.*

15. The last thing you need to do here in the
AddBookViewController.m is implement two IBActions, one for
the Save button and another for the Cancel button. Drag in the
"20 AddBookViewController.m IBAction" snippet from
DemoMonkey and place it just before the @end as shown in
Figure 8-33.

For the Cancel button, you have the cancelPressed: method

```
- (IBAction)cancelPressed:(id)sender {
```

in which you'll simply dismiss the ModalViewController without
saving any changes:

```
[self dismissModalViewControllerAnimated:YES];
```

In the savePressed: method,

```
- (IBAction)savePressed:(id)sender
```

will resign the First Responders (title, year, or description text
fields) if there are any. This will dismiss the keyboard if it's still
up:

```
[self._titleTextField resignFirstResponder];
[self._yearTextField resignFirstResponder];
[self._descriptionTextView resignFirstResponder];
```

You then verify that the user has modified any fields so that the book info dictionary has been created and isn't nil. And you create a new entity from the _bookDict dictionary using the DBBook helper method you implemented in Chapter 6:

```
if (_bookDict != nil) {
    DBBook *newBook = [DBBook createEntityWithDictionary:_bookDict];
```

Finally, you notify the delegate about the creation of this object so it can be added to the list of books right away if needed:

```
if ([self.delegate respondsToSelector:@selector(addBookVC:didCreateObject:)]) {
    [self.delegate addBookVC:self didCreateObject:newBook];
```

And dismiss the AddBookViewController:

```
[self dismissModalViewControllerAnimated:YES];
```

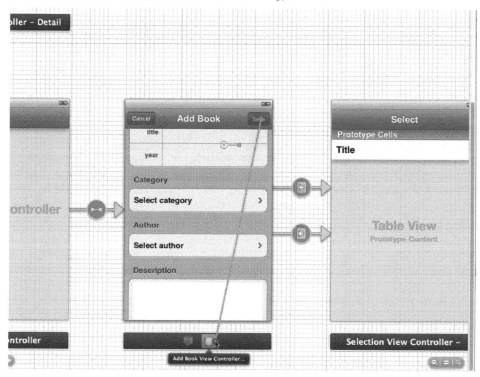

Figure 8-34. *Connect the IBActions you created.*

16. Now you need to connect the IBActions you created for the Edit
and Cancel buttons. So save your work and open the
Storyboard. Go to Add Book and Control-drag from the Save
button to the Add Book View Controller as shown in
Figure 8-34.

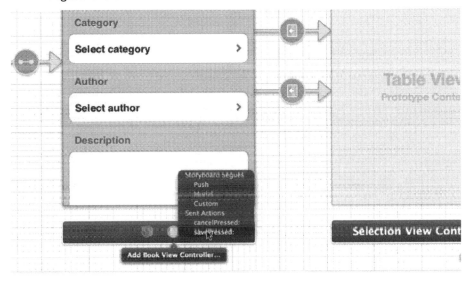

Figure 8-35. *Select savePressed: Sent Actions.*

17. When the pop-up appears, select the savePressed: method
nested inside the Sent Actions section as shown in Figure 8-35.

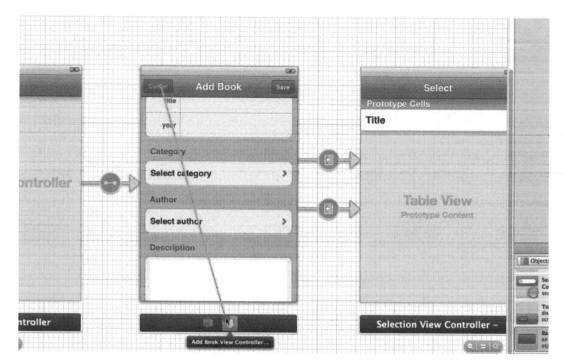

Figure 8-36. *Repeat for Cancel.*

18. Control-drag from Cancel to the Add Book View Controller as shown in Figure 8-36. This time, however, when the pop-up appears, select the `cancelPressed:` option nested inside the Sent Actions options as you did in Figure 8-35.

Hooking Up the Books Scene

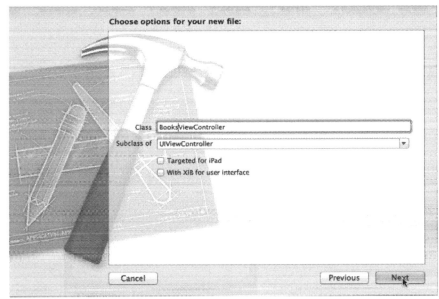

Figure 8-37. *Create the BookViewController.*

1. Let's move on now to the next View Controller. Press ⌘ ⏐ N to create a new subclass and after selecting the Objective-C class, click Next. Name it `BooksViewController` and make it a subclass of `UIViewController` as shown in Figure 8-37. Save it in its default location as you've always done in this book. When you're done, go back into Storyboard.

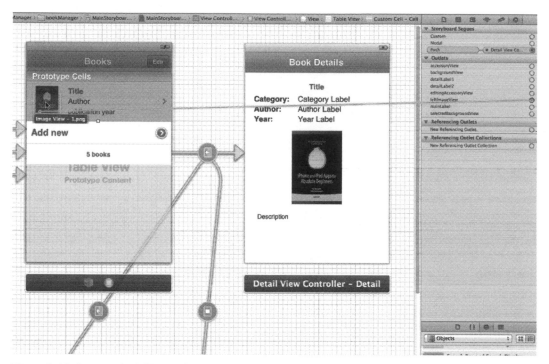

Figure 8-38. *Connect the leftImageView outlet to the Book cover image.*

2. Once you've opened up Storyboard, navigate to the Books scene. Remember that in the Books Table View you're using custom cells, so you need to connect the outlets to the custom cell subclass you created earlier in steps 1–4. Select the top cell containing the Book Image, Title, and so on, and then open up the Identity Inspector and in the Class field click CustomCell (refer to Figure 8-18 or 8-43 if you need a memory refresher). With the Cell Prototype still selected, open the Connections Inspector to see a list of all available outlets. Drag out from the `leftImageView` outlet and connect it to the book's cover image, which for now, in this case, is `1.png`. This is shown in Figure 8-38. This outlet will enable your connectivity to the SQLite database so you can display whatever associated image is saved in the database, not the static `1.png`.

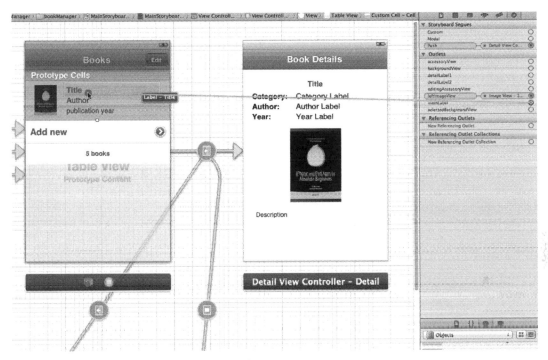

Figure 8-39. *Connect the mainLabel outlet to the Title.*

3. Control-drag from the `mainLabel` outlet and connect it to Title as
    shown in Figure 8-39.

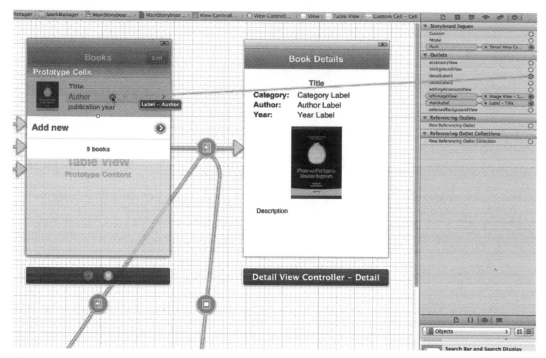

Figure 8-40. *Connect the detailLabel1 outlet to the Author.*

4. Control-drag from the detailLabel1 outlet and connect it to Author as shown in Figure 8-40.

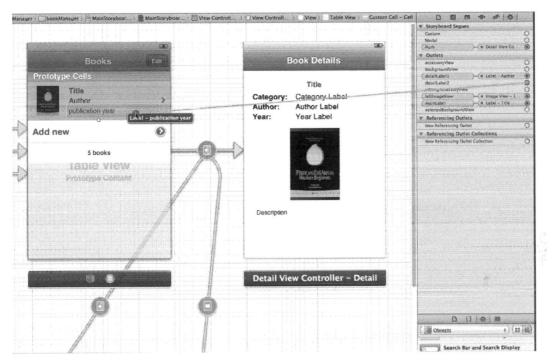

Figure 8-41. *Connect the detailLabel2 outlet to the publication year.*

5. Control drag from the detailLabel2 outlet and connect it to publication year as shown in Figure 8-41. Save it, and let's move on.

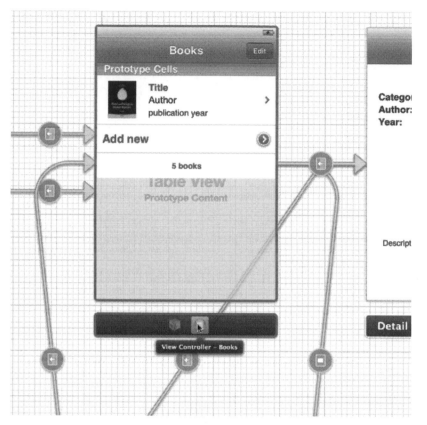

Figure 8-42. *Select the View Controller.*

6. You also need to create IBOutlets for the Table View and the Book count label. So select View Controller - Books as shown in Figure 8-42 so that you can assign a class to it.

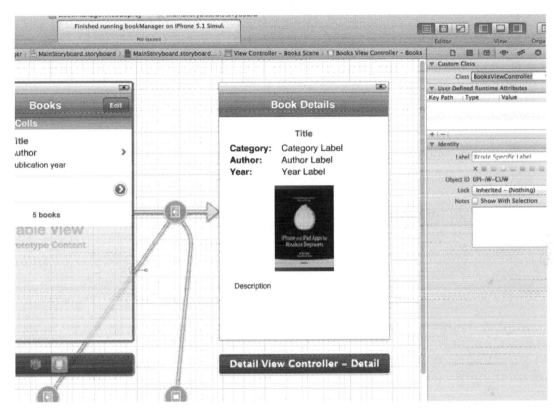

Figure 8-43. *Name the class BooksViewController.*

7. With View Controller - Books still selected, in the Identity Inspector click BooksViewController in the Class field as shown in Figure 8-43.

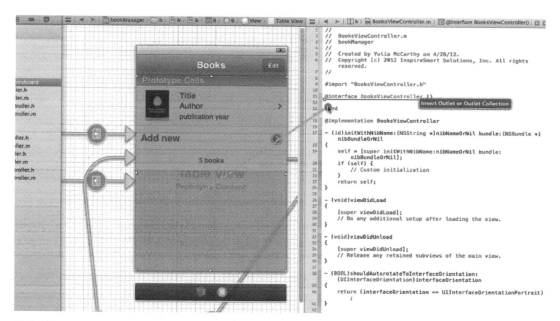

Figure 8-44. *Connect to the implementation file.*

8. Open the Assistant editor and make sure the
    BooksViewController.m file is the Xcode file that appears in the
    right-hand panel. Click once in the Table View section of Books
    and Control-drag over to the implementation file, releasing it
    right under the @interface as shown in Figure 8-44. When the
    pop-up appears, name it _tableView and leave all the other
    defaults of the outlet as is.

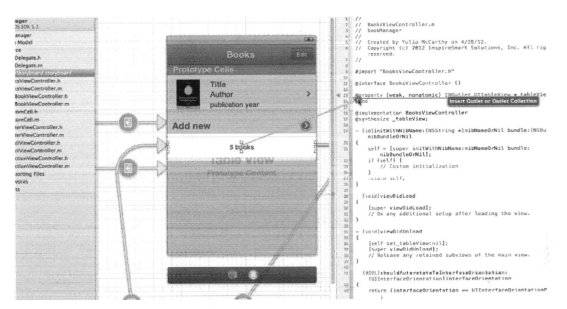

Figure 8-45. *Connect the _countLabel outlet.*

9. Now select the book counter and Control-drag over to the
    implementation file, dropping it right below the previous outlet
    as shown in Figure 8-45. Name it _countLabel and again leave
    the defaults as is. Save your work.

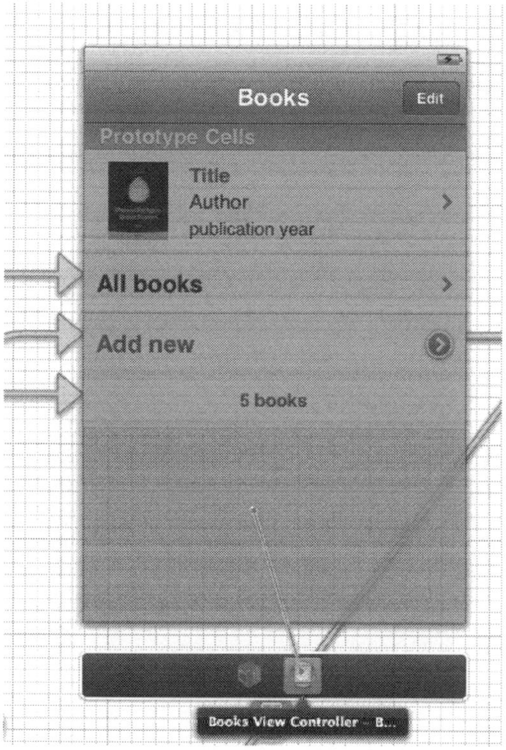

Figure 8-46. *Control-drag to the View Controller icon in the Dock.*

10. Lastly, Control-drag from the Table View to the View Controller icon in the Dock as shown in Figure 8-46.

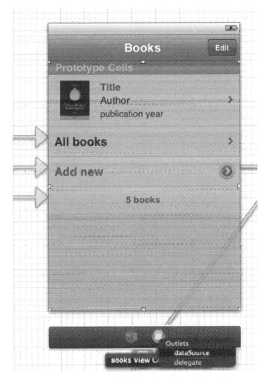

Figure 8-47. *Connecting the dataSource outlet*

11. In the dialog connection window that appears, select
    dataSource nested inside the Outlets option as shown in Figure
    8-47. Repeat the exact same procedure to connect the delegate
    outlet of the Table View.

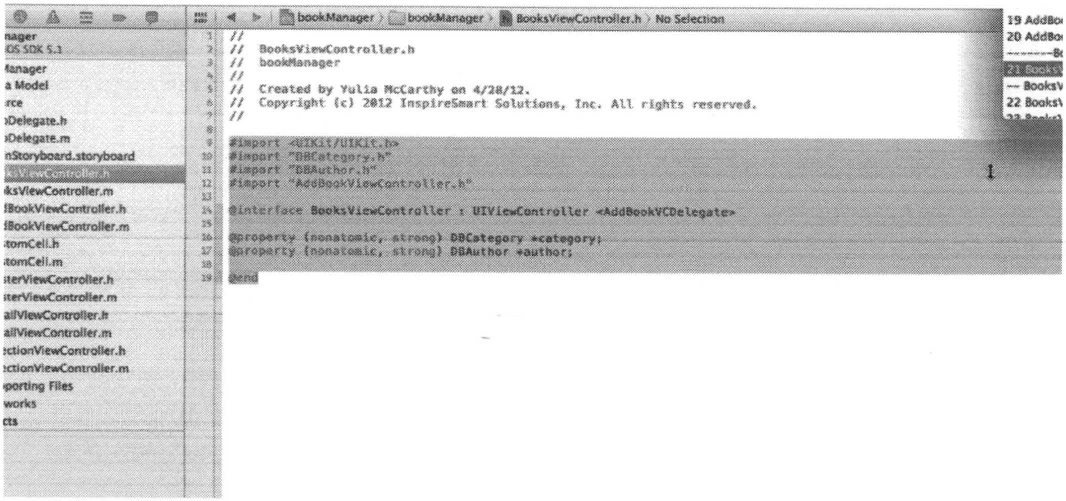

Figure 8-48. *Add in two additional properties of DBCategory and DBAuthor type.*

12. Open the Standard editor and open the `BooksViewController.h` file. Select all three lines of default code and delete it. You want to add two additional properties of categories and author into `BooksViewController`. Drag in the "21 BooksViewController.h Interface" snippet from DemoMonkey and place it in the body of the view as shown in Figure 8-48.

The two new properties are category and author:

```
@property (nonatomic, strong) DBCategory *category;
@property (nonatomic, strong) DBAuthor *author;
```

Figure 8-49. *Synthesize, import header files, and other tweaks*

13. Save your work, leave BooksViewController.h, and open its implementation file. Type in syntheses statements for _tableView, _countLabel, category, and author. Additionally, you'll need a variable to store the books in. Again, use a mutable array and call it _books. To do this, add its declaration to the private interface section right below the @interface. Make sure to enclose it in curly braces:

```
@interface BooksViewController () {
  NSMutableArray *_books;
}
```

Now you need to import the necessary header files. Drag in the "--BooksViewController.h Imports" snippet from DemoMonkey and place it directly under the only existing header file #import "BooksViewController.h" as shown in Figure 8-49.

Lastly, on `viewDidLoad` you'll populate the books array with `DBBook` objects. Drag in the "22 BooksViewController.m ViewDidLoad" snippet from DemoMonkey and place it in the `viewDidLoad` method directly under the `//Do any additional setup …` comment as shown in Figure 8-49 and as follows:

```
- (void)viewDidLoad
{
  [super viewDidLoad];
  // Do any additional setup after loading the view.

  if (self.category != nil) {
    _books = [NSMutableArray arrayWithArray:self.category.books];
  }
  else if (self.author != nil) {
    _books = [NSMutableArray arrayWithArray:self.author.books];
  }
  else {
    _books = [NSMutableArray arrayWithArray:[DBBook allBooks]];
  }
}
```

You can see you're using the category property `self.category` and the author property `self.author` to decide which books you need to display: the ones that belong to a specified category or a selected author. However, if none of those properties is defined by the user, you'll display all the books you have in the SQLite database:

```
else {
    _books = [NSMutableArray arrayWithArray:[DBBook allBooks]];
}
```

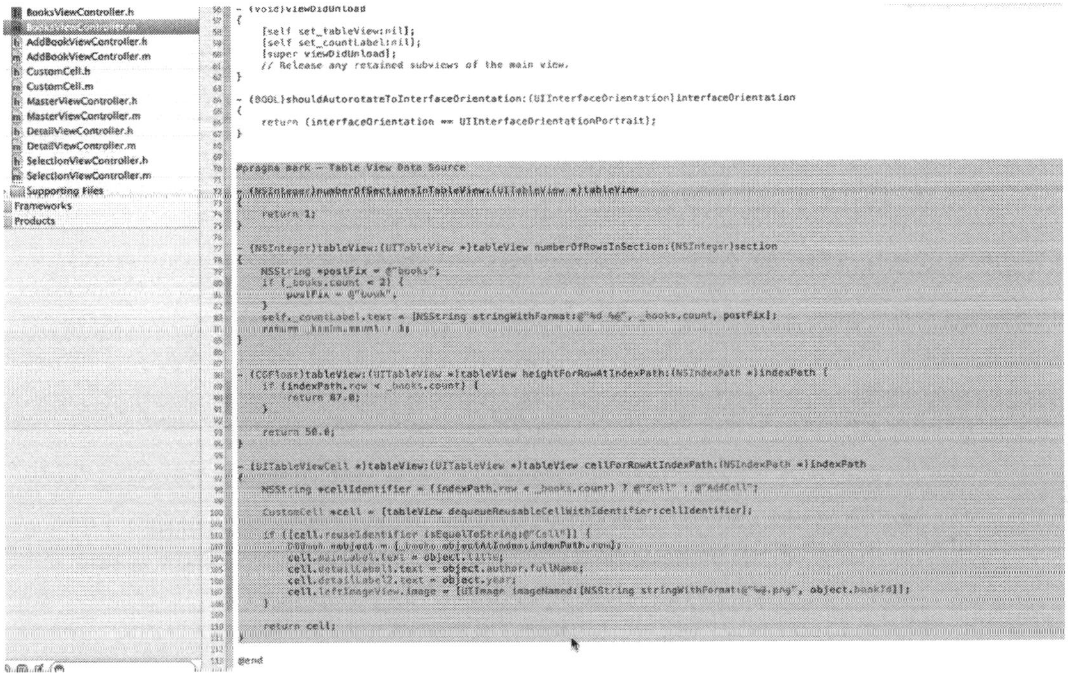

Figure 8-50. *Set up the Table View to display books.*

14. To display the books data in the Table View, you must implement the delegate methods. Drag in the "23 BooksViewController.m Display Books" snippet from DemoMonkey and place it right before the @end as shown in Figure 8-50.

    You want the very bottom cell of the Table View to display static content ("Add new" cell), which will be visible at all times, and tapping this cell will allow the user to create a new book record.

    To achieve that, you do a little trick here in

```
- (NSInteger)tableView:(UITableView *)tableView
numberOfRowsInSection:(NSInteger)section
```

    by adding one extra row to your Table View in addition to the number of objects you have in the _books array:

```
return _books.count + 1;
```

This guarantees that you'll always have at least one cell in the Table View, so you simply need to get your Table View to load the right Prototype cell from the Storyboard, based on certain conditions.

Notice that in this method you also update the text of the _countLabel—this way it's always up-to-date.

You de-queue the appropriate cell by its identifier, "Cell" or "AddCell," which you've specified at design time:

```
NSString *cellIdentifier = (indexPath.row < _books.count) ? @"Cell" :
@"AddCell";
  CustomCell *cell = [tableView
dequeueReusableCellWithIdentifier:cellIdentifier];
```

Based on the reuse identifier, you update the cell's content accordingly:

```
if ([cell.reuseIdentifier isEqualToString:@"Cell"]) {
    DBBook *object = [_books objectAtIndex:indexPath.row];
    cell.mainLabel.text = object.title;
    cell.detailLabel1.text = object.author.fullName;
    cell.detailLabel2.text = object.year;
    cell.leftImageView.image = [UIImage imageNamed:[NSString
stringWithFormat:@"%@.png", object.bookId]];
  }
```

> **NOTE:** The cell's reuse identifier is the means for you to tell your Table View what kind of Storyboard Prototype cell you want to be de-queued and displayed for a certain row. Thus, it's very important to set the identifiers correctly. If the identifier isn't set or is invalid, the dequeueReusableCellWithIdentifier:cellIdentifier method will return nil, and the app will crash. This is one the most common mistakes when prototyping Table View cells in a Storyboard.

Figure 8-51. *Set up editing mode.*

15. Add the methods that will allow the user to edit the Table View and remove the book records. Drag in the "24 BooksViewController.m Delete Books" snippet from DemoMonkey and place it right before the @end as shown in Figure 8-51. Here you implement standard `UITableViewDataSource` methods that are in charge of Table View editing. When the user taps the standard Delete button of the Table View while in Editing mode, they get the corresponding DBBook object for that row. This allows the user to remove it from the _books array, and then delete the entity from the database using MagicalRecord API. Finally, remove the Table View row for that record with animation, which is beautifully handled for you by the Table View itself:

```
if (editingStyle == UITableViewCellEditingStyleDelete) {
    DBBook *object = [_books objectAtIndex:indexPath.row];
    [object deleteEntity];
    [_books removeObjectAtIndex:indexPath.row];
    [tableView deleteRowsAtIndexPaths:[NSArray arrayWithObject:indexPath]
withRowAnimation:UITableViewRowAnimationFade];
}
```

Figure 8-52. *Implementing the prepareForSegue: method*

16. Next, drag in the "25 BooksViewController.m prepareForSegue:" snippet from DemoMonkey and place it right before the @end as shown in Figure 8-52. In the prepareForSegue: method, you look for two different segue identifiers: the ShowBookDetails identifier and the AddNewBook identifier. In the first case, you only need to send the selected DBBook object to the destination View Controller, which is the DetailViewController in your setup:

```
NSIndexPath *indexPath = [self._tableView indexPathForSelectedRow];
DBBook *object = [_books objectAtIndex:indexPath.row];
[(DetailViewController *)[segue destinationViewController]
setDetailItem:object];
```

In the second case, you need to set a delegate so that you can get the newly added object back from the AddBookViewController:

```
AddBookViewController *addBookVC = (AddBookViewController
*)navigationVC.topViewController;
[addBookVC setDelegate:self];
```

Also, remember that your AddBookViewController is embedded into the Navigation Controller. But here's the issue: in order to get to the AddBookViewController, you must follow the Navigation Controller hierarchy as indicated here:

```
AddBookViewController *addBookVC = (AddBookViewController
*)navigationVC.topViewController;
```

> **NOTE:** This is a very common pitfall. Remember that whenever your segue's primary destination View Controller is a Navigation Controller, you must access its topViewController and cast it to the appropriate class in order to get to the View Controller you're likely intending to prepare for segue.

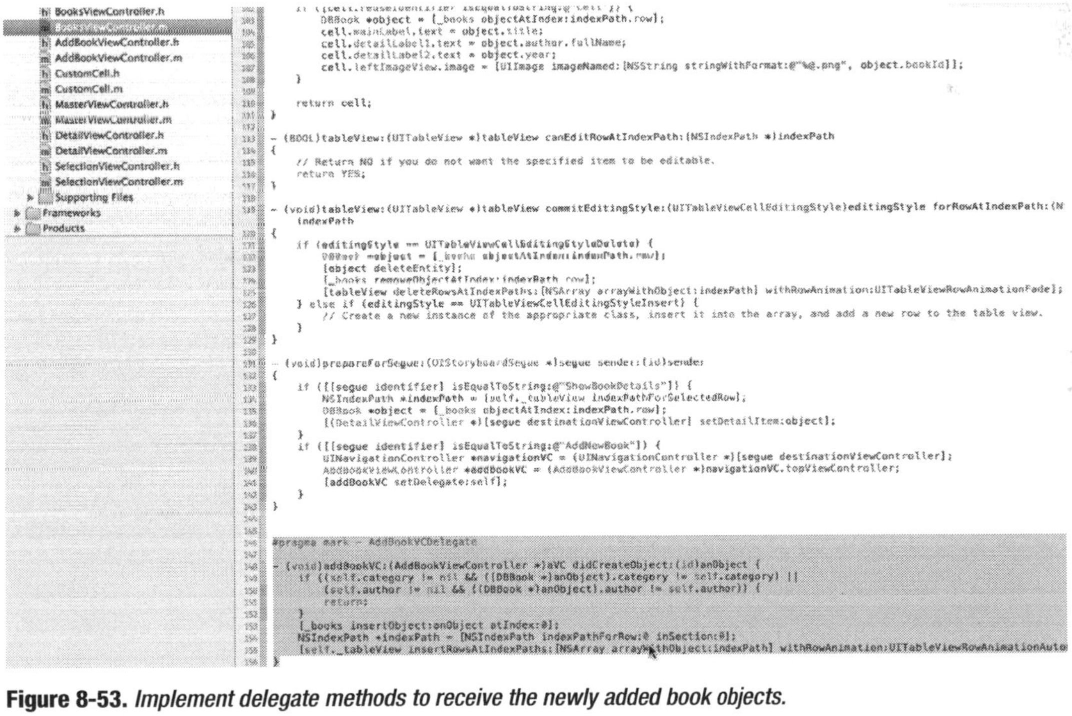

Figure 8-53. *Implement delegate methods to receive the newly added book objects.*

17. Additionally, you'll implement the delegate method for the AddBooksViewController, in which you can access the object that's been created by the user and add it to the Table View. Drag in the "26 BooksViewController.m Add Books" snippet from DemoMonkey and place it right before the @end as shown in Figure 8-53. In this method, addBookVC:didCreateObject:, you're checking whether you're currently displaying books per a certain category or per a certain author, and if so, whether the book you're about to add to the Table View belongs to one of those groups:

```
self.category != nil && ((DBBook *)anObject).category != self.category) ||
self.author != nil && ((DBBook *)anObject).author != self.author))
```

If that's not the case, you don't update the current list of books—otherwise, if the object passes the tests, you add a new row to the very top of the Table View:

```
NSIndexPath *indexPath = [NSIndexPath indexPathForRow:0 inSection:0];
[self._tableView insertRowsAtIndexPaths:[NSArray arrayWithObject:indexPath]
withRowAnimation:UITableViewRowAnimationAutomatic];
```

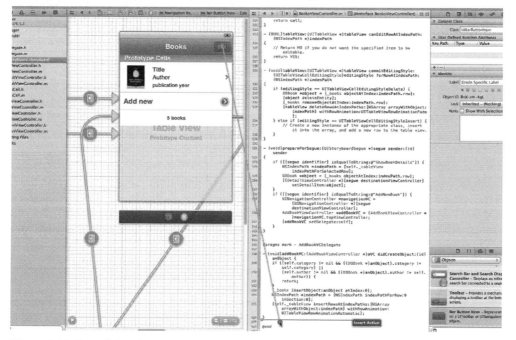

Figure 8-54. *Control-drag from the edit button to make an IBAction.*

18. Finally, you need to specify an IBAction for the Edit button in your Navigation Bar. Remember that once the user taps this Edit button, the Table View will switch to the editing mode, and the user will be able to delete cells. So open up Storyboard and navigate to Books Table View. Then open up the Assistant editor and make sure the right-hand pane is the implementation file of BooksViewController. Click inside it and scroll down to the bottom of the code. Now Control-drag from the Edit button down to just before the @end as shown in Figure 8-54.

In the pop-up dialog for the Action, name it editPressed. Now, make sure before you click Connect, because you've always been leaving everything in its default, that you select UIBarButtonItem from the drop-down menu in the Type field. Before proceeding, make sure your IBAction looks as follows:

```
- (IBAction)editPressed:(UIBarButtonItem *)sender {
}
@end
```

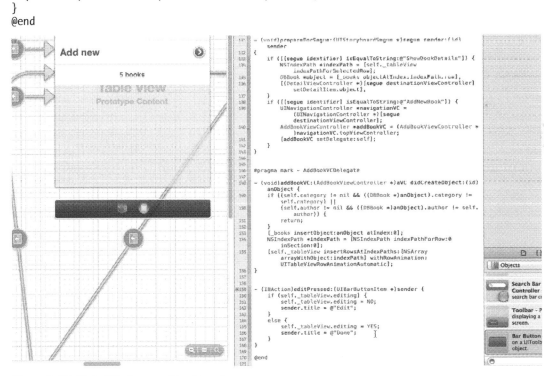

Figure 8-55. *Make IBAction capable of toggling.*

19. Press Return after the first bracket located after sender { and create a line between the beginning and ending brackets so that you can code inside the method. You need to write code so that you can toggle the editing mode for the Table View on and off. Type the following code:

```
- (IBAction)editPressed:(UIBarButtonItem *)sender {
  if (self._tableView.editing) {
    self._tableView.editing = NO;
    sender.title = @"Edit";
  }
  else {
    self._tableView.editing = YES;
    sender.title = @"Done";
  }
}
```

Refer to Figure 8-55 for details.

Adding Code for the Categories Scene

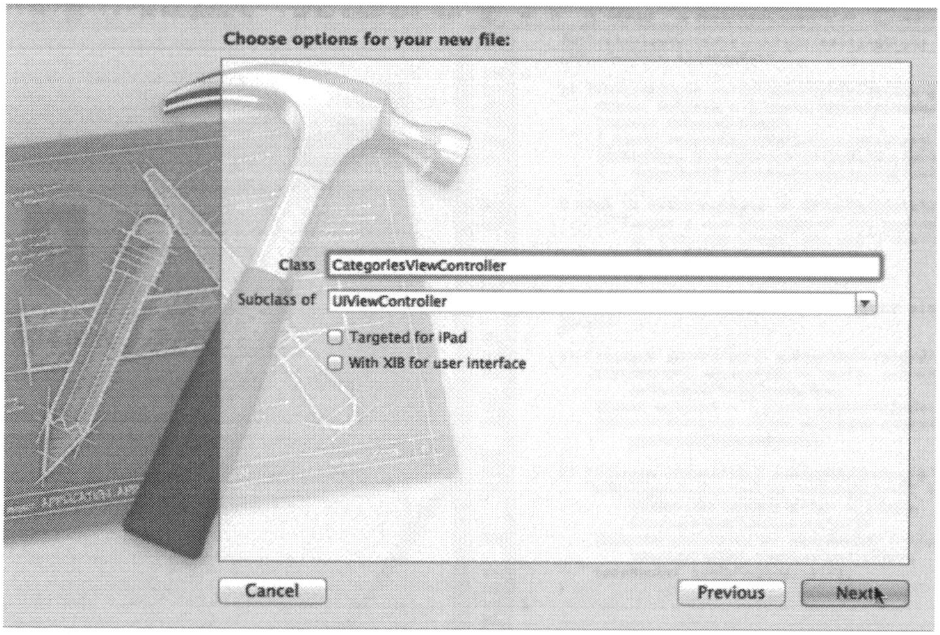

Figure 8-56. *Create the CategoriesViewController.*

1. The next View Controller you'll create is the Categories View Controller. Press ⌘+N to create a new subclass and, after selecting the Objective-C class, click Next. Name it CategoriesViewController and make it a subclass of UIViewController as shown in Figure 8-56. Save it in its default location.

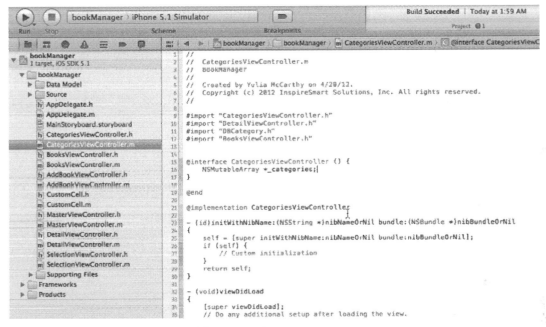

Figure 8-57. *Imports and an array to hold the categories*

2. Open up the CategoriesViewController.m file. Drag in the "--CategoriesViewController.m Imports" snippet from DemoMonkey and place it under the #import "CategoriesViewController.h" line.

You'll also need an array to store the objects from the database. You can just add this into the private @interface section. Type NSMutableArray *_categories; enclosed into a set of curly braces as shown in Figure 8-57 and as follows:

```
@interface CategoriesViewController () {
  NSMutableArray *_categories;
}
```

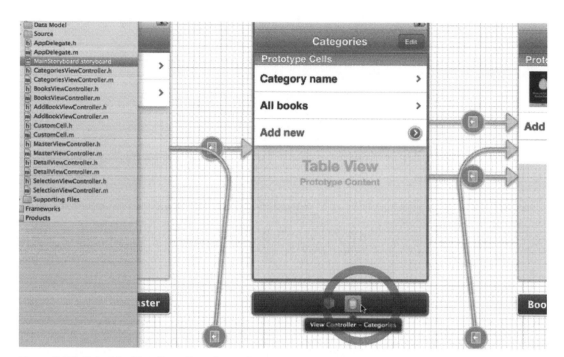

Figure 8-58. *Select the View Controller – Categories.*

3. You now need an outlet for the Table View that you have in the Categories Scene. Open up Storyboard and navigate to View Controller – Categories. Click it once to select it as shown in Figure 8-58.

Figure 8-59. *Set the Class for the Categories Scene.*

4. With the View Controller – Categories selected, open the Identity Inspector and set the Class to *CategoriesViewController* as shown in Figure 8-59.

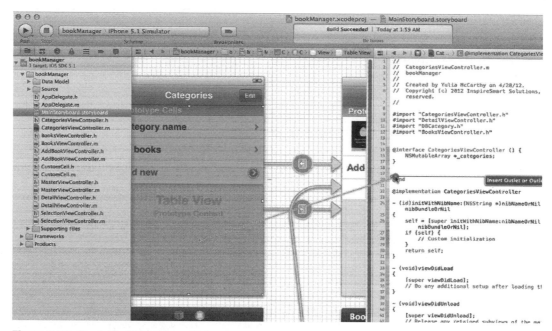

Figure 8-60. *Create the Table View outlet.*

5. Open the Assistant editor and make sure you have the
    CategoriesViewController implementation file on the right-hand
    pane of the Assistant. Now, Control-drag from the Table View to
    right before the @end as shown in Figure 8-60.

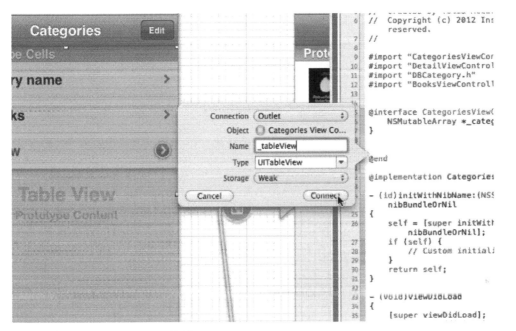

Figure 8-61. *Name the outlet _tableView.*

6. Name the outlet _tableView as shown in Figure 8-61. Click Connect and save everything.

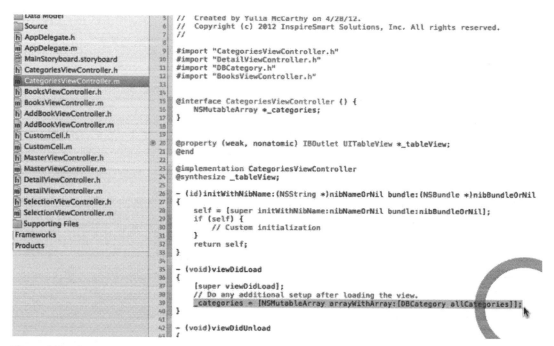

Figure 8-62. *Populate the _categories array with the objects from the database*

7. Open the Standard editor and then open the
CategoriesViewController.m file. You're going to populate the
_categories array with the objects from the database on
viewDidLoad: call. Drag in the "27 CategoriesViewController.m
ViewDidLoad" snippet from DemoMonkey and place it inside
the viewDidLoad: method as shown in Figure 8-62 and as
follows:

```
- (void)viewDidLoad
{
  [super viewDidLoad];
      // Do any additional setup after loading the view.
  _categories = [NSMutableArray arrayWithArray:[DBCategory allCategories]];
}
```

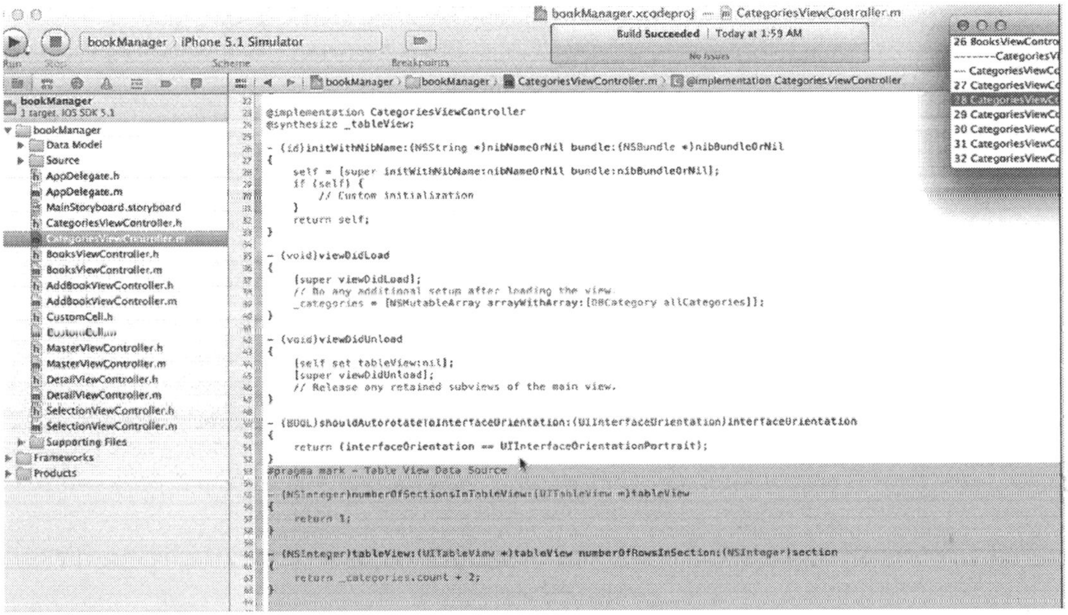

Figure 8-63. *Display the Items in the Table View.*

8. Next, you need to display the items in the
   `CategoriesViewController`. Drag in the "28
   CategoriesViewController.m Display Categories" snippet from
   DemoMonkey and place it right before the @end as shown in
   Figure 8-63.

   The way you display the items in the Table View is very similar
   to the one you did in the `BooksViewController`, except that here
   in the `(NSInteger)tableView:(UITableView *)tableView
   numberOfRowsInSection:(NSInteger)section` you display two
   static rows at the end of the Table View in addition to the
   number of book categories you have in the database:

```
return _categories.count + 2;
```

   Thus, you need to check for two additional cell reuse
   identifiers—`AllCell` and `AddCell`—when displaying the cells in
   order to load the proper ones from the Storyboard:

```
- (UITableViewCell *)tableView:(UITableView *)tableView
cellForRowAtIndexPath:(NSIndexPath *)indexPath
{
```

```
        static NSString *cellIdentifier = nil;
if (indexPath.row < _categories.count) {
        cellIdentifier = @"Cell";
        }
  else if (indexPath.row == _categories.count) {
    cellIdentifier = @"AllCell";
  }
  else {
    cellIdentifier = @"AddCell";
  }
```

Figure 8-64. *Bring in code that will delete the categories.*

9. You now need to bring in code that will delete the categories.
   Drag in the "29 CategoriesViewController.m Delete Categories"
   snippet from DemoMonkey and place it right before the @end as
   shown in Figure 8-64. You may notice that this is almost
   identical to Delete Books in Figure 8-51.

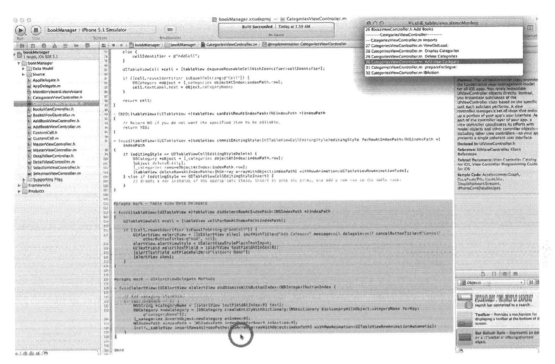

Figure 8-65. *Add a new category.*

10. Adding a new category is a little different, though. Because you only need to capture the category name, you don't need a whole new View Controller for that—you can do it using a UIAlertView. Drag in the "30 CategoriesViewController.m Add New Category" snippet from DemoMonkey and place it right before the @end as shown in Figure 8-65.

Here, once the user clicks the "Add new" cell

```
if ([cell.reuseIdentifier isEqualToString:@"AddCell"]) {
```

you simply pop a standard UIAlertView that contains a built-in UITextField:

```
UIAlertView *alertView = [[UIAlertView alloc] initWithTitle:@"Add Category"
message:nil delegate:self cancelButtonTitle:@"Cancel" otherButtonTitles:@"Add",
nil];
    alertView.alertViewStyle = UIAlertViewStylePlainTextInput;
    UITextField *alertTextField = [alertView textFieldAtIndex:0];
```

You then implement the UIAlertViewDelegate method:

```
- (void)alertView:(UIAlertView *)alertView
didDismissWithButtonIndex:(NSInteger)buttonIndex
```

> Save the category into the database and add it to the
> _categories array:

```
DBCategory *newCategory = [DBCategory createEntityWithDictionary:[NSDictionary
dictionaryWithObject:categoryName forKey:@"categoryName"]];
    [_categories insertObject:newCategory atIndex:0];
```

> Insert a new row into the Table View:

```
[self._tableView insertRowsAtIndexPaths:[NSArray arrayWithObject:indexPath]
withRowAnimation:UITableViewRowAnimationAutomatic];
```

Figure 8-66. *Implement the prepareForSegue: method.*

11. Next you'll implement the prepareForSegue: method. Drag in
    the "31 CategoriesViewController.m PrepareForSegue" snippet
    from DemoMonkey and place it right before the @end as shown
    in Figure 8-66.

    While storyboarding your UI, you specified two segues from the
    Categories Scene, between which you must distinguish:

```
([[segue identifier] isEqualToString:@"ShowCategoryBooks"])
```

and

```
if ([[segue identifier] isEqualToString:@"ShowAllBooks"])
```

In the first case, you set the Category property of the destination View Controller, which is BooksViewController, to the currently selected Category, and also reset its Author property to nil, in case it was previously assigned a value:

```
[(BooksViewController *)[segue destinationViewController] setCategory:object];
[(BooksViewController *)[segue destinationViewController] setAuthor:nil];
```

This way you make sure BooksViewController will only display the books that belong to the selected Category.

In the second case, you set both the Category and the Author to nil:

```
[(BooksViewController *)[segue destinationViewController] setCategory:nil];
[(BooksViewController *)[segue destinationViewController] setAuthor:nil];
```

In which case, you may remember, viewDidLoad BooksViewController will load all books you have.

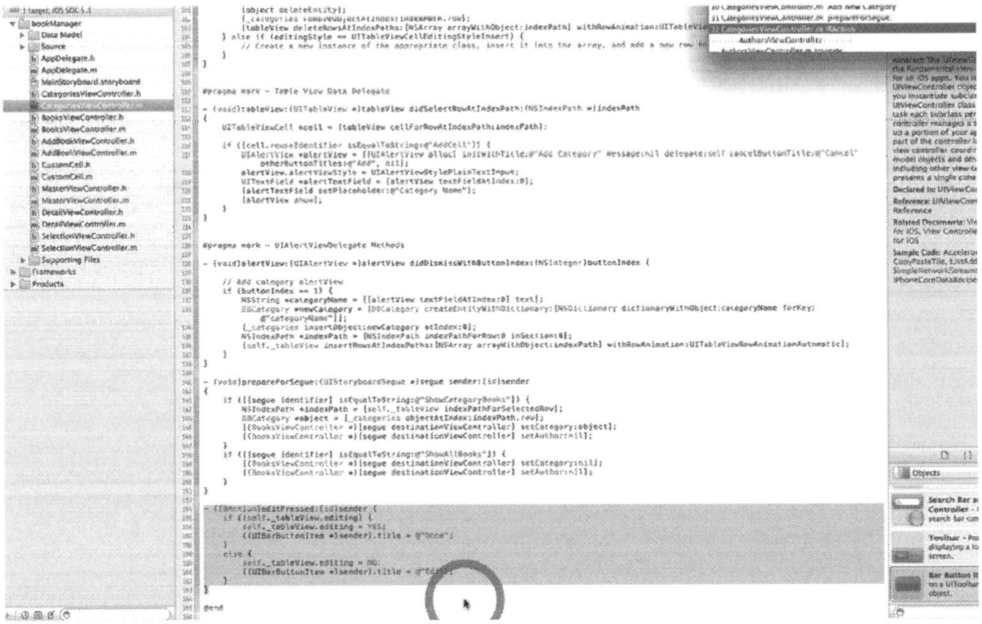

Figure 8-67. *Set up another IBAction for an Edit button.*

12. Lastly, you'll create the exact same `IBAction` method as you did for the `BooksViewController`, which will toggle the editing mode in your Table View. Drag in the "32 CategoriesViewController.m IBAction" snippet from DemoMonkey and place it right before the @end as shown in Figure 8-67.

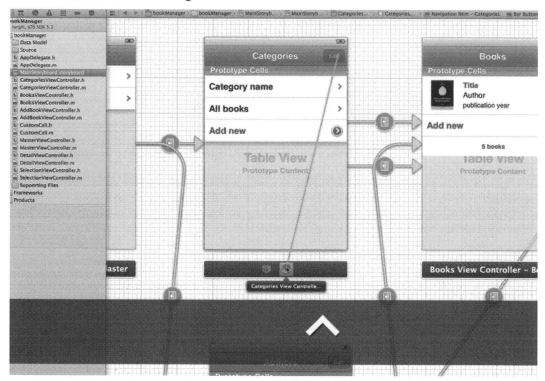

Figure 8-68. *Connect the Edit button to the Categories View Controller.*

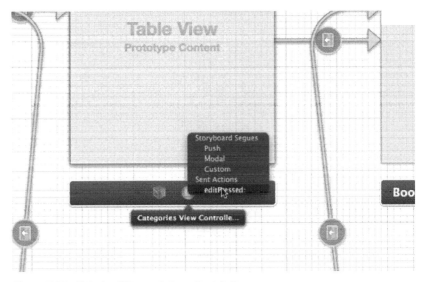

Figure 8-69. *Select editPressed: from Sent Actions.*

13. All you need to do is connect it to your Edit button on the View
Controller. In Storyboard connect the Edit button to the
Categories View Controller as shown in Figures 8-68 and 8-69.

Implementing the Authors Scene

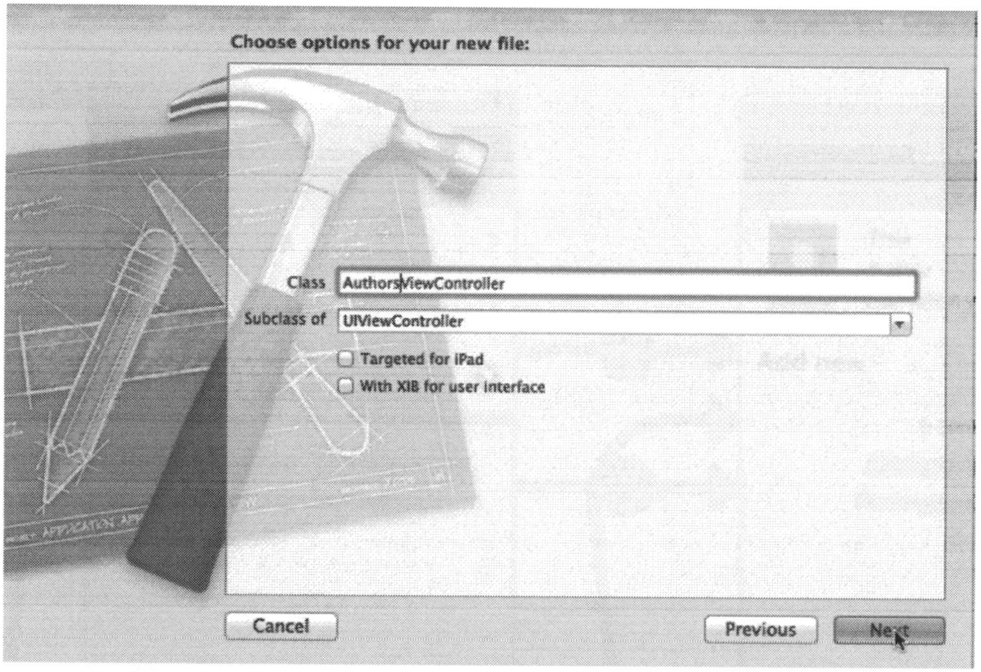

Figure 8-70. *Create the last View Controller class!*

1. The last View Controller you need to create is the Authors View Controller. Press ⌘+N to create a new subclass and, after selecting the Objective-C class, click Next. Name it *AuthorsViewController* and make it a subclass of UIViewController as shown in Figure 8-70.

NOTE: The next few steps for Authors repeat what you did for Categories, so these instructions will be brief. But we'll supply the images.

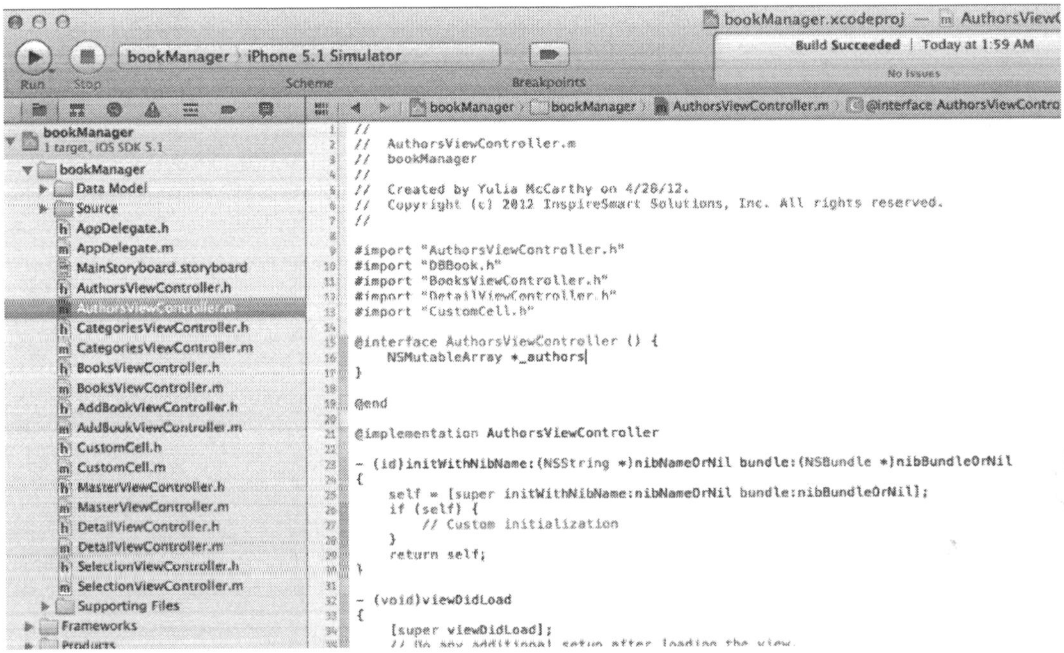

Figure 8-71. *Drag in the imports, Categories, and Author Display.*

2. Open up the AuthorsViewController.m file, drag in the "--AuthorsViewController.m Imports" snippet from DemoMonkey, and place it right under the #import "AuthorsViewController.h" as shown in Figure 8-71. These imports are DBBook.h, BooksViewController.h, DetailViewController.h, and CustomCell.h. Create the mutableArray just as you did for Categories.

Change @interface AuthorsViewController () to:

```
@interface AuthorsViewController () {
  NSMutableArray *_authors;
}
```

Drag in the "33 AuthorsViewController.m ViewDidLoad" snippet from DemoMonkey and place it inside the viewDidLoad: as you did for Categories.

Drag in the "34 AuthorsViewController.m Display Authors" snippet from DemoMonkey and place it right before the @end.

Figure 8-72. *Drag in the Delete Authors snippet.*

3.   Drag in the "35 AuthorsViewController.m Delete Authors" snippet from DemoMonkey and place it right before the @end as shown in Figure 8-72.

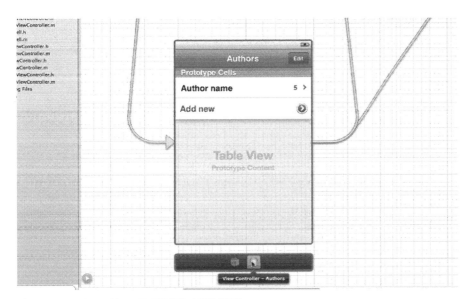

Figure 8-73. *Make the outlet for the Table View.*

4. You'll also need an outlet for the Table View. Open Storyboard and navigate to the Authors Scene. Click View Controller – Authors once to select it as shown in Figure 8-73.

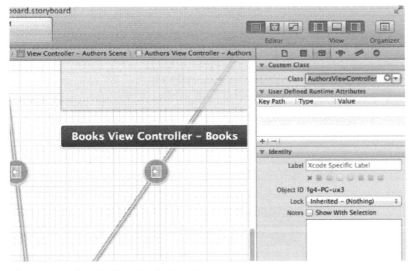

Figure 8-74. *Set the Class for Authors Scene.*

5. With View Controller – Authors selected, set the Class to *AuthorsViewController* as shown in Figure 8-74.

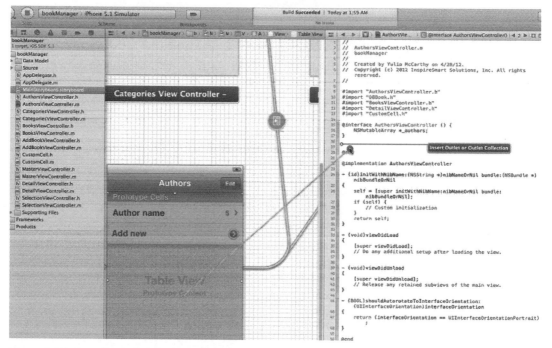

Figure 8-75. *Open the Assistant and create the outlet.*

6. Open the Assistant editor, make sure the AuthorsViewController.m is open in the right-hand pane, and drag from the Authors Table View to AuthorsViewController.m to create the outlet as shown in Figure 8-75.

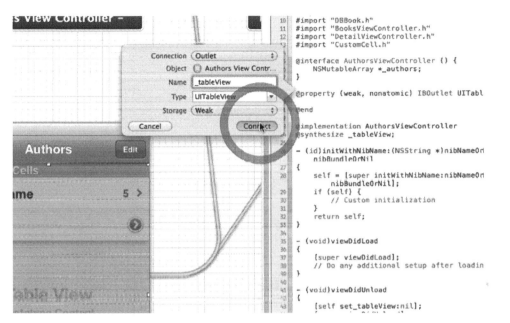

Figure 8-76. *Name the outlet _tableView.*

7. Once the Connection pop-up appears, name the outlet
   _tableView as shown in Figure 8-76.

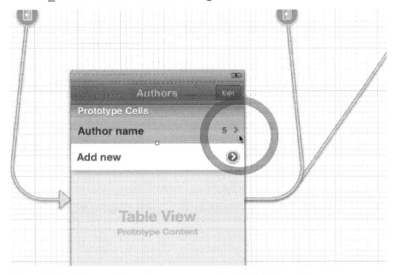

Figure 8-77. *Connect the outlets to your custom Table View cell.*

8.   Close the Assistant editor, go back to the Standard editor, and connect the outlets to your custom Table View cell. Click the cell once as shown in Figure 8-77.

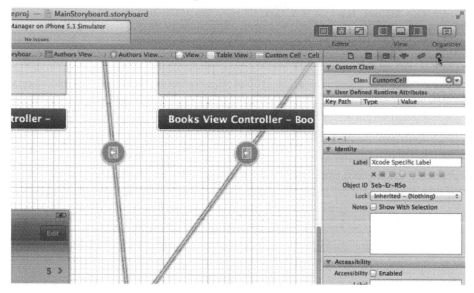

Figure 8-78. *Set the cell's Class to CustomCell.*

9.   Set its Class to *CustomCell* as shown in Figure 8-78.

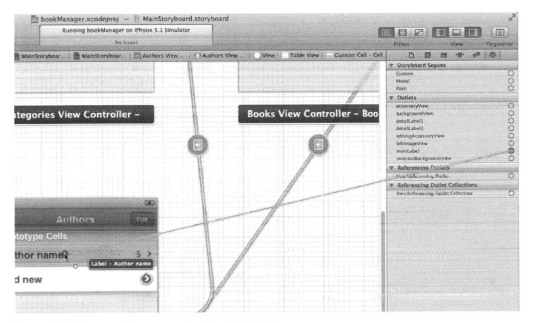

Figure 8-79. *Connect the mainLabel to "Author name."*

10. With the top cell still selected, open the Connections Inspector and connect the `mainLabel` outlet to the "Author name" label as shown in Figure 8-79.

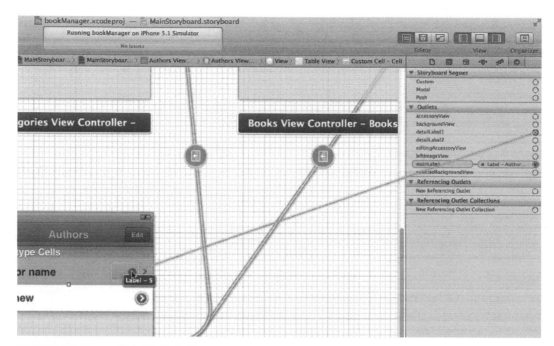

Figure 8-80. *Connect the detailLabel1.*

11. Connect the `detailLabel1` to "Label – 5" as shown in Figure 8-80.

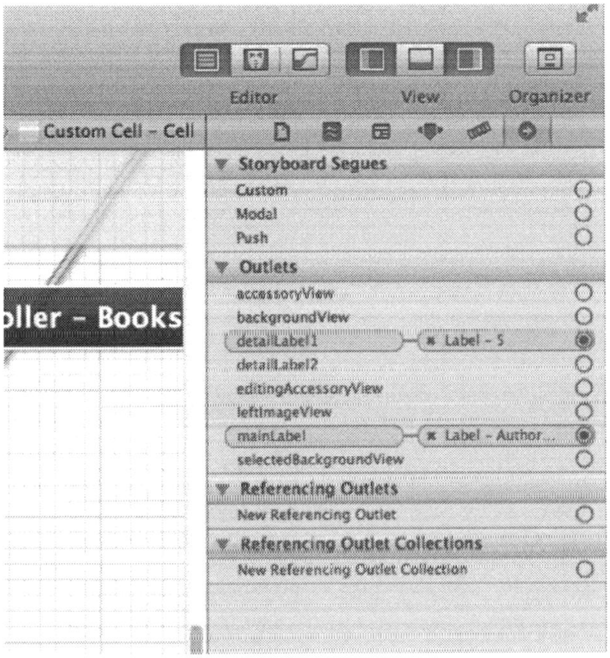

Figure 8-81. *Final connections*

12. Your final connections should look like ours as shown in Figure 8-81.

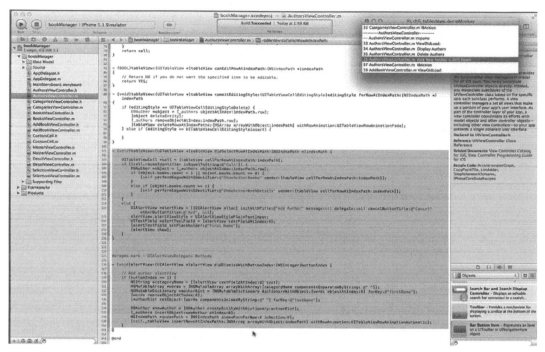

Figure 8-82. *Add new authors (slight variation).*

13. Now go back to the AuthorsViewController.m and drag in the
    "36 AuthorsViewController.m Add NewAuthors + Drill Down"
    snippet from DemoMonkey. Place it right before the @end as
    shown in Figure 8-82. As you may remember, when you were
    designing this scene you created two segues that originated from
    the Authors View Controller itself rather than a cell or a button.
    Thus, you must perform those segues manually from the code
    when certain conditions are met. In your case, you'll perform the
    segues once the user selects a Table View cell. In the
    tableView:didSelectRowAtIndexPath: method, you manually
    perform a segue with a specific identifier (ShowAuthorBooks or
    ShowAuthorBookDetail) based on how many books the selected
    author has:

```
if (object.books.count > 1 || object.books.count == 0) {
    [self performSegueWithIdentifier:@"ShowAuthorBooks" sender:[tableView
cellForRowAtIndexPath:indexPath]];
    }
    else if (object.books.count == 1) {
```

```
    [self performSegueWithIdentifier:@"ShowAuthorBookDetail" sender:[tableView
cellForRowAtIndexPath:indexPath]];
    }
```

If there's exactly one book, you'll perform the
ShowAuthorBookDetail segue to show the Book Details Scene for
this book; if the author has more than one book or no books at all,
you'll perform the ShowAuthorBooks segue to display the Books
Scene with the list of books associated with this author.

If the selected cell's identifier is not *Cell*, which leaves you with the
AddCell option, you'll pop up a UIAlertView with text field and Add
button, almost identical to the one you did for the Categories
Scene. Once the user taps the alert view's Add button, you create a
new author entity with the provided name. Now, add the new author
to the _authors array, and insert a new row at the top of the Table
View.

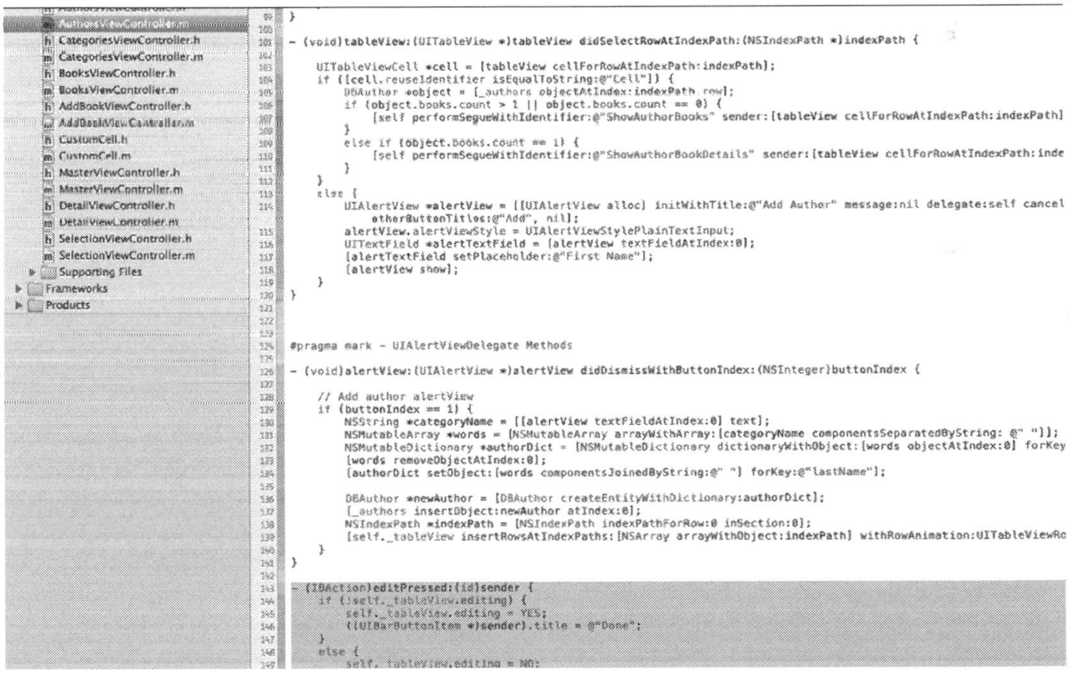

Figure 8-83. *IBAction same as for Categories*

14. The `IBAction` for the Edit button here is the same as in Categories. It toggles the editing mode for the Authors Table View in exactly same way. Drag in the "37 AuthorsViewController.m IBAction" snippet from DemoMonkey and place it right before the @end as shown in Figure 8-83.

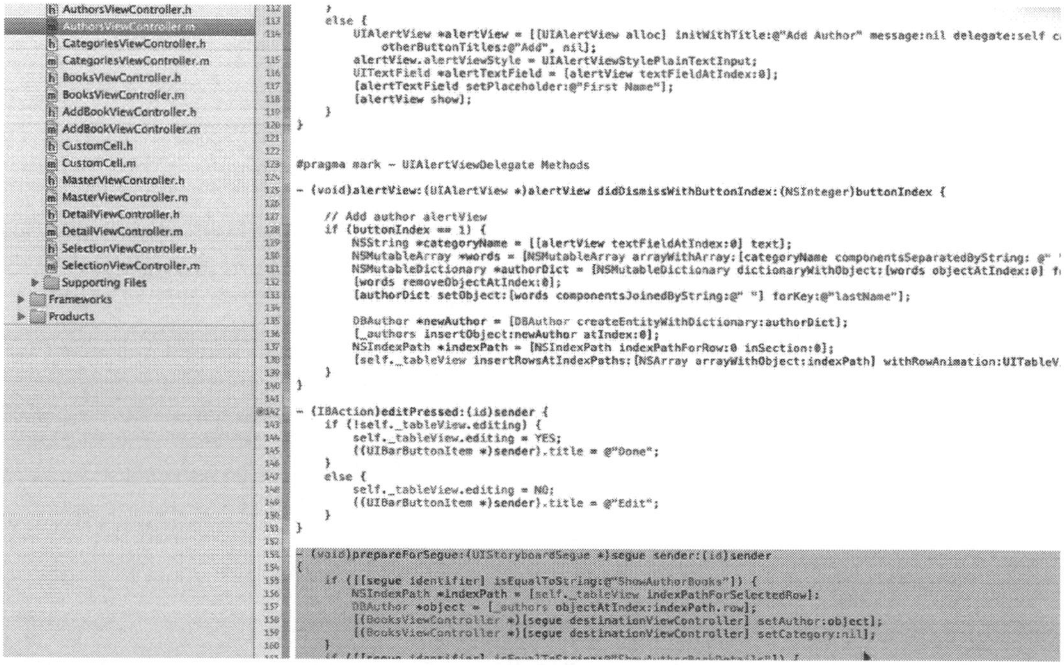

Figure 8-84. *Add the prepareForSegue: method implementation.*

15. Finally, you'll implement the `prepareForSegue:` method. Drag in the "38 AuthorsViewController.m prepareForSegue:" snippet from DemoMonkey and place it right before the @end as shown in Figure 8-84. The code here is a hybrid between the implementations you wrote for `CategoriesViewController` and `BooksViewController`.

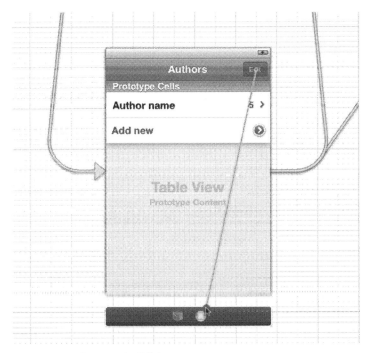

Figure 8-85. *Connect the Edit button.*

16. Back in Storyboard, Control-drag from the Edit button to the Authors View Controller icon in the Dock as shown in Figure 8-85. Select editPressed: from the pop-up dialog and save the file.

Wrapping Up and Loading Test Data

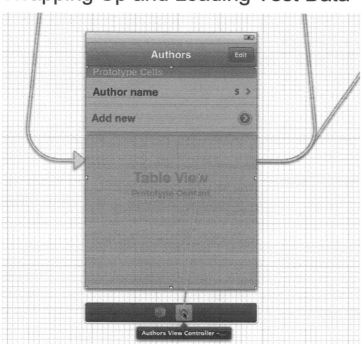

Figure 8-86. *Connect the first Table View.*

1. Control-drag from the Table View to the Authors View Controller icon in the Dock as shown in Figure 8-86.

Figure 8-87. *Select dataSource.*

2. In the Connection dialog that appears, select dataSource nested inside the Outlets option as shown in Figure 8-87. Repeat the exact same procedure to connect the `delegate` outlet of the Table View.

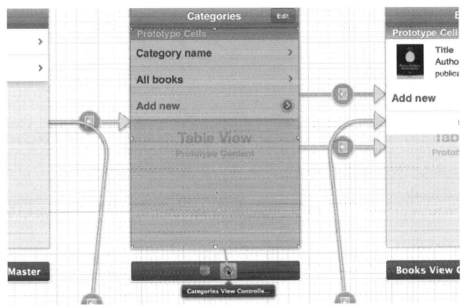

Figure 8-88. *Repeat for Categories as well.*

3. Now you need to repeat for Categories what you just did with Authors. Connect the Table View with the Categories View Controller icon as shown in Figure 8-88 and select dataSource from the Option dialog. Repeat again to similarly connect the `delegate` outlet.

```
       bookManager    bookManager    m AppDelegate.m    No Selection
 1   //
 2   //   AppDelegate.m
 3   //   bookManager
 4   //
 5
 6   #import "AppDelegate.h"
 7   #import "DBBook.h"
 8   #import "DBCategory.h"
 9   #import "DBAuthor.h"
10
11   @implementation AppDelegate
12
13   - (BOOL)application:(UIApplication *)application didFinishLaunchingWithOptions:(NSDictionary *)launchOptions
14   {
15       // Override point for customization after application launch.
16       [MagicalRecord setupCoreDataStackWithStoreNamed:@"MyDatabase.sqlite"];
17       // Temporary data
18       NSString *path = [[NSBundle mainBundle] pathForResource:@"bookdata" ofType:@"plist"];
19       NSDictionary *dataDict = [[NSDictionary alloc] initWithContentsOfFile:path];
20
21       if ([DBBook allBooks].count == 0) {
22           for (NSDictionary *dc in [dataDict objectForKey:@"categories"]) {
23               [DBCategory createEntityWithDictionary:dc];
24           }
25           for (NSDictionary *dc in [dataDict objectForKey:@"authors"]) {
26               [DBAuthor createEntityWithDictionary:dc];
27           }
28           for (NSDictionary *dc in [dataDict objectForKey:@"books"]) {
29               [DBBook createEntityWithDictionary:dc];
30           }
31       }
32
33       return YES;
34   }
35
36   - (void)applicationWillResignActive:(UIApplication *)application
37   {
```

Figure 8-89. *Populate the database with test data.*

4. You're almost ready to run your app! Although it's not required, and you should be able to run the app with an empty database, we recommend that you add one last piece of code. You've prepared a test database for this app, so you can test its functionality without the need to create many records yourself. Let's plug it in and see how the app works. Navigate to AppDelegate.m and drag in the "-- AppDelegate.m Imports" snippet from DemoMonkey. Place it below the #import "AppDelegate.h" line. Then find the following method:

```
- (BOOL)application:(UIApplication *)application
didFinishLaunchingWithOptions:(NSDictionary *)launchOptions
```

Drag in the very last "-- AppDelegate.m Data for Testing" snippet from DemoMonkey. Insert it at the end of the method implementation right below the following:

```
[MagicalRecord setupCoreDataStackWithStoreNamed:@"MyDatabase.sqlite"];
```

See Figure 8-89 for the final view of the AppDelegate.m after the two modifications you just made.

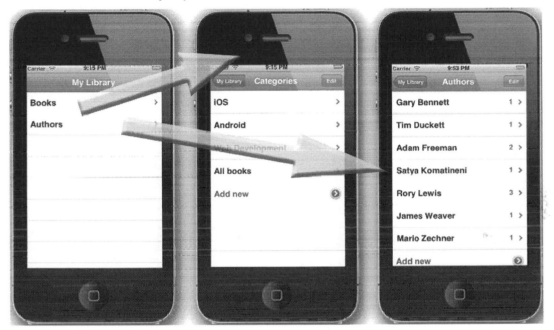

Figure 8-90. *Run it!*

5. Run it and test out the path from My Library to Books and then the path from My Library to Authors as shown in Figure 8-90.

Figure 8-91. *Three views working*

6. In Figure 8-91, the first image shows the Books View reached
    from Authors after selecting author Rory Lewis from the Table
    View. The middle image shows the Books View from Categories.
    The third image shows Deleting books. All working correctly.

Figure 8-92. *Adding*

7. The Adding Categories and adding Authors also works perfectly.

You can now say you've experienced, in detail, how you use the Master-Detail Application template to make an iPhone act like it was programmed with a Navigation-based Application template—or make an iPad act like it was programmed with a Split View-based Application template. This is huge, because now you know how to use the Master-Detail Application template when you want to work with lists, databases, and tables, particularly if you want to give the user the ability to drill down through your data in a hierarchical manner. You've also had experience now with the database component, and as mentioned, it's very difficult for employers to find Xcoders who have any experience at all with SQL.

Good job! Now get ready for your last app.

9

Chapter

Single View #3: wanderBoard Part I

In this final Storyboarding app, you'll build a simple maze-wandering game that allows the user to walk through a 3D maze that has one correct path among dead ends. As with the last app, this one is divided into three chapters: Chapter 9–11.

In this app you'll include a means to have the user graphically steer through the maze that implies motion. You'll be using mostly graphical images and Storyboarding techniques to develop this app while using as little code as possible. Similarly to Chapter 2's AlienView and Chapter 3's FlickrPhotoMap, this is also a Single View Application with Storyboards—but it's considerably more advanced. By the time you're done with this app, you'll have designed a serious graphical game using mostly Storyboarding.

wanderBoard: A Single-View App

We've designed the visuals to look as if you're in the maze looking left, right, or straight ahead. When you start the app you're dropped at the opening of a maze, as shown in Figure 9-0A, and you tap apparent openings in the walls to navigate from each location to the next. Occasionally, you wander down a path that goes nowhere and see a red arrow indicating that you can back up. Tapping the arrow returns you to your previous position in the maze, and you can keep tapping arrows to back all the way out of the dead-end path until the arrows stop appearing. Then you can continue forward in another direction to keep exploring the maze as shown in Figure 9-0B.

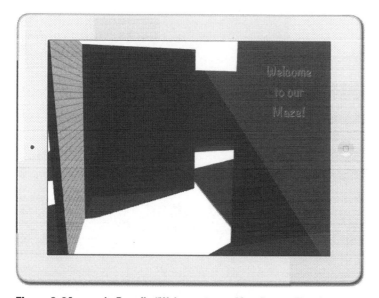

Figure 9-0A. *wanderBoard's "Welcome to our Maze" start: The view changes appropriately as the app keeps track of where you are in the virtual 3D space.*

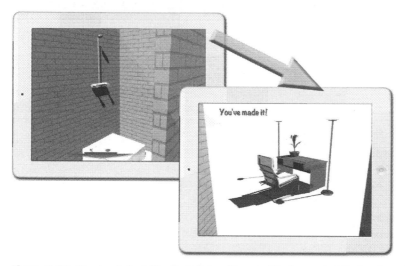

Figure 9-0B. *Dead ends look like the left-hand image. "You've made it!" signals you're out of the maze (right-hand image).*

We chose the iPad Landscape layout because it gives more room for maze presentation and room for navigation controls. The View Controller behavior is data-driven, meaning we encode information within the onscreen objects to control behavior of the application in a couple of ways:

- The object.tag property indicates mid-section or the end of dead-end paths.

- Segue identifiers indicate directions of travel Left, Right, or Forward, so the segue animation can also reflect the direction taken. This results in very little code being added to the View Controller template.

You'll use a Single View Controller object behind all 18 Maze Views. It's been given a special ability to determine whether and when to show a Reverse button (the red arrow) and it passes on segue direction by looking at the segue identifier and determining what to pass to the custom segue to affect its behavior. This View Controller uses a property of all View Controllers (isMovingToParentViewController) to determine when you're entering a dead-end path or leaving the path. Upon entry, the intermediate Reverse buttons are hidden, so you can't reverse until you get to the very end of a dead-end path. The ViewController code knows which buttons are intermediate by inspecting the .tag property of the Reverse buttons (which may or may not be present). The tag values are: tag=1 means mid-location, and tag=0 means end of path.

We also introduce some professional-level architectural designs in this app:

- A custom segue class handles the maze movement transitions (MovementSegue.m/.h).

- The Storyboard file encloses the Single View Controller within a Navigation Controller so that entering new locations and backing up when needed are simply push and pop operations. We configure the Single View as the entry to the maze and end by adding 17 more View Controllers, each with custom segues between them.

The wanderBoard app keeps track of how you move through a pseudo-geospatial area. In fact there are 18 scenes that the user can be in. Segues track where the user is by keeping track of which scene the user is in.

NOTE: There appears to be a bug in Xcode v4.3.2 (4E2002 in our case) wherein a duplicate of a UIButton from within Storyboard appears to occasionally fail to copy the "Shows Touch on Highlight" property. You may have to set this even though the button was duplicated! We will address this when we get there.

There will be a serious amount of repetition as you build the 18 scenes. And unfortunately, as noted in the nearby Note, there seems to be a bug with Xcode v4.3.2 that, as you will later see, prohibits us from completely automating the repetition of the 18 steps. With that in mind, we divide the project into four steps. First, you set up the files, adjust your project settings, and drag in your assets. Then you prep the Storyboard by adding your Navigation Controller, Image View, welcome label, and add the buttons. Next, you finish your View Controller header and implementation files. Finally, in MainStoryboard, you create the remaining 17 scenes (we give this step with and without assistance). This chapter covers the first two steps. The next two (the final one with assistance) are found in Chapter 10. The final step without assistance is in Chapter 11.

Preliminaries

As always, we supply you with all the files and code necessary for this chapter at http://bit.ly/sMRvAP. You can also download the final version of the app at http://bit.ly/Od8IUE. For an app of this size, you may want to download the Assets folder from http://bit.ly/Od9a5v and take note of the following: when you download the Assets.zip file, you'll see seven files/ These are: Default-Landscape@2x~ipad.png, Default-Landscape~ipad.png, icon72x72.png, icon144x144.png, MovementSegue.h, MovementSegue.m, and wanderBoard.demoMonkey, together with the two folders Images and Sources. You'll use the four .png files for icons and Landscape launch images. (We explain the MovementSegue files later, and of course you know what the demoMonkey file is all about.)

The Images folder contains 19 images, 18 of which you'll be using in the maze. Don't worry, we explain in detail how you can generate you own 3D landscapes. The 19th image is the red arrow image that tells users they have to start backtracking (shown in the left-hand image in Figure 9-0B). The Sources folder contains the OmniGraffle and Sweet Home 3D files we used to make the 3D images.

> **NOTE:** You may or may not want to find out how we created the 3D images used in the maze. If you're not interested in creating 3D imagery, skip ahead to the section "Step 1: Set Up the Files, Project Settings, and Assets." If you are interested, continue reading.

How We Created Our 3D Landscape

Because our focus is Storyboarding, we won't spend too much time explaining how to create 3D images. (We have an extensive 28-minute video of Stephen explaining exactly how to download, create, and integrate the OmniGraffle files with the Sweet Home 3D files at http://bit.ly/sMRvAP—see "Chapter 9_wanderBoard: How we created the 3D Maze for our Xcode" towards the bottom of the page.)

We used a simple tool called OmniGraffle to design the floor plan and camera views that users see as they go through the maze (Figure 9-0C). We then used the OmniGraffle images to guide our data entry into Sweet Home 3D to make the maze come to life with perspectives, walls and bricks, light sources, shadows, ornaments, desks, shelves, and other goodies we dragged into the file to create the scenes (Figures 9-0D and 0E). We're sure these two tools can be used in a much more sophisticated way. We've seen examples of what other people have done with these tools and they are absolutely amazing.

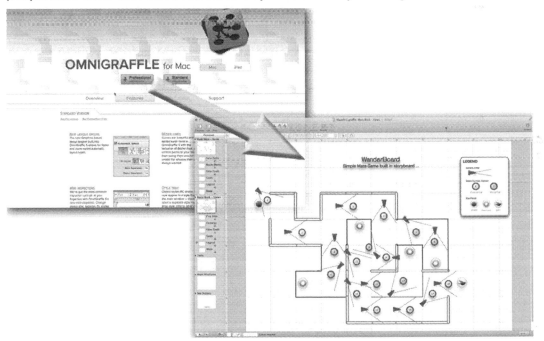

Figure 9-0C. *OmniGraffle provided a very easy, intuitive way for us to design the maze.*

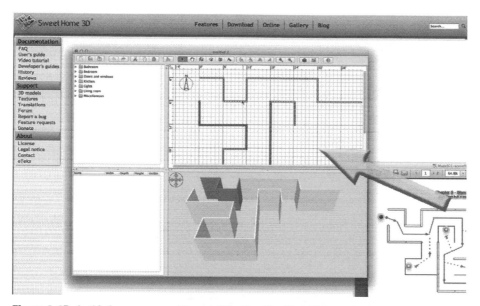

Figure 9-0D. *In this image we superimposed the OmniGraffle and Sweet Home 3D files on top of the Sweet Home 3D web site. We hand-entered the walls as shown in our drawing into Sweet Home 3D.*

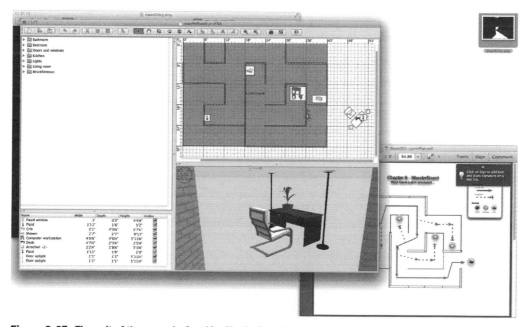

Figure 9-0E. *The exit of the maze in OmniGraffle depicted by the bird in the yellow circle at the bottom right of the image is replaced by a desk in Sweet Home 3D.*

Step 1: Set Up the Files, Project Settings, and Assets

As always, clear out your desktop. Then go to http://www.rorylewis.com/xCode/StoryBoarding%20in%20Xcode/Chapter07_WanderBoard-Assets.zipdownload the file, and unzip the folder to your desktop.

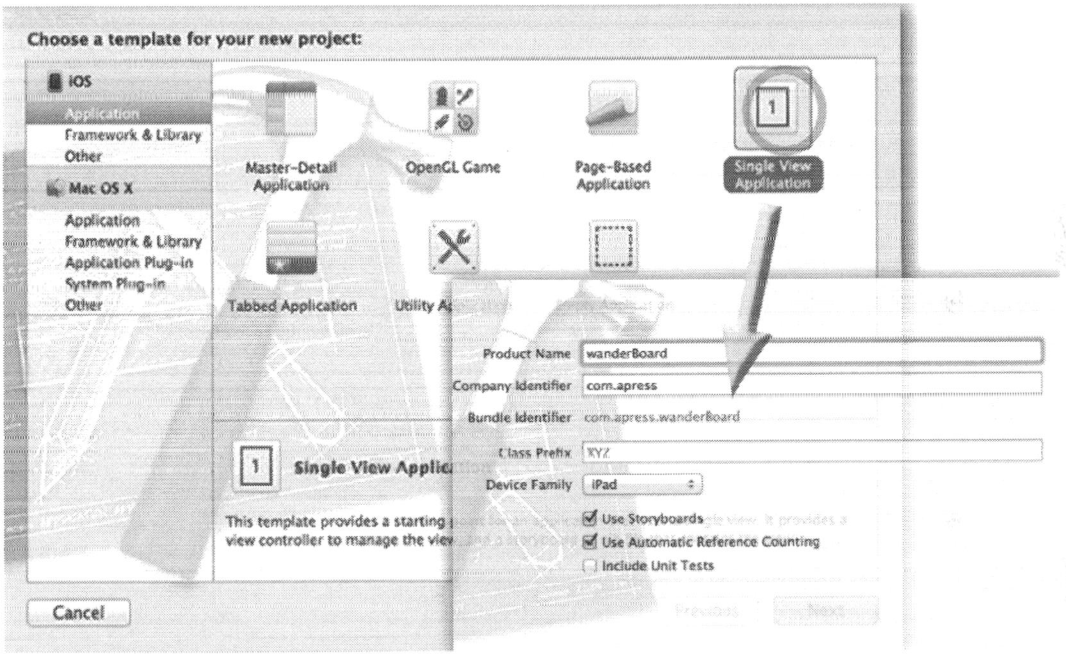

Figure 9-1. *Start a Single View Application and save it as wanderBoard.*

1. Open Xcode, press ⌘+⇧+N, and select a Single View Application. Name it *wanderBoard*. For Company Identifier, enter *com.apress* so if you have to compare or substitute some of our code with your code, it will all match. Select iPad because this app is an iPad-only app, you'll use Automatic Reference Counting and you'll of course use Storyboards as shown in Figure 9-1. Save it to your desktop.

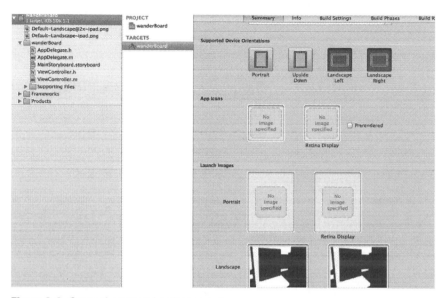

Figure 9-2. *Set up the app as Landscape-only.*

2. You're now going to set up our app and then drag in some of
    the assets from the WanderBoard - Assets folder you
    downloaded from the web. Make the app Landscape-only so
    you don't have to create a bunch of extra images for the
    different orientations (you already have 18 as it is—bear this
    caution in mind, by the way, if you create a game of your own
    that has many images). Uncheck the Portrait and Upside Down
    options in the Supported Device Orientations section in your
    Summary as shown in Figure 9-2. Figure 9-2 shows two
    Landscape images in the Launch Images section at the bottom
    of the figure—you accomplish that by dragging in your two
    splash screens Default-Landscape@2x~ipad.png and Default-
    Landscape~ipad.png together from your folder into your root
    directory as shown in the top left-hand corner in Figure 9-2.
    When you drop it in the directory, make sure to copy items into
    the project folder as always. What you will see is that as you
    drag them in, they automatically show up in the Launch Images
    because they're set at the proper resolutions and have the
    correct names.

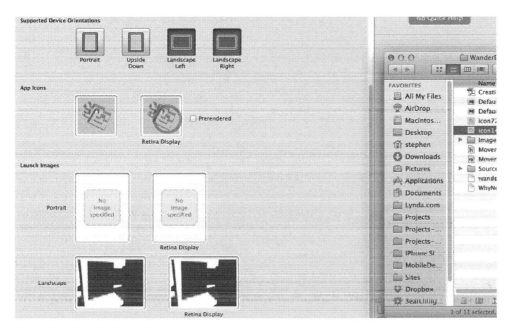

Figure 9-3. *Drag in the app icons.*

3. The last step automatically found the correct resolutions for the
   Launch Images and did the work for you. For the icons,
   however, it's a different story. Drag icon72x72.png and
   icon144x144.png individually from your folder into the App Icons
   slots, with the icon144x144.png icon going into the Retina Display
   slot as shown in Figure 9-3. Later you'll move these icons,
   currently stored by default in your project's root folder, into the
   Supporting Files folder.

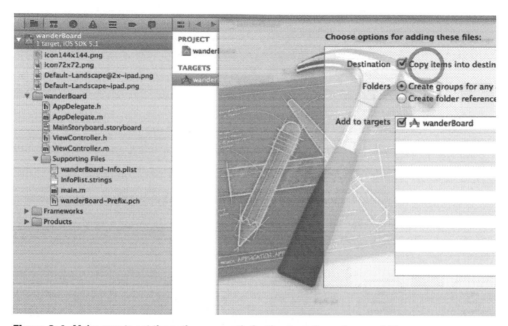

Figure 9-4. *Make sure to set the options correctly for the drag of your images folder.*

4. Now select your Images folder inside your downloaded folder
    and drag it into your Supporting Files folder. When the Choose
    Options dialog box appears, create a copy and groups as
    shown in Figure 9-4. Make sure your Supporting Files folder
    looks like ours. If not, you may have accidently placed them
    outside the Supporting Files folder.

Figuro 9-5. *Bring in the segue code.*

5. Now drag in the segue code MovementSegue.h and MovementSegue.m
    files we made for you into the wanderBoard folder as shown in
    Figure 9-5. Remember that Xcode doesn't know how to build
    the implementation file because this is an unexpected way for
    the framework to have been set up. So you need to set up a
    new compile source.

> **NOTE:** You added the class files differently than you've done in the past. Instead of
> selecting the group and then picking "Add files to {group}," you simply dragged the
> .m and .h files to the group from Finder. At the time of this writing, Xcode doesn't
> add the instruction to compile the .m file when you use this drag-and-drop method of
> adding class files. That's why you need the following step. If you used the "Add
> files..." method, you should find that the compilation of the .m file was already added
> for you.

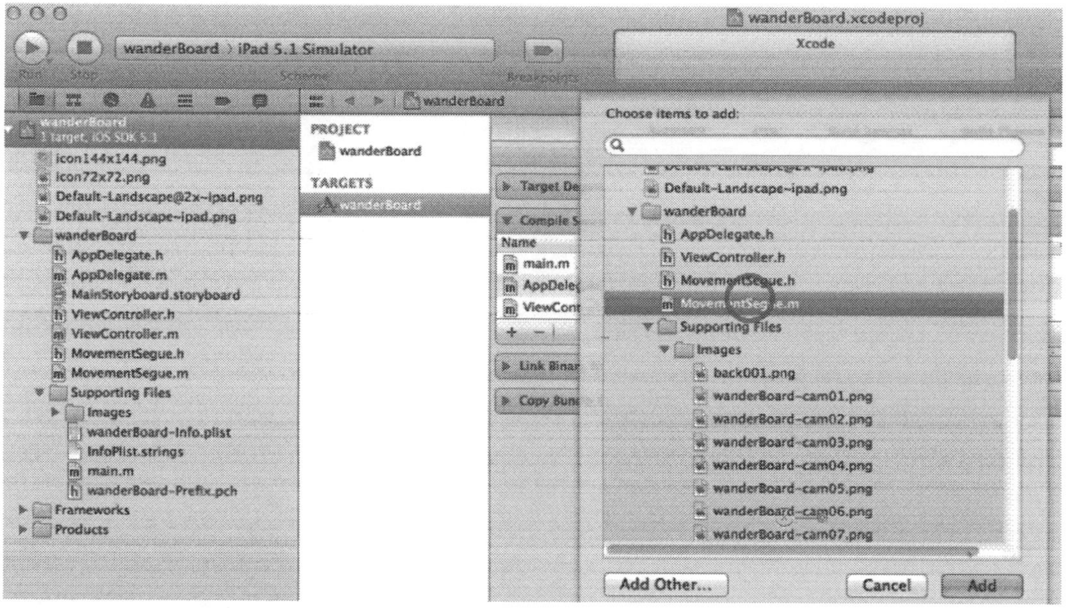

Figure 9-6. *Setting up a new compile source*

6. To create a new compile source for the segue class, click the Build Phases tab (visible in Figure 9-2 if you can't find it) and then select Compile Sources (3 items). You need to add a new compile source, which will be the segue. Click the + button under Sources (3 items) and select the MovementSegue.m file from the Finder dialog as shown in Figure 9-6.

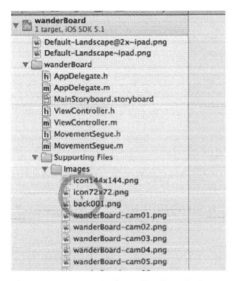

Figure 9-7. *Move the icon files into the Images folder.*

7. You're almost done dragging in the assets. You just need to do a little housecleaning now. Drag the two icon files icon72x72.png and icon144x144.png into your Images folder, located inside as shown in Figure 9-7.

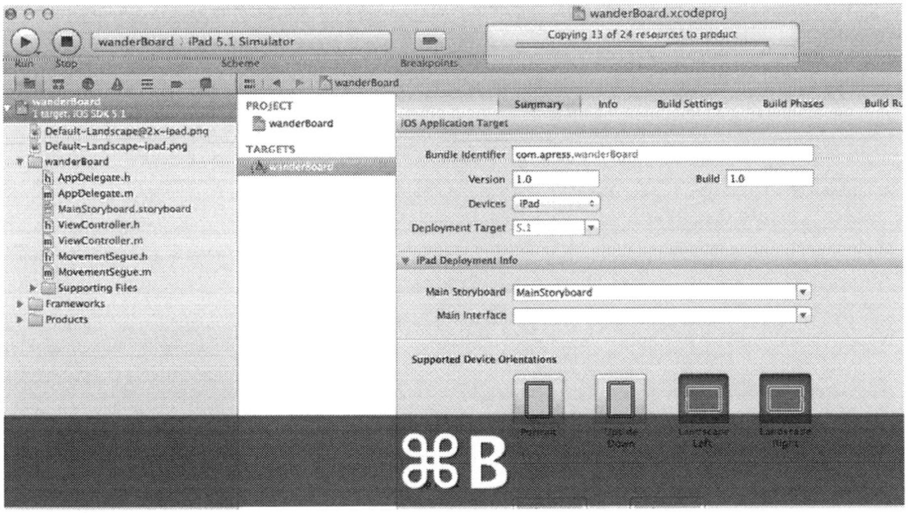

Figure 9-8. *Make sure you're set up correctly by building the code.*

8. You've now dragged all the assets into the project. Before moving on to the next section where you start programming the app, first make sure you've done everything correctly. Press ⌘+B as shown in Figure 9-8 and make sure it builds correctly. Note that in Figure 9-8 we've closed the Supporting Files folder. Yours may still be open.

Step 2: Prep the Storyboard

In this section you'll set up your Storyboard. You'll start by working on the first scene by adding your View Controller, UIImageViews, welcome label, and buttons. After you code this in the next section, bear in mind that you'll have to repeat it for the remaining 17 scenes.

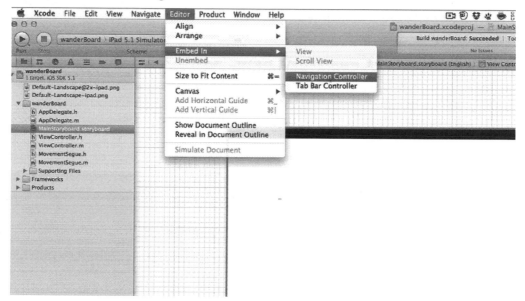

Figure 9-9. *Create the Navigation Controller.*

1. Open the Storyboard and you'll see the iPad default canvas on your screen. Think about this for a second. To make it easier to wander through a maze, where the user will often back up and then go forward again, it would serve you well to use a Navigation Controller inside your Navigation Controller as you've done in the past. Remember, doing so gives you the ability to push and pop views. Select the view on the Storyboard and choose Editor ➤ Embed In ➤ Navigation Controller as

shown in Figure 9-9. Now you'll see by looking at the Storyboard that you've taken your Single View, selected it, and embedded it inside the Navigation Controller so that everything begins from the Navigation Controller.

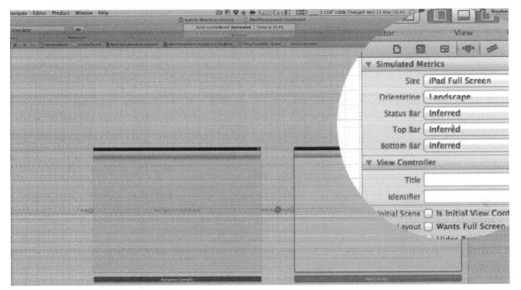

Figure 9-10. *Setting up metrics*

2. To set the metrics, click your View Controller (the one on the right-hand side) and open the Attributes Inspector. Navigate to the Simulated Metrics section, where you want to make sure that the size is iPad Full Screen and the orientation will stay Landscape. Leave everything else as Inferred as shown in Figure 9-10.

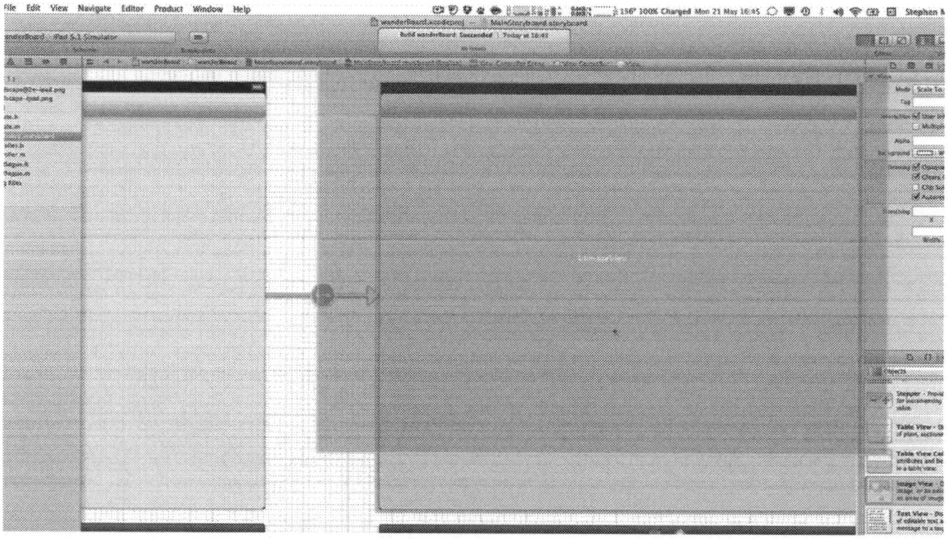

Figure 9-11. *Drag in an image view from the Library.*

3. Leave the View Controller you just set up in step 10 right there, because you'll be adding labels and buttons and things any project heavy with graphics would have. Start by bringing in an Image View from the Library. It will automatically size to the correct dimensions as shown in Figure 9-11. Once that happens, drop it into your view.

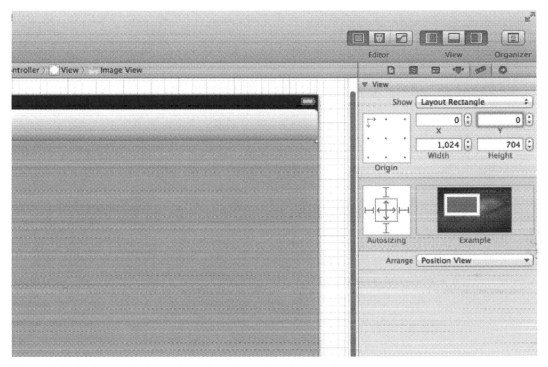

Figure 9-12. *Make sure the image is configured to automatically resize.*

4. You'll soon be taking out the Navigation Bar because you want your user to have the full-screen experience on the iPad. For our image to resize itself as we insert or take objects out of the view, we need to make sure now while we are creating this first scene that the Image View is set to automatically resize. Go to the Size Inspector and make sure the Autosizing option is configured as shown in Figure 9-12. While you're there, note that Interface Builder has resized the Image View to the size it needs to be with the Navigation Bar there. The x and y positions show that it's positioned in the upper left-hand corner which is correct.

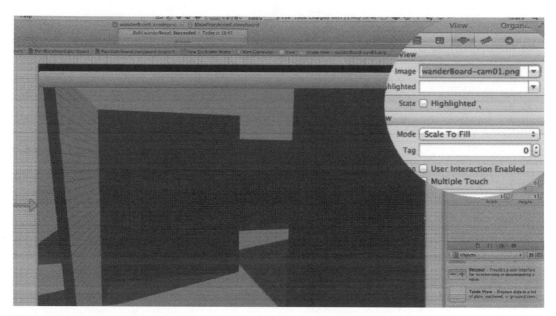

Figure 9-13. *Setting your first image.*

5. You're now able to set your first image. With the Image View still selected, in the Attributes Inspector select the image that shows the view from camera 1. This step is necessary because you may want to make sure, if you design a game with a 3D landscape, that you identify in your image filename, which camera number the view is coming from. Here, you're selecting camera view number 1, named wanderBoard-cam01.png from the drop-down menu as shown in Figure 9-13. If the filename of the image you want to show isn't visible in the list of images, you may need to scroll down to see more names.

Awesome! You're now standing at the entrance to the maze. You're now going to use Storyboarding and Xcode to walk a user through this maze, and that is a really cool concept.

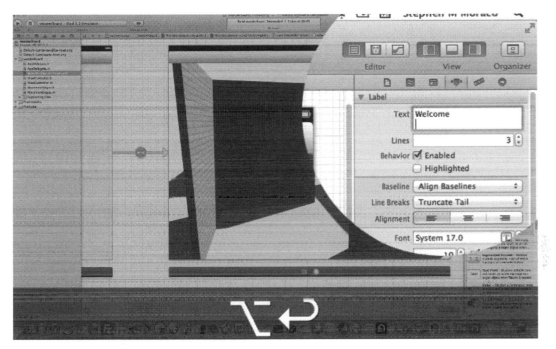

Figure 9-14. *Make a multi-line welcome label.*

6. You want to have a welcome label that greets users as they
    enter the maze. Grab a label from the Library, drag to the upper
    portion of the right-hand wall, and enlarge it a little. In the
    Attributes Inspector you're going to do something interesting
    that you may not have come across yet: make a multi-line label.
    You have to use a special key to make a soft return: In the Label
    text box, enter *Welcome* and press Option+Return to create the
    new line as shown in Figure 9-14. On the new line enter *to our*,
    create another new line, and enter *Maze!* as shown in Figure 9-
    15. Next you have to adjust the Lines count from 1 to 3 (as
    shown) before the label will show all three lines. Choose Mocha
    as the text color by selecting it in the crayon box color selection
    (Mocha is the left-most crayon in the 2nd row from the top).
    Also choose light grey for the shadow color, with the shadow
    offsets at a distance of 1 for Horizontal and 1 for Vertical.

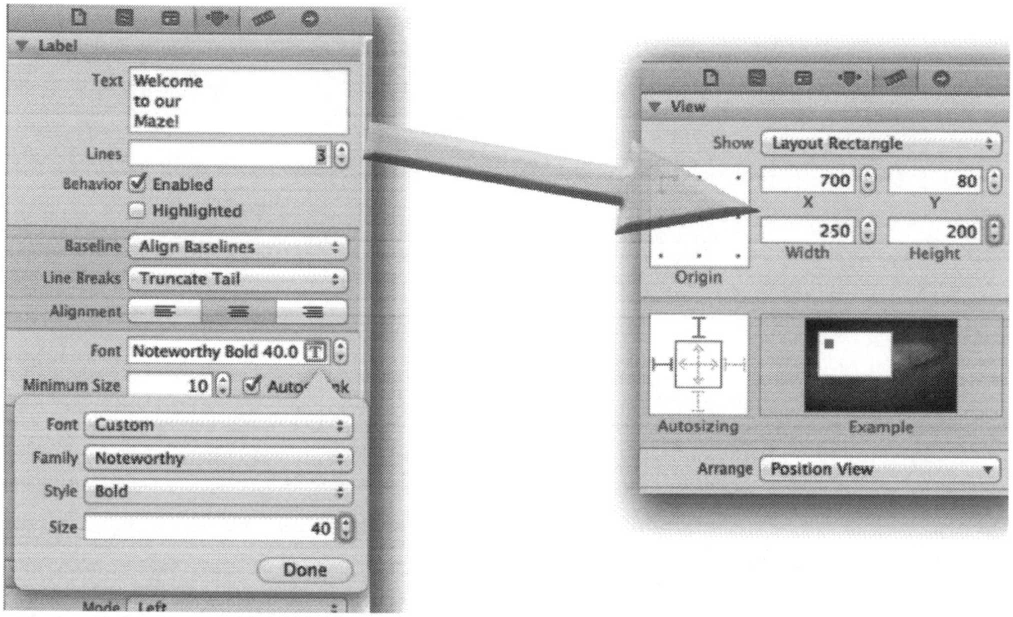

Figure 9-15. *Change the font style.*

7. While in the Attributes Inspector, with the font selected change the font to Noteworthy Bold by clicking the T icon in the drop-down menu and selecting Noteworthy. Select Bold for Style and 40 (points) for Size as shown in the left-hand image in Figure 9-15. In the Size Inspector make the x, y position 700, 80. Set the Width of the text box to 250 and the Height to 200 as shown on the right in Figure 9-15.

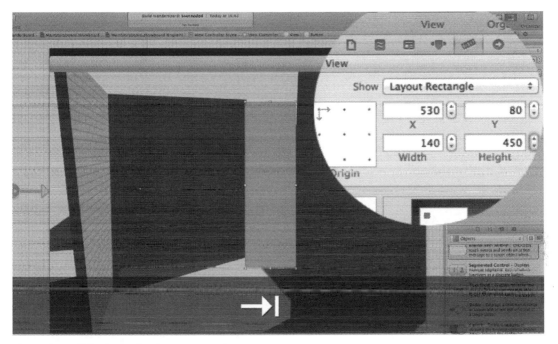

Figure 9-16. *Bring in the first button.*

8. To navigate from screen to screen, you'd like to use buttons, but you don't really want the user to see the buttons because that would give away which way to go. You'll use the Size Inspector to set the sizes and positions of buttons correctly. Then in the Attributes Inspector you'll make it invisible by changing it to Custom, which by default sets it to transparent.

    Drag in a button from your Library and place it about where you see ours in Figure 9-16. In the Size Inspector set the x-position to 530, y-position to 80, Width to 140, and Height to 450.

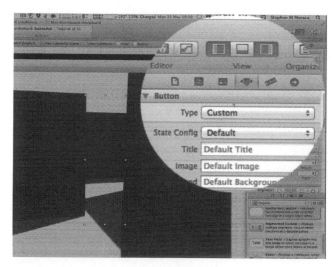

Figure 9-17. *Make the button invisible.*

9. To make the button transparent, in the Attributes Inspector select Custom for Type. The button will become transparent as shown in Figure 9-17.

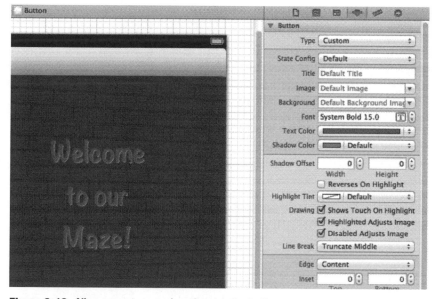

Figure 9-18. *Allow users to see when they tap the button.*

10. You've made the button transparent, but you need to let users see when they've tapped it. Put a check mark next to the Drawing attribute Shows Touch On Highlight so that when the user taps the button it creates a little flash that tells the user when the button got hit. This is shown in Figure 9-18.

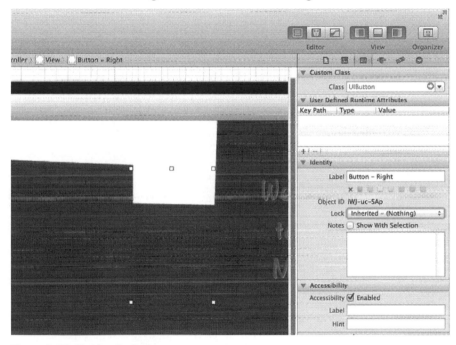

Figure 9-19. *Naming the buttons*

11. Even in this small 18-scene maze, each scene will have two to three options for where to go next, which could add up to 40 buttons. You need a naming system so you can easily identify buttons in your document outline just by name. This button you've selected allows the user to go to the right, so with the button still selected, in the Identity Inspector label it *Button - Right* as shown in Figure 9-19.

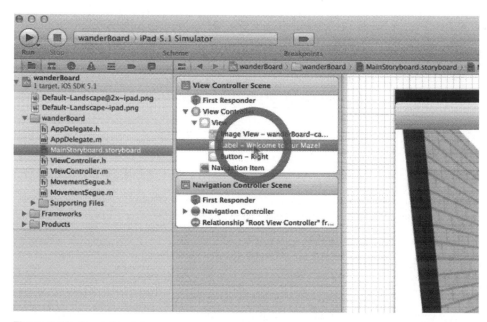

Figure 9-20. *Check the status.*

12. This is a critical step, so let's be overly cautious that this aspect
    of the project is working perfectly before moving on. First check
    it in the Document Outline and then run it. Open the Document
    Outline Panel in Storyboard if it's not already open and go to the
    View Controller Scene. Under View, if you open it up, you
    should see Image View..., Label - Welcome to our Maze!, and
    Button - Right as shown in Figure 9-20. Let's move on and build
    it. If it builds correctly, run it.

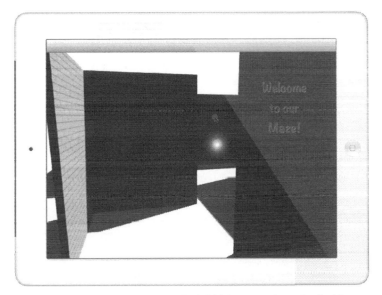

Figure 9-21. *Click the transparent (invisible) button and see the flash!*

13. When the iPad Simulator appears, click where you know the transparent button is. You should see a flash indicator as shown in Figure 9-21. Note that wherever you click, it will still show the flash. That's important because different people may choose different segments of the button. You've accomplished an important part of creating the app. Good job!

10

Single View #3: wanderBoard Part II

You've now set up the first scene. In this chapter, you'll add code to the View Controller's header and implementation files in Step 3. That sets you up for Step 4, in which you efficiently create 17 more scenes! Step 4 is divided into two parts. The first part, Step 4a, concludes this chapter, and for that step you will still receive assistance and guidance from us. Then in Chapter 11, we have you work on Step 4b, which comes with much less assistance.

Step 3: Finish the ViewController Header and Implementation Files

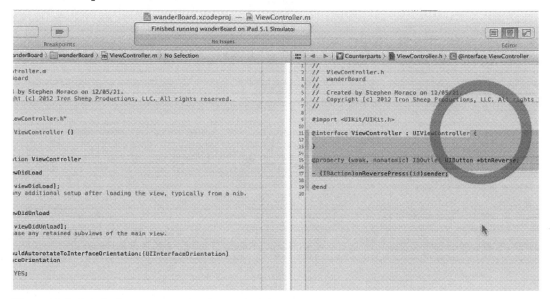

Figure 10-1. *Drag in the property and action method signature.*

1. Make sure you've opened up DemoMonkey and placed it in your favorite spot so you can access it while you code. Open the ViewController.m file and then open the Assistant Editor so that it opens up its header file in the right-hand pane. From DemoMonkey, drag in the first snippet "01 ViewController.h – add new property and action signature" and drop it at the end of the @interface line of code in the header file as shown in Figure 10-1 and as follows:

```
#import <UIKit/UIKit.h>

@interface ViewController : UIViewController {
}

@property (weak, nonatomic) IBOutlet UIButton *btnReverse;

(IBAction)onReversePress:(id)sender;

@end
```

All you're doing to the View Controller is adding a new property and an action method signature. You're setting up the ability for users to communicate that they need to back up in the maze when they get to a dead-end. They accomplish that with your reverse button (*btnReverse) which, upon being tapped, invokes this IBAction method. This is all you'll be doing to the header file, so it's time to on to the implementation file.

```
8
9    #import "ViewController.h"
10   #import "MovementSegue.h"
11
12   @interface ViewController ()
13
14   @end
15
16   @implementation ViewController
17
18   @synthesize btnReverse;
19
20
21   - (void)viewDidLoad
22   {
23       [super viewDidLoad];
24       // Do any additional setup after loading the view, typically from a nib.
25   }
26
27   -(void)viewWillAppear:(BOOL)animated
28   {
29       [super viewWillAppear:animated];
30
31       [self.navigationController setNavigationBarHidden:YES];
32
33       BOOL bIsMovToParent = [self isMovingToParentViewController];
34
35       // non terminal dead-end screens have a reverse button w/tag=1 (dead-end end screens have tag=0)
36       if(bIsMovToParent && self.btnReverse.tag == 1)
37       {
38           // we have arrived at this screen from another so hide our reverse button
39           self.btnReverse.hidden = YES;
40       }
41       else if(self.btnReverse.tag == 1)
42       {
43           // we have returned here by pressing reverse button at dead-end screen so show this reverse btn!
44           self.btnReverse.hidden = NO;
45       }
46   }
47
48   - (void)viewDidUnload
```

Figure 10-2. *Import viewWillAppear method code.*

2. Switching back to the Standard Editor (or simply working now in the implementation file on the left), you want to establish access to your custom segue object because, as shown earlier, you don't want to use custom segues. The custom segues, as you will see, are completely data-driven, meaning that data drives the behavior of the code. Put yet another way, the code looks at the view data and based on what it sees, it makes a decision on how to act. So go to DemoMonkey and drag in the "02 ViewController.m – add import of customSegue Object" and drop it after the `#import ViewController.h`. Now that in your public interface you've declared a property for a reverse button, you also need to tell the compiler to synthesize the reverse button property setter and getter code. To do this, drag in the "03 ViewController.m – add property synthesis," placing it immediately after the `@implementation` line.

As you can see in the implementation file, Xcode has, by default, instantiated the methods - `(void)viewDidLoad` and - `(void)viewDidUnload`. But when the view appears, you want to hide the Navigation Bar. So add a -`(void)viewWillAppear` method to do this. Drag in "04 ViewController.m – add viewWill Appear" and drop it in between the - `(void)viewDidLoad` and - `(void)viewDidUnload` methods as shown in Figure 10-2 and as follows:

```
#import "ViewController.h"
#import "MovementSegue.h"
@interface ViewController ()
@end
@implementation ViewController
@synthesize btnReverse;
- (void)viewDidLoad{ … }
-(void)viewWillAppear:(BOOL)animated {
  [super viewWillAppear:animated];
  [self.navigationController setNavigationBarHidden:YES];
  BOOL bIsMovToParent = [self isMovingToParentViewController];

  if(bIsMovToParent && self.btnReverse.tag == 1)
        { self.btnReverse.hidden = YES;}
  else if(self.btnReverse.tag == 1)
{self.btnReverse.hidden = NO;} }
- (void)viewDidUnload { …
```

> **NOTE:** To save space we deleted the comments in the preceding code.

From the code you can see that you're letting the super class do what it needs to do on viewWillAppear with [super viewWillAppear:animated];. Then you hide the Navigation Bar with [self.navigationController setNavigationBarHidden:YES]; and deal with how you arrived at this view. You want to know if you're heading toward a dead-end or backing out of a dead-end. The call [self isMovingToParentViewController] tells you part of the answer. You can see in the comments in the code (not shown in the preceding code) that for our non-terminal dead-end screens, you've given the reverse button a tag=1. Conversely, the dead-end end screens are given a tag=0. But if you arrived at this screen while heading toward the dead-end, then you hide the reverse button with self.btnReverse.hidden = YES. Finally, if the user returned to this point via a reverse button tap (backing out of the dead-end), then you do want to display the reverse button in this scene with self.btnReverse.hidden = NO; (if there is a reverse button in this scene).

```
30
31      [self.navigationController setNavigationBarHidden:YES];
32
33      BOOL bIsMovToParent = [self isMovingToParentViewController];
34
35      // non terminal dead-end screens have a reverse button w/tag=1 (dead-end end screens have tag=0)
36      if(bIsMovToParent && self.btnReverse.tag == 1)
37      {
38          // we have arrived at this screen from another so hide our reverse button
39          self.btnReverse.hidden = YES;
40      }
41      else if(self.btnReverse.tag == 1)
42      {
43          // we have returned here by presssing reverse button at dead-end screen so show this reverse btn!
44          self.btnReverse.hidden = NO;
45      }
46  }
47
48  - (void)viewDidUnload
49  {
50      [self setBtnReverse:nil];
51      [super viewDidUnload];
52      // Release any retained subviews of the main view.
53  }
54
55  - (BOOL)shouldAutorotateToInterfaceOrientation:(UIInterfaceOrientation)interfaceOrientation
56  {
57      // Return YES for supported orientations (our two landscape forms only)
58      return UIInterfaceOrientationIsLandscape(interfaceOrientation);
59  }
60
61  @end
62
```

Figure 10-3. *Replace code with code that allows both Landscape orientations.*

3. You now need to release the reverse button by dragging in "05 ViewController.m – add release button (inviewDid Unload)" and dropping it into `ViewDidUnload` right above `[super viewDidUnload];` as shown in Figure 10-3 and as follows:

```
- (void)viewDidUnload
{
  [self setBtnReverse:nil];
  [super viewDidUnload];
}
(BOOL)shouldAutorotateToInterfaceOrientation:(UIInterfaceOrientation)interfaceOr
ientation
{
  return UIInterfaceOrientationIsLandscape(interfaceOrientation);
}
```

The next thing to do is constrain view rotation to Landscape. Rather than say you support any orientation, you'll use a macro to ask whether you're in a Landscape orientation or not. To do this, drag in "06 ViewController.m – in 'shouldAutorotate …' replace" and drop it inside the `shouldAutorotateToInterfaceOrientation` as shown in Figure 10-3. It should replace the `return YES;` line that's already present in this method. You may need to remove this line after the insert of the new lines.

Instead of simply returning YES to all orientations, you now use the macro to determining if you're in a landscape orientation, `UIInterfaceOrientationIsLandscape`, and return its result.

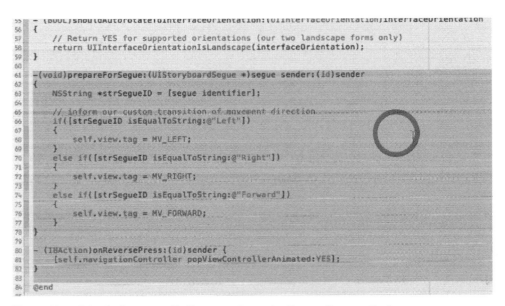

```
55  - (BOOL)shouldAutorotateToInterfaceOrientation:(UIInterfaceOrientation)interfaceOrientation
56  {
57      // Return YES for supported orientations (our two landscape forms only)
58      return UIInterfaceOrientationIsLandscape(interfaceOrientation);
59  }
60
61  -(void)prepareForSegue:(UIStoryboardSegue *)segue sender:(id)sender
62  {
63      NSString *strSegueID = [segue identifier];
64
65      // inform our custom transition of movement direction
66      if([strSegueID isEqualToString:@"Left"])
67      {
68          self.view.tag = MV_LEFT;
69      }
70      else if([strSegueID isEqualToString:@"Right"])
71      {
72          self.view.tag = MV_RIGHT;
73      }
74      else if([strSegueID isEqualToString:@"Forward"])
75      {
76          self.view.tag = MV_FORWARD;
77      }
78  }
79
80  - (IBAction)onReversePress:(id)sender {
81      [self.navigationController popViewControllerAnimated:YES];
82  }
83
84  @end
```

Figure 10-4. *Bring in the prepareForSegue:sender: and onReversePress: methods.*

4. You've spent some time creating transparent buttons to have your user navigate through the maze using your custom segues. You now have to bring in code that will respond to taps on these buttons. Drag in "07 ViewController.m – add prepareForSegue sender and onReversePress methods" and drop it in between the shouldAutorotateToInterfaceOrientation method and the @end statement as shown in Figure 10-4. You can see how you're looking for the user to choose to go left, right, or forward and you record this choice in the views "tag." If the user is instead trying to back out of a dead-end by tapping the back button, you execute a pop with popViewControllerAnimated:YES. Now do a build, and it should all build correctly.

Congratulations! You've finished all the code for this app. Yes, the aforementioned code is the sum of all the code you'll employ in this app. Now do a run and see what you have. You'll notice that now your beginning point looks like Chapter 9's Figure 9-0A in the sense that the Navigation Bar is no longer there, as it was in Figure 9-21.

From this point on, you'll be making the maze paths.

Step 4a: Create the Next Eight Scenes with Assistance

So far you've set up your app with its images and created the Storyboard and the code for the first scene. That's very often the case when you create a game with many scenes. At the University of Colorado at Colorado Springs Computer Science Department, we offer a Bachelor of Science in Gaming. It's often interesting to see how students panic when they realize that halfway through the semester they've yet to complete the code for the first scene, nor all the characters. The trick is to have the first scene and characters down so well that it makes creating the rest of the game a breeze.

Here, you have everything set up so you'll be as efficient as you can as you repeat the steps necessary to create each of the remaining 17 scenes.

> **NOTE:** You'll be using a 4-step process to create each new scene. We begin by explaining each step. As we move through and continue to repeat, we let the leash loosen a little by not always explaining each step and all its intricacies but merely reminding you to do it as you did previously.

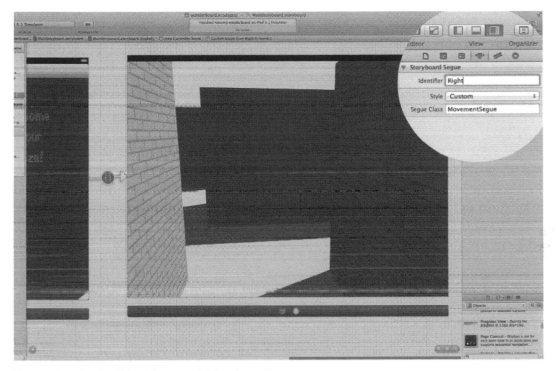

Figure 10-5. *Set the Title of first scene's View Controller.*

1. Before you begin our repeating methodology to efficiently create your remaining 17 scenes, you need to do a little house cleaning. The naming of scenes and entities is critical. Start by going back to the Storyboard. After clicking the View Controller's scene dock (the bar at the bottom of the scene on the canvas) and going to the Attributes Inspector, name it by setting the Title to *Opening Scene* as shown in Figure 10-5.

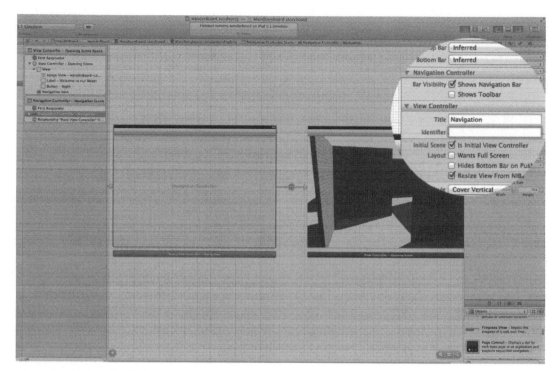

Figure 10-6. *Name the Navigator.*

  2. Click the Navigation Controller scene dock. You can just call this
      Navigation as shown in Figure 10-6.

Scene 2

You're finished cleaning up loose ends and can now focus on the steps you'll
repeat and grind through 17 more times. At a very high level, you'll be repeating
four steps:

  ▦ Scene #: Copy an existing scene.

  ▦ Scene #: Rename.

  ▦ Scene #: Organize graphics.

  ▦ Scene #: Make connections.

> **NOTE:** We'll indicate the **current step** or **sub-step** in bold so that you'll instantly know where you are in terms of the broader view.

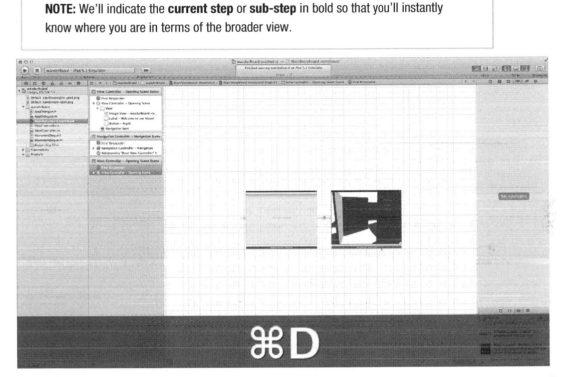

Figure 10-7. *Starting your first duplication, click Opening Scene's dock.*

1. You'll begin with step 1 for *Scene 2: Copy an existing scene*. You only have one existing scene to choose from, so go ahead and click the View Controller's scene dock and press ⌘+D to duplicate as shown in Figure 10-7. Immediately you'll see that it looks a little bit thicker. That's because the duplicated item is now sitting on top of the original scene.

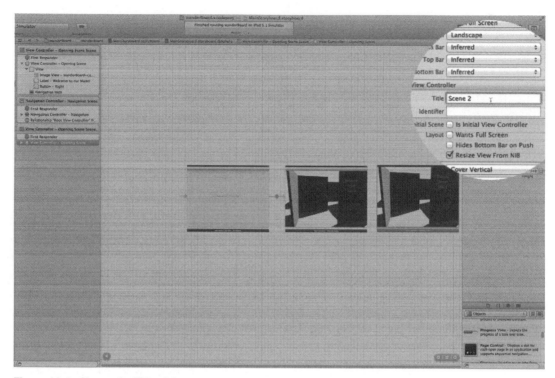

Figure 10-8. *Change the Title of the new scene.*

- Scene 2: Copy an existing scene.
- Scene 2: Rename.
  - Scene 2: Change the Title.
- Scene 2: Organize graphics.
- Scene 2: Make connections.

2. Select the duplicated scene and drag it to the right of the original scene. In the Attributes Inspector change the Title to *Scene 2* as shown in Figure 10-8.

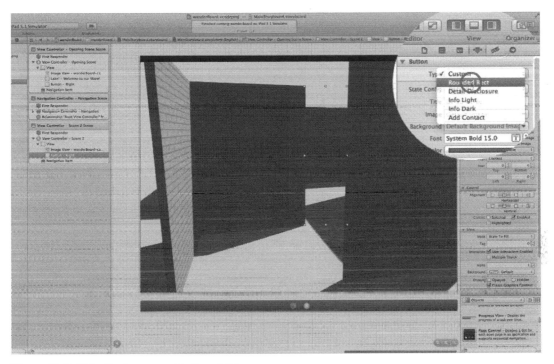

Figure 10-9. *Make the transparent button visible.*

- Scene 2: Copy an existing scene.
- Scene 2: Rename.
    - Scene 2: Change the Title.
- Scene 2: Organize graphics.
    - Scene 2: Hide inapplicable elements.
    - Scene 2: Edit buttons.
    - Scene 2: Make buttons visible.
    - Scene 2: Replace image with new image.
- Scene 2: Make connections.

3. Scene 2 doesn't have a welcome label, so select it and delete it. (Note that in all future scenes you create, you'll be hiding elements—in this case, you're deleting the label because it's unnecessary for any future scenes.) Scene 2 does have buttons in it, so you need to first make the transparent button visible so you can edit it. Select the transparent button still in place from scene 1 and, with it selected, in the Attributes Inspector make it visible by choosing Rounded Rect as shown in Figure 10-9.

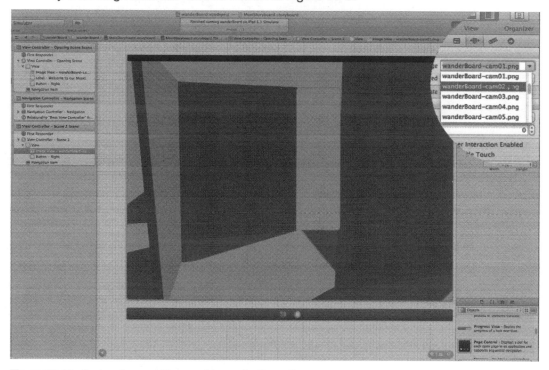

Figure 10-10. *Replace Image with correct image for Scene 2.*

- Scene 2: Copy an existing scene.
- Scene 2: Rename.
- Scene 2: Organize graphics.
    - Scene 2: Hide inapplicable elements.
    - Scene 2: Edit buttons.
        - Scene 2: Make buttons visible

◼ Scene 2: Replace Image with new image.

◼ Scene 2: Make connections.

4. You now need to get rid of the image background wanderboard-cam01.png and replace it with Scene 2's image wanderboard-cam02.png. To do this, select the view and with it still selected, in the Attributes Inspector change the Image name to wanderboard-cam02.png from the drop-down menu as shown in Figure 10-10.

> **NOTE:** See how the existing button from Scene 1 is still showing in Figure 10-10? This is correct. You want this. Editing the buttons is a two-step process.
>
> **First:** Make sure you have the correct buttons to transfer over to the new scene. Do that by making visible the existing buttons in the original scene (Organize graphics ➤ Edit buttons ➤ Make buttons visible) and/or hiding buttons (Hide inapplicable elements). So far, you haven't had to hide a button.
>
> **Second:** Change the dimensions and positions of the buttons so they're placed and fit correctly into the new scene. Then make them invisible again.

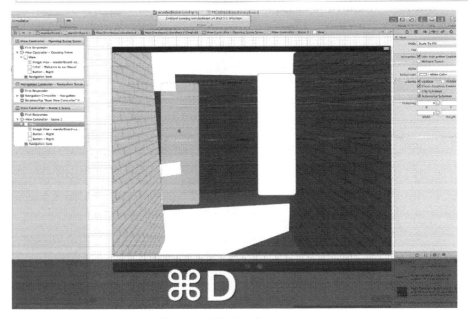

Figure 10-11. *Move duplicated button to left side of scene.*

- Scene 2: Copy an existing scene.

- Scene 2: Rename.

- Scene 2: Organize graphics.

  - Scene 2: Hide inapplicable elements.

  - Scene 2: Edit buttons

  - Scene 2: Replace image with new image.

  - Scene 2: Configure new buttons.

  - Scene 2: Duplicate buttons.

  - Scene 2: Reset parameters.

- Scene 2: Make connections.

5. In the new scene you can see that your user has two options here: go left or right. To accommodate this, you need to offer two buttons, one for each direction. Click the right-hand visible button and press ⌘+D to duplicate. Now move it roughly to the left-hand side of the scene as shown in Figure 10-11.

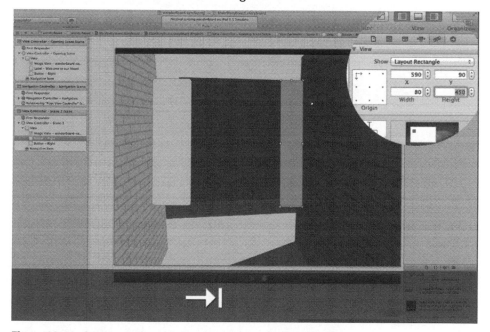

Figure 10-12. *Set the position and size of the original (right-most) button.*

- Scene 2: Copy an existing scene.
- Scene 2: Rename.
- Scene 2: Organize graphics.
  - Scene 2: Hide inapplicable elements.
  - Scene 2: Edit buttons.
  - Scene 2: Replace image with new image.
  - Scene 2: Configure new buttons.
  - Scene 2: Duplicate buttons.
  - Scene 2: Reset parameters of buttons.
  - Scene 2: Button Right.
  - Scene 2: Button Left.
- Scene 2: Make connections.

6. Make sure these two buttons are correctly placed and sized so it makes sense to the user. With the original button selected, in the Size Inspector enter the attributes. You'll be doing this a lot, so we'll give you the x and y coordinates that place the button on the scene, and then the vertical and horizontal dimensions of the button so that it fits snugly into position. We'll do this all in one set of numbers—we'll simply state: 590,90,80,450, and that means that the x-position is 590, the y-position is 90, the width of the button is 80 and the height is 450. We won't remind you that you need to select the button and go to the Size Inspector. 590, 90,80,450 means you go to the Size Inspector and enter the values as shown in Figure 10-12.

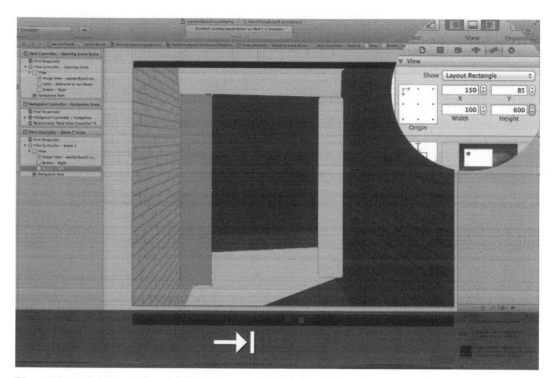

Figure 10-13. *Set the position and size of the new (left-most) button.*

- Scene 2: Copy an existing scene.
- Scene 2: Rename.
- Scene 2: Organize graphics.
    - Scene 2: Hide inapplicable elements.
    - Scene 2: Edit buttons.
    - Scene 2: Replace image with new image.
    - Scene 2: Configure new buttons.
    - Scene 2: Duplicate buttons.
    - Scene 2: Reset parameters of buttons.
        - Scene 2: Button – Right.
        - Scene 2: Button – Left.
- Scene 2: Make connections.

7. Before setting the new button's parameters, you need to always rename it because right now it has the name of the duplicated button. Select the new button and in the Identity Inspector, in the Label box rename it from *Button – Right* to *Button – Left*. Back in the Size Inspector set the parameters to 150,85,100,600 as shown in Figure 10-13.

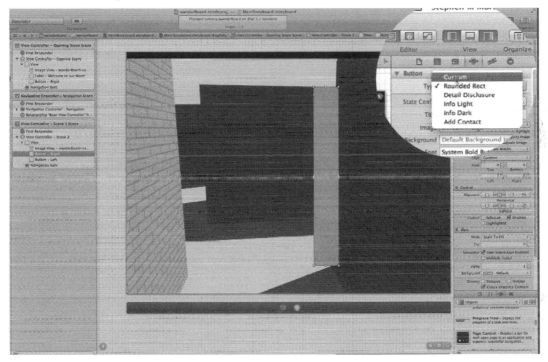

Figure 10-14. *Make all buttons transparent again.*

- Scene 2: Copy an existing scene.
- Scene 2: Rename.
- Scene 2: Organize graphics.
    - Scene 2: Hide inapplicable elements.
    - Scene 2: Edit buttons.
    - Scene 2: Replace image with new image.
    - Scene 2: Configure new buttons.

▪ Scene 2: Duplicate buttons.

▪ Scene 2: Reset parameters of buttons.

▪ Scene 2: Make all buttons transparent again.

▪ Scene 2: Make connections.

8. The last thing you'll always do after configuring the buttons of a new scene is make sure you make them transparent. Remember, you don't want to give clues away to the user. Select a button and in the Attributes Inspector choose Custom. We first performed this on the new button and then changed the second button to Custom as shown in Figure 10-14.

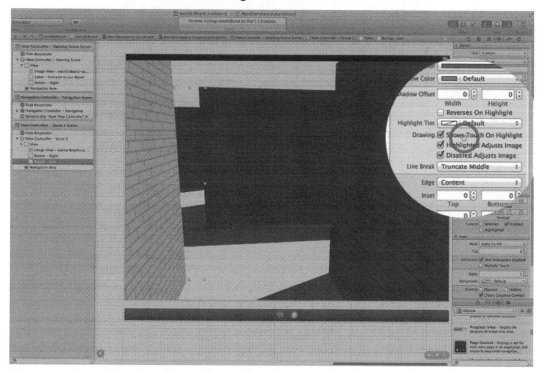

Figure 10-15. *Correcting the bug: make sure to set Shows Touch On Highlight.*

▪ Scene 2: Copy an existing scene.

▪ Scene 2: Rename.

▪ Scene 2: Organize graphics.

- Scene 2: Hide inapplicable elements.
- Scene 2: Edit buttons.
- Scene 2: Replace image with new image.
- Scene 2: Configure new buttons.
  - Scene 2: Duplicate buttons.
  - Scene 2: Reset parameters of buttons.
  - Scene 2: Make all buttons transparent again.
  - Scene 2: Correct bug if necessary.
- Scene 2: Make connections.

> **NOTE:** By the time this book comes out, a new version of Xcode will most likely have corrected the bug you're about to read about. We've alerted Apple and brought this to their attention. But this is the bug as it stands right now.

9. Notice that you duplicated a view where Shows Touch On Highlight was set for each button. but the duplicated buttons didn't have this value set correctly. Sometimes, for no apparent reason, the setting of this attribute isn't copied correctly, and because it's not consistent, that means there's a bug here. What you need to do is check that these buttons are going to show the touch on highlight. Select each button and change to Shows Touch On Highlight. We first corrected the right-hand button and then corrected the left-hand button as shown in Figure 10-15.

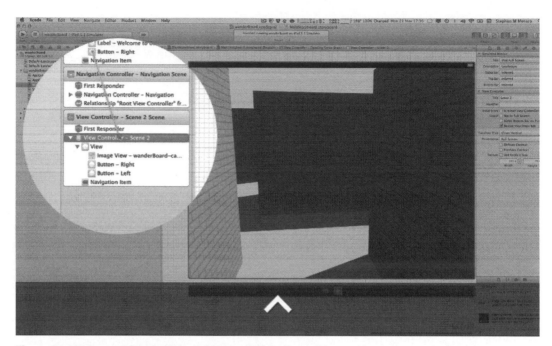

Figure 10-16. *Connect Opening Scene: Button – Right to Scene 2.*

- Scene 2: Copy an existing scene.
- Scene 2: Rename.
- Scene 2: Organize graphics.
- Scene 2: Make connections.
   - Scene 2: Control-drag from button to new scene.

10. The way the user gets to Scene 2 is by tapping on the right-hand button—in other words, selecting the right-hand portal in the maze. You're going to have to connect the right-hand button to the Scene 2 with a segue. If your Document Outline isn't open, open it, select Button –Right in View Controller – Opening Scene, and then Control-drag from it to View Controller – Scene 2 as shown in Figure 10-16.

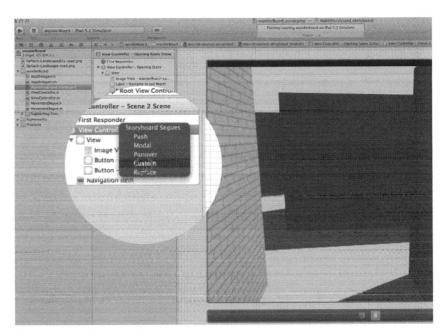

Figure 10-17. *Select the Custom segue type.*

- Scene 2: Copy an existing scene.
- Scene 2: Rename.
- Scene 2: Organize graphics.
- Scene 2: Make connections.
    - Scene 2: Control-drag from button to new scene.
    - Scene 2: Select Custom segue.
11. Once you've dropped the Control-drag over the View Controller – Opening Scene, select Custom from the Style menu as shown in Figure 10-17.

NOTE: We won't repeat this *Select custom segue* step because you'll always use a custom segue. From here on, we'll simply say *Control-drag from button (name) to new scene (name)*. You'll then automatically select the Custom segue option.

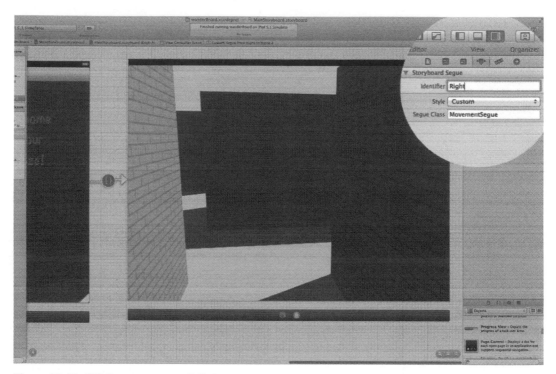

Figure 10-18. *Edit the new segues attributes.*

- ▦ Scene 2: Copy an existing scene.
- ▦ Scene 2: Rename.
- ▦ Scene 2: Organize graphics.
- ▦ Scene 2: Make connections.
    - ▦ Scene 2: Control-drag from button to new scene.
    - ▦ Scene 2: Edit the segue attributes.

12. You'll now see a new custom segue linking the two views. You can see that it's custom because it has the {} inside the segue linking the two views as shown in Figure 10-39. You need to associate the correct class with the new view. To do this, select the segue, in the Attributes Inspector name the Segue class MovementSegue, keep the Style as Custom, and change the Identifier to *Right* as shown in Figure 10-18.

> **NOTE:** Regarding the Identifier: you'll want to note that this is a right transition. By setting the Identifier value to *Right*, the Custom Segue class can look at the identifier, know that it's going right, left, or forward, and choose the appropriate animation to do so. Remember when we mentioned that your segues are data-driven? The *Right* value is the data that "drives" the selection of the correct animation.

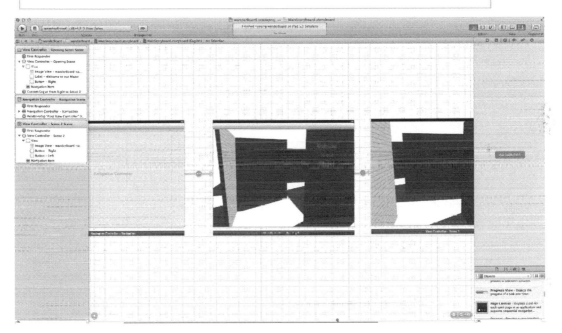

Figure 10-19. *Zoomed-out view of what you've just done*

13. Before you get too lost in the forest, zoom out for a second. You can see in Figure 10-19 that you have an opening scene and Scene 2. Scene 2 is the next location in the maze, and you used four essential steps to create Scene 2. Now you'll do Scene 3 with a little less hand-holding and explanation.

Scene 3

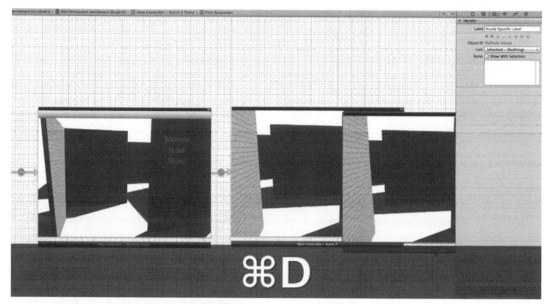

Figure 10-20. *Duplicate Scene 2 to create Scene 3.*

- Scene 3: Copy an existing scene.
- Scene 3: Rename
- Scene 3: Organize graphics
- Scene 3: Make connections

1. Similar to what you did in Figure 10-7, click Scene 2's dock, press ⌘+D to duplicate it, and then drag the duplicate to the right as shown in Figure 10-20.

Figure 10-21. *Scene 3: select the correct image.*

- Scene 3: Copy an existing scene.
    - Scene 3: Place above or below previous scene.
- Scene 3: **Rename**.
    - Scene 3: Change the Title.
    - Scene 3: Change the Image.
- Scene 3: Organize graphics.
- Scene 3: Make connections.

2. Now you're going to start a new convention. You can go left or right. Let's position the right scene on the bottom and the left scene on the top (left destination scene is above the right destination). So, from here on put the right turn on the bottom and the left turn on top. This way you can tell, just by looking at the Storyboard, that you're going to the right or left, travelling horizontally. As you did in Figure 10-8, you need to change the title—change the Title from *Scene 2* to *Scene 3* so you can remember what it is.

While you're here, change Image to `wanderBoard-cam03.png`, just as you did in Figure 10-10. This is shown in Figure 10-21.

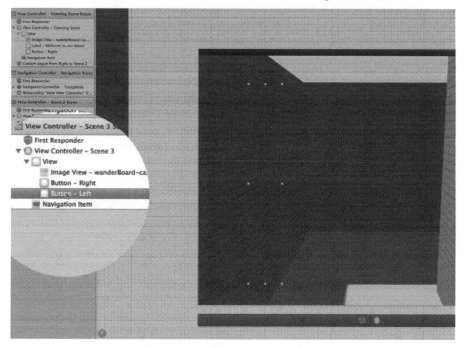

Figure 10-22. *Scene 3: Hide inapplicable elements: select Button – Left.*

- Scene 3: Copy an existing scene.
- Scene 3: Rename.
- Scene 3: Organize graphics.
    - Scene 3: Hide inapplicable elements.

▨   Scene 3: Make connections.

3.   Select Button – Left as shown in Figure 10-22 so you can hide it.

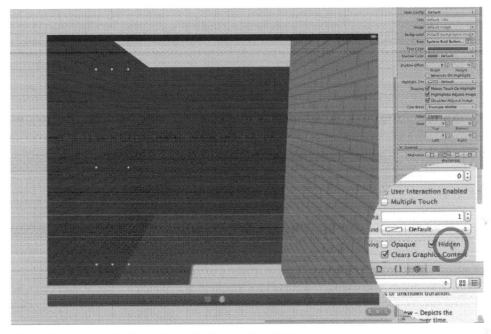

Figure 10-23. *Scene 3: Mark selected Button – Left as Hidden.*

▨   Scene 3: Copy an existing scene.

▨   Scene 3: Rename.

▨   Scene 3: Organize graphics.

    ▨   Scene 3: Hide inapplicable elements.

▨   Scene 3: Make connections.

4.   After you've selected Button – Left, check the Hidden option to hide it as shown in Figure 10-23.

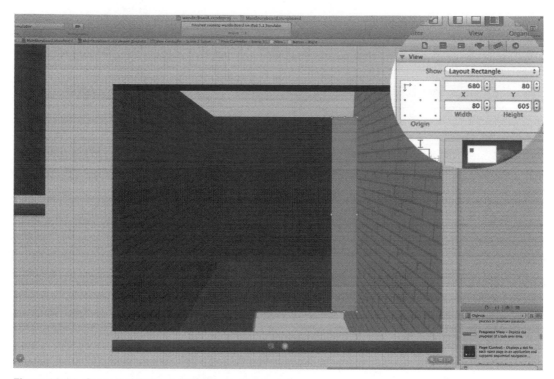

Figure 10-24. *Scene 3: Edit the right button position and size.*

- Scene 3: Copy an existing scene.
- Scene 3: Rename.
- Scene 3: Organize graphics.
  - Scene 3: Hide inapplicable elements.
  - Scene 3: Edit buttons.
    - Scene 3: Make button visible.
  - Scene 3: Replace image with new image (done).
  - Scene 3: Configure new buttons.
    - Scene 3: Duplicate buttons.
    - Scene 3: Reset parameters of buttons.
    - Scene 3: Button – Right.
      - Scene 3: Make transparent again.

       ▨ Scene 3: Correct bug.

  ▨ Scene 3: Make connections.

5.   Now select Button – Right and make it visible as you did in Figure 10-9. For the next step you need to make the right button fit appropriately into this scene. Select it and make it 680,80,80,605 as shown in Figure 10-24. Make it transparent again as you did in Figure 10-35. And lastly, as you did in Figure 10-15, correct the bug by setting it to Shows Touch On Highlight.

> **NOTE:** When there is no need to perform a step, I ~~strike it through~~.

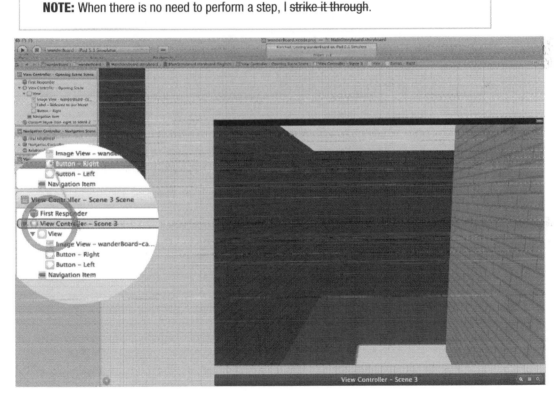

Figure 10-25. *Connect Scene 2: Button – Right to Scene 3.*

  ▨ Scene 3: Copy an existing scene.

  ▨ Scene 3: Rename.

  ▨ Scene 3: Organize graphics.

■ Scene 3: Make connections.

■ Scene 3: Control-drag from button to new scene.

6. Connect Button – Right in Scene 2 to the View Controller Scene 3 as shown in Figure 10-25.

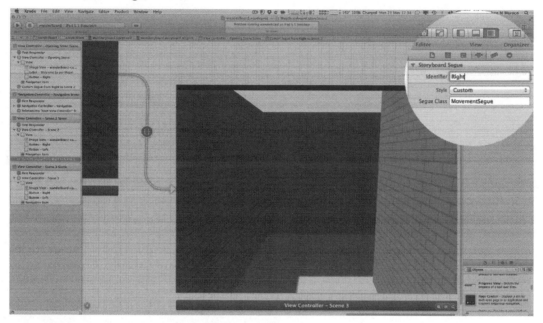

Figure 10-26. *Edit the new segue's attributes.*

■ Scene 3: Copy an existing scene.

■ Scene 3: Rename.

■ Scene 3: Organize graphics.

■ Scene 3: Make connections.

■ Scene 3: Control-drag from button to new scene.

■ Scene 3: Edit the segue's attributes.

7. Similar to Figure 10-18, select the segue, in the Attributes Inspector name the Segue class MovementSegue, keep the Style as Custom, and change the Identifier to *Right* as shown in Figure 10-26.

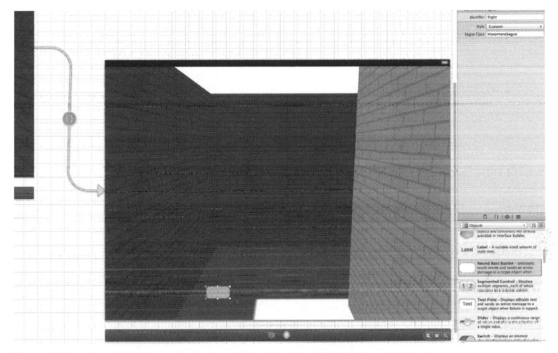

Figure 10-27. *Scene 3: Adding a new reverse button: drag Round Rect button onto the view.*

- Scene 3: Copy an existing scene.
- Scene 3: Rename.
- Scene 3: Organize graphics.
- Scene 3: Make connections.
  - Scene 3: Control-drag from button to new scene.
  - Scene 3: Edit the segue's attributes.
  - Scene 3: If dead-end, make button.

8. Now you're going to do something new. You may not know it yet, but you're heading down a dead-end. You'll need to repeat these steps each time you head down a dead-end. Essentially, you have to deal with the reverse buttons showing up so that once users get to the dead-end, they can backtrack. You undoubtedly remember all the code you did to enable this. You handle this by first dragging a new Round Rect button onto the canvas as shown in Figure 10-27.

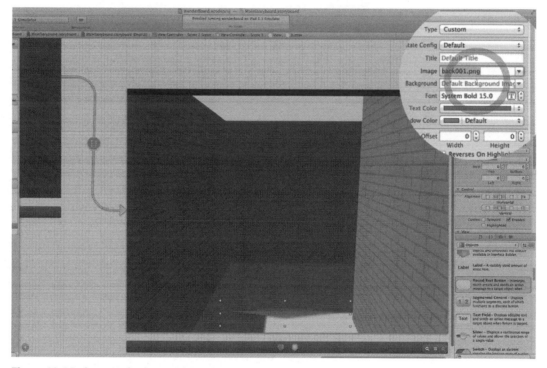

Figure 10-28. *Scene 3: Set Image of the new reverse button.*

- ▥ Scene 3: Copy an existing scene.
- ▥ Scene 3: Rename.
- ▥ Scene 3: Organize graphics.
- ▥ Scene 3: Make connections.
    - ▥ Scene 3: Control-drag from button to new scene.
    - ▥ Scene 3: Edit the segue's attributes.

░ Scene 3: If dead-end, make reverse button.

9. This reverse button is a custom button, and you have an image for it. In the Attributes Inspector, make it Custom and select back001.png for the Image as shown in Figure 10-28. Finally, set it up as 295,680,389,68.

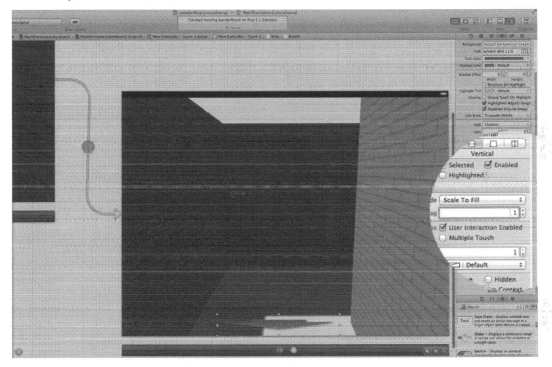

Figure 10-29. *Scene 3: Set Tag field value of 1 for new reverse button.*

░ Scene 3: Copy an existing scene.

░ Scene 3: Rename.

░ Scene 3: Organize graphics.

░ Scene 3: Make connections.

░ Scene 3: Control-drag from button to new scene.

░ Scene 3: Edit the segue's attributes.

░ Scene 3: If dead-end, make reverse button.

░ Scene 3: Edit Tag field.

■   Scene 3: Title the button.

10. You're also going to set up the tag for the reverse button using the second case of data being set. Nearly all objects in Storyboard have a Tag field. Set the Tag field to 1 in the view section of the Attributes Inspector as shown in Figure 10-29. You're going to use the tag of your red reverse button here so that when you head into a dead-end it has a Tag field of 0. As shown in the code, the button is hidden when the tag is 0 and is visible when the tag is 1. That way, users don't see the reverse button as they head into the dead-end. But upon hitting the dead-end they see the button, because now it's set to 1, and can navigate back out.

You also need to title the button. With it selected in the Identity Inspector's Identity section, enter *Button - Reverse* in the Label box. Now you're ready to move on to Scene 4.

Scene 4

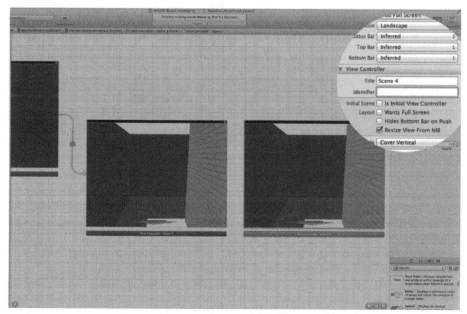

Figure 10-30. *Duplicate Scene 3 to create Scene 4 and drag it to right of Scene 3.*

⬜ Scene 4: Copy an existing scene.

⬜ Scene 4: Place above or below previous scene.

⬜ Scene 4: **Rename**.

⬜ Scene 4: Change the Title.

⬜ Scene 4: Change the Image.

⬜ Scene 4: Organize graphics.

⬜ Scene 4: Make connections.

1. This one is similar to what you did in Figure 10-20. Click Scene 3's dock and press ⌘+D to duplicate and then move the new scene to the right of Scene 3. Also change the Title to *Scene 4* as shown in Figure 10-30. Select the image and change it to wanderBoard-cam04.png, just as you did in Figure 10-21.

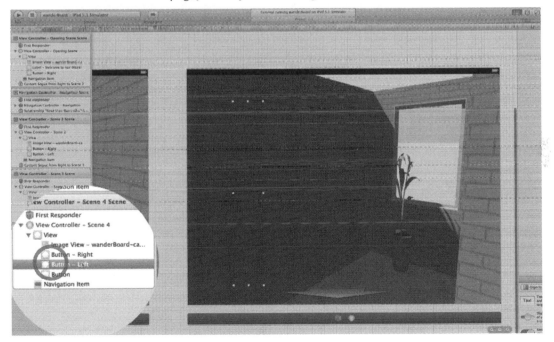

Figure 10-31. *Hide inapplicable elements: select Button – Left.*

⬜ Scene 4: Copy an existing scene.

⬜ Scene 4: Rename.

- Scene 4: Organize graphics.
    - Scene 4: Hide inapplicable elements.
- Scene 4: Make connections.

2. This is a dead-end, so you want to hide the right and left buttons, just as you did in Figure 10-22. See Figure 10-31.

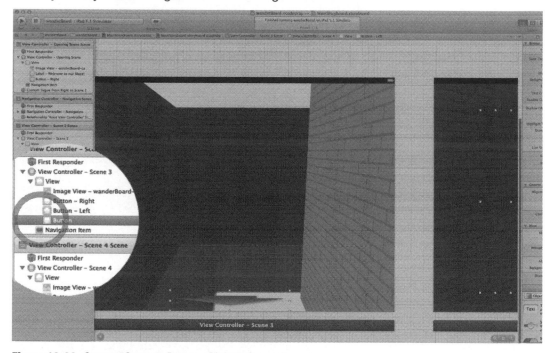

Figure 10-32. *Connect Scene 3: Button – Right to Scene 4.*

- Scene 4: Copy an existing scene.
- Scene 4: Rename.
- Scene 4: Organize graphics.
- Scene 4: Make connections.
    - Scene 4: Control-drag from button to new scene.

3. In View Controller – Scene 3 Scene, connect Button – Right to the View Controller – Scene 4 Scene as shown in Figure 10-32.

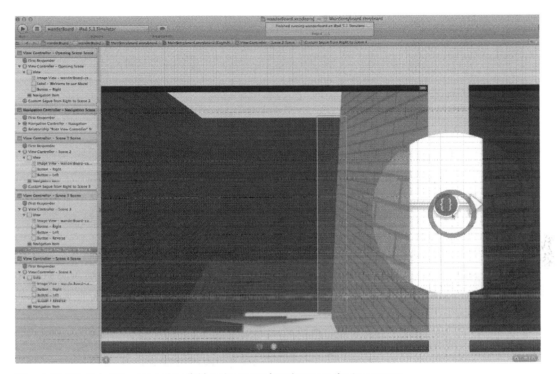

Figure 10-33. *Select the segue by clicking the segue icon between the two scenes.*

- Scene 4: Copy an existing scene.
- Scene 4: Rename.
- Scene 4: Organize graphics.
- Scene 4: Make connections.
    - Scene 4: Control-drag from button to new scene.
    - Scene 4: Edit the segue's attributes.

4. You know this is a right-hand turn from the button label, so select the segue as shown in Figure 10-33. In the Attributes Inspector name the Segue class MovementSegue, keep the Style as Custom, and change the Identifier to *Right*. Yup, you will be repeating this a lot! Notice how when you click the segue, it shows you what button is selected! This ends up being very helpful as things get complex.

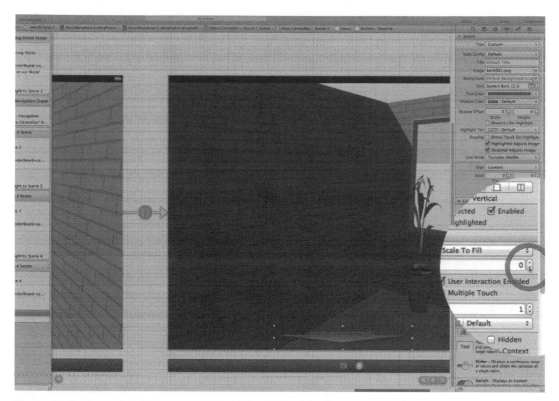

Figure 10-34. *Scene 4: Set the reverse button's Tag field to 0 (zero).*

- Scene 4: Copy an existing scene.
- Scene 4: Rename.
- Scene 4: Organize graphics.
- Scene 4: Make connections.
    - Scene 4: Control-drag from button to new scene.
    - Scene 4: Edit the segue's attributes.
    - Scene 4: If dead-end: Make reverse button.
    - Scene 4: Edit Tag field.

5. You want this reverse button here at the dead-end to be shown all the time, so set its Tag to 0 as shown in Figure 10-34.

Build and run and see what you have. Upon running it, you will
see that the reverse buttons don't seem to be working. It's
critical that you can debug at this point, and that's why you've
named your buttons within scenes. Let's go and debug now.

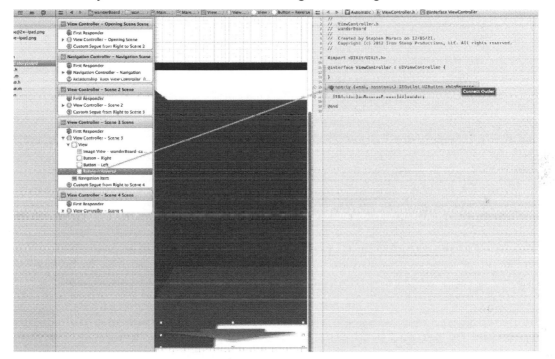

Figure 10-35. *Debugging Scene 3: connect the reverse button to its property.*

6. Go back into Storyboard, select the reverse button, open the
    Assistant Editor, and make sure your ViewController.h file
    appears in the right-hand side. You'll find you haven't set up what
    the button is and what action happens when you tap it (yup the
    stuff you did in helloWorld!). So here in your first view, View
    Controller – Scene 3 Scene, Control-drag from the reverse button
    to the header file btnReverse property as shown in Figure 10-35.

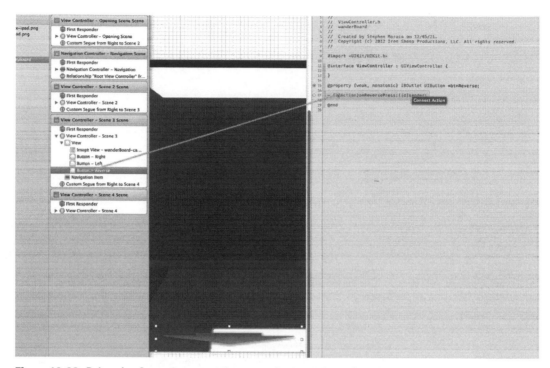

Figure 10-36. *Debugging Scene 3: connect the reverse button to the action method.*

7. You also need to set up the action you're going to take. Select
    the reverse button again and Control-drag out to the action
    method signature in the header file. The circle to the left of it
    that's empty in Figure 10-36 will now be full.

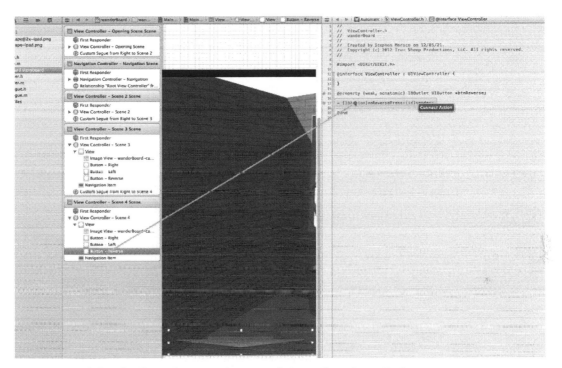

Figure 10-37. *Debugging Scene 4: connect the reverse button to the action method.*

8. In Scene 4 select the reverse button again, repeat part 1 as you did in Figure 10-35, and then part 2 as shown in Figure 10-37. As you can see, you're using the same ViewController object instantiated for each view. So, even though it says they have been hooked up once, you need to rehook them up for each view. That's what we "forgot" so we could really, really make this point.

Run it and you'll see when you go into the dead-end that the reverse buttons only show up once you get there, and that they now work to get you out.

Very good. You've accomplished a lot getting into and out of your first dead-end. You now have all the tools to fly through the construction of the rest of the maze.

Scene 5

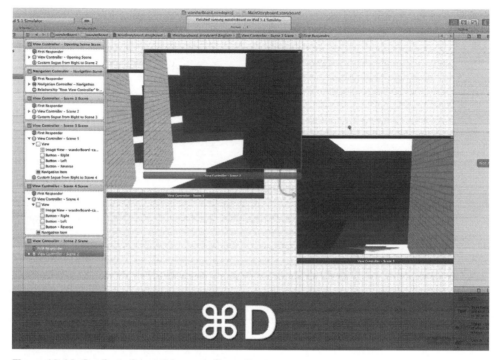

Figure 10-38. *Duplicate Scene 2 to create Scene 5.*

- Scene 5: Copy an existing scene.
  - Scene 5: Place above or below previous scene.
- Scene 5: **Rename**.
  - Scene 5: Change the Title.
  - Scene 5: Change the Image.
- Scene 5: Organize graphics.
- Scene 5: Make connections.

1. Up to this point you've taken, from the entrance, the right-hand path of the maze. Now you want to take care of the left-hand path. Switch back to Standard Editor mode. Start by selecting Scene 2 and duplicating it with ⌘+D as shown in Figure 10-38. Now move the duplicate above and to the right of Scene 2 and change the Title to *Scene 5* just as you did in Figure 10-8.

> **NOTE:** We used Scene 2 as Scenes 3 and 4 have reverse buttons, which we don't need for Scene 5.

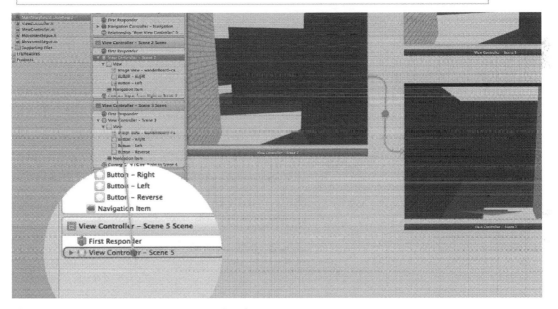

Figure 10-39. *Connect Scene 2: Button – Left to Scene 5.*

- Scene 5: Copy an existing scene.
- Scene 5: Rename.
- Scene 5: Organize graphics.
- Scene 5: Make connections.
    - Scene 5: Control-drag from button to new scene.
    - Scene 5: Edit the segue's attributes.

2. Control-drag from the left button in Scene 2 to Scene 5's View Controller as shown in Figure 10-39, just as you did in Figure 10-16. Select the created segue, in the Attributes Inspector name the Segue class MovementSegue, keep the Style as Custom, and change the Identifier to *Left*.

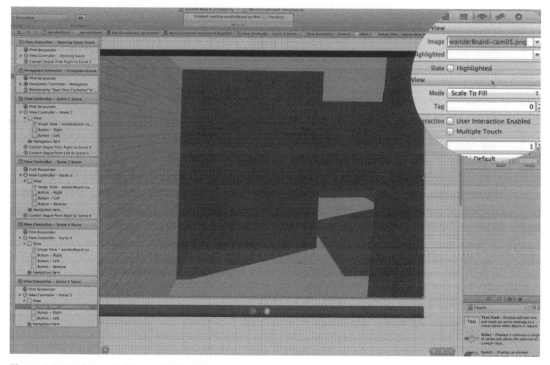

Figure 10-40. *Scene 5: Change the Image.*

- Scene 5: Copy an existing scene.
- Scene 5: **Rename**.
  - Scene 5: Change the Title.
  - Scene 5: Change the Image.
- Scene 5: Organize graphics.
- Scene 5: Make connections.

3. We went a little out of sequence here—change the Image to wanderBoard-cam05.png as shown in Figure 10-40.

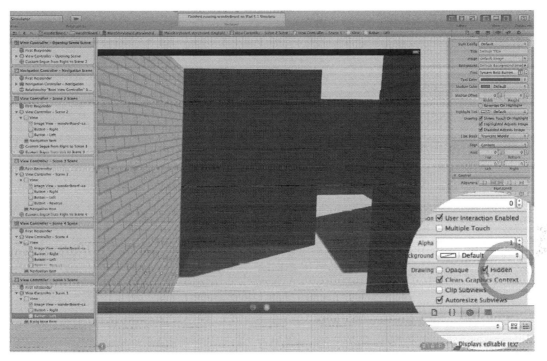

Figure 10-41. *Scene 5: Hide the left button.*

- Scene 5: Copy an existing scene.
- Scene 5: Rename.
- Scene 5: Organize graphics.
    - Scene 5: Hide inapplicable elements.
- Scene 5: Make connections.

4. For the buttons for Scene 5, you don't have a left outlet, so select Button – Left and hide it as shown in Figure 10-41.

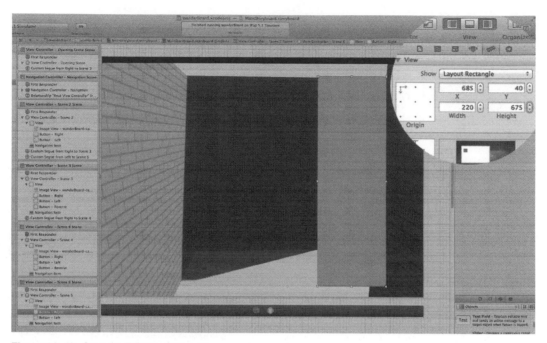

Figure 10-42. *Scene 5: Edit the right button.*

- Scene 5: Copy an existing scene.
- Scene 5: Rename.
- Scene 5: Organize graphics.
    - Scene 5: Hide inapplicable elements.
    - Scene 5: Edit buttons.
    - Scene 5: Make button visible.
    - Scene 5: Replace image with new image (done).
    - Scene 5: Configure new buttons.
    - Scene 5: Duplicate buttons.
    - Scene 5: Reset parameters of buttons.
    - Scene 5: Button – Right.
    - Scene 5: Make transparent again.
    - Scene 5: Correct bug.

■ Scene 5: Make connections.

5. You do have a right-hand button. And you know the drill now. Make it visible and set it at 685,40,220,675 as shown in Figure 10-42. Now correct the bug by setting it to Shows Touch On Highlight. Now let's move on to Scene 6.

Scene 6

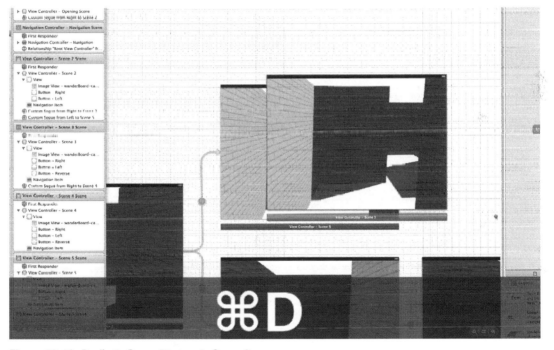

Figure 10-43. *Duplicate Scene 5 to create Scene 6.*

■ Scene 6: Copy an existing scene.

■ Scene 6: Place above or below previous scene.

■ Scene 6: **Rename.**

■ Scene 6: Change the Title.

■ Scene 6: Change the Image.

■ Scene 6: Organize graphics.

■ Scene 6: Make connections.

1. You know this is a right exit and that you have nothing special going on, so just duplicate the last one you made. Click Scene 5's dock and duplicate it with ⌘+D as shown in Figure 10-43. Change the Title to *Scene 6* and the image to wanderBoard-cam06.png.

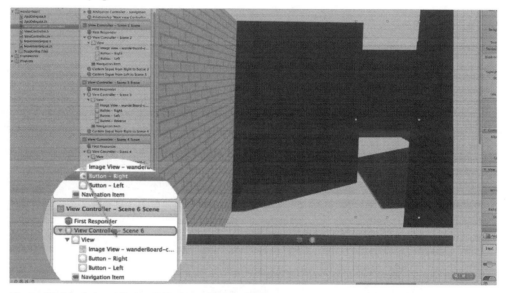

Figure 10-44. *Connect Scene 5: Button – Right to Scene 6.*

■ Scene 6: Copy an existing scene.

■ Scene 6: Rename.

■ Scene 6: Organize graphics.

■ Scene 6: Make connections.

■ Scene 6: Control-drag from button to new scene.

■ Scene 6: Edit the segue's attributes.

2. You need to make a segue to the right to get to Scene 6. Control-drag from the right button of Scene 5's View Controller of Scene 6 as shown in Figure 10-44. With this done, select the created segue, in the Attributes Inspector name the Segue class MovementSegue, keep the Style as Custom, and change the Identifier to *Right*.

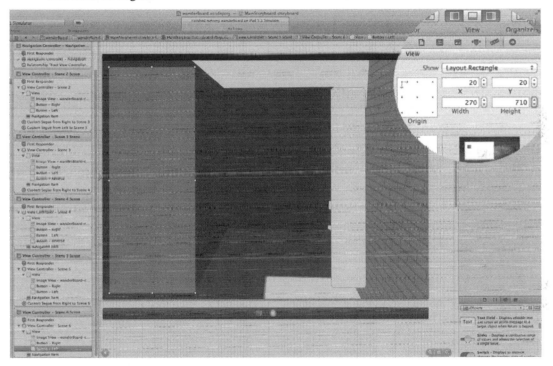

Figure 10-45. *Scene 6: Edit Button – Left.*

- ▦ Scene 6: Copy an existing scene.
- ▦ Scene 6: Rename.
- ▦ Scene 6: Organize graphics.
  - ▦ Scene 6: Hide inapplicable elements.
  - ▦ Scene 6: Edit buttons.
    - ▦ Scene 6: Make button visible.
  - ▦ Scene 6: Replace image with new image (done).

      ▓ Scene 6: Configure new buttons.

        ▓ Scene 6: Duplicate buttons.

        ▓ Scene 6: Reset parameters of buttons.

          ▓ Scene 6: Button – Right.

        ▓ Scene 6: Make transparent again.

        ▓ Scene 6: Correct bug.

    ▓ Scene 6: Make connections

3. In Scene 6 select the right button, make it visible, and set it at 720,85,110,630. Correct the bug by setting it to Shows Touch On Highlight. Select the left button, make it visible, and set it at 20,20,270,710 as shown in Figure 10-45. Correct the bug by also setting it to Shows Touch On Highlight. Make both buttons transparent, and let's move on to Scene 7.

Scene 7

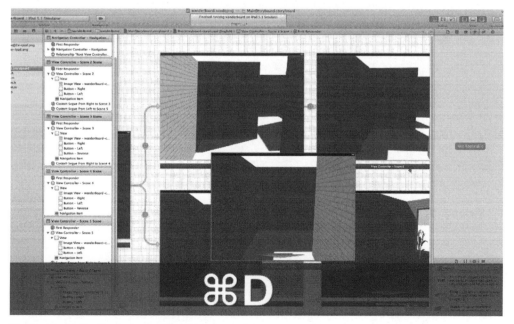

Figure 10-46. *Duplicate Scene 3 to create Scene 7.*

- Scene 7: Copy an existing mid dead-end scene.

  - Scene 7: Place above or below previous scene.

- Scene 7: **Rename.**

  - Scene 7: Change the Title.

  - Scene 7: Change the Image.

- Scene 7: Organize graphics.

- Scene 7: Make connections.

1. The left turn goes down another dead-end. This next scene will
   be a mid-dead-end scene, meaning en route to the dead-end.
   You want to duplicate the one existing mid-dead-end scene,
   which is View Controller – Scene 3. Select Scene 3 and duplicate
   it with ⌘+D as shown in Figure 10-46. Place it to the right of and
   slightly above Scene 6. Change the Title to *Scene 7*.

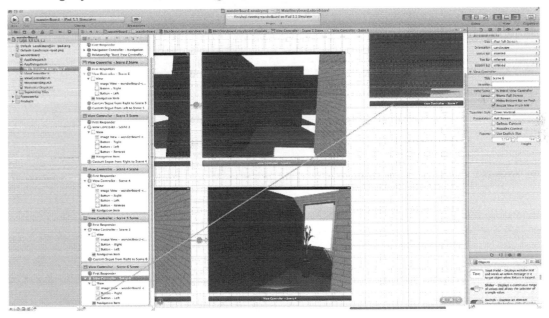

Figure 10-47. *Connect Scene 6: Button – Left to Scene 7.*

- Scene 7: Copy an existing scene.
- Scene 7: Rename.

■ Scene 7: Organize graphics.

■ Scene 7: Make connections.

  ■ Scene 7: Control-drag from button to new scene.

  ■ Scene 7: Edit the segue's attributes.

2. You'll connect the left button of Scene 6 to this new view. Let's do it in a slightly different way this time, just for fun. Control-drag from Scene 6's left button to the scene dock of View Controller – Scene 7 as shown in Figure 10-47. Select the created segue, in the Attributes Inspector name the Segue class MovementSegue, keep the Style as Custom, and change the Identifier to *Left*.

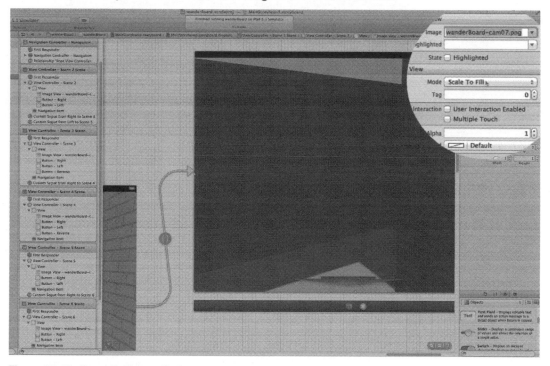

Figure 10-48. *Scene 7: Change the Image.*

■ Scene 7: Copy an existing scene.

  ■ Scene 7: Place above or below previous scene.

■ Scene 7: **Rename**.

- Scene 7: Change the Title.
- Scene 7: Change the Image.
- Scene 7: Organize graphics.
- Scene 7: Make connections.

3. Select the image and in the Attributes Inspector change Image to wanderBoard-cam07.png as shown in Figure 10-48.

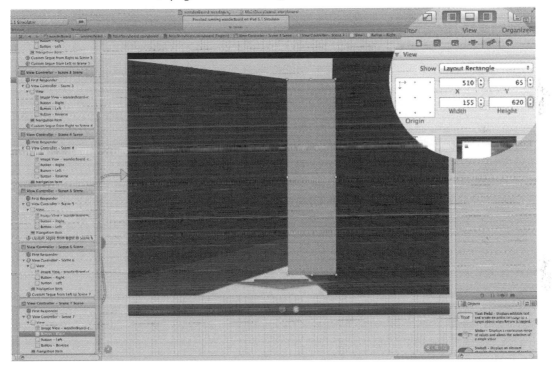

Figure 10-49. *Scene 7: Edit Button – Right.*

- Scene 7: Copy an existing scene.
- Scene 7: Rename.
- Scene 7: Organize graphics.
    - Scene 7: Hide inapplicable elements.
    - Scene 7: Edit buttons.
        - Scene 7: Make button visible.

- Scene 7: Replace image with new image (done).
- Scene 7: Configure new buttons.
  - Scene 7: Duplicate buttons.
  - Scene 7: Reset parameters of buttons.
    - Scene 7: Button – Right.
  - Scene 7: Make transparent again.
  - Scene 7: Correct bug.
- Scene 7: Make connections.
  - Scene 7: Control-drag from button to new scene.
  - Scene 7: Edit the segue's attributes.
  - Scene 7: If dead-end, make reverse button.
    - Scene 7: Edit Tag field.

4. Select the right button in Scene 7 and make it visible. Then select the left button and make sure it's hidden. The reverse button, of course, will be shown. Go back to the right button, select it, and set it to 510,65,155,620 as shown in Figure 10-49. Correct the bug by setting it to Shows Touch On Highlight and make it transparent. Don't forget to also click the reverse button and, keeping in mind it's an intermediate reverse button, set its Tag to 1. Time to move on to Scene 8.

Scene 8

Figure 10-50. *Duplicate Scene 4 to create Scene 8.*

- Scene 8: Copy an existing dead-end scene.
  - Scene 8: Place above or below previous scene.
- Scene 8: Rename.
- Scene 8: Organize graphics.
- Scene 8: Make connections.

1. This time you need to duplicate a dead-end scene. Select the scene dock of View Controller – Scene 4 and duplicate it with ⌘+D as shown in Figure 10-50. Place it to the right of Scene 7.

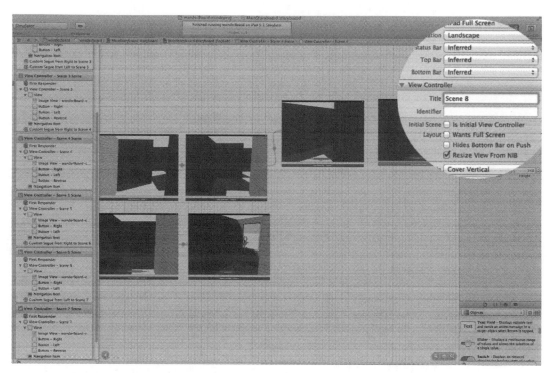

Figure 10-51. *Scene 8: Change the Title.*

- Scene 8: Copy an existing dead-end scene.
- Scene 8: **Rename**.
  - Scene 8: Change the Title.
- Scene 8: Organize graphics.
- Scene 8: Make connections.

2. Change the Title to *Scene 8* as shown in Figure 10-51.

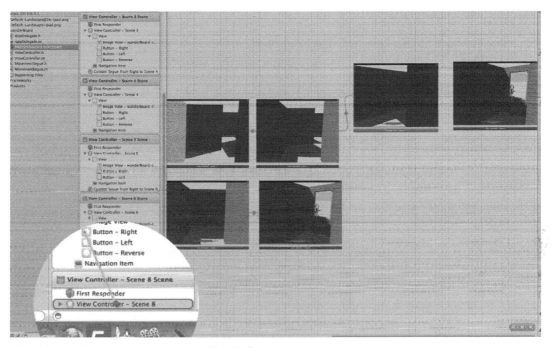

Figure 10-52. *Connect Scene 7: Button – Right to Scene 8.*

- ▨ Scene 8: Copy an existing scene.
- ▨ Scene 8: Rename.
    - ▨ Scene 8: Change the Title.
    - ▨ Scene 8: Change the Image.
- ▨ Scene 8: Organize graphics.
- ▨ Scene 8: Make connections.
    - ▨ Scene 8: Control-drag from button to new scene.
    - ▨ Scene 8: Edit the segue's attributes.

3. The right button from Scene 7 is your segue point, so Control-drag from it to the View Controller of Scene 8 as shown in Figure 10-52. Select the created segue, in the Attributes Inspector name the Segue class MovementSegue, keep the Style as Custom, and change the Identifier to *Right*. Select the Image and change it to wanderBoard-cam08.png. Now we can move on to Scene 9.

Scene 9

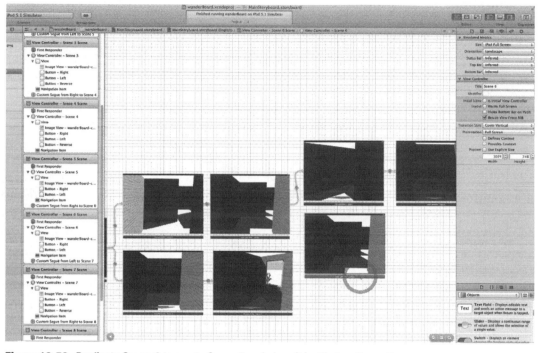

Figure 10-53. *Duplicate Scene 6 to create Scene 9 and place it just below Scene 7.*

- Scene 9: Copy an existing scene.
  - Scene 9: Place above or below previous scene.
- Scene 9: Rename.
- Scene 9: Organize graphics.
- Scene 9: Make connections.

1. To create the right side, duplicate Scene 6 and drag it to the right and slightly underneath Scene 6 as shown in Figure 10-53.

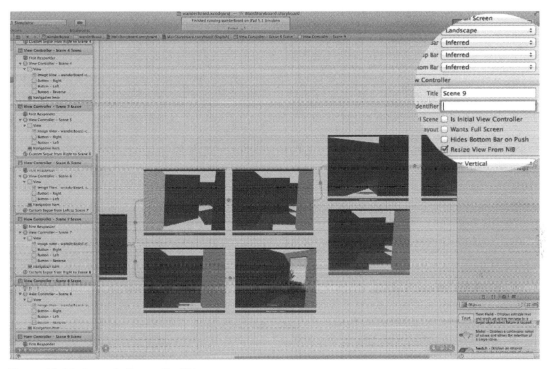

Figure 10-54. *Scene 9: Change the Title.*

- Scene 9: Copy an existing scene.
- Scene 9: Rename.
    - Scene 9: Change the Title.
- Scene 9: Organize graphics.
- Scene 9: Make connections.

2. Change the Title to *Scene 9* as shown in Figure 10-54.

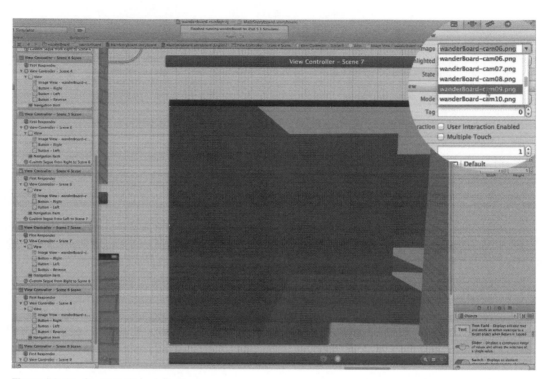

Figure 10-55. *Scene 9: Change the Image.*

- Scene 9: Copy an existing scene.
- Scene 9: Rename.
    - Scene 9: Change the Title.
    - Scene 9: Change the Image.
- Scene 9: Organize graphics.
- Scene 9: Make connections.

3. Change the Image to wanderBoard-cam09.png as shown in Figure 10-55.

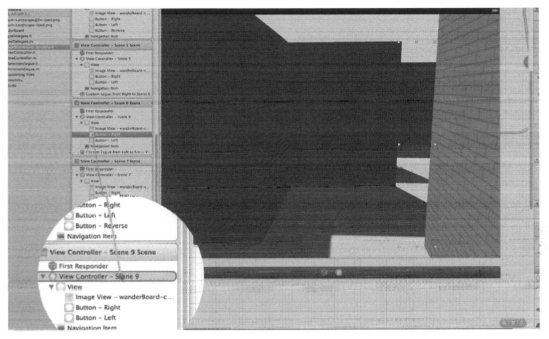

Figure 10-56. *Connect Scene 6: Button Right to Scene 9.*

- Scene 9: Copy an existing scene.
- Scene 9: Rename.
- Scene 9: Organize graphics.
- Scene 9: Make connections.
    - Scene 9: Control-drag from button to new scene.
    - Scene 9: Edit the segue's attributes.

4. The segue to Scene 9 starts at Scene 6's right button. Control-drag from it to Scene 9 as shown in Figure 10-56. Select the created segue, in the Attributes Inspector name the Segue class MovementSegue, keep the Style as Custom, and change the Identifier to *Right*.

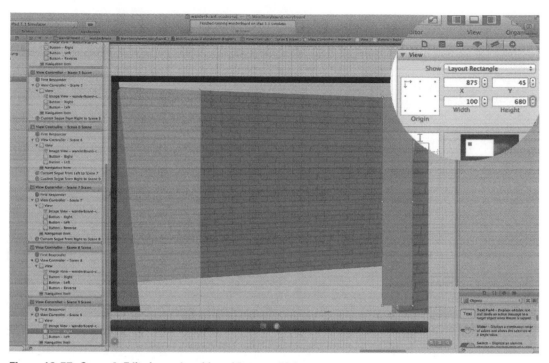

Figure 10-57. *Scene 9: Edit size and position of Button – Right.*

- Scene 9: Copy an existing scene.
- Scene 9: Rename.
- Scene 9: Organize graphics.
    - Scene 9: Hide inapplicable elements.
    - Scene 9: Edit buttons.
        - Scene 9: Make button visible.
    - Scene 9: Replace image with new image (done).
    - Scene 9: Configure new buttons.
        - Scene 9: Duplicate buttons.
        - Scene 9: Reset parameters of buttons.
            - Scene 9: Button – Right.
        - Scene 9: Make transparent again.

        ▨   Scene 9: Correct bug.

     ▨   Scene 9: Make connections.

5.   In this case, you do have two options for direction, so keep both buttons. First show the left button and then the right button so they're both visible. Change the right button from 875,45,100,680 as shown in Figure 10-57 to 875,45,100,680 and make the left button 20,20,100,710. Change them back to transparent and make sure they both Show Touch On Highlight.

You've reached the end of Step 4a and the end of this chapter. You've completed all the code for wanderBoard and have finished the implementation of the first nine scenes. Good job!

In the next chapter you'll finish the remaining scenes, making a few repairs along the way. By the end of the next chapter you'll be testing and running the completed wanderBoard application. You ready? Then read on!

11

Single View #3: wanderBoard Part III

At this point you've now created nine scenes and completed the code. In this final chapter you're going to complete the remaining scenes for the wanderBoard application.

Step 4b: Create the Final Nine Scenes

We think you've done this enough now that you just need a limited amount of instructions, such as a client, boss, or skilled co-worker/mentor may give you.

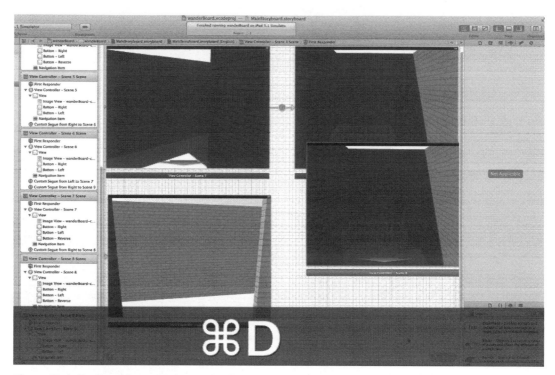

Figure 11-1. *Duplicate Scene 8 to create Scene 10.*

- Scene 10: Copy an existing dead-end scene.
    - Scene 10: Place above or below previous scene.
- Scene 10: Rename.
    - Scene 10: Change the Title.
- Scene 10: Organize graphics.
- Scene 10: Make connections.

1. This time you need to duplicate the dead-end scene. Select the scene dock of the View Controller – Scene 8 and duplicate it by pressing ⌘+D as shown in Figure 11-1. Place it to the right and slightly below Scene 9 and change the Title to Scene 10.

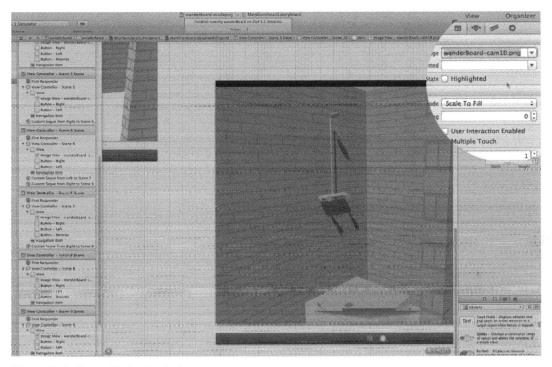

Figure 11-2. *Scene 10: Set the desired image.*

- Scene 10: Copy an existing dead-end scene.
  - Scene 10: Place above or below previous scene.
- Scene 10: Rename.
  - Scene 10: Change the Title.
  - Scene 10: Change the Image.
- Scene 10: Organize graphics.
- Scene 10: Make connections.

2. Change the image to wanderBoard-cam10.png as shown in Figure 11-2. Here you're creating another dead-end. You didn't complete the wiring up of the reverse button for the previous dead-end, so let's fix up Scenes 7 and 8 before we finish Scene 10.

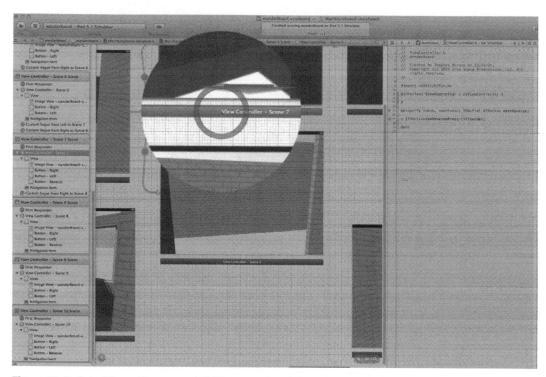

Figure 11-3. *Select Scene 7 so you can finish some missed steps.*

3. Remember when you ran your last test and had to go back and
    connect the red button to the code? Let's not repeat that
    mistake. Let's do that here. Select Scene 7 as shown in
    Figure 11-3.

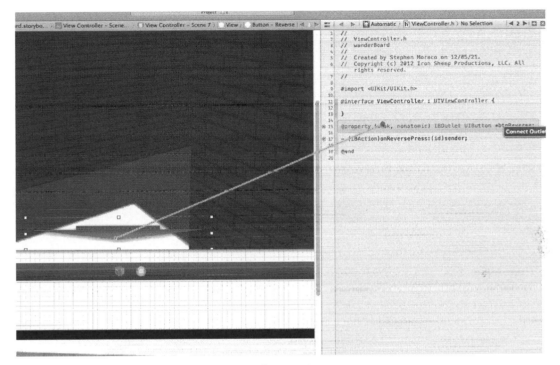

Figure 11-4. *Connect the Scene 7 reverse button to its property.*

4. Open the Assistant Editor and make sure your header file is on
    the right. Control-drag from the button to the header file as
    shown in Figure 11-4 to connect the button to its property.

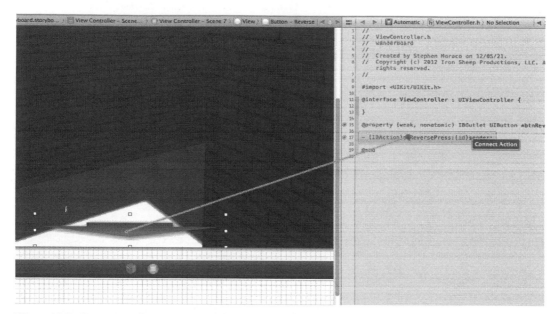

Figure 11-5. *Connect the Scene 7 reverse button to its action method.*

5. Control-drag from the button in scene 7 to the header file to connect the button to the action method as shown in Figure 11-5.

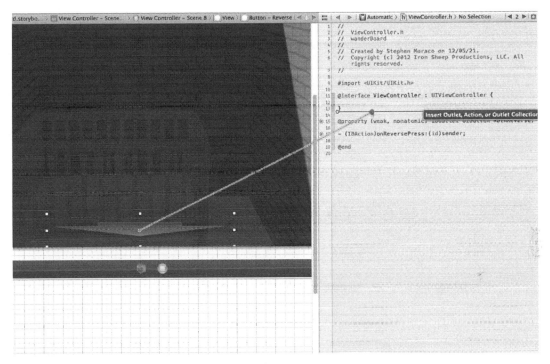

Figure 11-6. *Connect the Scene 8 reverse button to the property.*

6. Now do the same for Scene 8. After selecting Scene 8, Control-drag from the button to its property in the header file as shown in Figure 11-6.

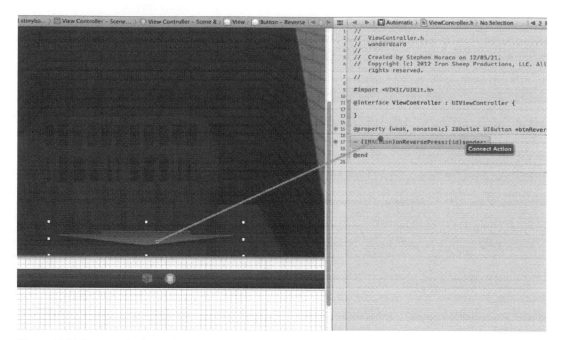

Figure 11-7. *Connect the Scene 8 reverse button to its action method.*

7. Control-drag from the button in Scene 8 to the header file to connect to the action method as shown in Figure 11-7.

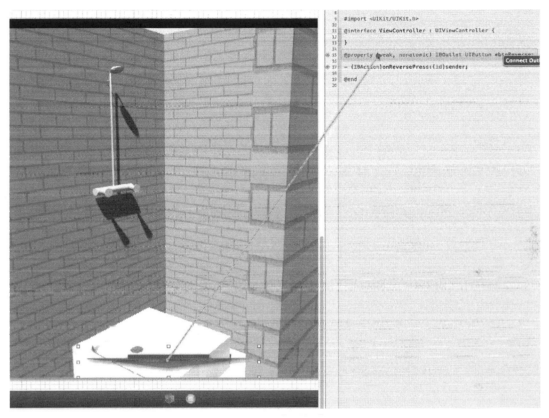

Figure 11-8. *Connect the Scene 10 reverse button to its property.*

8. Now, back to Scene 10. Select Scene 10 and Control-drag from the button to the header file as shown in Figure 11-8, establishing the connection to the property.

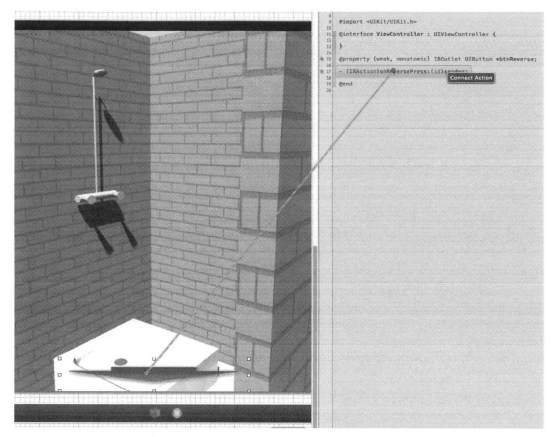

Figure 11-9. *Connect the Scene 10 button to its action method.*

9. Control-drag from the button in Scene 10 to the header file to
    connect the action method as shown in Figure 11-9.

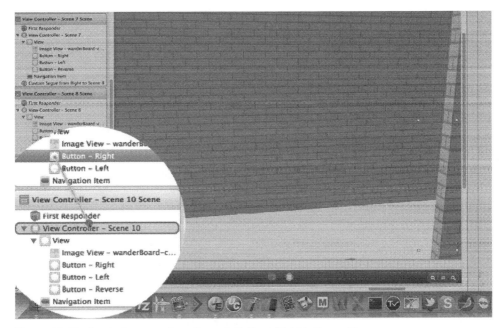

Figure 11-10. *Create the segue from Scene 9: Button - Right to Scene 10.*

▨ Scene 10: Copy an existing scene.

▨ Scene 10: Rename.

▨ Scene 10: Organize graphics.

▨ Scene 10: Make connections.

  ▨ Scene 10: Control-drag from button to new scene.

  ▨ Scene 10: Edit the segue's attributes.

10. As discussed, you need to go from the right button in Scene 9 to Scene 10, as shown in Figure 11-10. You can switch off the Assistant Editor, select the created segue, go to the Attributes Inspector, name the Segue class MovementSegue, keep the Style as Custom, and change the Identifier to Right.

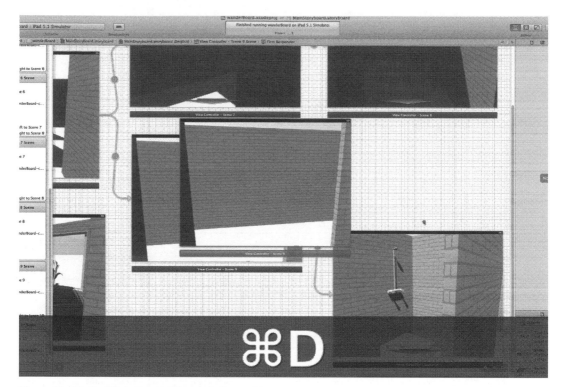

Figure 11-11. *Duplicate Scene 9 to create Scene 11.*

- Scene 11: Copy an existing dead-end scene.
  - Scene 11: Place above or below previous scene.
- Scene 11: Rename.
  - Scene 11: Change the Title.
- Scene 11: Organize graphics.
- Scene 11: Make connections.

11. Scene 11 is not going to be a dead-end, so take Scene 9 and duplicate it as shown in Figure 11-11. Drag over to the right and top of Scene 9—you'll notice it doesn't fit. Zoom out and move the upper run of views higher to make some space. Now change the Title to Scene 11.

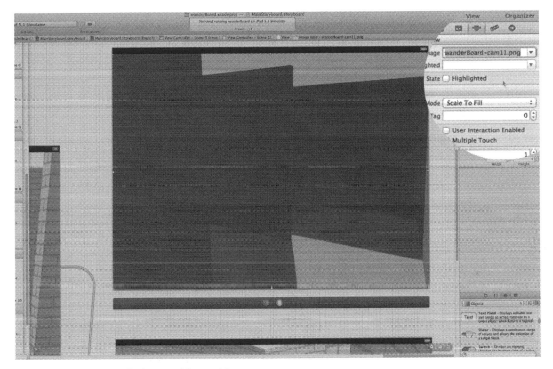

Figure 11-12. *Change the Image of Scene 11.*

▨   Scene 11: Copy an existing dead-end scene.

    ▨   Scene 11: Place above or below previous scene.

▨   Scene 11: Rename.

    ▨   Scene 11: Change the Title.

    ▨   Scene 11: Change the Image.

▨   Scene 11: Organize graphics.

▨   Scene 11: Make connections.

12. Change the Image of Scene 11 to wanderBoard-cam11.png as shown in Figure 11-12.

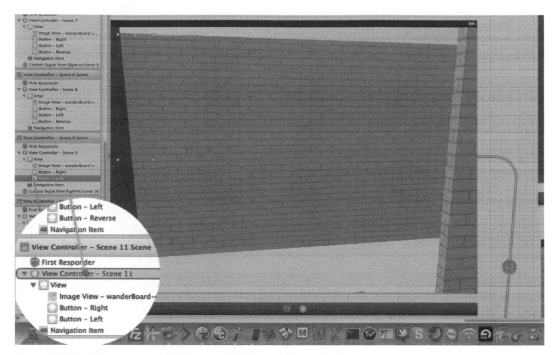

Figure 11-13. *Make the segue from Scene 10: Button - Left to Scene 11.*

- Scene 11: Copy an existing scene.
- Scene 11: Rename.
- Scene 11: Organize graphics.
- Scene 11: Make connections.
    - Scene 11: Control-drag from button to new scene.
    - Scene 11: Edit the segue's attributes.

13. Connect the left button in Scene 9 to Scene 11 as shown in Figure 11-13. Now select the created segue, in the Attributes Inspector name the segue class MovementSegue, keep the Style as Custom, and change the Identifier to Left.

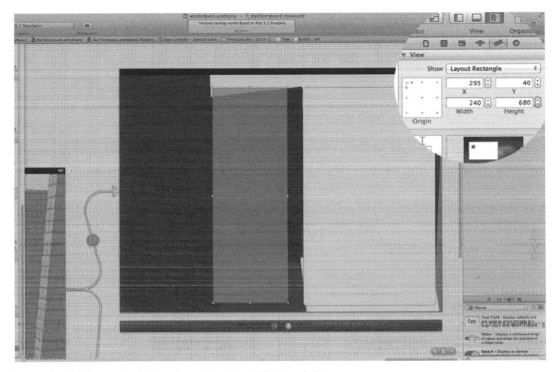

Figure 11-14. *Scene 11: Setting size and location of Button - Left.*

▓ Scene 11: Copy an existing scene.

▓ Scene 11: Rename.

▓ Scene 11: Organize graphics.

    ▓ Scene 11: Delete inapplicable elements.

    ▓ Scene 11: Edit buttons.

    ▓ Scene 11: Make button visible.

    ▓ Scene 11: Replace Image with new image (done).

    ▓ Scene 11: Configure new buttons.

    ▓ Scene 11: Duplicate buttons (done).

    ▓ Scene 11: Reset parameters of buttons.

    ▓ Scene 11: Button-Right.

    ▓ Scene 11: Make transparent again.

■ Scene 11: **Correct bug**.

■ Scene 11: Make connections.

14. Select Scene 11's two buttons and make them visible. Set the right button to 585,40,420,90 and the left button to 295,40,240,680 as shown in Figure 11-14. Now change them back to transparent and make sure they both show Touch on Highlight.

> **NOTE:** As you move on to Scenes 12–17 you'll no longer use the steps. We'll simply talk to you in prose, and you should be able to follow along at this point.

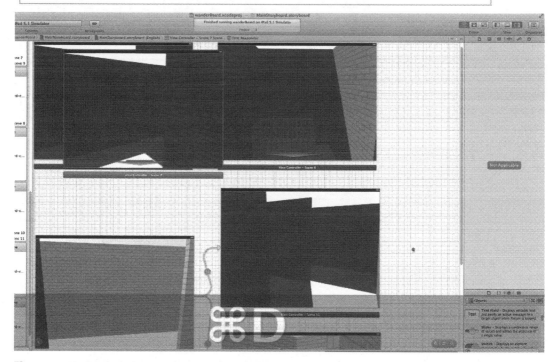

Figure 11-15. *Duplicate Scene 7 to create Scene 12.*

15. Scene 12 is going to be another dead-end—specifically, an intermediate dead-end. So duplicate Scene 7 as shown in Figure 11-15 and place it to the upper-right side of Scene 11. Change the Title to Scene 12 and change the Image to wanderBoard-cam12.png.

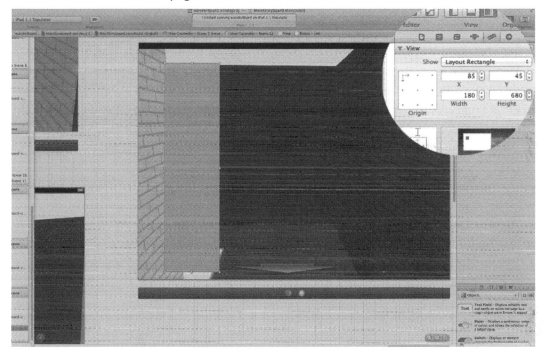

Figure 11-16. *Scene 12: Configure the buttons.*

16. For Scene 12 you can go reverse, and left but not right. So hide right and make left shown and visible at 85,45,180,680 as shown in Figure 11-16. Now make it transparent again and make sure it shows Touch on Highlight. Set the reverse button's tag to the intermediate level—so set it at 1. Remember to connect the reverse button to both the property and the action method!

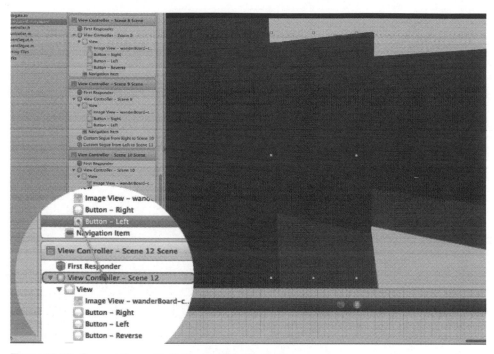

Figure 11-17. *Connect Scene 11: Button - Left to Scene 12.*

17. Connect Scene 11's left button to Scene 12 as shown in Figure 11-17. Now select the created segue, in the Attributes Inspector name the Segue class MovementSegue, keep the Style as Custom, and change the Identifier to Left.

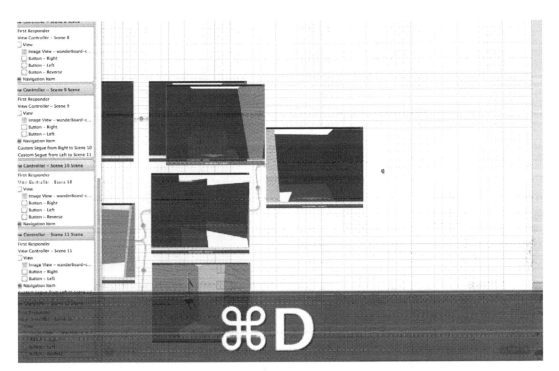

Figure 11-18. *Duplicate Scene 8 to create Scene 13.*

18. You know that after the intermediate dead-end of Scene 12
    comes the real dead-end, and that will be Scene 13. So
    duplicate Scene 8 as shown in Figure 11-18. Place it to the right
    of Scene 12. Change the Title to Scene 13.

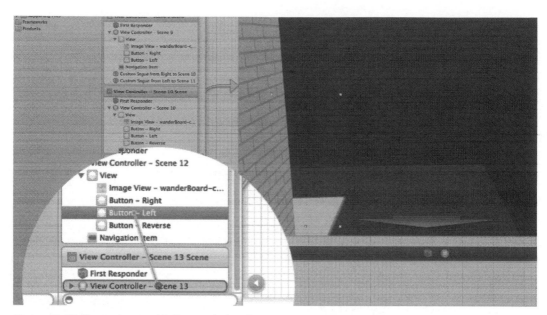

Figure 11-19. *Connect scene 12: Button - Left to Scene 13.*

19. Connect the left button in Scene 12 to Scene 13 as shown in
    Figure 11-19. Select the created segue, in the Attributes
    Inspector name the Segue class MovementSegue, keep the Style
    as Custom, and change the Identifier to Left. Change the Image
    to wanderBoard-cam13.png.

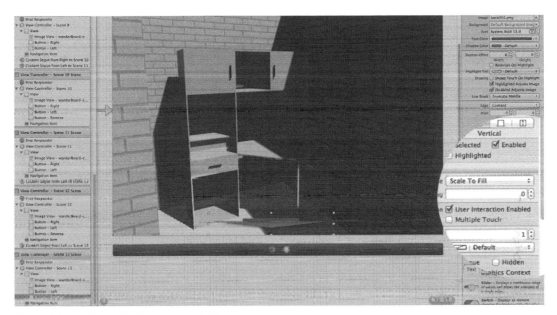

Figure 11-20. *Scene 13: Configure the buttons.*

20. Make sure the right button is hidden, the left button is hidden, and the reverse button is tagged at 0 as shown in Figure 11-20. Also, don't forget to hook up the reverse button to the property and the action method!

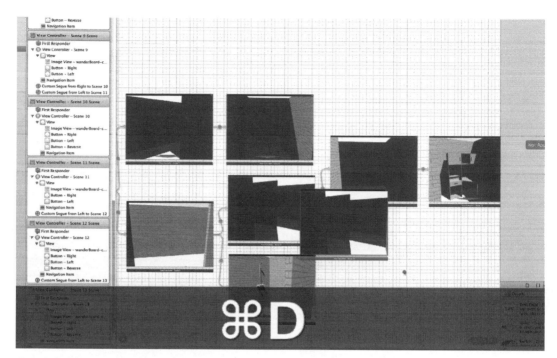

Figure 11-21. *Duplicate Scene 11 to create Scene 14.*

21. You're not going down a dead-end anymore, so duplicate Scene 11 as shown in Figure 11-21. Place it to the right and slightly under Scene 11.

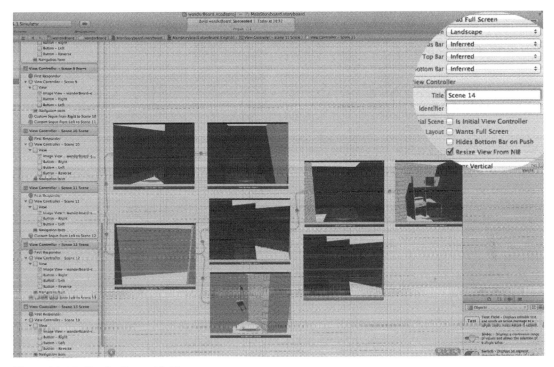

Figure 11-22. *Set the Scene 14 title.*

22. Set the Title to Scene 14 as shown in Figure 11-22.

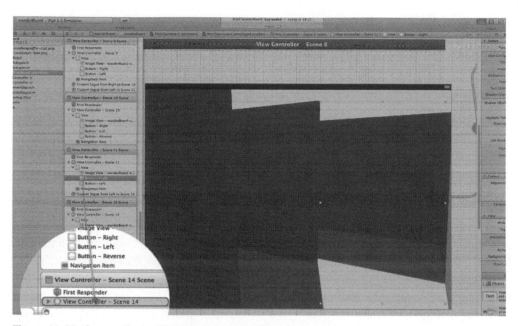

Figure 11-23. *Connect Scene 11: Button - Right to Scene 14.*

23. You need a segue from the right button of Scene 11 to Scene 14 as shown in Figure 11-23. Select the created segue, in the Attributes Inspector name the Segue class MovementSegue, keep the Style as Custom, and change the Identifier to Right. Change the Image to wanderBoard-cam14.png.

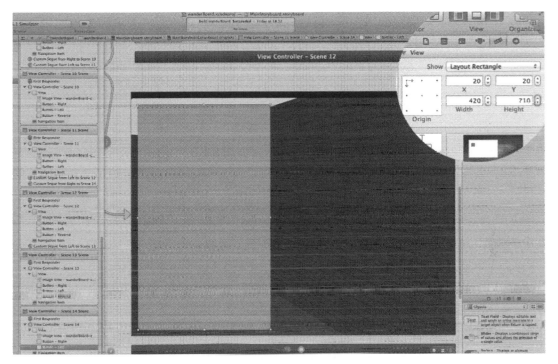

Figure 11-24. *Configure the Scene 14 buttons.*

24. You only have a single place to go, and that is left. So make the right button hidden. Make the left visible and then set it to 20,20,420,720 as shown in Figure 11-24. Then make it transparent and Touches with Highlight.

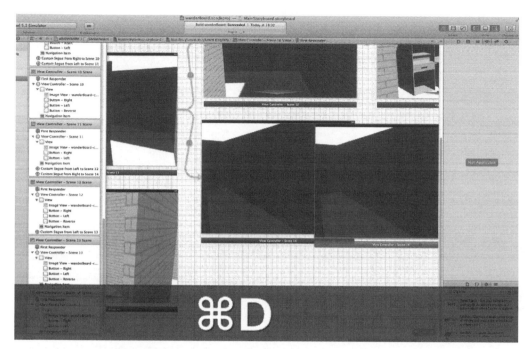

Figure 11-25. *Duplicate Scene 14 to create Scene 15.*

25. Duplicate Scene 14 as shown in Figure 11-25 and place it to the left of Scene 14.

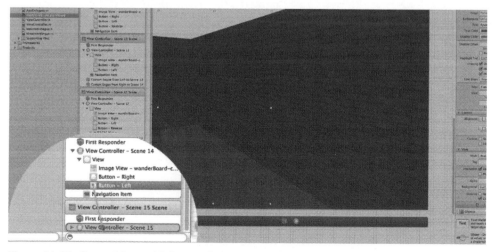

Figure 11-26. *Connect Scene 14: Button - Left to Scene 15.*

26. Change the Title to Scene 15. Because it can only go left, connect Scene 14's left button to Scene 15 as shown in Figure 11-26. Select the created segue, in the Attributes Inspector name the Segue class MovementSegue, keep the Style as Custom, and change the Identifier to Left. Change the Image to wanderBoard-cam15.png.

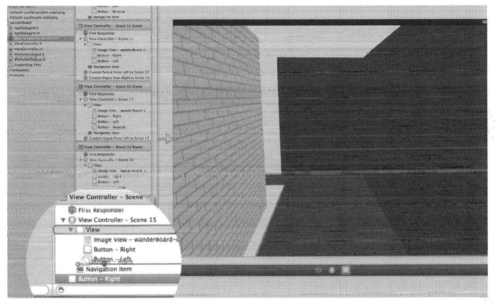

Figure 11-27. *Scene 15: Duplicate Button - Right to make a new forward button.*

27. You need to create a forward button. Duplicate the right button and then move it up as shown in Figure 11-27.

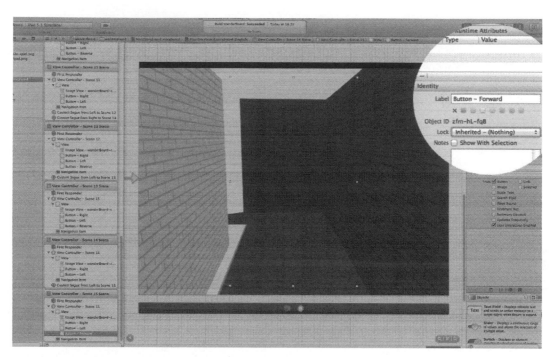

Figure 11-28. *Scene 15: Name the new forward button.*

28. Name the forward button Button-Forward as shown in
Figure 11-28.

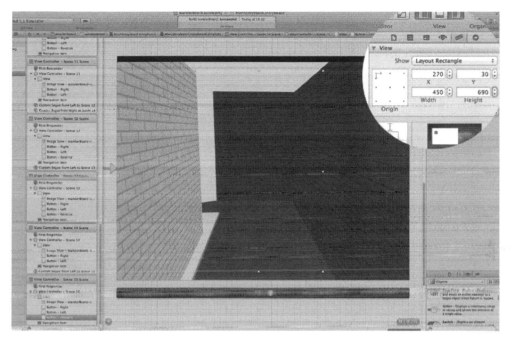

Figure 11-29. *Configure the Scene 15 forward button.*

29. Make sure that right and left are hidden and make the forward button be 270,30,450,690 as shown in Figure 11-29.

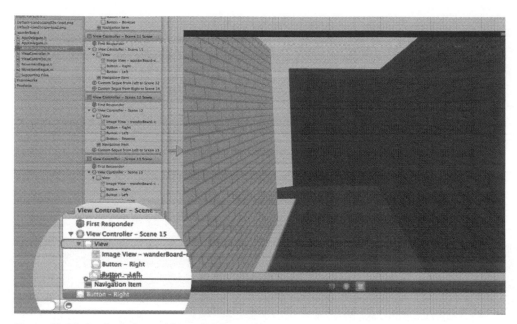

Figure 11-30. *Duplicate Scene 14 to create Scene 16.*

30. You don't need a forward button anymore, so just duplicate
Scene 14 as shown in Figure 11-30. Place it to the right of
Scene 15. Change the Title to Scene 16.

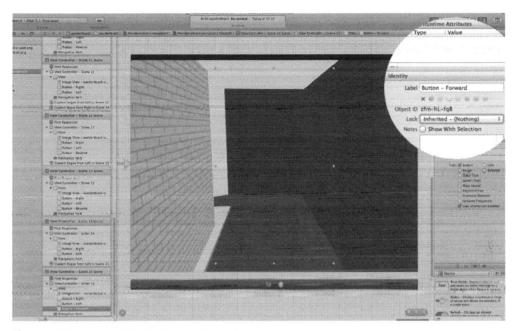

Figure 11-31. *Scene 16: Select Image View and change name.*

31. Sometimes it's easier to select the Image View in the side bar as shown in Figure 11-31 than try to pick things around the buttons. So select it and change the Image to wanderBoard-cam16.png. Also, because you copied this scene, your Button - Left may already be in the correct location, but please check that it's 20,20,420,710, not hidden, and that it's set to show Touch on Highlight.

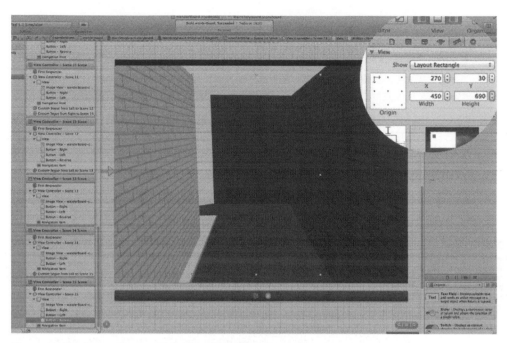

Figure 11-32. *Connect Scene 15: Button - Forward to Scene 16.*

32. Your segue goes from the special forward button you just made to Scene 16 here. So, connect them as shown in Figure 11-32. Select the created segue, in the Attributes Inspector name the Segue class MovementSegue, keep the Style as Custom, and change the Identifier to Forward.

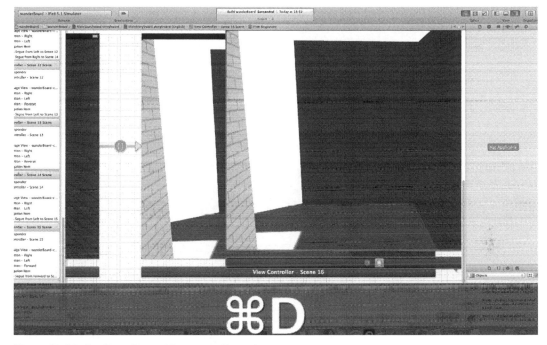

Figure 11-33. *Duplicate Scene 16 to create Scene 17.*

33. Duplicate Scene 16 as shown in Figure 11-33 and make it
Scene 17. Place it to the right of Scene 16. Set the Title to
Scene 17 and set the Image to wanderBoard-cam17.png.

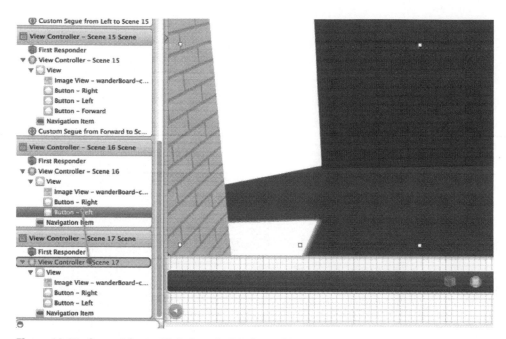

Figure 11-34. *Connect Scene 16: Button - Left to Scene 17.*

34. Connect Scene 16's left button to Scene 17 as shown in Figure 11-34. Select the created segue, in the Attributes Inspector name the Segue class MovementSegue, keep the Style as Custom, and change the Identifier to Left.

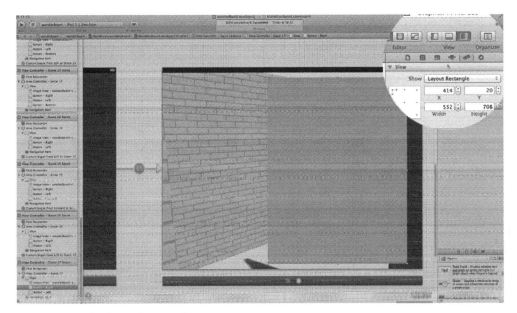

Figure 11-35. *Configure Scene 17 buttons.*

35. Back in the new Scene 17, let's configure the buttons. Ensure that your Button - Left is hidden (because you're not using it). Ensure that Button - Right is visible and change it from 414,20,552,708 as shown in Figure 11-35. Make it transparent and make sure it shows Touches on Highlight.

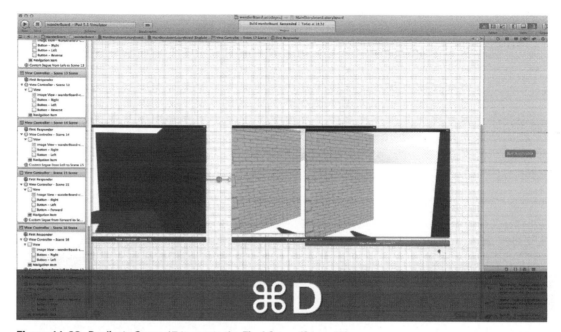

Figure 11-36. *Duplicate Scene 17 to create the Final Scene (Scene 18).*

36. Duplicate Scene 17 as shown in Figure 11-36. Place it to the right of Scene 17.

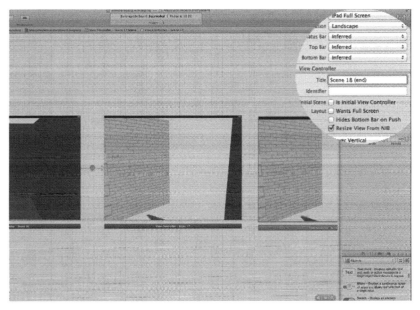

Figure 11-37. *Scene 18: Set the final Title.*

37. Change the Title to Scene 18 (end) as shown in Figure 11-37.

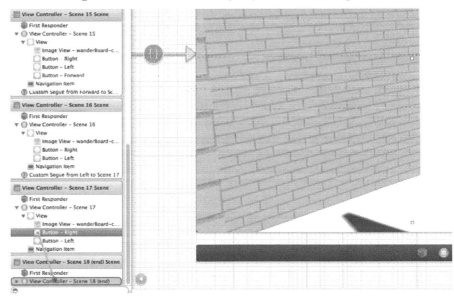

Figure 11-38. *Connect Scene 17: Button - Right to Scene 18.*

38. Connect the right button in Scene 17 to the final scene as shown in Figure 11-38. Select the created segue, in the Attributes Inspector name the Segue class MovementSegue, keep the Style as Custom, and change the Identifier to Right. You have no buttons on this one, so hide all the buttons by changing them to hidden.

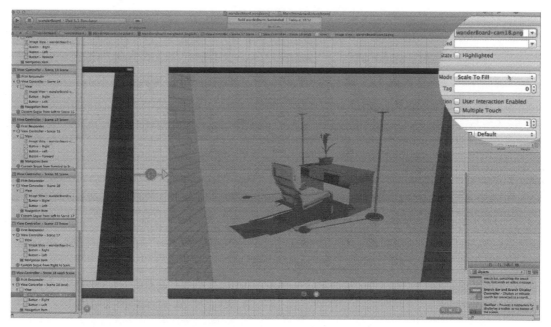

Figure 11-39. *Scene 18: Change the last image.*

39. You have finally reached the end of the maze! Change the Image to wanderBoard-cam18.png.as shown in Figure 11-39. Let's build it and run it. Uh-oh, we have some errors, with buttons not working.

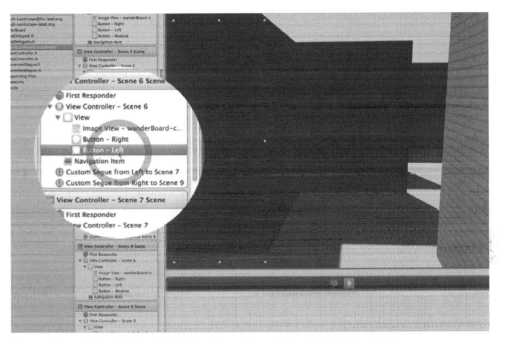

Figure 11-40. *Debug: Find and fix last problems (Scene 6, the first to find and fix).*

40. Our left button in Scene 6 wasn't working, so we select it as shown in Figure 11-40, and sure enough it was still hidden. Uncheck the hidden check box.

41. Repeat the same steps for the left button in Scene 9.

42. Repeat the same steps for the left button in Scene 11.

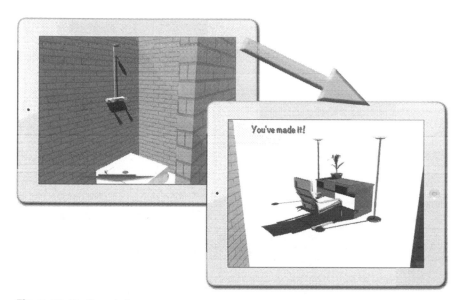

Figure 11-41. *It works!*

43. Run it and … Congratulations! It works (Figure 11-41)!

Congratulations on completing the wanderBoard app! In this application you've seen that with very little code and a bit of Storyboard content, you can create a rather fun but simple application. You've experienced the power of duplicating views on the Storyboard canvas when there are common components you want in each of the views. Duplicating really saves time compared to creating each view piece-by-piece from the ground up. The speed in which we were able to create this application really surprised us. We hope we've shared some of this surprise along with the fun of creating this app with you.

Chapter 12

How Far You've Come

This journey through Storyboards and iOS has covered the four fundamental concepts of Storyboards:

- Easily create transitions between views with little to no code.

- Pass information back from a Secondary View to a Main View.

- Send information to a Secondary View from a Main View.

- Transition between views with user-created visual effects.

You built applications that demonstrated these concepts. In fact, if you were working along with the book you've now written code yourself that had you exercising all four Storyboarding concepts. At this point you should feel very comfortable using Storyboards in your own applications.

How cool, right?!

Final Thoughts

As we were putting this book together, a few more aspects of Storyboarding came up in discussions we had with other developers and our online research:

- The ability to use multiple Storyboard files in a single application

- The effect that putting all the views/View Controllers in one Storyboard file (instead of many .xib files) has on team development

- The fact that not all scenes can be placed in Storyboard files

The first two of these topics are somewhat related. Let's look as each in a bit more detail.

Multiple Storyboard Files in One Application

Actually, using multiple Storyboard files in a single application is fairly easy to do. You'll want to review the class documentation for `UIStoryboard`, paying particular attention to two methods:

- *The class method*: `+storyboardWithName:bundle:`

- *The instance method*: `-instantiateInitialViewController`

The first establishes connection to your next Storyboard file, and the second (as its name implies) loads the initial scene as identified within your next Storyboard file. Sounds simple, but why would you want to create multiple Storyboard files?

The main reason to split up an application's scenes across multiple Storyboard files is probably best understood by looking at a hypothetical example. Let's say you have a main menu from which you can enter four independent regions of the application:

- Player selection with player configuration

- Game settings

- Scores for past games

- Help, which contains text-based help, image-based help, and a video tutorial

Each of these sections stands on its own, without the others, and each has a single entry point scene which one arrives at after choosing the appropriate menu item. In this example app, each of these sections could easily be its own Storyboard file. Keeping them in separate files does a number of good things for you. If you want to change the order of the help scenes (for example), or add one, and so on, you can simply edit the one Storyboard file that contains the help subsystem. It only contains help screens, so you can quickly rearrange things to get a new screen in place. And you know that, having only modified the help Storyboard file, it won't break or cause problems with any of the other Storyboards. In effect you reduce the numbers of scenes you have to wade through to get the fix in place, and you've isolated changes to only the help subsystem scenes. Make sense?

Having All .xib Files in One Storyboard Basket

This is really only a larger issue that often comes up when many developers work on a single application. If two developers both want to make changes to a single file, then changes have to be somehow later combined so that both sets of changes are delivered in the next release. We call this *merging the changes*. There are tools to help you merge text files, but there are no tools as of this writing that can help you merge Storyboard files. The only way to merge these files is to recreate the changes of one file into the second file. Of course, this inability to merge files isn't unique to Storyboard files. I think of any non-text file you have in a project (XML, HTML, CoreData object model diagrams/data, videos, and so forth)—these are all file types that make changes difficult to merge, if it's possible at all.

The software engineering community has developed a number of ways to deal with this need to merge changes. The simplest solution is to avoid the need to merge at all. In practice, this means that you don't allow two or more engineers to modify the same file if at all possible. Here are three ideas that can help you work around this problem:

- Assign engineers to work on different areas of the same application so their changes don't affect the same files.

- Make different changes in different releases, so that only one is being made for the next outgoing release.

- Separate functional areas within the application into separate files so that when changes are being made, the likelihood of overlap is lower.

As for the effect this has on Storyboard files, consider the transition from .xib files to the use of a Storyboard file—effectively, you're rolling up all the .xibs into this Storyboard file. It wonderfully increases your ability to see the overall shape of the application on one canvas and makes it so much easier to specify transitions between scenes on the canvas, but this transition also has the undesirable effect of focusing all your visual changes on this one Storyboard file. Multiple engineers now have to all work in this one file! Here is where these two topics are related: the best mitigation of this effect is to break up the Storyboard scenes into separate, but related, groups of scenes and placing each group into one Storyboard file.

Having more Storyboard files helps prevent changes from needing to occur in the same file because now you have more than just the one file. As our example tried to show, it can be fairly easy to find regions of related scenes in an application, and therefore it can be fairly easy to break an application into multiple Storyboard files.

What Do You Mean, Not All Scenes Are Appropriately Placed in Storyboard Files?

All through this book you've been seeing scenes segueing to other scenes. You've seen user actions cause a scene to change to another scene (by row selection or button press, for example), and you've specified which type of transition will occur when the new scene is presented. In fact, there is a requirement that all scenes within a Storyboard file are arrived at from other scenes in the same Storyboard file, except for the initial scene (the one that has the arrow pointing into it coming from nowhere).

However, it's not too hard to find types of scenes that don't come from a single point in the main flow from scene to scene. Think of messages like *Networking error*, *Invalid user name*, or *Failed to load page*, for example. These messages aren't generated from the main flow of an application; they often happen asynchronously to the application flow. You can also think of these messages as needing to be sent to the display from your code—not from user action in the application interface.

In the end, you'll find it to be a bit more effort and rather unnatural to use Storyboards for showing scenes whose display is caused by code, such as scenes showing custom alert views, custom pickers, or custom action sheets. You can place custom scenes each in their own Storyboard file and then show them from the code. And you can create visual effects and placement onscreen so that these custom scenes look and behave like their built-in counterparts— but as we said, it's a bit more effort.

Hey, I Have Questions!

If you have more questions about these final topics or, of course, about anything in this book, please visit our forums. We'll be glad to answer your questions. See you on the forums!

Index